The *Integrated Astrological* Guide
to
Self-Empowerment

Astrology for the transformation age.

Volume 1
"The Chalice of Arcturus"
The land and I are one in the same
Arthur The King

By Edmond H. Wollmann

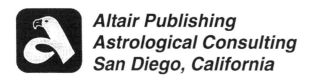

Altair Publishing
Astrological Consulting
San Diego, California

The *Integrated* Astrological Guide To
Self-Empowerment
By Edmond H. Wollmann

Published By:
Altair Publishing
P.O. Box 221000
San Diego, CA 92192-1000
United States of America

Library of Congress Cataloging-in-Publication Data:
Wollmann, Edmond H.
> The Integrated Astrological Guide to Self-empowerment:
> Volume 1 "The Chalice of Arcturus"/ Edmond H. Wollmann.
>> Includes bibliographical references and indexes.
>> ISBN 0-9663532-6-9

98-96089
CIP

Altair Publications/Astrological Consulting
P.O. Box 221000 San Diego, CA. 92192-1000 U.S.A.

Integrated Astrology Guides

These guides were inspired by the recognition that all disciplines fundamentally seek truth, serve a purpose, and are valid tools in the search for understanding the human condition. Whatever tools (disciplines) I believe serve in that understanding or topic are connected and referenced.

Much of what is written in these texts is fact. Some of it is inspired information, what I believe to be true, some empirical- some simply my best guesstimate through imagination. Most, the end result of many years of my own trials, tribulations and search for truth. It is an offering of the integration of differing systems of belief that are one thing, applied with astrology, and framed with understanding that we create our reality. Our experiences are there for us created by us, to serve us. Taking full responsibility for those creations using the tools presented, is the path to self empowerment and improving the quality of life. From that view I offer it as a service, a guide. If it serves you, you will find it useful. I in no way ask that it be regarded as any sort of ultimate truth or fact. My view is there is no such thing. I cannot prove its principles TO anyone. I believe each individual can prove it to themselves through practice and application.

Where astrology originated (history) is as interesting as *how it works* (physics). Neither of these questions is known with any great certainty. What is known and becoming more of a "fact" every day within many disciplines, is that our reality is much more pliable and manipulatable than we have perhaps believed it was in the past.

These guides incorporate the most accelerative perspectives about the world as we know it or as I can best discern them at the time of this printing from my view.

Knowing that astrology is valid infers that any discoveries in science, psychology, or spirituality can only support its use. From this relaxation of the "need to prove" I assert that all subjects and disciplines in this work are *allowed to fit.*

The proliferation of money making 1-900 numbers defeats astrological dignity. I opposed this idea when it started and still do not have one. I believe the astrological community prostitutes itself to the scientific community in its eagerness to gain "acceptance" and credibility, or to the public at large by seeking the popular view that paradigms are worthless unless scientifically proven or unless "for entertainment only." Compare other paradigms, i.e. earthquake prediction is considered a science and rarely if ever has been accurate. But this fact does not then require the scientific community to label this type of prediction "for entertainment only" and yet the consequences for being wrong can be quite devastating. This contradiction it seems, depends on who is doing the predicting, and *with what* that determines our level of acceptance based on *what we believe or have been taught to believe is true.* I believe all paradigms-science included-to be valuable and valid in the search for truth and seek inclusion, not exclusion, balanced, not dominant application.

Computers have now introduced us to the concepts of cyberspace and virtual reality. These conceptual constructs are reflected through the Uranus/Neptune conjunctions[1] and parallel the concepts initiated in this book, wherein the physical reality line of the real and the unreal, begins to blur.

When I began studying astrology in 1971 I was skeptical and set out to disprove it. However, any honest person who attempts this must become aware of the corroboration between astrological symbolism and a knowledge of self after enough investigation. Hence, the more I studied, the more mechanistically obvious it became that validity was there.

I began to see there were some serious reasons behind existence that were readily observable. There must be a reason I thought, for my own and others life experiences and needs being so different. However, this perspective raised more questions than it answered. If I had certain needs or characteristics as indicated by the horoscope, was I fated to experience only these? How do I change it? Where is the equalizer that balances the fact that some individuals never even hear about a religion let alone have this one life to

---

1Discussed in detail in chapter 13 and in general in the 1993 spring issue of Horoscope Magazine Yearbook-"The Uranus/Neptune Conjunction of 1993: A Collective Unconscious Awakening", also by the author.

redeem themselves. Why does one chart have numerous "negative" aspects and another numerous "positive"?

Learning about reincarnation as well as developmental psychological theories satisfied many of these questions. They were due to actions I had taken in "previous lives" or as the result of early environmental factors. Einstein's theories clarified to me that even the "time" factor was an illusion and all "lives" were all "happening" at once.

When I began counseling in 1979 I found that most needs and conflicts about self worth and status or other personality dynamics were tied strongly to the relationship with the parents and early environment. Noel Tyl (Professional Astrologer and Harvard psychology graduate) correlated this with psychological need and developmental theories introduced in his tremendous works in *"The Principles and Practice of Astrology"*. With these recognitions in mind I began counseling with the idea of assisting individuals in the recognition of these early schemas using the horoscope to find them. For example self worth is determined by the level (or lack of it) experienced as a perceived condition in the early environment and early support. These beliefs are then carried forward, often in an unconscious state and externalized in interaction with others and the environment in the adult life.

By the early 1980s I studied with great interest the channeling of "Seth" by Jane Roberts. Especially the volume entitled *"The Nature Of Personal Reality."* I also studied the Edgar Cayce material, the approach of the Rosicrucians, and Bashar and the association on reality creation in my search for understanding. Now there was a new concern. If we create our own reality, then why was the parental structure so influential in determining a person's reality experience? Why, or how, did we create the horoscope that we currently have? Where does the interaction of nurture and nature begin and end?

The *integral* conclusion was really not that hard to piece together. The horoscope reflects the belief momentum (past and present lives combined) and the resultant effects of such momentum, because the universe is simply idea and concept manifestation. The parental interaction is the catalyst that is unconsciously absorbed to manifest physically the best representation of the belief structure of the person involved, and the path chosen to unfold that momentum. The horoscope (picture of space at the time of birth) exists before parental interaction and must therefore be a template or a vibrational version of the momentum of the person and their belief "brought in" from the non-physical plane (soul self?) and is *reflected* through planetary geometric configuration.

The constellations and planets do not impel, compel, influence, energize or in any other way *determine* the identity of the individual. They reflect the signature of the schema "set" or probable personality. One version of "All That Is" or God looking at itself from another level, the physical level. The surrounding universe is the reflection of the momentum of the idea that we are at any given moment. Astrology is a tool to recognize the idea you are and its momentum or probable outcome as an effect of that definition. Tools of psychology, astrology or other awareness accelerators allow us the opportunity to own the reality and redefine it with preference through this knowledge of self.

An astrologer, or psychologist, can only serve as an artisan with a tool of self awareness. Self awareness is the only agent of change for a probable "fate" in the mirror of mind, matter. This book and the ones to follow are guides to understand that reflection and its illusory movement through time and space. They are guides to understanding our path and choices; to allow us to follow our development on as many levels as possible.

Dedicated to my mother,

whose transition to the other side

during this work,

in no way altered her loving support.

In Appreciation

To list the contributors at sum would be extremely difficult indeed, as the space required to list them would be greater than the length of the book. The list would date back to the beginning of recorded history and before.

This partial list includes astrologers, psychologists, channelers, theologians, scientists, astronomers, and teachers who have had a strong impact on my life and development, either directly or indirectly. In no special order they are; the horoscope examples in this book named and unnamed for the gift of their unique expression; special consideration to Noel Tyl (psychologist/astrologer) for his professional dedication to astrology and for his keen insights and astrological delineations. His psychological need theories form the psychological basis for many of my expanded interpretations. His works have been of great service in the astrological field.

Also special thanks to Darryl Anka (Bashar) who served me greatly by adding the philosophical pieces and empowering perspectives to trigger the insight and understanding I needed to complete my puzzle. To Kevin Ryerson (McPhereson, and John), Edgar Cayce, and Jane Roberts (Seth) for their willingness and patience with years of channeling, and clarification of difficult issues regarding the nature of reality. Joseph Campbell (the philosophical bridge between east and west philosophies), Donald H. Yott (astrologer) for Karmic astrological understandings and personal support, David McCall (psychologist), Jacques Vallee (UFO investigator), Albert Einstien (physicist), Carl Sagan (astronomer), Abraham Maslow, Karen Horney, Walter Mischel, Carl Rogers, Carl Jung (psychologists), Grant Lewi (astrologer), Vincent Van Gogh (artist), Paul McCartney, The Moody Blues (singers-musicians) Copernicus and Kepler (astronomers), Socrates, Christ, Buddha, Plato, Gandhi (philosophers-religions)...and many more, who, in my opinion, have shown a special level of sensitivity and/or integrity that inspires and adds required understanding and perspective to the thrust of this book.

My service is mediator of the apparently separate, into one.

When the white eagle of the north is flying overhead,
and the browns, reds, and golds of autumn lie in
the gutter, dead.

Remember then the summer birds with wings of fire
flaying come to witness springs new hope,
born of leaves decaying.

As new life will come through death, love will come
at leisure, love of love, love of life and giving,
without measure gives in return the wondrous yearn
for promise, almost seen.

Live hand in hand, and together we'll stand
on the threshold of a dream.

The Moody Blues

Table of Contents

Preface

"But man, proud man,
Drest in a little brief authority,
Most ignorant of what he's most assured,
His glassy essence, like an angry ape,
Plays such fantastic tricks before high heaven
As make the angels weep.
William Shakespeare, 1564-1616
Measure for Measure, II, ii.

Disciplines

The basis of this book and its tenets I put forth, will be reflected powerfully in the answer to one major question that pervades science, physics, psychology and metaphysics. That answer determines the direction of the next millennium, and the quality of life during it. The question is *whether reality exists independent of an observer.* Here we find it asked in two texts of completely different subject matter;

> "Science, you see, proceeds by a very fundamental assumption of the way things are or must be. That assumption is the very thing that Amit Goswami, with the assistance of Richard E. Reed and Maggie Goswami, brings into question in the book you are about to read. For this assumption, like its cloudy predecessors of the century before, seems to be signaling not only the end of a century but the end of science as we know it. That assumption is that there exists, "out there," a real, objective reality. This objective reality is something solid; it is made up of things that have attributes, such as mass, electrical charge, momentum, angular momentum, spin, position in space, and continuous existence through time expressed as inertia, energy, and going even deeper into the microworld, such attributes as strangeness, charm, and color. And yet the clouds still gather. For in spite of all that we know about the objective world, even with its twists and turns of space into time into matter, and the black clouds called black holes, with all of our rational minds working at full steam ahead, we are still left with a flock of mysteries, paradoxes, and puzzle pieces that simply do not fit. But

we physicists are a stubborn lot, and we fear the proverbial toss of the baby out with the bathwater. We still lather and shave our faces watching carefully as we use Occam's razor to make sure that we cut away all superfluous "hairy assumptions." What are these clouds that obscure the end of the twentieth century's abstract art form? They boil down to one sentence:

The universe does not seem to exist without a perceiver of that universe." Amit Goswami Ph.D. (Physics) "Self Aware Universe"

With regard to alien abduction;

‣   The most commonly debated issue, whether abductions are really taking place, leads us to the center of questions about perception and levels of consciousness.

The most glaring question is whether there is any reality independent of consciousness.

At the level of personal consciousness, can we apprehend reality directly, or are we by necessity bound by the restrictions of our five senses and the mind that organizes our worldview? Is there a shared, collective consciousness that operates beyond our individual consciousness? If there is a collective consciousness, how is it influenced, and what determines its content? Is UFO abduction a product of this shared consciousness? If, as in some cultures, consciousness pervades all elements of the universe, then what function do events like UFO abductions and various mystical experiences play in our psyches and in the rest of the cosmos? John E. Mack M.D. (Psychiatrist-Harvard) "Abductions"

It has been my observation through astrological application that it does not exist without the observer(s). It is redefined by belief and is in this text I seek to demonstrate how it empowers simply to know this.

This book demonstrates and presents possible observable answers to this question through astrological application and integration with other paradigms that reinforce that premise.

Copernicus on the reverence of the Heavens

"Among the varied literary and artistic studies upon which the natural talent of man is nourished, I think that those above all should be embraced and pursued with the greatest zeal which have to do with things that are very beautiful and very worthy of knowledge. Such studies are those which deal with the godlike circular movements of the world, the course of the stars, their magnitudes, distances, risings and settings, and the causes of the other celestial phenomena; and which finally explicate the whole form. For what could be more beautiful than the heavens which contain all beautiful things?" "Many philosophers have called the world a visible god on account of its extraordinary excellence. So if the worth of the arts were measured by the subject matter with which they deal, this art--which some call astronomy, others astrology, and many of the ancients the consummation of mathematics-- would be by far the most outstanding. This art which is as it were the head of all the arts and the one most worthy of a free man has nearly all the other branches of mathematics to support it. Arithmetic, geometry, optics, geodesy, mechanics, and whatever others, all assist it. And since a property of all good arts is to draw the mind of man away from vice and direct it to better things, these arts can do that more plentifully on account of the unbelievable pleasure of mind which they furnish. For who, after applying himself to things which he sees established in the best order and directed by divine ruling would not through contemplation of them and through a certain habituation be awakened to that which is best and would not admire the artificer of all things, in whom is all happiness and every good? For the divine psalmist surely did not say gratuitously that he took pleasure in the workings of God and rejoiced in the works of his hands, unless by means of these things as by some sort of vehicle we are transported to the contemplation of the highest good?

Now as regards the utility and ornament which they confer upon a commonwealth--to pass over the innumerable advantages they give to private citizens--Plato calls our attention to the right things, for in the seventh book of the *Laws* he says that this study should be pursued especially in order that through it the divisions of time into days, months, and years and the determination of solemnities and sacrifices should keep the state alive and watchful; *and he says that if anyone denies that this study is necessary for a man who is going to take up any of the highest branches of learning, then such a person is thinking foolishly; and he thinks that it is impossible for anyone to become godlike or be called so who has no necessary knowledge of the sun, moon, and the other stars.*"[1]

Copernicus on Approach

"...I confess that I shall expound many things differently from my predecessors,-although with their aid, for it was they who first opened the road of inquiry into these things."

These words were written by Nicholas Copernicus in 1540. And he refers to the wisdom of Plato, wisdom not dependent on technology, *that is timeless*. But the idea that these arts and sciences are based on inspiration as the effect of the **exploration** of the universe may have waned.

World Views

Evidence regarding the ancient Sumerian civilization suggests they lived and died by Astrological symbolism, and the Mayan culture expressed deeply their reverence of the heavens. The heavens are revered and awe inspiring. Great efforts were made to aspire to the heavens and to the "other" worldly or spiritual understandings. I submit-not from ignorance or fear, but from intelligent recognition.

In 1927, Anna Mitchell-Hedges found an anatomically correct quartz crystal skull in the Mayan city of Lubaantum, in the British Honduras. It has perfectly formed lenses in the eye sockets, so that if we shine a light through the bottom, it appears as if lasers are coming out of the eyes. It is perfectly balanced and has a detachable jaw. It has been estimated to be 3,600 years old and it cannot be duplicated with today's technology.

We can sense that some great wisdom of the past has been lost. Little is known of Earth's truer history and less of

---

[1] Author's emphasis. From "On The Revolutions Of The Celestial Spheres", book 1, not printed until he lay on his deathbed.

prehistory. Past cultures seem to suggest through their creations (like the Egyptian and Mayan pyramids) that physical manipulation was possible *without technological advances.* The Maya did not use the wheel. Remnants seem to make statements-as well as tell stories.

Current western world views are territorial, technological, material, and externally referenced in the complete assumption that physical reality exists outside of us. Disasters and difficulties are reported and measured in dollars and loss. Nature and reality against and opposed to man.

Our tendency is to conform to these views out of a fear of rejection socially and blind indoctrination of paradigmatic assumption (the effect of an externalized focus), *because we are taught helplessness from the beginning.*

▸   "It is our conditioning, our current collective world view that we were taught by our parents, teachers and society. This way of seeing things-the old paradigm-has aptly been called 'the hypnosis of social conditioning,' an induced fiction in which we have collectively agreed to participate."[2]

It is far more, we are learning, a phenomenological issue psychologically, "a term that refers to the individual's experience as he or she perceives it, because that is its most basic theme."[3] This psychological concept parallels the *quantum theory* that has become known as the new physics, and it supplies some of our most persuasive evidence yet that consciousness does have an effect on physical reality. Uncertainty is one of the primary ingredients to the quantum theory.

In general the quantum theory asserts that (at the sub-atomic level);

▸   "the atomic world is full of murkiness and chaos. A particle such as

---

2
    "Ageless Body, Timeless Mind" part 1, pg 3, by Deepak Chopra M.D., Harmony Books 1993.

3
    See the"Introduction To Personality" fifth edition 1993 by Holt, Rienhart and Winston, Inc.

an electron does not appear to follow a meaningful, well-defined trajectory at all. One moment it is found here, and the next there. Not only electrons, but all known subatomic particles-even whole atoms-cannot be pinned down to a specific motion. Scrutinized in detail, the concrete matter of daily experience dissolves in a maelstrom of fleeting, ghostly images.   Uncertainty is the fundamental ingredient of the quantum theory. It leads directly to the consequence of *unpredictability.* Does every event have a cause? Few would deny it... The cause-effect chain has been used to argue for the existence of God-the first cause of everything. The quantum factor, however, apparently breaks the chain by allowing effects to occur that have no cause."[4]

This side of the coin, so to speak, represents one side of the current accepted scientific paradigm-that of chaos theory and unpredictability. A view held by Danish physicist Niels Bohr, who accepted and believed that atomic uncertainty reflected and was intrinsic to nature.

In contrast to Bohr, Albert Einstein's perspective represents the other side of the paradigmatic coin;

▸   "God does not play dice", is one of his famous quotes. "Many ordinary systems, such as the stock market or the weather, are also unpredictable. But that is only because of our ignorance. If we had complete knowledge of all the forces concerned, we could (in principle at least) anticipate every twist and turn."[5]

The combining of the two polarized world views brings us to the central and most difficult concept of my work, to reconcile and convey, and yet is inherent in the conflict itself. *This concept asserts that the world that we experience is not a collection of individual but paired things, manifesting themselves in as many ways as is possible, and in infinite relationship.* Both world views are true and are in themselves a so-paired network of relationship.

For example, ideas have momentums which to some degree

4
    "The Experience Of Philosophy" second edition, Daniel Kolak-Raymond Martin, Part seven: Reality, *Reality and Modern Science: Paul Davies,* pg 342.

5
    Same reference, last note.

are predictable in their unfoldment once initiated. Discovery and anomaly changes and dislodges these momentums. It is awareness that determines the extent of dislodging and alteration of that momentum. Because this awareness of momentum then redirects, rearranges and catalyses into *new* trajectories of momentum. The ends of this "spectrum" of perspective are just different sides or views of the same thing, that is all *one* thing, that contains *both*.

Astrology

The study of astrology can be viewed as a reflective map of the momentum of the energy *and exploration of these relationship networks.* The belief momentum of mind (chaotic and mutable) which crystallizes into matter (deterministic and predictable) referred to in this book as the *mind/matter mirror.* Mind and matter are the same thing manifesting in all the ways that it can.

There are a few misconceptions about astrology that must be addressed before we can delve into this exploration, and therefore chapter one is completely devoted to definition clarification. But generally the reader should know these concepts (or misconceptions) about astrology first;

1. One aspect of Astrology, calculation and measurement, is a mathematically exacting science. The interpretations are not and requires much training. The horoscope is based on the exact time, date, and place of the birth of a person, idea, contract or any other type of "birth." It cannot be applied properly through a newspaper column, 900 phone number, or without sufficient preparation, examination, study and practiced application.

2. It is not necessary to "believe" in it. Astrology is not a religion or cult, *therefore faith is not required for it to function.* It is functionally evident *once it is learned.* Therefore understanding number one, dispels number two.

3. Astrology is an art/science. The scientific aspect is in the horoscope's construction, calculation and mathematical geometric interrelationship between astronomical bodies, and their placement against the backdrop of constellation reference (or designated area of space). The art aspect is in the intuited blending of astrological significators into psychodynamic awareness, application and/or psychological profiling.

4. Astrology does not have to be "proven scientifically" to be a valid application or tool. Astrology fathered science and it is *just one* of it's constituent elements. There are many ways to explore and understand the universe. Some creatures at the depths of the sea never experience light as those above. Which is the "right" way? The art of delineation and interpretation may be open to debate, but validity must be based on *service to client or subject,* as is psychology, stock market forecasting, earthquake prediction, or weather forecasting *none of which are unfailingly replicable working models.* Astrology's best use is NOT in the realm of prediction to begin with. It is in changing the definitions that *creates* probabilities of experience, through awareness.

5. Astrology does not influence human behavior. As quantum mechanics and holographic models depict, the observer determines, participates in, and affects the outcome of the event. This book holds that we create our reality utterly as the end product of *what we believe[6] or have been taught to believe is true-even if those beliefs are in a repressed or unacknowledged state.* And therein lies the most profound capability and utility of astrology; it reflects through the matter portion of the mind/matter mirror (outer space=inner space), the *momentum, intensity, configuration and trajectory or direction of those beliefs. This self-empowers the individual with self responsibility and the freedom to now chose and*

---

[6] Since the horoscope exists before any parental or environmental interaction, it is assumed the momentum inherent in the chart is the product of decisions made prior to incarnation and reflected through genetic structure.

change, because the reality is now owned.

Perspective

The earliest known horoscope was discovered to be approximately 4400 years old, found in ancient Babylonia. Our days are named after planets. The seven days of the week are one quarter of the Moon's cycle, a month one lunar cycle, one quarter of Earth's orbit represents each season. Celestial symbology and mythology gave birth to our current conception of an ordered society. The connection was so powerful that to be separated from the cosmos or stars spawned the word *disaster.*

About 2000 years ago Jesus the Christ was born,[7] which set a powerful tone for religious changes, the church and Christianity in general. Like most religions it has fallen asleep and been ritualized.

The precession of the equinox by the coincidence of the equator and the plane of the ecliptic (the zodiac) allows for a regression through the astrological signs at a rate of approximately 30 degrees or one sign of the zodiac every 2000 years. Christ was born during the dawning of the age of Pisces ♓, symbolically representing the savior, sacrifice, sorrow and physical suffering as an effect of the physical focus of material reality, and it's toll from *the illusion of duality and the limitations of physical focus.* The sign Pisces is symbolized by two fish swimming in opposite directions. Modern day Christians display little magnetic fish on the back of their automobile as their symbol of their religion-*and yet are vehement in their belief that astrology is satanic.*

Fundamentalists fight the scientific view for prominence in the educational system and texts on the issue of creation vs evolution (two fish swimming in opposite directions). Assisted

---

[7]
Although there is very little if any evidence of his birth, his existence is known with some certainty. Please see "New Testament Story", second edition, David L. Barr, Wadsworth Publishing, 1995.

suicide takes center stage as a way to empower the individual to end self suffering. These are all the effect of the culmination of the Pisces age, and the beginning of the age of transformation wherein suffering is seen as a *choice of definition-not a given.*

The three "wise men" (Magi Greek from Persian meaning diviner or astrologers) followed the stars (or horoscope) because of their recognition of the uniqueness of astrological configurations[8] not because of objects in the sky. We need very little science to recognize that you cannot follow an astronomical object (such as Hale/Bopp Comet) and be lead to somewhere on the globe. *Yet this explanation is more widely accepted than the astrological one!* Canonization lead to an "acceptable and proper" Christian attitude. This is because organized religion is, analytically, the science of following. *"For religious devotion is a collective phenomenon that does not depend on individual endowment."*[9] Conventional religious attitudes and approaches are a defense psychologically against religious (spiritual) experience.

"O ye of little faith"[10] was intended to generate the idea that every individual "was as powerful as they need to be to create whatever they desire to create in their reality, without having to hurt themselves or anyone else in order to create it."[11] This is the concept of self-empowerment. "I am the *way*, the truth,

---

[8]
    See "Prediction in Astrology" Noel Tyl, "The Birth Of Jesus", Chapter 1 pg 11, Rectification to 7 B.C..

[9]
    "The Collected Works Of C. G. Jung, Psychological Types, Volume 6", pg 124 on "Schiller's ideas on the type problem".

[10]
    Matthew 6:30. King James Version.

[11]
    Darryl Anka channeling "Bashar", "The New Metaphysics".

and the life: no man cometh unto the father, but by me"[12]; this is a model of *behavior* not who to praise, glorify, or follow. "All that is" or God, is all one thing. Each individual is one of the expressions of that all (Chapter 1 will cover whether negative or positive in that expressing).

Science on the other hand separates nature from man, *Deus ex machina,* (deity separate from the machine) a perspective adopted as a bi-product of extreme focus, and an effect of commercialism and the technological/territorial perspective. This delusion of grandeur and blind faith with its religious adherence to rigid paradigmatic dogma, has created infinite number of substances "known to cause Cancer in laboratory animals", other fallacies of inductive reasoning,[13] have created a medical industry nightmare (by the x axis), an out of control insurance industry based on statistics (by the y axis), a rapidly decreasing ozone layer, the illusion of using propulsion for interstellar space travel (now recognized as fallacious), etc., etc.. Yes science has given us many wonderful devices, *that have led us away from the awe inspiring sight of a starlit night* (now we watch the television instead of the sky). Empirical approaches can lead us away from the re-cognition of our connection to it. Science is valuable in its place and gives great understanding of the physical. When it reinforces doubt and cynicism it detracts from significance and meaning. We then bow to the letter of the law, and violate its heart-the search for truth.

DNA patterns follow astrological patterns, *the initial template.* Understanding both reveals parallels and the universal template. One reflects the other, there is no contradiction-there is no conflict.

12
John: 14:6, King James version.

13
Properly defined as having something new in the conclusion, that is not presented in the premise. See "A Concise Introduction To Logic", Patrick J. Hurley, Wadsworth Publishing.

The *Age of Aquarius* has dawned. No longer do we need to worship or follow saviors or dicta. Aquarius is ruled by the planet Uranus, *the great awakener* (Buddha and Christ consciousness). Aeons ago Uranus was brushed by the dark body *Nemesis*,[14] counterpart of our Sun and was tipped on it's axis. This reflected the aspect of consciousness that was sacrificed to the unconscious as an effect of focus (Saturn) and hence the direct line to the creator was severed, as one pole of this planet faces toward the sun and one away. We have played the game of forgetting and limitation to it's end. Time for the second coming. *Which will happen within each individual.* The glyph of Aquarius ≈ reflects the electricity and sensation of waking up to the *avant garde* (advanced group or forward guard) recognition that we create our reality 100% even when we use 99.999% to create the illusion that we only have the remaining .0001%. The conscious decision to recognize the validity of the individuality of each and every individual as a "co-creator" is the way to "a new world order". Taking full responsibility for one's reality creations=absolute freedom. But we must first see them, own them and cease blaming. This book serves in that way. To allow that awakening.

The astrologer can serve as that forward guard.

How to use this book

It is assumed that you are reading this book, not only to understand yourself better, but perhaps to gain insight into a broader purpose to living and understanding your place in it as a path. Therefore, a diverse base knowledge of some of the currently accepted postulates (not necessarily deep) will certainly help in understanding how and why I come to connect or conclude certain issues.

14
    Greek myth, goddess of divine retribution. The astronomical body proposed by astronomers to account for the perturbation and descent of comets from the Kuiper belt and Oort cloud at the outer limits of the solar system.

A basic knowledge of astrology is helpful but not necessary, the same goes for psychology. I have defined some aspects that I will use most often and every chapter will have a summary and lists of terms or definitions if important. I will suggest some books to use in conjunction with this one at the end of this preface and most chapters-if needed. We will move right into application of astrology from chapter 8 and onward with comments on how these conclusions are determined. The best way to learn if you are not knowledgeable is application, and to see how conclusions are reached regarding clients if you are. It may be frustrating for the beginner, but the better the keys are learned the easier it will be. Manipulation of the keys comes with experience-but they never change-only their level of meaning.

No calculating is done either (except perhaps to explain what we need to know to understand and continue) because the computer age allows us accurate charts in seconds or for a few dollars. Organizations and sources for chart calculations and ordering and for reading lists and books available on this aspect are listed in the back of this text.

This book is not intended to be all inclusive. It is what I believed to be necessary basics. Although it has delineations, they are only keys. What is said is all that needs be said about certain positions until they are incorporated into the horoscopic pattern. Things fall into place and come to light through thorough delineation or when the client arrives that often the imagination could not fathom-but still fit and apply quite easily. Recommended (not essential) reading companions;

"Holistic Astrology" and *"Astrology 1-2-3-"* Noel Tyl, Llewellyn Publications, 1984, 1991.

"The New Metaphysics", Darryl Anka, Light and Sound Communications, 1987

"Black Holes and Time Warps" Einstein's Outrageous Legacy, Kip S. Thorne, W W Norton & Company, 1994.

"The Experience of Philosophy," Daniel Kolak and Raymond Martin, Wadsworth Publishing, 1993.

"The Power Of The Myth," Joseph Campbell , W/Bill Moyers. New York: Doubleday.

"The Nature Of Personal Reality," Jane Roberts A Seth Book. New Jersey: Prentice Hall. 1974

"Edgar Cayce On Atlantis" Edgar evens Cayce
New York: Paperback Library. 1968

"Revelations," and *"Challenge to Science, The UFO enigma."* Jacques Vallee, New York: Ballentine Books. 1991-1966

"Holy Bible," New Revised Standard Version, Oxford University Press.

"The Holographic Universe," Michael Talbot, Harper Perennial, 1992.

"Contact Cards," Carlsberg & Anka, Bear & Co. 1996

"Introduction to Personality" Walter Mischel, Fifth edition. Harcourt Brace Jovanovich Publishers. 1993 (or at least College level psychological text equivalent.)

Chapter 1

Crystalline Definitions
Part one

"Cold hearted orb that rules the night,
removes the colors from our sight,
red is grey, and yellow white,
but we decide which is right;
which is an illusion."
The Moody Blues from
"Days Of Future Passed"

Validity, The illusion of prejudice

All creations in the universe are essentially neutral, without meaning or status. Things and events within the universe are given meaning by us, by what we believe and/or we are taught to believe they mean. Because "All that is" or God is *all* one thing, how is it possible that one part can be "better" than another? There may be ways that we need to think parts of it *should* be, but that is an expectation, and that is a judgment.

The *knowledge* of "good and evil" was the symbolic forbidden fruit that Adam and Eve were deceived into taking a bite of.

▸　　　"But the tree of the knowledge of good and evil, thou shalt not eat of it: for in the day that thou eatest thereof thou shalt surely die"[15]

They then became *aware* of their nakedness and were ashamed. This assignment of values began the *judgment of paradise.* This metaphor symbolizes the belief that we must do something special in order to deserve to exist, and our *clothing*

---

[15] Genesis :2,17

is psychological as well as physical. These psychological clothes or shells define belief parameters and limit our experience[16] in the world of opposites and polarity pairs.

In *"Ageless Body, Timeless Mind,"*[17] Deepak Chopra lists 10 assumptions that underlie our shared world view and redefines them according to a more expanded perspective based on quantum mechanics discovery and new physics. The redefinition is meant to remove limiting perspectives from our accepted references, and expand the ***new world view*** that we create our reality by what we define ourselves to be. For most of us this recognition can be disconcerting. Because it is difficult to reconcile ***determinism vs. chaos or fate vs. free will.*** Metaphysical dualism is itself a belief parameter.[18]

Webster/Lexicon dictionary defines "valid" as; *validus=strong, powerful* "1) Sound, just, well founded. 2) Producing the desired effect or results. 3) *(logic)* So constructed that if the premise is so asserted jointly, the conclusions cannot be denied without contradiction."All that Is" (God) is *all that is!* Which part of it can be deemed not "sound, just, or well founded?" Logically, if all that is, is a derivation from the infinite creator, all is valid.

From this perspective all truths are true. They may not be what we prefer or expect, *but must be there for a reason and serve a purpose.* Only in physical reality does the validity of polarity pairs seem to create conflict and paradox. In dream reality conceptual understanding occurs.

We assign ***subjective value judgments*** because the

16
    The serpent also a part of this story, sheds its skin, a symbol like Eve that affirms life through the transformation of spirit to matter.

17
    Chopra, Deepak, M.D.. Ageless Body, Timeless Mind, San Diego: Harmony Books, 1993.

18
    Theological dualism holds that the two real's are God and nature, and that God transcends nature.

conscious mind is limited in it's cognitive ability to understand *how* things fit and is biased in expectation on how they *should* fit. These expectations or "shoulds"[19] reflect personal and collective psychological needs in interaction, which allow us to validate ourselves and justify our existence within *certain belief parameters.* These **archetypal** parameters presented in the paragon of astrology, are what allows awareness or the **discernment** of the chosen parameter. Astrology is a tool of discernment to understand how we *value judge* universal archetypal reference.

On discernment vs. value judgment

Without a thorough and holistic awareness of the entire self (conscious + unconscious), function is reduced to a value judgment perspective, simply because we are not aware of the parameters of our *own* perspective and the paradigms and hidden assumptions we have. This prevents understanding and dulls the psychodynamics[20] of our self-actualization[21] process.

Lexicon/Webster defines judgment as "an opinion or notion formed by judging or considering"; "a determination of the mind so formed." The "mind" referred to here is obviously the conscious level of the mind. But this does not negate the many levels of mind. Greater understanding of multiple levels of mind, results in greater discernment. Discernment being defined as; (Lexicon/Webster) "Acuteness of judgment; the

---

19
  For those interested in a greater explanation of the "Tyranny of the shoulds", see *Personality Theories,* Bem P. Allen, Allyn & Bacon 1994, Chapter 5, Karen Horney, page 118.

20

The process through which a personality is regulated.

21

A concept or personality theory introduced by Carl Rogers wherein it is "best conceptualized as a tendency toward fulfillment, toward actualization, toward the maintenance and enhancement of the organism" (1963 pg 6).

power to perceive differences between things or ideas, as well as their relationships." When used in matters of psychic material or mind, discernment is the ability to separate and distinguish the **projection** of one's beliefs as opposed to the clear-sighted **observation** *of* a belief parameter or system of thought. Although no system of understanding or paradigm is bias free, understanding the psychological dynamics behind the creation of beliefs frees our discernment to a greater degree.

> ▸ "The recognition and taking to heart of the subjective determination of knowledge in general, and of psychological knowledge in particular, are basic conditions for the scientific and impartial evaluation of a psyche different from that of the observing subject. These conditions are fulfilled only when the observer is sufficiently informed about the nature and scope of his own personality. He can, however, be sufficiently informed only when he has in large measure freed himself from the levelling influence of collective opinions and thereby arrived at a clear conception of his own individuality . . . "The collective attitude hinders the recognition and evaluation of a psychology different from the subject's, because the mind that is collectively oriented is quite incapable of thinking and feeling in any other way than by projection."[22]

These levels of mind are reflected in the horoscope. The levels are outlined in detail in *chapters (3) Experiential Template, and Geometric Basics (4)* and establish the premise for four bases and three levels (as in DNA compounds) with counterparts making six and bipolar representations in all totaling 12.[23] For the discussion at present, the levels of mind

---

[22]

Carl Jung, Psychological Types, *The Type Problem in Classical and Medieval Thought.* pg 10, paragraphs 11, 12.

[23]

That is responsible for the pattern and structure of Deoxyribonucleic acid or DNA pairing of strands of nucleotide monomers.

discussed are:

- ***Materialized Mind***- Physical objects that act as "props" to accelerate reality experience. (I.e., Roman architecture, a chair, etc.).
- ***Mind***-The unconscious and conscious processes that perceive, conceive, comprehend, evaluate and reason.
- ***Conscious mind***- The upper level of mental life marked by awareness; The part of the mind comprised of psychic material of which the individual ego is aware and supported by. By reading this, you are focussed in this realm of psychic material, however the other levels permeate and affect this one, *always.*
- ***Unconscious mind***- The part of the mind comprised of psychic material of which the ego is unaware. In psychoanalytic theory, it is the part of the personality of which the ego is unaware but that profoundly affects actions, behaviors and beliefs.
- ***Collective Unconscious mind***- Racially and/or generationally inherited psychic material present in the individual unconscious or the combined consciousness of a generation or generations experiencing mass idea expression. These represent the "primordial images" introduced by Carl Jung, and serve as a sort of root directory to all levels of consciousness (reflected in DNA).
- ***Higher consciousness or self***- A totally non-physical (as we know physicality) level that encompasses and synthesizes all psychic material on all levels the identity or oversoul contains-past, present and future. There is much debate about the reality of this level (i.e. near death experience reports, psychic experience reports etc.)

The focus of the conscious self and mind is the starting point for the compartmentalization of psychic material. Value judgments increase the distance between this and higher levels. The unconscious contains all psychic material just below the awareness level of the conscious mind function, and where we place all fears and unresolved conflicts, especially those that threaten ego orientation.[24] All levels conscious or unconscious are still responsible for the creation of one's experiential reality. It is for this reason that many individuals find it difficult to "believe" they create their own reality, because it is assumed that it means the psychic material they are *aware of* is the only part responsible. This results from a completely unbalanced and *empirical orientation,* resulting in an *empirical* type of reality experience. This orientation reflects the belief that there is a separate "reality" that functions independently of the observer. We create our reality experience by what we believe; Does the tree make a noise when it falls in the forest with no one present to hear it? The proverbial tree does not even exist, let alone make a noise when it falls, if no one perceives it, because the perception *is the creation.*

The ego (conscious mind level of psychic focus) is not the entire identity but an effect of conscious mind functioning and a locus of control for the general identity in physical reality. It is in essence, an artificial construct, resulting in the **persona**, (personae) meaning **mask or false face** created by the necessary focus of physical reality. The persona reinforces the concept of separateness and the idea that physical reality exists outside the self. This functioning is based on only one bank of psychic material and less than full utilization of the "other" levels of the psyche. This focus deludes us into thinking that the self we are is *all* we really are. Things are then deemed to be either "good" or "bad". This is a subjective value judgment.

▸   "I know and am persuaded by the lord Jesus, that there is

---

24

There are more levels of course, as well as types of consciousness. These are dealt with more in depth in the section on psychology.

nothing unclean of itself: but to him that esteemeth anything to be unclean, to him it is unclean."[25]
"There is nothing good or bad, but thinking makes it so."
Hamlet-Shakespeare

Psychology recognizes schematic functioning as "*encoding* (categorizing, construing, interpreting, explaining) and their *expectancies* (anticipations)" . . ."In our culture, a major dimension of encoding that is relevant for most people (Osgood et al., 1957) concerns evaluation (good-bad, able-unable, success-failure)."[26] These concepts or value judgments are in themselves artificial constructs, stemming from our habitual patterning in emotive instead of cognitive forms of communication rampant in the 90s (i.e., emotive "spin" designed to persuade rather than inform).

In Algebra, an expression is *evaluated* by substituting the numerical values for the *variables*. The value can be removed without removing a discernable function. We do this in our day-to-day experience as individuals in order to limit the impact of change threatening situations and maintain sameness.

The concepts of good and bad are subjective value judgments. We return then, to our initial assertion of neutral meaning but discernable function. These primary discernable functions are positive and negative expressions of everything. These positive and negative manifestations are best represented geometrically by the *double pyramidal octahedral (physical) and tetrahedral (non-physical) structure* [27] because

---

25

Romans 14:14.

26

"Introduction To Personality", 5th edition, *Encoding, Constructs, and Expectancies*, Chapter 15, page 419, Walter Mischel, 1993. Holt, Rinehart and Winston, Inc.

27

See *The New Metaphysics, Template Metaphysics* by Bashar and The Association, channeled by Darryl Anka, chapter 7, pg 87, Light and Sound Communications Inc., 1987.

they reflect the four bases and three levels with counterparts making six and bipolar representations in all totaling 12 (introduced on page 4). This is the basis for the primordial first six signs of the horoscopic mandala (Aries through Virgo).

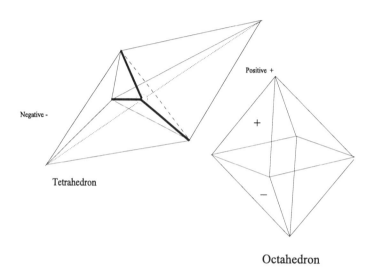

Tetrahedron

Octahedron

Positive and Negative Energy

<u><-8 -7 -6 -5 -4 -3 -2 -1 0 1 2 3 4 5 6 7 8 ></u>

In mathematics the number line represents the concept of the infinite *negative* numbers left of the centerline 0, and the infinite *positive* numbers to the right of centerline 0.

Integrative or positive energy

The **positive** manifestation of "All That Is" to the right of centerline 0:

▸　　Integrative and unifying; allows all creations to exist for a reason; Constructive, expansive and unbiased.

Chooses by preference; Acts as a conviction of belief definition.

The key word in positive energy is ***integrative***. This energy allows for the synthesization of different ideas in a harmonious and supportive way. Acting in integrity means that the identity recognizes that the power is within and that therefore changing any aspect of reality is an internal process. Confirmation of this internal change, is reflected in positive action.

> ▸ As long as you are in physical reality you always create an identifiable symbol to reflect to you the idea going on. Since you have created physical reality to be something outside yourselves, then understand that everything you perceive in physical reality is a physiological symbolic extension of processes, interactions, which are actually going on, more or less, inside yourselves. Not truly outside yourselves, but inside yourselves. You are the actual interaction, the actual process.[28]

Because all *levels* of psychic material are only apparent (actually all one), it is important to note that these levels must be connected. The connection between levels can be likened to shining a flashlight in the dark. We know everything else still exists, but we can only see a specific segment until we broaden the illumination. All the levels of consciousness are still there. We cannot increase our interconnectedness with the "All That Is", we are as connected as we will ever be. We can therefore only increase our *awareness* of this interconnectedness. Awareness of these "other levels" and their incorporation into conscious awareness and consideration leads to positive expression in the form of self-empowerment; knowing that we are as powerful as we need to be to create anything, with integrity. Discernment utilizes more than one bank or level of consciousness and is unifying, therefore positive. Being balanced is in itself a positive state of being (i.e. as the infinite expressions of the number line suggests.)

---

[28] Bashar, "Blueprint For Change", 1990, Luana Ewing, New Solutions Publishing.

Segregative or negative energy

The **negative** manifestation of "All That Is" to the left of centerline 0:

▸ Is segregative, separative, limiting and constrictive; Reflects cynicism rather than unification; Enhances polarization and is judgmental; *Re*acts to defend against perceived threats.

The key word in negative energy is ***segregative***. Judgment relies on only the conscious portion or bank of psychic material and is therefore negative. Ideas such as "survival of the fittest", "no pain, no gain" are ideas connected with the ego or with the conscious mind's physical focus. The ego believes itself to be a separate entity. Therefore the need to defend the self from the perceived externals, the need to reinforce the importance and significance of the identity, and the need to *disbelieve* that everything is unfolding as it needs to, are in evidence in behavior.

Judgment reinforces the ego in its assessment that things are not "the way they should be." If we invalidate the reality we are experiencing at any given moment, then we cut off other levels and aspects of the self that may be trying to communicate with the conscious mind, ideas that we need to learn, to look at, and to integrate in order to get on with a more expanded self-definition. In the integrated perspective, "hope" is not necessary to overcome implied despair.[29]

Principles of positive\negative energy, self-empowerment and reality creation take on special meaning for those in the counseling professions. Placing the power outside the self is commonplace. All reality experiences are ways that "All That Is" has of exploring itself. All are reflective and in a sense insubstantial. Scientists blame genetics, natural forces and

---

[29]

Hope implies things are not as they "should be", despair follows as a "last resort." Bashar, "Perfection" 2/21/87.

chaos for their physical experiences. Without integral awareness, Astrologers blame the planet's positions. Psychologists blame early environment and conditioning. These tools of inquiry lose power without discernment and understanding the application of negative/positive energy.

Discernment allows for the capability to re-cognize (rethink); to perceive a different belief system and its reinforcing logic without buying into or being affected by it.

Judgment is a value, status and condition loaded perception, based on the observers personal belief system and corresponding logic. We can usually tell more about the observer through this type of mind set, *than the observed.* Since the observer and the observed are aspects of the act of observation, discernment is the only way an individual has of breaking a habitual response to interaction with its creations.

In projection, one's own unacceptable temperament is inhibited and attributed to another person.[30] This behavior is the effect of **judging** the unacceptable quality. It is for this reason that it is difficult and often impossible for someone to *discern* a life or a level at which they themselves are not or have not functioned. It is a matter of vibrational levels, mechanics. The discerner *must necessarily* be at a higher vibrational frequency. When the higher meets the lower, for the lower it can sometimes be a fearful experience.

▸ ..."but the idea many times of the reasons that those fears occur in your society, when you are interacting with beings from other societies in that way, no matter what level you are interacting with them, the reason that many of those fears occur is because-let us say-and again in no way, shape, or form, is this meant to be a comparative judgement that you are any less than any other being. But the way you create yourselves to be, the way you have been taught to think of yourselves, creates within you the ability to hide and suppress many portions of your consciousness from

---

30

Sigmund Freud presumed that this form of behavior reduced anxiety.

yourselves, and in doing so you function on a lower vibratory frequency very often. When you come in contact with a being that operates on a very high vibratory frequency because it is willing to know itself as completely as it can, then those two frequencies when they come together, will usually create the effect of the higher frequency in a sense overwhelming the lower frequency, and forcing the lower frequency to rise in pitch. In forcing the lower frequency to raise in pitch, that will bring to the surface all the things that you have been keeping buried within you, and bringing those things to the surface when you are not ready to face them, can be a very fearful experience for many of you. *That* is where the fear comes from." [31]

Phobias can often result as an effect of patterned fears.[32]

Summary

I.   Things within the Universe (or more appropriately Multiverse since it contains infinite levels) are not valid because we judge them to be so, but rather simply *because they exist.* In physical reality we see "All That Is" as polarity pairs of opposites (i.e., male/female, right/wrong, darkness/light).

II.   Discernment and judgment reflect two different types of energy. *Discernment* is the ability to observe and analytically evaluate a belief system without becoming caught up in the belief system. *Judgment* more closely resembles projection and/or reaction formation,[33] and

---

31

Darryl Anka channeling "Bashar" on "Perfection" Feb. 19, 1987, in answer to a question about fears involved with dreams of extraterrestrials, and not feeling well after the event.

32

In traditional and classical conditioning, an unconditioned stimulus is paired with a conditioned stimulus which results in a conditioned response. An unconditioned stimulus from the author's point of view however, is a rigidized and physicalized belief.

33

A defense term wherein replacement in consciousness of an anxiety-producing impulse by its opposite occurs.

the individual mistakes their own belief system with its reinforcing logic, for an attitude on the part of the observed. The Horoscope reflects the archetypal pattern of belief structures and their physical manifestations.

III.   There are many levels of manifested mind or *psyche* (meaning soul) the initial activating force of "All That Is" exploring itself. All of these levels are responsible for each individual's experiential reality, and the collective experience when combined as a whole.

IV.   The ego is the *effect* of our focus upon the material or physical aspect of mind, and is to a great degree an artificial construct. It is made up of and relies on specificity.

V.   The concepts of "good" and "bad" are subjective value judgements, and tell us little about the type of energy being expressed. There is however, **Positive** *expression,* which is recognizable by its integrative, unifying, constructive, expansive, unbiased and supportive characteristics. It reflects a belief in self-empowered action as a conviction of belief. **Negative** *expression* is characterized by its segregative, separative, limiting, constricting, cynical, polarizing and reactive qualities. It reflects a belief in reality existing only outside the self and the resulting "battle" between it and physical reality. Negative is reactive and is therefore disempowered.

VI.   Fear/suppression of the unconscious portions of psychic material is the effect of negative energy and results in *projection* of the fears into relationships. It may be projected on to things in the form of phobias.

VII.   The vibrational level of a being is determined by the willingness and capability of that being to know itself on *as many levels as fully as it can.* Fear may be the result when we resist acknowledging certain beliefs that we may hold as an effect of repression or resist our own growth. If we accept that we create our reality, we can surmise that we cannot experience anything that is not a part of us on some level. The logical conclusion is the creator is within us.[34]

▸   "He who has so little knowledge of human nature as to seek happiness by changing anything but his own disposition, will waste his life in fruitless efforts and multiply the griefs which he proposes to remove."   Noah Webster

Part two

"Motor of love, motor of love
heavenly father look down from above,
I can't get over your powerful
motor of love"
"Motor Of Love" from "Flowers In The Dirt"
Paul McCartney

Spirit
Physics describes forces in many ways, and we could discus forces such these at great length. This would give us no more information of the primal force that drives them all than when we started. This is because science seeks to reduce and separate as a mode of investigation rather than expand and integrate the "something" that drives the inquiry.

▸   "The myth brings us into a level of consciousness that is spiritual . . . there is a condescension on the part of the infinite to the mind of man, and that is what looks like God."[35]

Spirit is the essence or mode of movement behind all

---

[34]   This is why the concept of the external or absolute other God must by definition be an illusion.

[35]   Joseph Campbell on "The Power Of The Myth", with Bill Moyers, 1987.

manifestations in the Multiverse. Matter reflects or symbolizes the feminine aspect of spirit because it is a ***receptacle for the animated*** spirit. Matter is mind or spirit in physical terms. Matter reflects the physical translation of spirit, which is the propellant of idea exploration in the Universe.

Physical and non-physical realities are *aspects* of reality. Waking or dreaming states reflect the ***degree of focus*** within reality, and are aspects of conscious and unconscious psychic material interchange and permeation.

> ▸ "The brain can be called simply the physical counterpart of the mind. By means of the brain the functions of the soul and intellect are connected with the body. Through the characteristics of the brain, events that are of nonphysical origin become physically valid. There is a definite filtering and focusing effect at work, then. Practically speaking, you do indeed form the appearance that reality takes through your conscious beliefs. Those beliefs are used <u>as</u> screening and directing agents, separating certain nonphysical probable events from others, and bringing them into three-dimensional actuality."[36]

Separation does not really exist between waking or dreaming, conscious or unconscious realities. Separations may be experienced as the effect of the conscious mind and ego focusing on the matter portion of spirit. The more dissolved an ego focus is, the greater the experience of self (i.e., trance and sleep states, meditation, LSD experiences). The more focused, the greater the ability for exacting applications, but the less that opportunity exists for knowingness[37] (i.e., autism).

The supra conscious or higher consciousness, manifests awareness of spirit through the "feminine" portion (matter) to the conscious mind through the "props" of physical reality.

36

Jane Roberts channeling "Seth" in "The Nature Of Personal Reality", 1974 Prentice-Hall, Chapter 14 "Which You? Which World?", pages 319-320.

37

The self-awareness of "All That Is" of itself.

Thus in myths and in physicality it is the female who is the giver of forms, time and space. Recall it was *Eve* not Adam who received the forbidden fruit. The snake sheds its skin and the Moon (the symbol of feminine forms) sheds its shadow. These symbols reflect the affirmation of physical life and regeneration. **Archetypes** are universal images or symbols within these levels of psychic material expressing patterns for the organization of experience. It is my assertion that the basic archetypes for all of experience in this system (solar system) are symbolized in the division of the heavens or Zodiac.

In dream reality the "props" take the form of symbology and the conscious mind constantly receives an education. *It is this recognition consciously that allows us the power of preference and choice.* The conscious mind is not necessarily the primary source of mind exploration, rather it is just one format.

Spirit is the motivating force or *mode* of myriad manifestations, both physically or nonphysically as expressions of "All That Is". The divine agency working in the heart of all things. We have little understanding from what spirit emanates, no more than we do the Universe. We see effects, not causes.

The mystery or **mystical experience** leads to spiritual rebirth (Christ). To be **born again** is to participate in the mystical and mythical experience of life. Albert Einstein said;

▸ "The most beautiful and most profound emotion we can experience is the sensation of the mystical. It is the sower of all true science. He to whom this emotion is a stranger, who can no longer wonder and stand rapt in awe, is as good as dead. To know what is impenetrable to us really exists, manifesting itself as highest wisdom and the most radiant beauty which our dull faculties can comprehend only in their most primitive forms-this knowledge, this feeling is at the center of true religiousness."

The Christ consciousness experience is to die to the flesh and be re-born to spirit. The tree *back to Eden* and non-duality, is represented by the Christ consciousness.

The Holy Grail or **chalice** is attained and realized by those who follow their bliss,[38] excitement or inspiration and attain their achievements through natural aggression, without separation from the natural self, where ritual is not necessary. Orthodox religions separate spirit and nature. There is an unwillingness to engage in the sublime. From the perspective of the sublime the ego diminishes and allows for the identity to become one with nature. Nature *intends the Grail.* This attitude was evident in the native American cultures who understood nature and being supported by it and one with it. Because of their less focused dominance perspective, they were unprepared and unable to understand their demise as the stewards of this continent.

▸   " How can you buy or sell the sky-the warmth of the land? The idea is strange to us. We do not own the freshness of the air or the sparkle of the water. How can you buy them from us? . . We know that the white man does not understand our way. One portion of the land is the same to him as the next, for he is a stranger who comes in the night and takes from the land whatever he needs. The earth is not his brother but his enemy, and when he has conquered it, he moves on. He leaves his fathers' graves, and his children's birthright is forgotten. . . There is no quiet place in the white man's cities. No place to hear the leaves of spring or the rustle of insect's wings. But perhaps because I am a savage and do not understand, the clatter only seems to insult the ears. And what is there to life if a man cannot hear the lovely cry of a whippoorwill or the arguments of the frogs around a pond at night? The Indian prefers the soft sound of the wind darting over the face of the pond, and the smell of the wind itself cleansed by a midday rain, or scented with a pinon pine. The air is precious to the red man. For all things share the same breath the beasts, the trees, the man. The white man does not seem to notice the air he breathes. Like a man dying for many days, he is numb to the stench. . .When the last red man has vanished from the earth, and the memory is only the shadow of a cloud moving across the prairie, these shores and forests will still hold the spirits of my people, for they love this earth as the newborn loves its mother's heartbeat. . . One thing we know-our God is the

---

[38] Refer to Joseph Campbell *"The Power Of The Myth."*

same. This earth is precious to Him. Even the white man cannot be exempt from the common destiny. Sealth, a Duwamish chief, 1865."[39]

Western society's focus on the individual has become so great that it seems that *spirit* has been divorced from the individual and spirit's rightful place as the only true, invisible means of support. Abundance is not assumed, but something to be achieved.

Psychology

Psychology is the study of the interplay or interchange of psychic material between these different levels, or the lack of it. Behavior results from the integration or segregation of levels and archetypes, which become patterned to serve the emotional security definitions of the conscious self. Some aspects of definition expression are allowed and others not. These definitions are developed in response to the self validation of certain aspects and needs and to not contradict archetypes not included, and that do not serve, the definition choice.

Developmental **conflict** occurs when the self's need to resolve apparent contradiction and paradox within the world of duality (the physical world) seems opposed to that self definition.

The experience of living (in the conscious realm) is the examination and exploration of the process of becoming in time, what we already are, out of time on less focused levels.[40]

Thus, living is an experience of ever changing combination and recombination of archetypal references that we meet from

---

[39] Peter Matthiessen, *"Indian Country"*, Penguin Books, 1992.

[40] As an extension of "All That Is" in its exploration. Time is not a "thing" that occurs, it is an artificial construct for talking about and measuring the occurrence of events.

these levels in our life through time.[41]

The horoscope reflects the combination and interplay of these archetypes from many levels, and results in probable behavior from the effect of new levels of interchange, (i. e., focus, fulfillment, expression and resolution, as we will see later in planetary aspect development). We then meet the archetypal conflicts on the stage of physicality. The process, cycle or quadrature, will be referred to as the *four dimensions template* (which defines four temperament types, the four DNA nucleotide bases, and the four cardinal points etc.).

Psychological theories and teachings necessary to understand the basic psychology in this text, follow. The definitions are not all inclusive and only parts deemed relative or helpful, are explored. They have been updated and integrated with principles discussed thus far.

A glossary of terms and definitions necessary to operationalize and lead a more comfortable use of this text follows at the end of the chapter.

Definitions of Personality

What is a personality? It is sometimes associated with some social skills or effect upon others, or as the person's most striking characteristic. The *persona* is a mask or face presented by the ego mainly as the effect of the identity's archetypal orientation. Some definitions from the psychological perspective include;

- ...a person's unique pattern of traits (Guilford, 1959, p. 5).
- ...the dynamic organization within the individual of those psychosocial systems that determine his characteristic behavior and thought (Allport, 1961, p. 28).
- ...the most adequate conceptualization of a person's behavior in all its detail (McClelland, 1951, p. 69).

- "Now, recognize that the personality is not who nor what you are.

---

[41] Again this is reflected in the recombination of chromosomes through the process of meiosis, one haploid cell from each parent into a diploid cell.

> Personality is, we shall say, an artificial construct, a facade (not in a negative term, but a mask) created so that you can have and express, in your physical reality, the idea that you call mentality: thought, analysis, rationalization, reason. With this tool of personality, you can, then, know that you have created a specific mechanism or channel for the consciousness' point of view or philosophy and, therefore, that philosophy will be expressed in your own unique way, colored, if you will, by the unique personality or mentality that has been created to express it."[42]

Whether personality results from traits, is the effect of the organization of psychic systems, or simply the product or appearance as the effect of behavior is not clearly presented in psychology. Because astrology is not accepted as a valid study (currently) in psychological academia, the effect is a sort of broad "fishing" by personality theorists of what it is. Astrology fits with both biological as well as psychological models while mirroring archetypal images, because *it defines them.* Astrology is the study of the system or template from which these patterns arise.

It is the combination and organization of *Archetypal traits* that produces what is known as a personality.

The materialists view, whose concepts of biological traits as being responsible for personality foundation, is the theory of most improbable viability. From where does the template arise to create biological patterns? Because recognizing a *pattern* is a conceptual cognition which the materialists view argues is the *effect* of materiality, a concept of pattern cannot exist if perceptions are "caused" biologically. A contradiction in principles denies the validity of this assertion. A pattern is an idea. An idea is a concept. A concept may manifest physically, but an idea is the template that allows that concept to manifest physically. Psychology "results" from the interaction of the personality (archetypal images) psychodynamics, with the mental field (psyche) on all levels.

---

[42] Darryl Anka channeling "Bashar" in *"The New Metaphysics"* 1987 Light and Sound Communications, Inc. page 12 third paragraph.

Psychodynamics

Until Sigmund Freud's ideas of the unconscious, it was generally understood that our behavior was under our conscious or rational control. Freud laid the foundation for the recognition that perhaps there were underlying or **unconscious** reasons for behavior. He postulated that the unconscious was driven by basic impulses, (e.g., sex and aggression), and asserted that these drives were suppressed by the conscious mind. The **Ego** mediated the impulses of the id and the superego. Conscious mind inhibited these base impulses. This reflects a negative orientation of the psychodynamic relationships between levels of the psyche.

The perspective of self-empowerment maintains (as the horoscope will later show), the **ego** (or **identity definition**) is indeed the conscious aspect of the self. But is the **effect** of conscious focus with the benign higher self focused through conscious mind. Somewhat like the protocol of a modem in computer terminology. The protocol (ego) determines the method and pattern of transmission of information by *archetypal orientation*. Protocols (egos) only act as a mediators of the types of archetypes will be at issue or allowed through

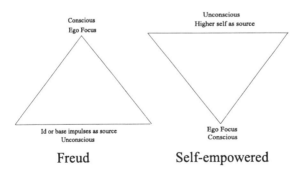

Conscious
Ego Focus

Unconscious
Higher self as source

Id or base impulses as source
Unconscious

Ego Focus
Conscious

Freud   Self-empowered

and in what *method* from this higher self sea of consciousness. The personal **unconscious** is a personal sea, with depths that increase as the self moves further away from conscious focus and into a more expanded and undefined higher self sea. Often, the triangle is used to convey the concept of the conscious mind as being the "tip" of the iceberg in consciousness terms. In the above, the expanded view would simply be the result of *positive energy* and be more representative if inverted, with the most base level, the conscious mind.

The main difference between Freud's perspective and the positive perspective is that the motivations of individuals, although some may be unconscious, are **inherently** *positive* and seeking integration and unification, rather than being subdued because they are inherently negative and seeking drive reduction satisfaction. They may *become negative* through disintegration, and the erosion of self-empowerment by cutting off or *unlearning* natural assertion. This most often occurs through the early environment or societal structure and subjective value systems of belief adoption. Post-modern society places all validity in the ego. In the limited idea that the self we are, *is all we are,* and are not responsible for it because it is biologically caused.[43] It is not the pleasure principle (Freud's tension reduction theory which satisfies id's needs) but the **God principle** (the theory that the identity seeks idealized fulfillment through realization) that motivates the identity. The drive reduction theory places the power outside the self and therefore *must* be negative.

The **reality principle**, according to Freud, is the ego's need to test reality and to delay discharge of tension until the appropriate object and/or circumstances are found. Again this perspective ignores the possibility of creation of environmental experience by the higher self. A more positive perspective asserts that the environment is created by the higher self and

---

[43] Acknowledging that some traits and activities are biologically caused. But an ideological or Archetypal template is responsible for the biological pattern. That pattern, at least in this solar system is reflected in astrological measurement and celestial configuration.

tests the ego's (conscious self) ability to perceive what it's beliefs *about* reality create. The higher self communicates to the conscious self in this way.

The **Superego** is not the censor of primal drives, but the conscience realized and experienced as the effect of the higher self and it's prescriptions of developmental growth. There is a learned sense of responsibility and duty garnered from the experience, with external reality as the "props" and educational tools of the higher self.

Conflict ensues when the integration of apparently polarized archetypes are sought to be integrated at a higher level of awareness by the higher self, and the conscious mind resists this growth. This is what is meant in this text when we speak of *psychodynamics.*[44] **Pain** (physical and psychological) is the effect of this resistance to growth and beliefs in separation.

Defense mechanisms result from the ego's inability or unwillingness to acknowledge the origin of conflict. **Anxiety,** the negative expression of excitement or bliss, is the unwillingness to accept responsibility for creation of one's reality experiences and the judgment of them. *Defense mechanisms* are developed out of the belief that ego is not served by the events and/or experiences it perceives and creates. Thus defense may result from being taught that reality is only outside of the self and therefore requires a defense to protect itself from attack as a carry over from its proper place in protecting the physical self from injury etc. Our physiology and physical experiences then mimic this concept.

Guilt reflects the ego's conflict with higher self conscience when integrity has been violated. It can also be the effect of a judgement of a behavior deemed "wrong" or a thought believed not "good." A defense mechanism may be used to cover up this violation. The violation is placed in an

---

[44] This is not what the psychological community considers the driving force in dynamics, they would consider it a clash between impulses and restraining forces of the identity.

unconscious mode until the identity is ready or willing to negotiate its resolution. The ego's primary job is to effect functioning in the physical world. If ego-self believes acknowledging flaws and errors undermine its status and power, those ideas will be rejected forcefully (this is the negative expression of ego). It may hold on to a pattern of behavior beyond usefulness. A *habit* is a mechanism that is unconsciously performed and resists extinction because reinforcement is strong and hides the integrity violation.[45]

A comprehensive understanding of the fears of the ego are essential to understanding human nature. These fears are reflected through the functions of defense mechanisms. Defense mechanisms are faulty reasoning on the part of the ego because of its heavy reliance upon external reality feedback that has been misinterpreted and patterned. The primary fear of the ego is "loss of control," which from a metaphysical understanding it never fully has anyway, since the will of the higher self must be followed to some degree (this concept will be explored further in the chapter on universal premise).

The following are some of the most important defense mechanisms. Understanding them fully is critical, they will later be tied to astrological patterns. By understanding them, effective counseling and reflective remediation can be employed. Defense mechanisms result from guilt and perceived threats to the status and identity (efficacy) of the ego. Needs that the identity defines as its persona (the personality, the chosen mask) are the issues being defended against or deemed in deprivation or at issue.

Denial must be acknowledged as a possible defense to other networks or defenses. Denial may occur in especially difficult issue confrontation, or if the counselor has not gained

---

[45] A habit of course can be positive and in integrity, but will necessarily be unconscious to be a habit. Extinction is the weakening of a response through the withholding of reinforcement.

the trust of the client. The identity believes that there is nowhere to escape from confrontation, and no way to save face. The sensitivity of the counselor and experience are essential to accurate determinations of the state of the client (refer to vibrational levels in the first section).

Repression occurs when the outright denial of a situation or attitude flies in the face of objective facts. This repression reflects the ejection from the conscious level of psychic material, ideas and issues the identity chooses to ignore. It remains subconscious, because there is an indecision factor, and the concept is in a state of reassessment. Guilt and judgment have complicated expression of the repressed archetype or concept, and hesitation replaces confidence.

Repression is exceedingly important in analysis. It reflects the idea of the spirit's or soul's game of forgetting other aspects of the self as the effect of physical focus and subjective value judging certain archetypes as "bad."

The issues that are repressed present threats to emotional security of the beliefs of the identity. Repression is strongly connected to past life unresolved issues. Actions taken from a powerless perspective lack integrity,[46] create guilt feelings and (depending on the state of the conscience) are repressed. They are either dealt with on an internal level, or are reassessed until the higher self creates developmental scenarios that demand resolution (crisis). Hesitancy and procrastination often accompany repression. *Action reflects conviction of belief.*

The *overcompensational pendulum* is the effect of dramatic guilt from actions that oscillate often wildly from repression to aggression. It can occur within a lifetime or from life to life. Let us say that in one life an individual is unusually assertive and dominating (perhaps the picture of today's

---

[46] Integrity is the recognition that we are as powerful as we need to be to create whatever we desire, without hurting ourselves or anyone else in order to create it. Connected (integrated) with higher self awareness.

politician may serve as a good example). Actions are taken far removed from inspiration, integrity or a sense of service. People are hurt or affected negatively from these actions. Guilt, remorse or a simple sense of conscience may not come about until death (it can come about at a saturation point of momentum in the current life of course) when an assessment instills a sense of perspective about the lack of integrity with actions taken.[47]

When the conscience point reaches remorse, an exaggerated sense of inhibition or repression of natural aggression functioning ensues. Hesitancy and procrastination predominate, creating an unnatural *resistance* to self

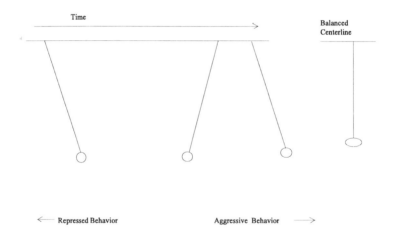

fulfillment. After enough restriction, a belief in the loss of positive expression can produce excessive aggression

---

initiating the cycle all over again.

In **projection** a person's own unacceptable beliefs and attitude are inhibited from recognition, and the source of anxiety is attributed to another person. For example, one's inability for sensitivity or empathy are attributed to another person. The other person is viewed as not "understanding" or listening and sensing the needs of the person projecting. This form of denial is almost always accompanied by some forms of repression and ego or identity insecurity. The archetypal issues in need of resolution are the concepts projected upon others. There is not usually a hierarchy to projection, but someone important (i.e., husband/wife) becomes the screen or recipient of an archetypal conflict with some other important figure (i.e., parental figure).

Because these issues are placed in the unconscious and not dealt with, they become a very strong determinant of behavior (habit). The individual then interprets these repressed issues as a feeling it receives about others, when in reality they are its own definitions. When issues are dealt with from this level there is little will[48] and the identity primarily *re-acts* to its own creations.

A **feeling** is a reaction to a belief. *No one "just feels" a certain way without first having a belief or estimation of this issue(s) being "felt" about, although it may be and most often is unconscious.* An emotion therefore is the e-motion or energy-momentum behind a belief, *that produces a "feeling"* (Bashar).

Rationalization occurs when self-deceiving excuses and justifications serve only *to avoid acknowledging* these projected or repressed feelings. For example, if an individual wishes to terminate a relationship because they do not wish to acknowledge their lack of willingness to examine aspects of themselves through the interaction, they may seek to find as

---

[48] Defined as; the control the mind has over its reactions.

many flaws in the partner as possible. In this way justifying terminating the relationship as necessary because of the *partner's* inability or unwillingness to examine his/her faults, with which the former is exasperated and can no longer cope.

Because the mother is extremely important in early development, some issues that are unresolved with her identity may be acquired by the child. **Anaclitic identification** is the idea that the child's intense dependency on the mother early on makes her influence profound. A hierarchy of needs is thus established from this early interaction.

Fixation was thought by Freud to be the preoccupation or over-identification with one of his "stages" of development. The fact that there are critical periods in development I would submit are a given is because the identity is in an acclimation stage until about 7 (acclimation to physicality). In this text **Anaclitic identification** will be more closely associated with the **reigning need** of the personality's hierarchy of needs discussed above (please refer to Noel Tyl supplemental reading). It is the aspect of the Anaclitic identification that the child believes was *not* nurtured by the mother, was deprived, and hence requires fulfillment above all other needs. The other extreme is the preoccupation with the issue by the mother transferred to the child. All other needs and aspects of the persona work to fill this need. It is a "hallway" willed by the higher self,[49] that one must "go down" to fulfill certain explorations of reality (momentum of belief).

Understanding the psychodynamics of one's persona functioning can aid in the alteration of behavior, and change the probabilities of future experience. Being self-empowered means being self-aware. Greater awareness, leads to greater free will of the physical self to understand and implement the free will of the higher self, and in so doing, serve "All That Is."

---

[49] A choice made by the non-physical self previous to incarnation.

Carl Jung

Carl Jung developed his own theories of psychoanalysis which retain the concepts of the unconscious, but he added a **collective unconscious** that is an inherited (both physically and psychically) aspect of the consciousness. The collective unconscious contains **Archetypes** or **primordial images** individually rearranged and recombined, and form the foundation of astrological archetypal reference. Archetypes are universal in primordial form. How they may be interpreted from solar system to solar system, in different languages and signs, is another matter. They occur in dreams, myths, art, and as behavior patterns and in my opinion *physically*. Archetypes form the basis for the hierarchy of twelve personality needs. The Mayan civilization used the thirteenth harmonic and if their perspective can be fully deciphered we may have a truly new (or old) astrological approach.[50]

The **shadow self** is an unconscious part of the psyche representing polarity aspects of the aware self, and is gradually incorporated into the persona if a successful unfoldment of personal growth occurs over the life of an individual. This allows for more coherent and complete expressions of identity in the world of polarities. It corresponds to the "Dark body" *Nemesis[51]*, proposed by some astronomers as being responsible for the perturbation of comets and other material in the Oort cloud surrounding our solar system. It would be the "Shadow" of our Sun symbolically and archetypically.

According to Carl Jung each individual has a masculine and feminine side. The masculine, positive or *active* is the **animus** and feminine, negative or *passive* is the **anima**. The successful integration of these aspects within each individual allows for the defensive aspects of personality to be virtually

---

[50] Please refer to *"The Mayan Factor"*, by Jose' Arguelles, Bear & Company, 1987.

[51] Orbiting the solar system every 26,000,000 years.

non-existent, and dis-ease all but eliminated. Biologically, this concept corresponds to the active and passive transport of nutrients and chemicals in a cell (see chapter 2 "Universal Premise").

Jung took Astrology seriously and regarding it as fundamental, and representative of his ideas in example to the *Mandala.*

* "Originally he regarded astrology as a function of time...but must be understood as a "stream of energy filled with qualities,"[52]so that the time quality peculiar to that moment of a man's birth also attaches to his character and possibly to his fate as well.

   The old astrological stellar myths are expressions of these intuitively grasped time qualities. They are archetypal images, involuntary creations of the "knowing unconscious," which primitive man projected upon the stars. Jung wrote in a letter in (June 1960): '"We must bear in mind that we do not make projections, rather they happen to us. This fact permits the conclusion that we originally read our first physical, and particularly psychological, insights in the stars. In other words, what is farthest is actually nearest. Somehow, as the Gnostics surmised, we have "collected" ourselves from out of the cosmos.'"[53]

The *Mandala* is almost always a circular shape (which symbolizes the soul or whole self, see the section on *Geometric Basics*) that contains designs, and is often divided into four parts. The horoscope, although a mathematically correct representation of relative celestial positioning, is also a Mandala, and therefore requires an Art/Science approach to delineation.

52
       Letter, January 1934.

53
       From *"Jung's Last Years",* Aniela Jaffe`, Spring Publications, 1984, pages 29, 30, Chapter 1, *"Parapsychology: Experience and Theory".*

- "Jung's conception of personality is complex...His observations often dwelled on the multiple, contradictory forces in life: 'I see in all that happens the play of opposites' (1963, p. 235). Yet he was also one of the first to conceptualize a *self* that actively strives for oneness and unity. Jung saw the self (the striving for wholeness) as an archetype that is expressed in many ways. The expressions of the striving for wholeness include the **Mandala** (a magic circle archetype) and various religious and transcendental experiences. He devoted much of his life to the study of these expressions in primitive societies, alchemy, mythology, dreams, and symbols. To achieve unity and wholeness, the individual must become increasingly aware of the wisdom available in his or her personal and collective unconscious and must learn to live in harmony with it..."[54]
- Mandala....Well, it is just one typical archetypal form. It is what is called *ultimo exquadra circulae,* the square in the circle, or the circle in the square. It is an age-old symbol that goes right back to the pre-history of man. It is all over the Earth and it either expresses the Deity or the self; and these two terms are psychologically very much related, which doesn't mean that I believe that God is the self or that the self is the God. I made the statement that there is a psychological relation, and there is plenty of evidence for that."[55] "It is, we should say, the main archetype."

The Four Dimensions Template

Jung described four ways that individuals experience the world **sensing, intuition, feeling,** and **thinking.** These different approaches to experiencing reality are temperament styles and ways of experiencing the world (the four sides of the square in the circle). They are **backdrops** of belief and archetypal patterns. They form the canvas for the personal consciousness to "paint" upon. The styles of **introversion** and **extroversion** are also temperament styles. All of these approaches can be tested and evaluated using the **Keirsey Temperament Sorter and the Myers-Briggs Type Indicator**

---

[54] "Introduction to Personality" chapter 3 "Ego Psychology and Object Relations"p 69, Walter Mischel, Columbia University, Harcourt-Brace, 1993.

[55] "Conversations With Carl Jung", by Richard Evans, Van Nostrand, 1964.

(see figure on the following page).[56]

I highly recommend that this form of personality assessment be used in conjunction with an accurately prepared horoscope. No one is a pure type. We are all different configurations and intensities of each. We will tie these temperament styles to the

Characteristics frequently associated with each type

	Sensing types		Intuitive types	
Introverts	**ISTJ** Serious, quiet, earn success by concentration and thoroughness. Practical, orderly, matter-of-fact, logical, realistic, and dependable. See to it that everything is well organized. Take responsibility. Make up their own minds as to what should be accomplished and work toward it steadily, regardless of protests or distractions.	**ISFJ** Quiet, friendly, responsible, and conscientious. Work devotedly to meet their obligations. Lend stability to any project or group. Thorough, painstaking, accurate. Their interests are usually not technical. Can be patient with necessary details. Loyal, considerate, perceptive, concerned with how other people feel.	**INFJ** Succeed by perseverance, originality, and desire to do whatever is needed or wanted. Put their best efforts into their work. Quietly forceful, conscientious, concerned for others. Respected for their firm principles. Like to be honored and followed for their clear convictions as to how best to serve the common good.	**INTJ** Usually have original minds and great drive for their own ideas and purposes. In fields that appeal to them they have a fine power to organize a job and carry it through with or without help. Skeptical, critical, independent, determined, sometimes stubborn. Must learn to yield less important points in order to win the most important.	**Introverts**
	ISTP Cool onlookers—quiet, reserved, observing and analyzing life with detached curiosity and unexpected flashes of original humor. Usually interested in cause and effect, how and why mechanical things work, and in organizing facts using logical principles.	**ISFP** Retiring, quietly friendly, sensitive, kind, modest about their abilities. Shun disagreements, do not force their opinions or values on others. Usually do not care to lead but are often loyal followers. Often relieved about getting things done, because they enjoy the present moment and do not want to spoil it by undue haste or exertion.	**INFP** Full of enthusiasms and loyalties, but seldom talk of these until they know you well. Care about learning, ideas, language, and independent projects of their own. Tend to undertake too much, then somehow get it done. Friendly, but often too absorbed in what they are doing to be sociable. Little concerned with possessions or physical surroundings.	**INTP** Quiet and reserved. Especially enjoy theoretical or scientific pursuits. Like solving problems with logic and analysis. Usually interested mainly in ideas, with little liking for parties or small talk. Tend to have sharply defined interests. Need careers where some strong interest can be used and useful.	
Extraverts	**ESTP** Good at on-the-spot problem solving. Do not worry, enjoy whatever comes along. Tend to like mechanical things and sports, with friends on the side. Adaptable, tolerant, generally conservative in values. Dislike long explanations. Are best with real things that can be worked, handled, taken apart or put together.	**ESFP** Outgoing, easygoing, accepting, friendly, enjoy everything and make things more fun for others by their enjoyment. Like sports and making things happen. Know what's going on and join in eagerly. Find remembering facts easier than mastering theories. Are best in situations that need sound common sense and practical ability with people as well as with things.	**ENFP** Warmly enthusiastic, high-spirited, ingenious, imaginative. Able to do almost anything that interests them. Quick with a solution for any difficulty and ready to help anyone with a problem. Often rely on their ability to improvise instead of preparing in advance. Can usually find compelling reasons for whatever they want.	**ENTP** Quick, ingenious, good at many things. Stimulating company, alert and outspoken. May argue for fun on either side of a question. Resourceful in solving new and challenging problems, but may neglect routine assignments. Apt to turn to one new interest after another. Skillful in finding logical reasons for what they want.	**Extraverts**
	ESTJ Practical, realistic, matter-of-fact, with a natural head for business or mechanics. Not interested in subjects they see no use for, but can apply themselves when necessary. Like to organize and run activities. May make good administrators, especially if they remember to consider others' feelings and points of view.	**ESFJ** Warm-hearted, talkative, popular, conscientious, born cooperators, active committee members. Need harmony and may be good at creating it. Always doing something nice for someone. Work best with encouragement and praise. Main interest is in things that directly and visibly affect people's lives.	**ENFJ** Responsive and responsible. Generally feel real concern for what others think or want, and try to handle things with due regard for the other person's feelings. Can present a proposal or lead a group discussion with ease and tact. Sociable, popular, sympathetic. Responsive to praise and criticism.	**ENTJ** Hearty, frank, decisive, leaders in activities. Usually good in anything that requires reasoning and intelligent talk, such as public speaking. Are usually well informed and enjoy adding to their fund of knowledge. May sometimes appear more positive and confident than their experience in an area warrants.	

astrological significators when we begin the section on the Experiential Template (Chapter 3).

Sensing types are practical, need for functional adequacy, are experience oriented, sensible, rely on past experience and facts, tend to material orientation, and basically experience knowing through the sensory systems.

Intuition types rely on possibilities, hunches, fantasy, imagination, inspiration, and their hopes for the future are very important. They are spontaneous, unrestrained, and fear being ignored. They usually have good insight into underlying sensory inputs.

Feeling types are subjective, personal, express sympathy, are emotionally oriented and fear being taken advantage of. The desire for significance, security and compassion are

---

56
    Refer to *"Please Understand Me"* character and temperament types by David Keirsey & Marilyn Bates, Prometheus/Nemesis Book Co. 1978.

strong. The evaluation of emotional experience is strongly valued.

Thinking types are objective, impersonal, analytical, intellectual and social. Their focus is on abstract reasoning and thought. They have a strong fear of being unappreciated for their uniqueness, intellectually and socially.

Extroverted types reflect the concept of animus and are energetic, externally oriented, extending, expending and maintain breadth. This attitude more accurately corresponds to the conscious mind functions discussed earlier.

Introverted types reflect an orientation more closely associated with the anima or; the subconscious mind functions and are internal, need solitude, intensive, conservatively oriented and maintain depth.

For individuals interested in a more comprehensive understanding of the types please refer to "Volume 6 of The Collected Works of C. G. Jung, *Psychological Types*" Bollingen series XX, Princeton University Press.

Here are some notable excerpts from interviews and statements from Carl Jung relative to this text's perspective. Question from Dr. Evans;

• Dr. Jung, there has been much discussion about how certain experiences in the early years influence the formation of the ego. For example, one of the most extreme views concerning such early influences was advanced by Otto Rank. He spoke of the birth trauma and suggested that the trauma of being born would not only leave a very powerful impact on the developing ego, but would have a residual influence throughout the life of the individual.

Dr. Jung;

• I should say that it is very important for an ego that it is born; this is highly traumatic, you know, when you fall out of heaven.[57]

• "Mythology is a pronouncing of a series of images that formulate the life of archetypes."

---

[57] "Conversations with Carl Jung", Richard I. Evans, Van Nostrand, 1964.

• "If somebody is clever enough to see what is going on in people's minds, in their unconscious minds, he will be able to predict."

Summary

VIII. Spirit is both physical (matter-feminine) and energetic (non-physical-masculine). Levels of spirit are determined by vibrational speed.

IX. Spirit is the divine agency working within all things which we will call "All That Is." Separations between levels is an illusion.

X. Mystical experience is the *Mode* of manifestation that leads to spiritual rebirth or being "born again." The Christ consciousness is the collective consciousness of all ideas within our solar system integrated.

XI. Spirit and nature are one. Back to Eden is the integration of conflicts to non-duality. The "Grail" or "Chalice" is this integration achieved through following one's bliss or excitement, acting with the whole self with integrity.

XII. Psychology is the study of the interplay and interchange of the levels of psychic material. Behavior is the result of the integration or segregation of these levels that manifests in the form of needs or conflict with them.

XIII. The resolution of apparent conflict and contradiction is the experience of living in physical reality, and the examination of aspects of the self in their apparent fragmented expression through time.

XIV. A "personality" is not all that we are, but is represented by the ego, an artificial construct that we use as an interface with physical reality. Archetypal images that are in conflict or specific organizations produce needs that infer a personality. Biological traits in genes are generational and collective belief patterning carried through incarnation. They are "caused" by the archetypal template (beliefs), not vice-versa.

XV. As we move into a more expanded version of the self

we go deeper into the unconscious. Psychodynamics is the interaction and regulation of the personality through need fulfillment and resolution. Natural aggression is the positive expression and assertion of an individual acting in integrity. Integrity is the recognition of power that does not require external domination to be fulfilled.

XVI. Defense mechanisms are the psychological effect of the individual's unwillingness to acknowledge and discern archetypal conflict and accept responsibility for the creation of reality experiences that arise from definitions. The idea that we are powerless and need protection from ourselves promotes this concept. Anxiety is the negative expression or judgement against following one's bliss or excitement. Guilt is the recognition of acting without integrity.

XVII. ***Action is the conviction of belief.*** The overcompensational pendulum is the oscillation of guilt patterns that swing wildly and in the extreme from actions of repression to actions of aggression. This can occur within the life and from life to life.

XVIII. Feelings are reactions to beliefs. All of reality is created by beliefs, concepts and definitions. The reigning need of the personality drives the development and nurturing of belief definition acquired most often through attachment in the early environment (first past life-then early environment in this life). This is how we fulfill the higher self and therefore indirectly the exploration of "All That Is" of itself.

XIX. The shadow self is the unconscious expression and polarity of the conscious self. All attitudes and archetypes are expressed in masculine and feminine terms. The Mandala is the primary archetype that permeates all consciousness. In accordance with this concept is the four primary temperament styles(along with the DNA bases forms the ***Four dimensions***

        Template) and the extroverted and introverted expression of them.

XX.   The key to the prediction of behavior and experience is the conscious awareness and understanding of unconscious belief patterning and definition.

Key Definitions

Abnormal-Deviation from a "type" or standard. Every individual is absolutely unique and expresses a specific idea, therefore, there really is no such thing.

Abundance-The ability to have and create whatever experiences or things that you need when you need them. You always have this ability and what you need, even if you do not recognize it until later. If we believe everything is there for a reason, we will find it much easier.

Accelerate-A change in vibration to a higher level or pitch in consciousness that is more aware and encompassing in perspective, usually achieved through the incorporation of psychic material previously held in an unaware state. (*see introspection*).

Accident-Everything happens for a reason and therefore this is simply the conscious mind's interpretation of unexpected events that occur suddenly and without sequential reference.

Accord-A lack of resistance to developmental growth exhibited by a lack of dis-ease and/or disintegration.

Accurate-Exact conformity to truth as an effect of analytical discernment. (Whether this truth is the preferred truth or not is another question).

Acknowledge-To own or recognize through some act. In this text we have said that we create our reality by what we believe. If we wish to change any aspect or our reality, we must change definitions. We cannot change definitions we are not willing to acknowledge or "own". (*refer to the defenses of the ego*).

Action-The physical manifestation and/or movement of belief conviction.

Actualize-To real-ize.

Addiction-The giving up of creative power (the illusion of it) to anything that denies the power of definition in the present.

Affect-Emotion and feeling as a response to belief. General mood based on perspective and beliefs.

Aggression-Two types. Natural aggression is the healthy

assertion and belief that the idea you are expressing deserves expression just because you exist. Unnatural aggression usually results as an overcompensation from prolonged judgment and repression of the identity and its validity. (*see the overcompensational pendulum*).

Alienation-This usually happens when the vibrations of individuals or groups become so different as to be unable to relate.

"All That Is"-God. Since we are an extension of "All That Is" it cannot be accurate to label it another being. It is not outside of us. Literally, all that is.

Alternative (or Parallel) lives-"...or alternate lives will simply be extensions of your soul self. The creation of personality fragments of a sort that extend themselves into alternate dimensions of reality, rather than the one that you relate to as your particular universal time track, although you can have alternative lives in the present time track, and you can call them counterparts."[58]

These lives intrude upon the consciousness of this life because in actuality they are one thing, experienced sequentially.

Anxiety-The negative expression and resistance to developmental tension and growth otherwise felt as excitement.

Archetypal Symbology-The unconscious substream of collective consciousness that manifests as symbols and concepts experienced by the mass consciousness. Some aspects of it may be unique to specific solar system configuration, and some are universal in nature.

Atonement-The allowance and experience of things as they are.

Attitude-Is the signature of expectation. It can therefore be a strong deterrent to the experience of spontaneity, synchronicity

---

[58] "The New Metaphysics" by Bashar, Light and Sound Communications, 1987.

and possibly discernment. Perhaps the best attitude is one devoid of expectation.

Availability Heuristic-A principle that suggests that the more easily we can imagine something or think about it, the more we believe it to be likely in physical reality. If we acknowledge that there are different levels to the psyche, then if we can imagine it, *it must be manifestable or real on some level.*

Awake-Typically is meant to signify conscious mind focus at the expense of other levels of psychic material. We may be more awake, however (in touch with broader aspects of ourselves) in the dream state or when we encounter unexpected aspects (or accidents) of ourselves through unconscious creation and experience. "Waking up" then could be the acknowledging of aspects ourselves through reality encounters.

Aware-The incorporation and integration of divergent levels of consciousness and focus.

Balance-The recognition that you (and all of reality) contain all divergent and apparently contradicting polarities and dichotomies, both positive and negative.

Belief system-Is one of the three aspects of the persona, the other two being *emotion* and *thought.* It is one of the ways that the free will of the physical self is determined and expressed. The specific configuration of the archetypal reference that a being *trusts* into manifestation.

Better-The conscious mind judgment of a *different scenario* that does not allow present situations to be of service or to "fit."

Bible-The *Age of Pisces* inspired book meant to assist in the relaxation of conscious mind preoccupation and focus toward the expansion of perspective for the *Age of Aquarius.*

Biofeedback-The use of equipment to provide feedback and information on biological functions of the body created by the entirety of the levels of the psyche.

Buddha-Sanskrit for "the awakened one" or enlightened one.

Cause-The apparent physical or possibly non-physical

initiation of any momentum. Since there really is no such thing as time, all causes are effects as well.

Channel-Anything that functions as a carrier to express vibrations, levels and ideas.

Childlike-Without the fear of, or addiction to, only the physical dimension of reality- and a lack of the "seeing-is-believing" mental attitude associated with it.

Christ   Consciousness-The   integrated   combined consciousness of all archetypal reference within this solar system. The "psyche" of this system.

Co-creation-Participation through relationship of two or more co-creators within the Multiverse ("All That Is").

Cognitive restructuring-A therapy such as rational emotive, that allows the individual to think about their perceived problems more constructively and less irrationally. The effect of questioning underlying beliefs. (*See discernment*)

Coherent-Logically and integratively consistent.

Co-incident-The unifying agreement between more than one system of belief through vibrational relevance. Corroboration not accident.

Collective unconscious-Mass idea expression that extends into archetypal reference, by which all of our physical reality experiences are made possible mentally, through the projection of them as reflection into material objects and experiences.

Common sense-A trust (belief) in "self-evident" concepts. Commonly held beliefs and prejudices internalized by the approximate age of 14 years. Albert Einstein pointed out that every new idea one encounters in later life must combat this accretion of self-evident concepts.

Conditioning-The acceptance by the unconscious level of psychic material of a *belief, emotion or thought.*

Con or Co-fusion-The dissolution of focus by the conscious mind upon the matter portion of spirit caused by the expansion of perspective and introduction of previously unaccepted psychic material.

Conscience-Intuitive and/or conscious recognition of integrative behavior. Functioning at the level of discernment.

Conscious Commandment-The decision process and ability of the adult or mature mind (conscious mind of course) to redefine itself through awareness and will. (see willpower).

Conservation and classification abilities-Characteristics of the *concrete operational stage* of children at the age between 6-12 proposed by Jean Piaget (Piaget & Inhelder, 1969), wherein children begin to recognize that certain properties of an object remain the same, even when other superficial properties change. This initiates and corresponds with the critical stages of development reflected in astrology by Saturn's cycle at ages 7, 14, 21, 28 etc. The conscious mind reaches critical stages of concretization and conscious commandment at these ages.[59]

Control-There are two types. Negative control is the belief that reality exists only outside of the self and requires domination. Positive control entails the recognition that you are the reality you previously thought you existed within. Therefore positive control results in the transformation of perspective through the incorporation of experiences through the reflective interaction with the environment or *response-ability*.(see responsibility).

Conviction-The willingness to fulfill the purpose of living, which is to express with fervor the idea you are within the "All That Is", diligently, by following your bliss or excitement.

Counselor-An individual that assists or allows another individual to re-member or re-cognize ideas already contained in the personal or collective unconscious material. "You cannot teach a man anything. You can only help him discover it within

---

[59] See *The Development of Children,* second edition, Michael and Sheila Cole, UCSD, 1993, *Scientific American Books, Pt IV Middle Childhood.*

himself."[60]

Death-Cessation of the physical vehicle when *idea* expression has been exhausted.

Depression-A state of being created by the individual to allow for a psychologically inward focus, when value judgements about situations seek contradiction resolution. A time to go within. Chronic depression is a symptom of more serious issues that need resolution.

Destiny-The unfolding of physical events and experience that represent the most strongly held belief system and character definition in unfoldment.

Dichotomy-The apparent effects of "All That Is" manifesting itself as counterpart concepts in three dimensional reality.

Dis-aster-State of perceived separation from the stars and cosmos.

Discern-Perceptual ability to discriminate between belief projection and belief momentum acknowledgement.

Dis-ease-Hyphenated to emphasize the original meaning of the word. A state of being wherein aspects of the self, not considered to be the self, are denied integration and contradiction resolution. Developmental tension results as an effect of paradox or contradiction the conscious mind is unwilling to psychologically integrate or co-fuse. Therefore, as an expression of the overall state of vibrational level integration, dis-ease is not simply external organisms attacking the biological structure, but a state of being that allows this to occur.

Disempowerment-Addiction to the concept that physical reality exists only outside of the individual, independently. *(see section on science)*

Distance-A perceptual illusion based on three dimensional focus. Real while you are physical but an illusion none-the-less.

---

[60] Galileo.

Emotion-The energy motion of a belief or definition that "causes" feelings.

Enlighten-The effect that occurs when unconscious forgotten awareness is re-membered.

Excitement-The vibratory energy sensation that is felt when an individual is allowing the experience and participation in the frequencies that are most representative of the self definition and level. It is reflective of the easiest fulfillment path of the individual's "hallway", the chosen path or destiny of idea expression and fulfillment *in the current life.*

Fact-One of the elements of a paradigm or system of thought. Anything that we can imagine must exist on some level, therefore, it also can be regarded as anything actually existent. But that existence is not necessarily determined by manipulability. Its *conceivability* makes it "real".

Fate-Unrecognized choice. The physical manifestation of belief definition usually misinterpreted as anything from "God's will" to chaotic and random acts of the universe. Fate is the experiencing of the most likely events to occur as an effect of definitions of the individual, if the energy does not change. Therefore, the less the awareness of belief definition, the easier it is for an astute analyst to predict behavior *and experience.*

Fear-The experiencing of definitions that the individual has failed to acknowledge through introspection. The higher self and unconscious bring these definitions to the forefront of conscious mind recognition either through perceived threats to security or physical threats through the "props" of the material world. More positively, the emotional response necessary to physical survival.

Feeling-The emotional sensation felt as a reaction to deep seated belief or cognition. We must *believe* something first before we *feel* any way about it because the universe has no built-in meaning.

Free will-There are two types but we always have free will to redefine ourselves at any moment. The free will of the higher self manifests more in the appearance of a destiny or path. The free will of the physical self or persona then has its own free will to determine the *quality of experience* in the hallway or definition parameters determined by the higher self, as reflected through the horoscope. Either way it is the exercising of the chosen purpose.

Friendship-Similarity in vibrational frequency enough that five factors occur; 1) common ground activities are shared. 2) communication clarity. 3) information exchanges. 4) conflict resolution. 5) reciprocity and positive reinforcement. (John Gottman 1983).

Genetics-The physical reflection of the momentum of belief patterning prescribed by the higher self and the collective unconscious.

Genius-The allowance and expression of all levels of consciousness, including some past and some future selves, in the present incarnation.

Higher-order motive-In psychology this is known as a "hypothetical" motive because it does not involve physiological changes that can be measured as the "cause" of the motive. The perspective of this text is that this is the primary and *ultimate motive* although it may be quite unconscious.[61]

Ideas-All the different ways that God or "All That Is" has of expressing itself within the creation that it is, labeled or not.

Illusion-The discounting of the present experiences through the judgement of the conscious mind, of not being the ideal. An antonym of discernment.

Implied-To contain an inference, suggestion or hint through discernment, logic, or psychological interpretation or action, an idea that may contradict or reinforce conscious mind argument and recognition. To show to be involved with-*implicate.*

---

[61] Because of the homogenous oneness of "All That Is" its creations cannot logically be of a different motive.

Integrity-Functioning as an integrated whole. Actions and behavior that reflect the awareness and recognition that you are as powerful as you need to be to create whatever you desire to create as an experiential reality, without having to hurt or malign anyone or anything else in order to do so, simply through redefinition and the *trusting* of the new definition. A person acting with integrity is moved to action only by unifying, spontaneous excitement as the effect of inspiration and following ones bliss. They are not moved through the perceived loss of control, threats, strategic block, or the negative effects of any other vibration. Positive energy dissolves barriers through understanding, negative energy seeks to overpower or flee barriers which paradoxically creates a more difficult barrier-because the barriers are created by the self for a *reason*.

Intention-The most important factor in the experiencing of reality. The type of energy and belief that initiates momentum, action and experience.

Intuition-Automatic discernment without the process of analysis. Accuracy is determined by the extent of self knowledge. From *intueri:* to look into or upon.

Karma-The self imposed balancing of polarity experience through momentum.

Knowledge base-The base of conceptual storage that determines the quality of mental functioning and memory. Research has shown that the more a person knows about a topic, the easier it is to recall items that pertain to that topic or base.[62]

Learned helplessness-A negative belief spiral that allows for passive endurance of situations not believed changeable.

Learned optimism-The belief in the ability to induce a positive

---

[62] *The Development of Children,* second edition, Michael and Sheila Cole, University of California, San Diego, *Scientific American Books,* Part IV, Chapter 12, Cognitive and Biological Attainments, pages 447, 448.

reality.

Light-The basic component and stuff of which the Multiverse is made.

Love-Empathic sychronistic accord and recognition of vibratory levels between *any-things* in the Multiverse. There is no guilt or sense of responsibility involved in unconditional love. Those are issues of power, not love.

Mathematics-The organized symbolic expression through numbers of the "mechanics" of "All That Is".

Matter-The physically manifested version of mind.

Mind-The non-physical version of idea expression. The essence of "All That Is".

Moral-The prevailing value judgments of good and bad based on the awareness of the current collectivity.

Mythology-A symbolic language used to interact with archetypal reference.

Natural-Energy and momentum taking the line of least resistance. Normal implies expectations and conditional standards that reinforce the ego in its assessment of "correct and proper." Natural is infinite in expression. *(see excitement, bliss, and integrity)*.

Occult-To obscure, such as one planet crossing over the face of another. The study of knowledge hidden by the preoccupation with conscious mind functioning.

Oversoul-The collective name for the entirety of the identity, physical and non-physical.

Paradox-The expression of polarity in physical reality. It appears as a discrepancy, but is a signal that all sides are contained within your consciousness.

Perfection-"Allow us to refresh ourselves on the idea and the concept of, perfection. We have discussed many times with you, the idea that in your lives very often you are taught, that even when you create the idea and the notion in your lives of what you call, a spiritual path. That the reason for this is for the a-ttainment and the a-chievement of perfection. But recognize once again as we have shared many times our perspective is that you will never a-chieve perfection, because you are already perfect. The idea does not mean that you will not grow, not expand, not change, not transform, not learn something new. But it is simply an allowance, a recognition of allowance in your lives, that at any given moment, the idea you are being, the reality you are expressing, the events you are experiencing, are for their *own reasons* perfect in themselves. This relaxation, this attitude, this backing off from yourself in that way rather than applying so much pressure to the idea to BE MORE PERFECT, is what allows you to know that you can always become a *different* type of perfection at any given moment, perhaps a more expanded type. But you will always be, at any given moment, the absolute perfect manifestation of whatever idea you are being at that moment. Your willingness to allow that moment to be perfect in and of itself, is what paradoxically allows you to *create* the next and different perfect moment. Because unless you are willing to allow whatever moment you are experiencing to be complete in and of itself on all levels, then you are not allowing yourself to view and perceive all facets of that experience, because if you do not think it is perfect as it is, if you invalidate it and judge it in that way, in a negative point of view, then you yourself may be shutting off aspects of that event, of that moment that you need to see, need to be aware of, to incorporate them into the totality of yourself so that you can get on with the next step. Every moment is a stepping stone to the next moment, and if you invalidate any stepping stone then you yourself remove from the path you are, the ability to get to the next stepping stone. Always allow each and every moment of your lives to be perfectly valid as they are. This does not mean that you must accept that the things that are occurring in your life are what you "should" accept or prefer. You can always prefer your life to be the way you desire it to be. But the way to allow yourself to *create it* to be the way that you desire it to be, is to accept that the way it is now SERVES A PURPOSE and is a PART of the path you have created yourself to be, and that what you are learning is there for a reason, *your reason!* That there is something within the scenario you want to see, you want to reflect on, you want to learn from. And in accepting and acknowledging the way your life does unfold, that is what gives you the recognition of the empowerment you have, to create your life to unfold in the direction and in the manner you most desire it to be.

So simply do allow yourself to reflect at any given moment, that no matter what your choices, every scenario, *for what it is,* is a perfect manifestation of that scenario. You can prefer perfect harmony and perfect ecstasy, or you can prefer perfect misery. But both are perfect expressions of the idea you are reflecting at that moment. And when you ***allow it to be there for a reason***, then you can extract from that scenario, what will most assist you in reforming the idea, redirecting yourself and creating what it is you desire to experience most in your reality.

Many individuals will pressure themselves in many different ways to *strive, to struggle, to try,* to be more perfect. Will set themselves goals and ideals in that way, *that continually denies the validity they possess, at that moment.* In that way you deny yourself all that you truly desire as well. For if you do not believe yourself complete in that moment, then you, by your own definition, insist that you do not have the capability of creating what it is you say you desire to attract into your lives. Knowing that you are complete, perhaps focused not in a way you prefer to be, but knowing you are complete, gives you the opportunity to know that at any given moment you have the ability to refocus yourself in any direction you desire-you *lack nothing!* You have all the tools and all the abilities you require at any given moment to be ***anything*** you are willing and bold enough to believe you can define yourself to be!"[63]

Perspective-A separated viewpoint that allows for analytical discernment. The fragmentation of the ideas of "All That Is".

Primacy-Paths and belief definitions taken early in life, especially early deprivation patterning, become the most significant issues throughout the life. This is known as primacy.

Prove-To demonstrate viable evidence through discernment as opposed to belief.

Puberty-The primary stage of cognitive development that corresponds to Piaget's *Formal Operational Stage,* and to the peak cycle of Saturn at approximately age 14, that concretizes through physical reality and experience, the identity's greatest fears of limitation in conscious commandment.[64] *(see conservation, commandment, willpower, conscious mind).*

Reality-The systems or portions of "All That Is" that one experiences, as the effect of belief definition and conviction.

Reality;"Will simply be an idea being expressed and experienced." Bashar, Darryl Anka, "The New Metaphysics", Light and Sound Communications, Beverly Hills CA., 1987

Recognize-The recalling of information.

Reflection-The creation of separated symbols that are a reminder to the self of its creations. This is what the horoscope and the study of astrology is.

Relative-The logic that applies to a specific system of belief.

Religion-To re-link the self to its origin in the cosmos or macrocosm. You cannot *belong* to a re-linking, it is a state of being not a thing. Orthodox religions of present day have nothing to do with this idea. They are habitually ritualized organizations that promote the science of following for those powerless enough to believe that any other individual has more

---

[63] Darryl Anka channeling *Bashar and the association,* February 19, 1987, Los Angeles, California.

[64] See previous footnote.

power than they do to re-link. Placing the power outside of themselves they are necessarily disillusioned. Christ said, "The kingdom of God cometh not with observation: neither shall they say, lo here! or, lo there! for, behold, the kingdom of God is within you."[65]

Responsibility-The ability to respond to your own creations, through increasing awareness of the definitions within the self that created them. We are not responsible *for anyone,* we are only responsible *to them* by being all that we can be in service, through unconditional love. However, this should not be taken to mean that we are not somehow always either a *part of the solution to issues, or a part of the problem. (see self efficacy, learned helplessness, self-empowerment).*

Self-efficacy-The belief and trust in the performance and experience of reality that is reinforced by acting on things that inspire and represent the essence of the energy of the individual. The opposite of learned helplessness which creates feelings of inferiority.

Should-A conscious mind judgment that gives more value to one idea over another. If you are following your excitement or bliss, whatever occurs needs to and is a part of the path you chose to be. Therefore, there are no "shoulds". *(see excitement, integrity and co-incident).*

Status-An artificial condition or rank derived from value judgment. Belief in self-efficacy.

Telepathy-Strong identification with a vibrational frequency that allows for attunement to that frequency.

Template or Templet-The foundational symbology upon which a system of reality is derived.

Threshold of believability-The level at which actions begin to reflect beliefs other than what is professed. The intensity level or conviction contained with the idea you say you are. I.e., if you say you wish to be abundant, when do you believe this is

---

[65] Luke 17:20, 21, King James Version

possible? If you say within a year, then this time period reflects to some degree your willingness to accept the abundance. If you believe tomorrow is when, the threshold is high, if 2 years the threshold lowers. It is a way to discern the reality of the momentum of a belief and the strength of a person's convictions.

Time-The measurement of events, and experiencing of ideas sequentially that actually exist all at once. The effect of conscious mind focus and limitation.

True-The absolute conforming of an event or experience to the belief system and reality that created it.

Trust-The conviction of belief that manifests mind into matter and experience.

Victim-The belief that one can experience calamity originating from outside of the self. We cannot experience anything that is not a part of us *on some* level. Similar vibrations affect each other by *agreement within the same system of belief.*

Will or willpower-"That sum of psychic energy that is disposable to consciousness" (C.G. Jung from *Psychological Types*). The conscious commandment or control the upper level of mind has over its psychic reactions emanating from *all levels.*

Index

Supplementary reading.

Anka, Darryl. The New Metaphysics.
California: Light & Sound Communications Inc.,
        1987
Arguelles, Jose'. The Mayan Factor.
New Mexico: Bear & Company.
        1987

Barnett, Lincoln. The Universe And Dr. Einstein.
New York: William Morrow & Co., Inc..
        1966 second edition.
Barr, David L.. An Introduction-New Testament Story. Second edition.
California: Wadsworth Publishing.
        1995
Brill, E.J.. The Gospel According To Thomas.
New York: Harper and Row.
        1959
Bruder, Kenneth and Moore, Noel Brooke. Philosophy, The Power of Ideas.
California: Mayfield Publishing Co.
        1993
Campbell, Joseph. The Power Of The Myth, W/Bill Moyers.
New York: Doubleday.
        1988
Fix, William R. Pyramid Odyssey
Virginia: Mercury Media.
        1984
Holy Bible. Bible. With Apocrypha.
New York: Oxford University Press.
        1989
Keirsey David, and Bates, Marilyn. Please Understand Me.
San Diego: Prometheus/Nemesis Book Co.
        1978
Mader, Sylvia S.. Inquiry Into Life. Seventh edition.
Iowa: Wm. C. Brown Publishers.
        1994
Matthiessen, Peter. Indian Country.
New York: Penguin Books.
        1992
Mischel, Walter. Introduction to Personality. Fifth edition.
Texas: Harcourt Brace Jovanovich Publishers
        1993
Talbot, Michael. The Holographic Universe
New York: HarperCollins
        1991

Chapter 2

Universal Premise

> "The world was created by
> the word of God so that
> what is seen was made out
> of things which do not appear."
> Saint Paul

Perspective on Science/Religion/Art

The Universe is infinite. There are many levels of it that we have yet to discern. The limitation of our conscious perception is most easily depicted by a diagram of the scale of known waves. The spectrum of visible light is minuscule compared to just the known or *discovered* waves. The unseen obviously outweighs the seen. Yet scientists believed in the early part of the twentieth century, that all that there was to be known in physics, was known. Absence of evidence, is obviously not evidence of absence.

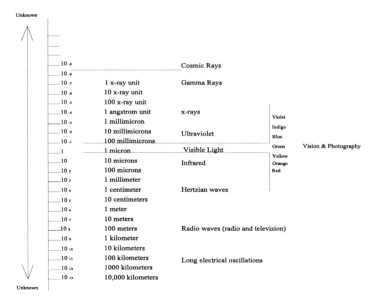

This is known as the fallacy of "Appeal to ignorance" (Argumentum ad ignorantum). When the premises state that nothing has been **Proved** one way or the other about something, and the conclusion then makes a definite assertion about that thing, the argument commits "an appeal to ignorance". The issue usually involves something that is incapable of being proved. (At least at the present moment). Example:

"People have been trying for centuries to provide conclusive evidence for the claims of astrology, and no one has ever succeeded. Therefore, we must conclude that astrology is a lot of nonsense."[66]

Of course in all fairness, absence of evidence is not evidence of presence either. But not knowing how to look for that evidence also makes it difficult to confirm presence. The scientific community had no less difficulty accepting Einstein's theories of relativity at the time, than it now does the probability of astrological validity. Many theories are confirmed-refuted-reconfirmed or remain unknown over time. But science does not seek out **anomaly** (deviation from the common rule).

▸   "The decision to employ a particular piece of apparatus and to use it in a particular way carries with it an assumption that only certain sorts of circumstances will arise. Normal science research is a strenuous and devoted attempt to force nature into the conceptual boxes supplied by the professional education. Anomalies are disregarded because they do not articulate the paradigm."
Thomas Kuhn-Author of the widely acclaimed "The Structure of Scientific Revolutions".

Paradigms or belief systems of thought taught by academic communities, research and compile information to further articulate that system of thought rather than to find discrepancies or contradictions of anomaly. They do until the discrepancies outweigh the consistencies, which then creates another paradigm for research and experimentation.

▸   "We believe every effort should be made to study abnormal

---

66
        Logic, 4th Edition Hurley, University of San Diego, Wadsworth Publishing, 1991, page 128, "Informal Fallacies".

behavior according to scientific principles. It should be clear at this point however, that science is NOT a completely objective and certain enterprise. Rather, as we can infer by the comment from Kuhn, subjective factors, as well as limitations in our perspective on the universe, enter into the conduct of scientific enquiry. Central to any application of scientific principles, in Kuhn's view, is the concept of a paradigm, a conceptual framework or approach within which a scientist works. A paradigm according to Kuhn, is a set of basic assumptions that outline the particular universe of scientific enquiry... In addition to injecting inevitable biases into the definition and collection of data, a paradigm may also affect the interpretation of facts. In other words, the meaning or import given to data may depend to a considerable extent on a paradigm.[67]

Normal science (or puzzle solving) however, is based on past scientific achievements, which provides its basic foundation for further research. Astrology can be considered normal science[68] since it has been explored and reworked for at least 5000 years. The University systems however, were created by the church and even Galileo and Copernicus know the price to be paid for presenting anomaly (i.e., Sun centered system). Fortunately astrologers must only endure uninformed badgering in this day and age.

Science (*scientia,* knowledge) is the systematic study of knowledge gained through the operation of laws. Scientific knowledge is skeptical and never complete. This definition qualifies most of astrology as a science. The reason why the scientific community does not deem it to be so is A) because science does not question life from the holistic view, let alone as a paradigm requiring puzzle solving; B) because it contains a very large propensity for anomaly, C) It has yet to be accepted as a paradigm for further articulation by the academic community, D) it is thought to be a subject requiring belief and faith to function. E) from the holographic or holistic view, the whole organizes the parts and the observer co-

---

[67] *"Abnormal Psychology"*, University of Southern California, State University of New York" Davidson and Neale, 6th edition, 1996. Wiley and sons publishers.

[68] Please refer to *"The Structure of Scientific Revolutions"*, Thomas S. Kuhn, second edition, University of Chicago Press, 1970.

creates the observation. Science is simply one methodology or format for exploring the physical universe.

> ▸ "All this talk of science should not leave you with the impression that it is good and other approaches are bad. It is neither good nor necessarily better than other orientations; science just is...Some covered theories (in this text) will meet the scientific criteria better than others. Theories that fail to meet criteria well will be subjected to appropriate criticism-so will more scientific theories that are flawed in other ways. But no theories will be dismissed solely on the basis of failure to meet scientific criteria. There are good reasons to include theories that do not meet scientific criteria well. In fact, strengths in the non-scientific realm may make these theories more valuable than some more scientific theories.
> Sometimes a well thought-out philosophical position, although it is too abstract to be tested scientifically, can have more merit than a 'hard science' point of view."[69]

Astrology was not a part of astronomical study as scientists profess it was in the past. Astronomy was a part of *astrological* study. The idea of blending paradigms is encouraged from this author's view. The more comprehensive scientific information we have about planetary movement etc., the greater the accuracy and predictability of astrological measurement.

As the EM wave scale shows, if we adhere to the "seeing is believing" perspective we will limit the believable reality to a very small band indeed. We had to *believe* the other bands of waves existed before we would ever "see" them. It is **believing is seeing, not seeing is believing**. Critical thinking persons consider that the Universe is a never ending treasure trove of exploration and discovery.

The word **Hell** is derived from the old English *helan,* meaning to cover over or to hide from consciousness. **Heaven,** then, is obviously *dis-covery,* and both are *states of being.*

> ▸ "Some readers may be puzzled: Didn't we learn all about the foundations of physics when we were still at school? The answer is "yes" or "no," depending on the interpretation. We have become

---

[69]
"A final word about science", Bem P. Allen Western Illinois University "Personality Theories" page 15 introduction, 1994 Simon & Schuster.

acquainted with concepts and general relations that enable us to comprehend an immense range of experiences and make them accessible to mathematical treatment. In a certain sense these concepts and relations are probably even final. This is true, for example, of the laws of light refraction, of the relations of classical thermodynamics as far as it is based on the concepts of pressure, volume, temperature, heat and work, and of the hypothesis of the non-existence of a perpetual motion machine.

What, then, impels us to devise theory after theory? Why do we devise theories at all? The answer to the latter question is simply: because we enjoy "comprehending," *i.e.,* reducing phenomena by the process of logic to something already known or (apparently) evident. New theories are first of all necessary when we encounter new facts which cannot be "explained" by existing theories. But this motivation for setting up new theories is, so to speak, trivial, imposed from without. There is another, more subtle motive of no less importance. This is the striving toward unification and simplification of the premises of the theory as a whole (*i.e.,* Mach's principle of economy, interpreted as a logical principle)."[70] It is the theory that determines *what* we can observe.

The scale of waves metaphorically reflects "All That Is" as a continuous interlocking configuration of vibrational frequencies. Analogous to the radio, our particular view is the station our "dial" is tuned to and is the one we "get." All disciplines give us different pieces of the puzzle and allow us to receive different stations on the "scale of waves." It behooves us to have as many pieces as possible in our understanding of the "truth." Enormous amounts of information, bring us to *tentative* truths.

It is not a matter of chance that pieces of these puzzles come at certain times, or that these pieces fit so well when we seek alignment with them. After review, it is cogent to assert that there is intelligence behind universal manifestation. The universe is a two way ***mind/matter mirror.***

- ▸ *"In the beginning God created the heaven and earth...*
  One intriguing observation that has bubbled up from physics is that the universe seems calibrated for life's existence. If the force of gravity were pushed upward a bit, stars would burn out faster, leaving little time for life to evolve on the planets circling them. If the

---

70
Albert Einstein *"On the Generalized Theory of Gravitation",* Scientific American, Volume 182, no. 4, April 1950, page 1.

relative masses of protons and neutrons were changed by a hair, stars might never be born, since the hydrogen they eat wouldn't exist. If, at the Big Bang, some basic numbers-the "initial conditions"-had been jiggled, matter and energy would never have coagulated into galaxies, stars, planets or any other platforms stable enough for life as we know it. And so on."[71]

It is ridiculous to speculate "what if" these conditions did not exist; they do. The fact that we possess intelligence is evidence to this author that the universe that produces these beings, must also be intelligent. Science is not the reason for speculation that the universe is of intelligent design, nor will it ever be, it is the insight that discoveries bring that make this so. Insight is derived from the simple fact that existence without purpose is *senseless, and with this understanding, this purpose is evidenced everywhere.*

All of existence must fit together. We can sense that a universal template and premise brings it into being. Science seeks to validate the *functions* of this templet, not determine whether it is sensed. The heart of the law is the search for truth; if we bow to the letter and violate the heart, we've missed the point. It is the sense of detachment from "All That Is" that creates the illusion.

> ► "According to general relativity, the concept of space detached from any physical content does not exist. The physical reality of space is represented by a field whose components are continuous functions of four independent variables[72]-the coordinates of space and time. It is just this particular kind of dependence that expresses the spatial character of physical reality.
>
> Since the theory of general relativity implies the representation of physical reality by a *continuous* field, the concept of particles or material points cannot play a fundamental part, nor can the concept

---

[71] *"What does Science Tell Us About God?"*, Time Magazine, December 28, 1992, page 40, sixth paragraph.

[72] Referred to throughout this text as the *four dimensions template* manifesting in many ways.

of motion."[73]

Einstein's relativity theories, holographic and physics theories *validate astrological viability.* The concept of space detached from its physical content *cannot exist at its spiritual root.* The all is simply "something" differentiated. Physical reality is just one way that we have of looking at ourselves. Our consciousness is not *in* our body, **our body is in and moves through our consciousness** (Bashar, 1987).

The four dimensions template is reflected though these four independent variables, the four forces (subatomic particle physics) four Cardinal points (east-west, north south), the four elements (fire, earth, air and water), and the *four* nucleotide bases of DNA (adenine, thymine, cytosine and guanine, see diagram next page) all of which manifest in masculine and feminine polarized pairs (purines and pyramidines). Each nucleotide of DNA is a complex of *three* subunits.

Even the Bible carries this numeric symbology in the form of the four Gospels and is woven throughout Revelations. The four dimensions template I believe, is woven archetypally throughout the world (perhaps physical universe) and is the unified field theory templet for physical manifestations.

I also believe this is the reason for the glorification of the pyramidal structure (the externalized portion of the octahedron outlined in chapter 1) both in Egypt and Central America by the Mayan civilization (also listed on U.S. currency). Why would a civilization spend so much effort on such monstrous work as the Pyramid at Giza *other* than a statement of truth? Why such an attribution of importance? I believe it is symbolic information handed down from the same civilization that used to exist somewhere in the location of the Bermuda rise, *Atlantis.* Upon destruction of the island perhaps some of the survivors went east to Egypt and some went west to end up in Central America. The archaeological similarities between these two

---

[73]
    "On The Generalized Theory of Gravitation", Albert Einstein, Scientific American, Vol. 182, No. 4, page 3, 1950.

First Base	Second Base				Third Base
	U	C	A	G	
U	UUU phenylalanine	UCU serine	UAU tyrosine	UGU cysteine	U
	UUC phenylalanine	UCC serine	UAC tyrosine	UGC cysteine	C
	UUA leucine	UCA serine	UAA *stop*	UGA *stop*	A
	UUG leucine	UCG serine	UAG *stop*	UGG tryptophan	G
C	CUU leucine	CCU proline	CAU histidine	CGU arginine	U
	CUC leucine	CCC proline	CAC histidine	CGC arginine	C
	CUA leucine	CCA proline	CAA glutamine	CGA arginine	A
	CUG leucine	CCG proline	CAG glutamine	CGG arginine	G
A	AUU isoleucine	ACU threonine	AAU asparagine	AGU serine	U
	AUC isoleucine	ACC threonine	AAC asparagine	AGC serine	C
	AUA isoleucine	ACA threonine	AAA lysine	AGA arginine	A
	AUG (*start*) methionine	ACG threonine	AAG lysine	AGG arginine	G
G	GUU valine	GCU alanine	GAU aspartate	GGU glycine	U
	GUC valine	GCC alanine	GAC aspartate	GGC glycine	C
	GUA valine	GCA alanine	GAA glutamate	GGA glycine	A
	GUG valine	GCG alanine	GAG glutamate	GGG glycine	G

cultures is amazing.[74] This format that spirit takes when it manifests physically, is what I have termed *the universal premise*. When we place man and his awareness at center we have the mystical significance of the number 5. This is reflected in the physiological fact that man has the development of the fifth *opposable* digit of the hand, the thumb. Symbolized in this, is mankind's creative prowess by free will over the *four dimensions template*.

The universal concept of the four dimensions is also reflected in the biological process of cell division called mitosis. Cells

---

[74] *"Edgar Cayce on Atlantis"* by Edgar Evans Cayce, 1968 by The Association for Research and Enlightenment.

reflect the polarity of the masculine and feminine forces that are always required for completeness. Peptide bonds are polar and proteins have a primary (linear sequence of amino acids), secondary (helix), tertiary (3-d shape) and quaternary (2 or more linked polypeptides) again reflecting the template.[75]

Evolution theorists have asserted that cosmic rays (and x-rays) may have been involved with the effects on chromosomal mutation (a radical change from previously existing qualities or patterns) especially in albinism. This idea reinforces astrology to some degree and corroborates microcosmic and macrocosmic reflectivity and mutual reception. As above, so below is a physical and universal mechanism, not just a metaphor. The universal premise is always revealed as the templet base of 4 expressed in modes of 3.

The ancient Chinese and other civilizations also had the recognitions of the premise of the sexagenary period (a "cycle of cathay") obtained by combining two by two the twelve (the multiple of 4/3) earthly branches or signs of the zodiac (*shih erh ti chih*) with the ten heavenly stems or planets *(shih tien kan).* All examples of duality were expressed in *yin and yang.*[76] These yin and yang lines when combined form the possibility of 64 hexagrams which is precisely the effect of the 20 known amino acids with their three letter codes which combine in 64 ways. The ancient Sumerians also used the sexagesimal systems and it is no coincidence that they were based on the number 60, it is the base for the 120 degree triangle. The Babylonians were also responsible for the cuneiform languages and the division of the circle by 360 degrees that we use to this day. The seven day week is also their invention. The numerical pattern in **Revelation** *the apocalypse of John,*

---

[75]
   "Inquiry Into Life", Wm. C. Brown Communications Inc. 1994.

[76]
   George Sarton *"The Dawn of Science", The Orient and Greece".*

follows the same 3, 4, 7, 10, 12 patterns.[77]

These are but a few corroborations that can be made by an enquiring mind of this universal premise I propose from my limited knowledge base and several historical references. The academic community probably within its vast knowledge base has "proof" that astrology is not as divorced from academic viability as is commonly believed. If paradigms were "married" instead of reduced to separate unrelated topics I believe the growth in each would be far greater than alone. Paradigms can be woven into a cohesive cogent representation which would serve a metaphysical premise, without any danger of a loss of integrity to the specific paradigm of study. We must move from a segregated investigative process to an unifying one. Now that computers are capable of cross referencing information there will be an explosion of informational exchange that must prepare us for the coming shift in consciousness due from 2012 to 2015.[78] Physics will become metaphysics. Einstein's relativistic theories imply that time is an illusion and that everything is actually "existing" at once. This perspective allows the acknowledgement that all connections to past history *still exist* and are accessible to the consciousness capable of changing its dial, and tuning in, and tapping it.

The way that we tune into these other levels is through following our excitement and bliss. All bliss is connected a thread that leads to all other excitement and discovery (Bashar, 1986). We limit the fullest expression we can be if we are not doing this. This is the primary purpose of anyone's present incarnation; to be the you you chose to be to the fullest extent. The horoscope helps us understand these choices and agreements and whether they are based on anxiety or

---

[77] Please see *"The New Testament Story"*, second edition, David L. Barr, Chapter 11, page 397.

[78] The Mayan civilization predicts this as a period of great transformation. Even though they had no evidence of the existence of the Planets Pluto and Uranus, which astrologically confirm that prediction by their configuration on this date.

excitement and bliss (negative or positive energy).

The current religious and political structure is an **Orion**[79] remnant in which domination and control are the primary tenets. Following one's bliss with trust and integrity is the *release* from Orion and the science of following (control) relied upon by politics and religious fundamentalism. The belief in powerlessness (and fear) is a necessary element of physical and psychological domination, without it, the powerful *are powerless*. These structures survive from the giving away of power by the populace because we are taught to believe that we need "protection."

We create institutional structures to protect us from things we are unwilling to take responsibility for. They may also protect us from things we may not *want* protection from.

Art
"Starry, starry night, flaming flowers that brightly blaze,
swirling clouds in violet haze, reflect in Vincent's eyes of
china blue, colors changing hue,
morning fields of amber grain,
weathered faces lined in pain,
are soothed beneath the artist's loving hands."
"Vincent", Don McClean

Art is a common language that utilizes the natural discernment abilities of every individual. Art requires intuited responses and observation, and it uses more than one level of psychic material within the mental field and is therefore integrative. Likewise astrology uses this form of perception to a great degree because the nuance of geometric configurations is a gestalt field delineated very often through *impression* (once the factual and mechanical aspects are learned of course).

---

[79] The ancient civilization from Orion was negative in the sense of domination and control. *Bashar, The New Metaphysics, 1987.*

We will use the horizontal line (associated with rest) as a diagonal (motion), in angularity (agitation), and as a curve (calmness or gracefulness). An axis describes a visual direction, and can act as implied directions and visual suggestions. Art, like mythology and the horoscope, conveys more than a sum of its parts. The "beautiful" is that which expresses more than an ordinary significance.

Colors, sound and shape are the effects of vibrational frequency as well, (i.e., red reflects the idea of the driving force of physicality-as in the case of *planetary rays*). Any color, sound or shape therefore is a manifestation of a wave. This can be seen with a prism refracting light in the same way that

spirit is refracted into physical reality. White light (consisting of all colors) is separated into its polarity components. When vibrational frequencies are lowered to manifest in physical reality, pairs consisting of these components result. Astrology reveals these conceptual pairs of our consciousness to us in the form of *signs*. Astrology is an art as well as a science. We tie these angles, lines and axes together. With the *3* primary colors, we draw conclusions; a "portrait" of the persona seen through the gestalt field of the horoscope.

Time and Space (reincarnation)

"Gazing past the planets,
looking for total view,
I've been lying here for hours,
you've got to take the journey,
out and in, out and in, out and in.
And if you think its a joke,
well that's alright do what you want to do,
I've said my piece and I leave it all up to you."
The Moody Blues, "To Our Children's Children's Children"

Perspective on Space

Some still think it strange to "believe" in the existence of intelligent extraterrestrial life. In November 1995 (and several times since then, the latest, May 1998) through the *Hubble* telescope it was discovered that a planet larger than Jupiter *in another solar system,* a star in the constellation Pegasus (and supposedly others in formation) were found. Statistically, at best, our planet is a very small planet, one of the smaller in orbit around a minor star, at the furthest edge of a common and inconsiderable galaxy.

Scientists generally believe it illusion that intelligent life elsewhere in the universe would be able to visit here, or would want to come if they could. In 1988 Whitley Strieber catalyzed the psychological recognition of this phenomena with *"Communion".* However, the phenomena entered our psyche collectively in earnest in the 1940s.

> ▸ As early as 1946 Jung had begun to collect data on unidentified flying objects-newspaper clippings, reports issued by groups dedicated to their study, statements from the scientific, military, and governmental establishments, letters from people all over -and he read virtually every book on the subject. His published letters give us a vivid notion of his preoccupation with the phenomena.[80]
>
> Typically, in February 1951 he wrote to an American friend:

"I'm puzzled to death about these phenomena, because I haven't been able yet to make out with sufficient certainty whether the whole thing is a rumour with concomitant singular and mass hallucination, or a downright fact. Either case would be highly interesting. If it's a rumour, then the apparition of discs must be a symbol produced by the unconscious. We know what such a thing would mean seen from the psychological standpoint. If on the other hand it is a hard and concrete fact, we are surely confronted with something thoroughly out of the way. At a time when the world is divided by an iron curtain-a fact unheard-of in human history-we might expect all sorts of funny things, since when such a thing happens in an individual it means a complete dissociation, which is instantly compensated by symbols of wholeness and unity. The phenomenon of the saucers might even be both, rumour as well as fact. In this case it would be

---

[80] C. G. Jung: Letters, selected and edited by Gerhard Adler in collaboration with Aniela Jaffe, Vol. 2 (Princeton, page 75). From editorial note *"C. G. Jung, Flying Saucers, A Modern Myth of Things Seen in The Sky",* Translation by R.F.C. Hull, 1978, Princeton University Press, from Volume 10 of his collected works.

what I call a synchronicity. It's just too bad that we don't know enough about it." [81]

If *we* are capable of recognizing the probability of space constructed format being a four dimensional type fabric (Einstein's theories), it is certainly an egocentric delusion of grandeur to think that a civilization maybe a thousand years ahead of us is not capable of moving along that fabric.

Observe that as our egocentric notions of our place in the universe become more realistic (such as the change from geocentric to heliocentric, from finding no planets to discovering some) our awareness and acceptance of other world probabilities increase, our significance is levelled, our world gets smaller, people are more accepting. Political and religious structures, albeit unconscious, want to slow this awareness because it detracts from the ability to control and dominate. As individuals become more self-empowered, they become less of followers, hence, the demise of the sciences of following.

Statistically, it is more probable that life is a common event rather than not. There are as many stars in our galaxy alone, as there are grains of sand on all of earth's beaches *combined.*[82] Why would I *need* a scientist or government official to tell me there is probably intelligent life on at least half of all the planets orbiting them?

---

[81]
     Ibid., p. 3 (to Beatrice M. Hinkle, 6 Feb. 1951).

[82]
     There are 100 billion or more knowable galaxies (meaning their light is not so far away that we have not received it yet) each containing roughly 100 billion stars each.

Reincarnation

"The thing that hath been, it is that which shall be;
and that which is done is that which shall be done;
and there is no new thing under the Sun.
is there any thing whereof it may be said, see this is new?
it hath already been of old time which was before us.
There is no remembrance of former things;
neither shall there be any remembrance of things that are to
come with those that shall come after."

Ecclesiastes 1:9-11

From what we can see, surmise and understand, time and space are the *coordinates* of the four dimensions template. We will learn "in time" that the only way we will be able to traverse space, is to include the aspect of time. To continue our analogy of the wave chart, it is easy to imagine that our "lives" reincarnationally are not actually sequential but are all "happening" now. All the frequencies are already there, we just get the one we are tuned to. When we change our attitude (dial) we move accordingly up and down the scale.

> ▸ "Space has no objective reality except as an order or arrangement of the objects we perceive in it, and time has no independent existence apart from the order of events by which we measure it."[83]

Our lives (future and past) are like the frames of a filmstrip; they all exist at once but we experience them frame by frame.[84] It is through the conscious concentration on this particular frame that we are denied remembrance of frames that have passed, or ones that are about to come up, since at birth we are disoriented to this reality, as we mature our increasing focus allows us to gradually forget the life just lived (described by Saturn's quadratures to the birth position and in psychology as conservation and classification stages-see Chapter 1, page

---

[83] *"The Universe and Dr. Einstein"*, Lincoln Barnett, Bantam Books, 1968.

[84] Please refer to "*Bashar: Blueprint For Change*", "*The Filmstrip analogy*", pages 116-118.

40). How many of us can remember what we had for breakfast last week? Sometimes we do remember a vague glimmering of a past or future event, and when we do we call it *deja vu*.

Astrological Premise
"Men at some time are masters of their fates:
"The fault, dear Brutus,
is not in our stars, but in ourselves
that we are underlings."
Shakespeare, Julius Caesar, Act 1 : scene 2, 130

In chapter 1 we discussed the idea that physical reality is the manifestation of archetypal concepts and symbols. The EM chart gives us an outline of some of the known frequencies. Forms follow frequencies. Function follows symbology. The horoscope is the "scope" of the frequency you are, you (the physical you) are the frozen version of that frequency at the time of birth (time) that is reflected through the signature of galactic geometric relationship (space).

The universal premise is that "All That Is" is *vibration in relationship* and *IS* the 4 and 3 template in its physically manifested form. The physical aspects of these vibrations are the mirrors of its consciousness. The planets, stars and asteroids that we read in horoscope delineation are not outside of us, they are reflective aspects of *ourselves*, and we are a reflective aspect of "All That Is". Every moment and every movement of these bodies reflects all of the different ways that "All That Is" has of dreaming and exploring itself into existence. We are our brothers keeper because we are our brother. Our link to the stars was forged from the beginning when we arose from them. That connection cannot be broken.

The mirror of the horoscope does not cause, compel, impel, influence or in any other way affect us-**IT** is the *effect* of us. Physical reality is an agreed upon and collective creation or parameter of agreement upon which we play out the game of being separate from the *rest of creation.*

We use the mirror to see what we look like. If we wish to

change any aspect of our reflection, we simply change ourselves and the reflection has no choice but to follow suit. We don't really need to know anything about a mirror in order to use it. We need not know about optics to use it. Neither science or religion alone will answer why the connection exists and why astrology works as it does. But it does and is operationally and functionally obvious to anyone who has made a sincere effort to learn it. I believe the theories of relativity imply confirmation of astrological premise. To simply discount the use of a mirror because of a lack of mechanical knowledge of optics, reflection and refraction, would be a fools act or argument. A word to the wise is sufficient. Astrology is operationally observable. The idea of the nonlocal premise described in *"Holographic Universe"* describes this idea well;

▸ The main architects of this astonishing idea are two of the world's most eminent thinkers: University of London physicist David Bohm, a protege of Einstein's and one of the world's most respected quantum physicists, and Karl Pribram, a neurophysiologist at Stanford University and author of the classic neuropsychological textbook Languages of the Brain.

Pribram and Bohm Together

Considered together, Bohm and Pribram's theories provide a profound new way of looking at the world: Our brains mathematically construct objective reality by interpreting frequencies that are ultimately projections from another dimension, a deeper order of existence that is beyond both space and time: The brain is a hologram enfolded in a holographic universe. For Pribram, this synthesis made him realize that the objective world does not exist, at least not in the way we are accustomed to believing. What is "out there" is a vast ocean of waves and frequencies, and reality looks concrete to us only because our brains are able to take this holographic blur and convert it into the sticks and stones and other familiar objects that make up our world. How is the brain (which itself is composed of frequencies of matter) able to take something as insubstantial as a blur of frequencies and make it seem solid to the touch? "The kind of mathematical process that Bekesy simulated with his vibrators is basic to how our brains construct our image of a world out there," Pribram states.' In other words, the smoothness of a piece of fine china and the feel of beach sand beneath our feet are really just elaborate versions of the phantom limb syndrome.

According to Pribram this does not mean there aren't china cups and grains of beach sand out there. It simply means that a china cup has two very different aspects to its reality. When it is filtered through the lens of our brain it manifests as a cup. But if we could get rid of our lenses, we'd experience it as an interference pattern. Which one is real and which is illusion? "Both are real to me," says Pribram, "or, if you want to say, neither of them are real." This state of affairs is not limited to china cups. We, too, have two very different aspects to our reality. We can view ourselves as physical bodies moving through space. Or we can view ourselves as a blur of interference patterns enfolded throughout the cosmic hologram. Bohm believes this second point of view might even be the more correct, for to think of ourselves as a holographic mind/brain looking at a holographic universe is again an abstraction, an attempt to separate two things that ultimately cannot be separated. Do not be troubled if this is difficult to grasp. It is relatively easy to understand the idea of holism in something that is external to us, like an apple in a hologram. What makes it difficult is that in this case we are not looking at the hologram. We are part of the hologram. The difficulty is also another indication of how radical a revision. Bohm and Pribram are trying to make in our way of thinking. But it is not the only radical revision. Pribram's assertion that our brains construct objects pales beside another of Bohm's conclusions: that we even construct space and time.

For the counselor, a tool that does not place power with the client as the service is fallacious. A fallacy is a defect in an argument. A false premise for an argument is a defect. The premise that the counselor has some power greater than the client to change their reality is a false premise, and defective arguments and *remedies* must necessarily follow. If the power is outside of us, we cannot **own or control it.** If the constellations and planetary configurations *affect* us, it implies we cannot control them, therefore we lose power. Counselors in astrology may, in their zealous need to prove their craft, say "this is happening *because"* of such and such configuration. This removes power from the client and places it with the configuration.

A prediction of future probabilities is a sensing of the most likely events to happen *if the energy doesn't change.* Acting as a mirror, the horoscope allows us to see the other levels of our psyche to determine how definitions are manifesting so that if we don't prefer them we can redefine them. The horoscope allows us to discern them through discernment or accurate empathy[85] moving us toward self actualizing motivations, intentions and experiences.

> ▸ "The general actualizing tendency an "inherent tendency of the organism to develop all its capacities in ways which serve to maintain or enhance the organism." (Rogers, 1959, p. 196)

In conclusion, to say that difficulties are arising from a configuration astrologically or otherwise is a *fallacious and defective argument* regarding counsel and service. Definitions create reality, redefinition recreates it. Everything we have and are is the result of awareness and redefinition *effort.* The counselor's service is to assist the client's efforts in the *allowance* of redefinition towards desired preference. And if the counselor is following *his/her* bliss and excitement, it is always a spontaneous explosion of synchronicity, and an enlightening exploration of camaraderie and sharing.

The self reflective nature of the Multiverse is evidenced by the ability to have recognitions that move beyond the self, that allow for transcendence, that allow for the existential view. If you live in a "Valley" the landscape of that valley is all you know, and are not real clear on the appearance of that valley while you are in it. Except from the perspective of being "in" the valley. When you climb to the mountaintop you are now able to view the valley from a different perspective, to get a bigger picture-an awareness of the "landscape" of the valley. Before you climbed this mountain there would have been a habitual way of perceiving the valley which has now changed through the removal of the lens of the self and its participation in the landscape of the valley.

If you have a habit, it is unconscious. If you have a recognition through awareness of the habit you no longer-by definition-have the habit. This ability for a recognition outside of or beyond is in a sense proof that consciousness must be of

---

85
   Accurate Empathy is psychologist Carl Roger's term for the ability to accurately perceive the client's internal world in a non-evaluative way. See "Personality Theories" Bem P. Allen, Chapter 9, page 223.

a non-physical nature to begin with, for the ability to view the pattern from another point of view is to stand outside the paradigm that you are. The infinite and non-physical requirements for this self reflective ability is implicate and necessary for a Multiverse that cannot be "hard wired." A "hard wired" or close-ended Multiverse would not contain a parameter for transcendent perspectives to be created if it were. It is a loop or a mirror; another view other than what you define yourself to be that *implies* something beyond the reality you immediately inhabit. The ability to move beyond the valley and to the mountain is the effect of self-awareness. The goal of any metaphysical and self improvement endeavor is awareness. The ability to move beyond the physical illusion of time, allows us to recognize that we actually exist everywhere at once as non-physical and infinite co-creators with "All That Is". We are the reality that conscious mind, deceived by the physical senses, believes it exists within (See Bashar, "Self Awareness, 1/88).

Therefore it is not a matter of *whether* we fit within the infinite "path" but how. The more conviction and trust we express in the creation of our reality-the less time it takes to get to this mountaintop. Transcendence and transformation are not the product of mediocrity, *not* the product of placing power outside the self, *not* the product of acquiescence, and *not* the product of conscious mind recognitions alone.

We *cannot* experience a reality and vibration that we do not believe to be true for us-on all levels. All experience serves to tell us the vibration we are at any given moment.

> ▸   "Vibration is the impingement of consciousness upon the homogenous field that creates physical reality, or that is created to create physical reality. It is a reflection of the ability to create distinct, or as your physicists say, discontinuous reality, so as to have the ability to create many different ideas of reality that can interact in the same basic universe, while not necessarily occupying the same time frame or space referential point. It creates the idea of being able to be out of phase with something else so as to not interfere with it, so that it can be a parallel reality existing in the same basic referential place and time, but not experienced to be doing so." "The New Metaphysics" Bashar and The Association

Light and Sound communications 1987.

From this view, the future and the past are created from the present, cause and effect are illusions. Nothing is pre-determined, set in stone, or not redefine-able when you trust, and act on what you are capable of acting on that is your bliss with integrity. Experiences are momentums of the self with degrees of intensity, formed by belief as the most likely reality to be experienced. Successful living is the recognition that life is a matter of preference and choice on some level. The proof is in the acting, the acting in conviction, the conviction from belief, and the belief from definitions and preference. There are no other requirements and there need be no other proofs.

Summary

I.   The universe is infinite in *vibrational* manifestation. Implied are more unseen levels of vibration than seen. Absence of evidence, is not evidence of absence.

II.   *Science* consists of belief systems of knowledge called *paradigms*. A paradigm is a set of assumptions. A paradigm does not seek to resolve *anomaly* (deviation from the common rule), but seeks reinforcement of "facts" to support the further articulation of the paradigm. This is reflective of every system of belief which possesses it's own reinforcing logic.

III.   *Normal science* is puzzle solving based on achievements providing a foundation for further research. This definition qualifies astrology as normal science. Science is the *systematic study of knowledge* gained through the operation of laws.

IV.   Astrology is not accepted by the scientific community because it is not an accepted paradigm for further study and articulation. Science has not *seriously looked at it,* and has a large propensity for anomaly from the exercising of free will.[86] A common misconception is

---

[86] The planets can only line up in relatively similar positions once every 25,000 years.

that it requires faith to function. A well thought out philosophical postulate can be as useful if not more so, than a collection of "facts."

V.   ***Heaven and hell*** are states of being based on the extent of covering up or discovery of consciousness with regard to ourselves. Experiential reality is not the result of ***seeing is believing*** but ***believing is seeing*** and is the process of manifestation in the "real" world.

VI.   Physical and non-physical reality is likened to a ***mind-matter mirror.*** Everything in the universe is a continuous interlocking vibratory web wherein space cannot be detached from any physical content within it.

VII.   Our consciousness is not in our body, ***our body is in and moves through our consciousness.***

VIII.   Einstein's theories of relativity (gravitation- i.e., that space is not "empty") reflect precisely the concept of astrological premise. The four dimensions template manifests in bases of ***four*** and modes of ***three.*** The pyramid reflects this basic format and structure.

IX.   It appears ancient civilizations had much of the universal premise already in application. Because time and space are essentially illusions, this information still exists and is accessible through states of mind. The number bases of 360 and 60 are very important to astrological application and perspectives as a mathematical templet.

X.   The current religious and political structures exist because we give them our power from the belief that we as a society are inherently negative and need protection.

XI.   ***Art*** is the integrated expression and reception of the beautiful received through the intuited use of more than one level of psychic material. Colors, sound and shape are the effects of the perception of vibrational frequency. The prism's refraction of light provides a good model of how spirit manifests in matter. Astrology is an art as well as a science.

XII.   Our planet and place within the Universe is very small and insignificant (at least physically). Intelligent life manifesting elsewhere is statistically and logically more of a given than a possibility.

XIII. Through process of reincarnation we experience different aspects of the soul self. These selves are actually existing "all at once." We forget our past selves because we refocus to material existence after birth.

XIV.   **Astrology** is the study of the interlocking vibratory frequencies that reflect ideas and beliefs that are being expressed physically or psychologically at any given moment.

XV.   The counselor cannot participate in the science of following. We can only help an individual rediscover things within him or herself that they prefer to create and experience. There is no such thing as a prediction of **THE** future because the future is determined to a great extent by decisions and awareness acted upon now. All futures have equal probability of manifestation when acted upon with trust. Astrologers predict the future through a sensing of present energies *that may change* depending on the awareness of the individuals involved. Accurate empathy equates to analytical discernment in many ways.

Index of terms and Concordance

Supplementary Reading

Barnett, Lincoln. The Universe And Dr. Einstein.
New York: William Morrow & Co., Inc..
　　　1966 second edition.
Carlsberg, Kim, & Anka, Darryl. Contact Cards
New Mexico: Bear & Company
　　　1996
Campbell, Bernard G.. Humankind Emerging.
New York: HarperCollins Publishers Inc.
　　　1992
Campbell, Joseph. The Power Of The Myth, W/Bill Moyers.
New York: Doubleday.
　　　1988
Cayce, Edgar Evans. Edgar Cayce On Atlantis.
New York: Paperback Library.
　　　1968
Einstein, Albert. On The Generalized Theory of Gravitation.
Scientific American: Volume 182, No. 4,
　　　April 1950
Hull, R.F.C.. Flying Saucers, A Modern Myth of Things Seen in The Sky.
New York: MJF Books, Princeton University Press.
　　　1978
Kuhn, Thomas S., The Structure of Scientific Revolutions. Second edition, enlarged.
London: The University of Chicago Press.
　　　1970
Kuhn, Thomas S. The Copernican Revolution.
England: Harvard University Press.
　　　1985
Mader, Sylvia S.. Inquiry Into Life. Seventh edition.
Iowa: Wm. C. Brown Publishers.
　　　1994
Nemett, Barry. Images, Objects and Ideas. Viewing the Visual Arts.
San Diego: Harcourt Brace Jovanovich College Publishers.
　　　1992

Sagan, Carl. Cosmos.
New York: Random House
        1980
Time Magazine. What Does Science Tell Us About God?
December 28, issue, page 40.
        1992
Talbot, Michael. The Holographic Universe
New York: HarperCollins
        1991
Thorne, Kip S.. Black Holes & Time Warps.
New York: W W Norton & Company.
        1994

Chapter 3

Experiential Template (Zodiac)
Template Definitions
"Just as Maxwell and Faraday assumed that a magnet
creates certain properties in surrounding space,
so Einstein concluded that stars, moons, and other
celestial objects individually determine the properties
of the space around them. And just as the movement of a
piece of iron in a magnetic field is guided by the structure
of the field, so is the path of *any body* [87] in a gravitational
field determined by the geometry of that field."
Lincoln Barnett in "The Universe and Dr. Einstein"

Just outside Bombay India in an eighth century temple
stands the sculpture the *"Mask of Eternity."* In the center of the
relief is the mask, a face which looks straight forward. On each
side of the forward looking face are two other faces, male and
female that look out and away from center. These two faces
represent the duality of the masculine and feminine, when as
a spirit upon incarnation into physical reality, we are polarized
and lose transcendence. God, the face in the center, looks
straight ahead and transcends duality.

When we divide the vault of the heavens of 360 degrees
around the earth by *three* we end up with the *twelve* houses or
signs of the zodiac[88] each 30 degrees. We will refer to it as the
experiential template because it reflects the arena of every
possible experience in this solar system from our perspective.
The Christ consciousness is the combination of all archetypal

---

[87] Author's italics.

[88] There is confusion to some about this. Tropical (most common) Astrology is based on the *division* not on the constellations, so it doesn't matter if they have moved since the creation of the astrological premise.

symbology in this solar system and is reflected in this template.
The vault of the heavens is constantly being reviewed as earth spins on its axis. The symbolic zodiac in this plane of the ecliptic reflects the agreed upon archetypal parameters of experiential probabilities to be experienced in this system. It acts as a backdrop to planets that move through it as they orbit the Sun (from our view on Earth). This template is our connection to the rest of the Universe as a fragment of a more

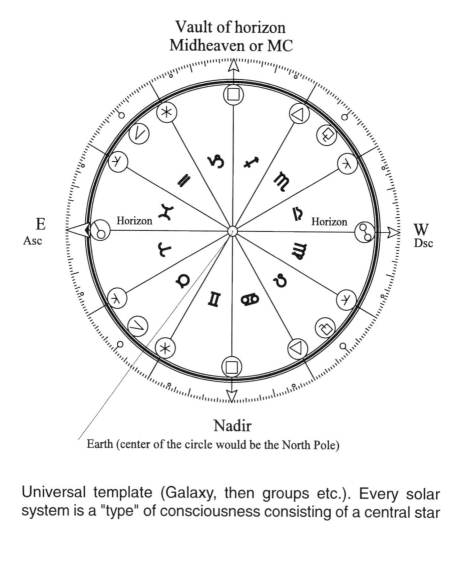

Earth (center of the circle would be the North Pole)

Universal template (Galaxy, then groups etc.). Every solar system is a "type" of consciousness consisting of a central star (or two) as a Sun, orbiting planets, asteroids, moons companion stars, and dark bodies etc.. As we make forays outside this system we will have to learn to interpret the vibrational frequencies of a collection of combined consciousness', a galactic astrology. But for now this geocentric astrology defines the experience of this system *relative* to the universal consciousness outside the system. If you are familiar with the appearance (proposed or inferred) of a spiral DNA strand, the orbital plane of the planets and the zodiacal division would symbolically represent a "slice" of macrocosmic DNA, with the horoscope and its sign polarities as the base paired acids.

When we are viewing a chart, horoscope, zodiac or dial (all these names refer to the same basic configuration) it is to be viewed symbolically as if we are lying on the earth (always in the center) face up feet pointing south. Our left arm would be east, right arm west. Outstretched they would define the vault of sky or the horizon that we could see, east to west. The other half of the circle (or earth) would be described by the area from behind our back from arm to arm, with the Nadir (meaning deepest point) being on the other side of the earth, at the center of our back.

The horoscope is a mandala that is a facsimile or map of the solar system viewed from above with the symbols of the planets and their relationships placed within the circle of the heavens. It reflects the actualization and manifestation of spirit through polarity into the physical world. It symbolizes a macrocosmic molecule of consciousness. When we delineate planetary geometric configurations within it, we are simply determining the state or frequency of that consciousness, very much like the determination of an element by its atom's shells electron orbits and weights about the nucleus.[89] It reflects the "mask" of spirit when physicalized, or the mirror of mind through matter.

---

[89]
See *"Inquiry into Life"*, seventh edition, Sylvia S. Mader, Wm. C. Brown Publishers, 1994, page 18-23, also *"From Quarks to The Cosmos"*, Scientific American Library, 1989.

The beginning of the sign sequence always begins with Aries. The imaginary line or division beginning is called a ***Cusp***.[90] The beginning of the house sequence always begins at the ***east point***. This is the point rising in angularity to the point on the earth where the individual is, often this is where the sun rises. This is because the earth is rotating "into" it or east as it moves counterclockwise in its spin. This point is profoundly important in any chart, because it represents the "now" of any moment and establishes the cuspal arrangement at any given moment of the horoscope. In other words the issues or archetypes that will represent the face or ***mask of the persona*** or person are established by the direction the earth is facing relative to the template at the time of birth or ***natal chart***.

This book will not cover horoscope construction. If you have not already done so, a computer service order form is available in the back of this text to order one. Send your birth time, (listed on your birth certificate) date, and place to the address listed. It is strongly recommended that you familiarize yourself with the concept of the horoscope so that errors can always be detected, *i. e.,* if you were born at noon the symbol for the Sun *must* be located somewhere close to the midheaven (noon).

The ***natural chart*** (page 80) is the zodiac or template that begins with the sign Aries and is established not by the birth of a person, but by the birth of spring or the spring equinox. This is the point every year when the Sun's apparent path in the sky moves north of the plane of the ecliptic when the days and nights are equal in length.[91] But the concepts of birth and beginning are always associated with both the first house (the east point) and the sign Aries. This concept, of sign and house

---

[90]
    At this point it is strongly suggested that for a more complete technical understanding of mechanics, a companion text such as *"Astrology 1-2-3"* by Noel Tyl, Llewellyn Publications, 1984, or *"The Astrologers Handbook"* by Sakoian & Acker or others that are recommended, be used in conjunction with this book.

[91]
    Anyone who is serious about understanding astrology, must familiarize themselves with at least the level of Astronomy 101-109 offered at the community college level.

correlates will apply to all signs and all houses.

In each solar system every sign of the template (30 degree division) has a planetary correlate. Other astrological texts say that the planet "rules" the sign. Aries is "ruled" by Mars for example. Now for the sake of eliminating confusion we will also say it this way in this text. Our solar system however, is a fragment of the overall consciousness of a collection of systems, as well as a fragment of the overall system or universe. Therefore it is more logical to say that the planet *in* the solar system *focuses* the energy of the *sign* that is *outside* of the solar system that extends beyond it. Similar to the way that a lens focuses the light outside the camera to form the picture inside on the film. It is the way that the galactic or universal consciousness is distilled and brought into the consciousness of the physical organisms within the system. It is our connection to the "rest" of the Universe, and like the photo will always be an incomplete representation.

The experiential template of astrology proves the interconnectedness of "All That Is" and our part in it by its interlocking layers and levels. There are blue galaxies that we can "see" at the outer limits of the universe that are at least 15 billion light years away (and therefore that far back in time). With this vastness "God" cannot be limited with any type of judgement in the way that many subscribe to and orthodox religions express it. Of course they are free to see it and create it that way if they wish. Just because we believe (create) ourselves separate from the Multiverse, is not evidence of a *Deus ex machina* (deity separate from the machine).

The flow of the template

The following is the natural delineation and flow of the manifestation of *any* idea, person, place or thing imaginable in this system. We will interpret the energy or frequency of these polarity pairs at as many levels as possible from the highest (non-physical) to lowest (physical) as well as the accompanying effects psychologically and mundanely. Beliefs are delineated in both positive and negative terms.

The symbols for the signs and planets are an art form.

Therefore they convey a language that is much more than the sum of the parts. They convey the essence of the idea they represent.

> ▸   "In astrology, the meanings of the heavens and their organization in relation to man are enormous in scope. Abbreviations become necessary. But the symbology of these meanings, developed throughout history, offers an infinite scope of significance, brought to life within man and through the astrologer's deductions. "The Sun" says little in comparison with the *symbol* for the sun: ☉, the circle of life and man within."[92]

The first *three* signs of the template (1/4 or a quadrature) form the basis for what we have defined in previous chapters as the prism of the persona that is formed from the ***three*** modes of functioning now described as ***belief/emotion/thought*** (Bashar). Belief initiates idea manifestation. Emotion reflects the e-motion or energy motion of the belief, the threshold of believability behind it. Thought is best represented as the dissemination and diversification of the belief and e-motion contained within it. These three modes of functioning are materialized through the ***four*** elements of the four dimensions template (time and space). Macrocosmic DNA.

The first three signs of the template form the most specific and personally focused aspects of the persona and of spirit manifesting in specific definition. The formation of the definition and identity (Aries/belief), the consolidation of the worth of the idea (Taurus/emotion), and the conscious awareness and dissemination of itself and interaction with polarity (Gemini/thought).

The planetary "lenses" that focus or rule these signs are the rocky spheres of Mars (Aries), Venus (Taurus), and Mercury (Gemini). The closer the planets are to the Sun in orbit, the more focused are the symbolically reflected aspects of the persona (ego) and experiences in physical reality. They reflect subjective experience of the self and separateness. True

---

92
    "Astrology 1-2-3", Noel Tyl, Llewellyn Publications, 1984, Chapter 4, *The Calligraphy.*

subjectivity is to this author empirical conscious mind focus.

All throughout nature we can see the symbolism of this first quadrant. On the savannah an Impala is born (Aries), quickly accumulates functioning power (Taurus), and is mobile in minutes (Gemini). A plant seed germinates (Aries), sends roots into the ground for nutrients for establishment (Taurus), and absorbs carbon dioxide from the air, and when mature releases pollen, spores, or seeds (Gemini).

When the circle ("All That Is") is divided by four (physicality), we have the four dimensions template of time and space. The first quadrant of the experiential template is the spring that brings forth and establishes *Identity.*

Part 1 The Self
Spring
Aries 1st house experience March 21-April 19

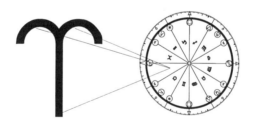

The polarity of Identity (♈) *reflection* (♎)

Symbolism-Aries represents the birth of the identity, ego, self and singularity of definition. The symbol is reflective of the Ram's horns, a seed springing up from the ground, a power scepter and the incarnation of any idea; The thrust of a geyser. The beginning. It is the masculine component of identity definition. The artificial persona construct self presentation and approach.

Spiritual-The fragmentation of the consciousness of "All That Is" in its exploration of specificity as one idea.

Psychological-The need of the personality to prove its

independent ego validity importance through being the pioneer or first. Martial and fiery. Fear of being ignored. (For psychological need theories see Noel Tyl, 1972).

Belief

+ Trust that following the self's excitement and bliss leads to identity fulfillment. Natural aggression.

- The belief that the self can be thwarted by others leads to impatience, pushiness and participation in actions of dominance.

Physiological-External sex organs, bladder, muscular system, head, face, eyes, and the sense of taste. Accidents or illness to these parts of the body indicates unresolved developmental issues with Arian concepts.

Mundane-War, physical dominance and assertion, metals and artillery.

House correlate-First/identity definition and efforts at validation. The self.

Planetary Lens or Ruler-Mars ♂ The need to prove the self. Energy applied to physicality.

△ **Element**-Fire/The trinity of identity.[93]

☐ **Mode**-Cardinal/The quadruplicity of **Belief**.

Taurus 2nd house experience   April 20-May 20

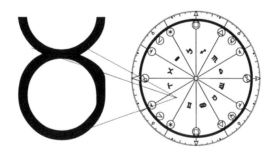

---

[93] Both Modes and Elements will be discussed more fully in the chapter on Geometric Basics to follow.

The polarity of Worth (♉) *interaction* (♏)

Symbolism-Taurus is the sign of the accumulation of energy and value structures of the identity. The symbol is of the self receiving resources from the Multiverse that will support the identity. We cannot have an integral desire of identity need that is *not fulfillable in some way.* The reception symbolized by the crescent is that of abundance and stability through the unconditional support of "All That Is". The Bull and its horns reflect this stability and it is through this sign or house that we will delineate feelings (beliefs) about self worth.

Spiritual-The reflective sense of deservability[94] and abundance that attracts the necessary tools for use by the identity in physicality. The ability to have what you need, when you need it.

Psychological-The value structures that an individual holds in order to maintain relative stability of the ego. The need to keep things as they are, and to accumulate more of the same that is seen to serve the identity and reinforce its definition. Venusian and structured. Fear of functional inadequacy.

Belief

\+ Conviction of the worth of the identity definition. Functional and material self-sufficiency. Personal reflection through the mind-matter mirror.

\- Invalidation of portions of the self as less than deserving of manifestation and expression. The scarcity perspective. Belief in the "survival of the fittest."

Physiological-Throat, Kidneys, the back at the beltline, sense of touch.

Mundane-Material possessions and money, banking and all things of finery.

House correlate-Second/worth and beliefs of self support. Resources.

Planetary Lens or Ruler-Venus ♀ Personal and social

94
  The thresholds of believability (outlined in the definitions list) and deservability are intensity measurements or momentums that a person may hold of a belief (Bashar).

reflection in the mind-matter mirror (easy to remember because it looks like one). The need to see the self in things and others.

△ **Element**-Earth/The trinity of physicality.

□ **Mode**-Fixed/The quadruplicity of **Emotion.**

Gemini 3rd house experience   May 21-June 20

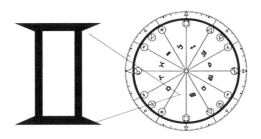

The polarity of Thought (Ⅱ) *interaction* (♐)

Symbolism-Gemini is the symbolic reference to the world of polarity pairs. The dissemination of ideas and their articulation, more commonly known as knowledge of the physical world. Its symbol of the twins reflects of the "Mask of Eternity" and the inherent duality of physicality. The thought aspect of the persona is the conveyance and communication of the identity (first house) and its worth (second house). Because of this conveyance, diversity is the effect and the requirement.

Fleeting mentality and the need for appreciation in the realms of intelligence are signified. The application of intelligence to ideas and their expression are symbolized by this Mercurial sign.

Spiritual-The experience of conscious awareness as the effect of physical focus and alignment. Mind viewing itself as matter.

Psychological-The need for acceptance and appreciation for diversity and intelligence. Fears of not being appreciated for intelligence or being seen as knowledgeable. The diversification of worth requires successful articulation and this is the primary need and fulfillment desire of this sign.

Belief

+ Trust in the conscious perceptions as the mediators between the inner and outer realities. Objective analytical discernment and distribution of information.

- Focus on the conscious mind at the exclusion of other levels of psychic material. The concept that the conscious mind is the "real" mental realm and others are disregarded. This leads to empty, superficial talk and thoughts.

Physiological-Solar plexus, lungs, arms, hands, tongue, nervous systems, sense of sight. The distribution systems of the body.

Mundane-Technical modes of communication and travel. All forms of delivery systems and messages. Applied intelligence.

House correlate-Third/information. The communication, thinking and dissemination of information profile of the identity.

Planetary lens or ruler-Mercury ☿ The needs for thinking and articulation of information and ideas. The "reception" of matter consciously is symbolized by the dish above the mind/matter mirror.

△ **Element-**Air/The trinity of idea interaction.

☐ **Mode-**Mutable/The quadruplicity of **Thought.**

The second three signs of the experiential template begins the second quadrant (or first square 90 degree angle) of the mode of belief to itself. This simply reflects the physicalization of the definition and belief from Aries. What was initiated in Aries seeks stabilization and establishment in Cancer. The e-motion of the initiated belief now "takes root" in Cancer as the first sign of the second quadrant of belief. Belief is "made real" and established internally as a subconscious pattern or internal "status". It is very important to determine the nurtured belief in this sign and house because it forms the archetype that is responsible for the physicalized form that will be experienced in the external world concretely, called status.

The Moon is the lens or ruler of Cancer. Because we create ourselves in such a focused fashion, we create an unconscious and apparent separation between the masculine and feminine principles. It is this inner feminine and receptive function of belief that Cancer represents. Our early environment and maternal interaction acts as the trigger of belief that catalyses and establishes internal definitions from which we will later project our beliefs about reality, into reality.

This house and the other unconscious houses (8th and 12th) form the matrix of the unconscious where the e-motion of belief is dealt with in an empathic level-meaning the recognition of vibrational frequencies on an intuitive level.

The identity that was established as an idea in 1 begins to form materially in 4 and encounters the first apparent contradiction; the fact that a part of itself (the mother, the rain, any external factor required for nurture) appears to be outside of it and out of its control. Therefore behavior may reflect this "insecurity" with the apparent loss of control. Certain behaviors arise in an attempt to communicate needs to the external, and emotional security needs are born in house 4 and the sign Cancer. The 4th house and angle begins the contradiction and paradox of the "mask" of persona and descendance of self into matter out of the transcended "All That Is" center. If the belief in identity is strong, its emotional security and internal status will be as well, and vice-versa.

It is this operance of emotional security that either keeps creative extension healthy and empowered, or fearful and retreating. Upon the establishment of the healthy sense of internal status lies the ability to extend and give love in Leo and the 5th house. If we believe we are one of the valid ways that "All That Is" has of expressing itself and are nurtured and loved in the establishment of it, giving love and creating is effortless and reflective of ourselves and our definition in Leo.

The lens of Leo or ruler is the Sun. Since it is a source of light rather than a lens, it drives and maintains the life giving force of the identity. This truly is reflected in the idea "that in giving we receive." Leo reflects the energy of "All That Is" coming "through" the Sun and warming the creations in this system to motivate and support them in their continuing exploration. Its life giving energy is returned to the identity to begin the cycle of expression all over again of the initiation and extension of the self in Aries. It is creative extension through any form, be it children, art work, giving love or any type of "channeling oneself" with trust, that strengthens the self expression and serves others as well. It is the first square to Taurus on 2 that is being externalized. The beliefs in worth and abundance are seen in the creative extension and love given here. If the belief in abundance is strong, creative extensions will be as well.

The extraction, dissemination and practical use of these extensions are reflected through the sign Virgo and the 6th house. The internal status is established in Cancer, extended as creations in Leo, and reaped or discriminately separated to be applied and used in service through Virgo and the 6th. It is here where the "wheat is separated from the chaff" and the individual through service begins to meet the projections of themselves that will be in full externalization through this belief initiation process from the 1st to the 7th. It is here where the **perspective** and its limitations or fears of the identity at 1 will begin to be seen. This manifests as analytical correctness or "what will work" out of the myriad extensions of the 5th and Leo. It is the discrimination of preference that is the positive end result goal. If the mental state and information is secure and diverse in 3, the perspective is clear at 6. Dis-ease or health problems can be seen as the effect of a lack of positive or integrative approach or thought. The inability to critically assess negativity allows for the state of being known as dis-ease. Obviously at this point the greater the development, awareness, and understanding of the components of identity and co-operation of them, the healthier the persona will be.

Each quadrant initiates through **belief**, structures and supports through **e-motion,** and disseminates it through *thought* and behavior. The second quadrant is the summer that establishes and extends the identity in its first interaction with *projected forms*.

Summer
Cancer 4th house experience June 21-July 23

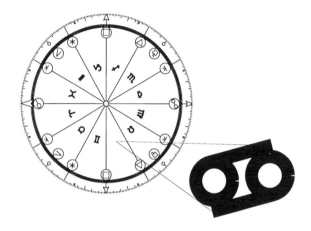

The polarity of Status (♋) *Belief* (♑)

Symbolism-Cancer reflects the self's first interaction and confrontation with the unconscious portions of the self. It reflects the individual's sense of establishment and identity root, hence emotional security concerns. This house and sign are profoundly important with regard to early environmental concerns and the unconscious habit patterns. The symbol can be interpreted as the woman's breasts, a crabs claws, or two moons all representing the nurturing and protective aspect of the psyche. The feminine function is to nurture regardless of political correctness or philosophical bent, but there are many ways to nurture. The home is delineated through Cancer and the 4th. The changeability phases of the moon and the woman's cycles are represented here. The moon sheds its shadow and reaffirms the pulse of birth and life. The moon has been greatly revered in all cultures. It also can reflect the Yin/Yang and balance point of inner awareness, the "place" we need to go to find the inner self.

Spiritual-The access point or vortex to the oversoul, higher self and/or inner self. The place of perfect peace.

Psychological-The need to establish and maintain emotional security. The effect of the insecurities felt when the identity encounters the threat of things outside itself. Cancer carries with it the fear of being taken advantage of from "the outside penetrating" and affecting the soft interior. The successful establishment of identity depends on a secure sense of self and vice-versa.

Belief

+ A strong sense of emotional security springing from the belief in identity from within. A status inwardly and validation of what the self represents.

- Power is placed outside the self and security is sought through the external environment through collecting or securing things.

Physiological-Breasts, stomach, female functions, brain matter, left eye in males, right eye in females, and the lymph nodes and fluids in the body.[95]

Mundane-The drive to maintain and secure a home or territorial pursuits. Environmental nurture and structure. Restaurants, food etc.

House correlate-The Fourth/status. The connection or state of knowingness of the identity's validity through the connection to the inner self.

Planetary lens or ruler-The Moon ☽ The reigning nurturing and personality needs of the identity. The reflector of the Sun's light and energy, and the processor of that energy through the unconscious.

△ **Element-**Water/The trinity of emotion.

---

95 Except for the spinal fluids that are ruled by Neptune.

☐ **Mode-**Cardinal/The quadruplicity of **Belief.**

Leo 5th house experience July 24-August 23

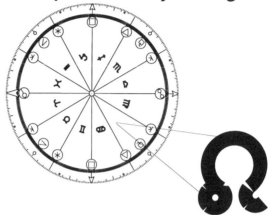

The Polarity of Extension ⟨♌⟩ Emotion ⟨♒⟩

Symbolism-Leo the heart of creative force supports the self definition through creative extension. It reflects the mane of the Lion, the crown of the king, the solar flare of fiery life force. The king and the land are one. There are no security concerns here. Here the life force is deployed, extended and results in the creator being defined by the creations it extends. The passion of love giving either through a warm hearted embrace or a passionate one. This is the house and sign that is the worth of the sense of security when one finds their base in the inner self. It is self empowerment, action in the form of re-creation, the word for fun. The trinary extension is in the creative force and apex manifestation the higher self, the three points of the triad or triangle that creates the stability necessary for existence in physicality.

Spiritual-Creation as the natural extension of any creator. The image that we were created in, is that of co-creators. Life is given through creation and extending the idea that you are.

Psychological-The need for dramatic ego reinforcement. To be the center, authority and to establish identity through creative extension.

Belief

+ Trust in the empowering and automatic extension of the self. Creation as the effect of simply existing. The joy of self expression.

- Self defensive, overinflating importance in the attempt to counter the disbelief in the self's ability to create whatever it desires without having to hurt itself or someone else in the process. Domination.

Physiological-Upper back and heart area, right eye in males left eye in females.

Mundane-The dramatic arts, actors, the stage. All forms of creative extension and love giving. Romance. Children. Self-empowerment.

House correlate-The Fifth/extension. The creative extension of self into physical reality, giving love, and the accumulated worth of inner discovery.

Lens or ruler-The Sun ☉ The core energy of the self. Spirit at the center of creation. The center about which creations revolve.

△ **Element-**Fire/The trinity of identity.

☐ **Mode-**Fixed/The quadruplicity of **Emotion**.

Virgo 6th house experience August 24-September 22

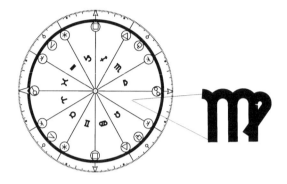

The polarity of Perspective (♍) *Thought* (♓)

Symbolism-The adjustment of perspective through analytical discernment. Here the fruit of the creations are distilled, distributed, and determined through discrimination to be "correct" or proper, useful or practically applicable. Virgo is where the wheat is separated from the chaff. A refinement of creations and their worth (the 6th is the 2nd of the 5th) is delineated here. Dis-ease as the effect of judgement and lack of introspective perspective adjustment will be read through this polarity. It is part of the quadruplicity of thought/perspective and reveals that dis-ease, illness, confinement and other limitations in physicality are the effect of our thinking and perspective. The individual's service as the outgrowth of following their bliss in creative endeavors is the "fruit" of the identity definition here, and the ideal of this polarity is the efficacy sought by the identity through refining and redistribution of the creations of itself.

Spiritual-The effect of the ego definition in physicality and its specific focus of exploration as an aspect of "All That Is".

Psychological-The need to be correct and proper analytically or judgementally. This carries with it beliefs in efficacy and a fear of losing control. Functionally adequate. These concerns can be overdone and with no breadth of vision, this can turn into righteousness or "good and bad" value judgements.

Belief

+ The capability for objective analytical discernment. Specificity and versatility. Critical thinker.

- Judgements of right and wrong, good and bad. Sees the trees at the expense of the forest. Tunnel vision.

Physiological-The digestive tract and all extracting systems, the nervous system.

Mundane-Services rendered to others, the sense of service to society as the effect of specific focus and one's "craft". Illness and disease as the effect of invalidating portions of the self or the environment. Fears of inadequacy. Small animals as fragment projections of the self in physicality.

House correlate-The Sixth/perspective. The resultant perspective and orientation of belief through the thinking profile and definitions (3/9).

Planetary lens or ruler- Mercury. ☿ The way one needs to think and disseminate information. Conscious awareness of the mind/matter mirror. The filter and lens of the consciousness of the Sun. The conscious manipulation and participation in and of polarity.

△ **Element-**Earth/The trinity of physicality.

□ **Mode-**Mutable/The quadruplicity of **Thought.**

These six houses or experiences we covered are the first and *subjective* basis for externalized factors we will discuss and discover in the next six. The first 6 are the persona or personal factors in identity expression and creation. As we move to the 7th house we will begin to see the externalized versions. These next six are the polarized reflection of the definitions of the first six, and in analysis we will always look to the next six (houses) as a way to delineate the identity's interaction with others and the environment. The shadows of the self that are encountered to reflect upon itself and its creations.

We will rise up above the horizon at 7, and as we do the consciousness that was once subjective and internal will be seen, encountered and experienced through interactions with others in a co-created "external" arena. The self in this way becomes objectively aware in its open ended exploration as an idea within the mind of "All That Is".

The identity (1) worth (2) thinking (3) identity establishment (4) creative extensions (5) and the applications of them (6) are brought to full externalization and reflected back at the horizon of awareness at 7 through the apparently external mirror of mind to the self in interaction with others.

Index of terms and Concordance

Part 2 The Other

The polarity experience is the effect of choosing to create ourselves separate from the rest of "ourselves" and to act as an observer. From this point of view things appear to be outside of us. The archetypal reference for this begins at the horizon line of the natal and natural horoscope. This horizon line establishes the identity and the apparent self and other, or inner and outer realities. It is the focal point of this pairing of opposites along with the MC and IC (the Cardinal points). The ancients and native civilizations appear to have had good reason behind their preoccupation with the Cardinal points. It becomes the "cross-hair" so to speak of identity, marking a point within the space/time continuum.

The 7th to 12th houses above the horizon are actually the vault of our view when we look from east to west, north to south. They are everything we "see" of the heavens from our earthbound perspective and reflect the "observed aspects" of the self. The aspects below the horizon, reflect the unconscious or unseen portions of the self from which the observed aspects spring. This model of reality creation will evidence powerful validity when we begin to delineate the identity and its creations in this text. The inner definitions below the horizon define the parameters of experience above. Below is inner and/or dream reality experiences, and above the external or physical reality experiences.

The projected versions of early environmental interaction are seen in the 4th and carried as projected images and versions in 7. Although the other exists in their own right, we still create and project our versions of what they are, and in this way as much can be discerned about the observer through the experiences in this house as the observed.

The realities one experiences are unique, and we observe that although siblings are from the same families with the same parental structure (usually but not always) their perception of the parents and "their" early environment can be seen very differently by each.

The 7th house initiates (Cardinal) the quadrant wherein the distillation of the identity's perspective (6th) now determines the portions of self that will be experienced and encountered. The 7th is the worth or resource of the 6th (2nd of 6th). The more fully we analytically discern aspects of the self, the less dramatic the distinction between the self and others. The others are then perceived as compliments of the self or reflections of the self that serve and illuminate these undefined aspects.

Partnerships and marriage traditionally seen in the 7th are the effect of reconciling this balancing of the unknown portions of the self with the known. In this way the 7th cusp is where the unseen shadow aspects of the self are **encountered.** The psychological counterpart of Aries; the need for **social acceptance** at 7, is the action that moves us to merge with those portions of mind reflected through the mirrored interaction by **relationship.**

When we move to the 8th house, others values and our interaction with them and the resultant transformation of **perspective** by them becomes evident. At 6 and 8, there is an adjustment of thinking and perspective required by the ego self from the definition at 1 that requires flexibility and reassessment. In the 8th house however, this transformation may be traumatic as the support system of the identity established in 2, may need complete revision. A death, reconstruction and resurrection. If the worth of the identity is not secure, the clash of rigid value structures can act as a catalyst for **perspective alteration** in the search for **significance.**[96]

This transformation, depending on its level, leads us to greater more expanded insight and experience of ourselves and others at 9. The beliefs and interaction in higher educational pursuits will be reflected here-formally or

---

96
Real or implied meaning.

informally. Here in 9, the ***thought interaction*** or ideological exchange between us and "others" and their thinking, opens the door to greater insights of life and higher self awareness,[97] and the ***expansion*** of the self definition initiated in 1. Or it can lead to conflict through interaction with those "other" ideas. Either way, this leads to the full application of self defined belief manifesting physically in 10. Or again by derivative measurement, the worth of the transformative encounter in 8 can be seen in interaction with another's thinking (the 9th is the 2nd of the 8th). We can take any house this way and apply it in any relationship around the wheel. The 9th is the 5th (creative product or extension) of the 5th. Our extensions (5th) are consciously acknowledged (9th is the 3rd of the 7th and the 9th is the 5th of the 5th) by the other.

Fall
Libra 7th house experience September 23- October 22

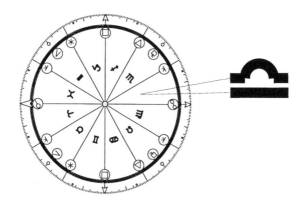

97
Meaning the interaction with greater levels of the self and consciousness.

The polarity of identity $(\triangleq)$ *reflection* (Υ)

Symbolism-Libra is the symbol of the setting sun on the horizon. It is the balance of the identity that is not recognized except through interaction and relationship. The arena where identity is "weighed." The scale is the symbol that reflects this balance. It is the next in the series of *belief* signs that are the motivators of the artificial construct called personality. Libra is the receiver of Aries. We now see the projected version of ourselves through others. Half of the setting sun is in the upper hemisphere (conscious awareness) and the other half submerged below the horizon (the unconscious portions of the self). Libra defines the identity through **acceptance** by others through chameleon like behavior, whereas Aries needs to be first and stand out as a singularity, Libra seeks reinforcement by mirroring and harmonizing. In the game of baseball for example this is shown clearly as the team up to bat as the "Aries" team while the "libra" team takes the field.

Spiritual-The polarized pair counterpart fragmenting of the self as the effect of (Arian) focus and exclusivity. Finding the self in "All That Is."

Psychological-The needs are for social and romantic acceptance, and the fear of not being appreciated in like terms. Rejection fears. Venusian and complimentary.

Belief

+ Trust that one cannot experience anything that is not a part of them in some way, shape, or form on some level.

- Difficulty defining the identity. Being untrue to the self, and placing power outside the self. Seeing all sides as an end.

Physiological-Kidneys lower back at the belt-line. Social disease.

Mundane-Marriages, social events, peace agreements, etiquette.

House correlate-Seventh/identity blending and efforts at acceptance. The other.

Planetary lens or ruler-Venus ♀ Social and personal reflection, the mind matter mirror.

△ **Element**-Air/The trinity of idea interaction.

□ **Mode**-Cardinal/The quadruplicity of **Belief.**

Scorpio 8th house experience October 23-November 21

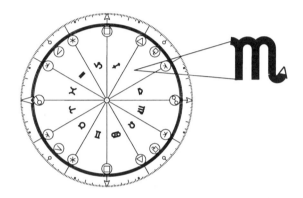

The polarity of value (♏) *interaction* (♉)

Symbolism-The Scorpion is the symbol of the sting of emotional impact that occurs when either a part of the ego is transformed (more typically stated as "lost") or the significant portions of the self are realized and manifested. The Eagle is another symbol reflecting the great heights and freeing of the soul that occurs either in actual physical death or in the death of negative ego.[98] The psychological need to idealize or place significance upon the identity upon death is the Scorpionic archetype. Because the ego fears its loss of control and wishes to immortalize the self in some way; the consciousness it once knew, maintaining that identification *beyond* death appeals (opposite Taurus and the need to maintain the Earthly

---

[98] Defined as the more clinging and fearful aspects of the identity, where power is given to physicality.

resources). The ancient civilization of Egypt is symbolized by Scorpio, with its mummification rituals and other attempts to continue the conscious ego focus beyond material life (Yott, Karmic Astrology).

The mysteries of life will be reflected here in Scorpio. Along with the momentum from past lives that the ego has refused to transform to higher levels.

The 8th house is also the legacy, values and monetary or worth significance encountered through others. It reflects the interchange of values that occur in sex. The ego is "exposed" to an evaluation of its worth in interaction, hence sexual drives may be found here as well as the 5th. In the 5th however, it is on the level of recreational exchange and romance, here a transformation can occur when the rigid structures of ego defense are allowed to dissolve in the drive for significance. Or a crisis in importance if they don't. This is also the house of obsessive/compulsive drives. It also has dominion over the psychodynamics and psychoanalysis aspects of the interaction of psychic material levels as in psychotherapy.

Spiritual-The transformation of perspective essential to move from level to level, and dimension to dimension wherein the ego begins to recognize that it is the reality that it thought it existed within.

Psychological-The need for emotional significance through value exchange and interaction. Fears of being taken advantage of through the empathies.

Belief
+ Trust in the significance of the identity and its experiential reality. Everything happening for a reason. Validations of the unseen portions of the self in others. Confidence in the unseen.
- The loss of power and significance, the belief in the loss of meaning in transcendence and transformation. Futility breeds manipulation to avoid loss of advantage.

Physiological-Sex organs, reproduction, rectum, eliminative functions.

Mundane-Mortgages, mortuaries, partnership financial

dealings, death, perspective transformations through personal loss or crisis, encumbrance.

House correlate-Eighth/others worth and beliefs of value interaction.

Planetary lens or ruler-Pluto ♀ The transformation from powerlessness to powerfulness or vice versa. The alteration of perspective. Spiritual transformation in physicality. The collective consciousness. Power struggles and race issues.

△ **Element-**Water/The trinity of energy motion or e-motion.

☐ **Mode-**Fixed/The quadruplicity of **Emotion.**

Sagittarius 9th house experience November 22-December 21

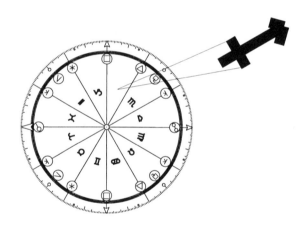

The polarity of Thought (♐) *interaction* (♊)

Symbolism-The higher thought interaction and expansion that occurs when ideas are blended. The thinking of others enhances our own knowledge, understanding and ability to comprehend concepts. Fire fuels thoughts. The arrow of inspired conceptualization hits its target-the higher self. Thinking is the best way to travel, and journeys of mind, soul and body are contained within the archetype of Sagittarius.

The law is an ethical agreement between men and intellectual behavior is the proposed result. Justice and equity. The thinking of others in interaction with our own requires compromise and convergence, and in this way the ideas of one expand and enlarge with the ideas of others. Academia is the result. The higher thought and self expands through concept and expands the identity definition. This sign is the apex of self expression in interaction with "All That Is".

The needs of inspired acceptance for the intellect can lead to great heights of intellectual accomplishment and world travel.
Spiritual-The recognition of the synchronicity, interconnectedness, and harmonization of all ideas and concepts within the "All That Is".

Psychological-The need to have the identity's beliefs, thoughts, opinions and intellect respected, ego reinforced by others, and the fear of them being ignored.

Belief

+ Trust in the aspects of intuition, imagination and intellect working in harmony. The belief that all ideas enhance the greater good.

- Preoccupation and concern about the beliefs and opinions of others, or society as a whole. Arrogance and intellectual snobbishness.

Physiological-The blood, arteries, thighs, liver, right ear, sense of smell.

Mundane-The effects of the collection of and interaction by many minds in philosophy, academia, laws, and international travel and communications.

House correlate-Ninth/information. The thinking profile of the identity in interaction with other minds.

Planetary lens or ruler- Jupiter ♃ Expansion and opportunity that is created in physicality through accretion of mental prowess and inspired interaction with thoughts and ideas. The apex of identity fulfillment. Philosophy; The foundation of the Multiverse.

△ **Element-**Fire/The **Apex** of The trinity of identity.

☐ **Mode-**Mutable/The quadruplicity of **Thought.**

From this point forward all the signs element apex is achieved. This means that the apex of synthesis of the first two signs are blended and expressed through the third point. This culmination point manifests physically in *interaction*. The third square or quadrature initiated by Capricorn is the apex of the modal expression and manifests physically through physical *action and creation. This is symbolized on US currency as the top of the pyramid with the all seeing eye.*[99]

The foundations laid down in the first three houses, became externalized expressions in the next three. The 7th cusp initiated the externalization of the identity through relationship reflection, now the culmination of identity finds its manifestation in physical reality externalization and concretization.

The MC or Midheaven (cusp of the 10th house) is extremely important in the horoscope. It reflects the life path, the purpose and full externalization in physical reality of the identity. This is the testing ground where belief manifests. The effects of belief momentum accrue in the final quadrant (9-12) and the reaping of its effects-both in difficulty or positive and expanded experience, will be reflected through this "final" maturation area.

The identity will find full work and participation in *manifesting* itself in Capricorn and 10, exchanging and *co-creating* in interaction with other beings in Aquarius and 11, and begins to *merge and blend* back with "All That Is" as the negative aspects of ego are lost and empathy and understanding takes precedence over ego assertion in Pisces and 12. The readying for a new cycle, a new incarnation and focus of another idea at 1, where the cycle begins all over again.

Saturn begins this quadrant as the ruler of Capricorn. Saturn from *sero* or *satum* meaning to sow, is the accumulated unconscious habit patterning absorbed through the early

---

99 All but one of the framers of the constitution were freemasons.

environment in 4 and Cancer ***now physicalized as material reality.*** Capricorn is the experience of physicality. It is the opponent or deceiver of spirit. Saturn/Capricorn is where power is given to the material world and perceived as ***status***, our buying into it determines levels of empowerment. Capricorn is the worth (2nd of the 9th) of the expanded perspective of idea interactions in Sagittarius. The dissemination of the others values and worth (3rd of the 8th), and the emotional security and identity establishment of the other(s) (4th of the 7th).

The worth of the 10th or our full externalization is found through the creative interaction with others in 11 (the 11th is the 2nd of the 10th). The 11th is the accolade and love received from others.

The dissolving of these accumulated definitions is the mutable dissemination of the final sign Pisces. The psychological momentum issues that ***limit*** and dissolve self definition. All 12th house derivations limit the expression and require insightful introspection of the house that follows; To undo the e-motion or momentum, is to dissolve and to co-fuse.

Winter

Capricorn 10th house experience December 22- January 20

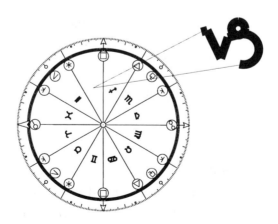

The polarity of Status (♑) *Belief* (♋)

Symbolism-The mountain goat at the peak of the mountaintop. The practical, austere, and efficient climber to the heights. With agility and remarkable diligence dangerous paths are easily traversed.

  Capricorn is the pinnacle of the earth signs, the apex of material and physical efficiency and economy. Here the ambition and excitement of the "career" path culminates and manifests from the feelings of inner security established in 4. The outer reflects the inner man. As Christ said "a tree is known by its fruit" and here the fruit is found, the fruit of the *belief* (Cardinal apex) in the self and its threshold of believability in application. Capricorn reflects the path we are and have envisioned or "imagined" we would become as the reflex to house 4 and Cancer from belief and definition.

Spiritual-The matter portion of the mind/matter mirror. The spirit in physical version.

Psychological-The needs for strategic effectiveness, survival instincts, and fears of functional inadequacy. The father figure and authority. The superego.

Belief

+ Trust that the earth is a material version of spirit and the self's right to manifestation in it. The taking of full responsibility for the self and its reality creations.

- Belief in a "battle" and bombardment from the "external" world. The struggle between good and evil. No pain, no gain beliefs. Giving of power to material things.

Physiological-The teeth, bones, spleen, knees, left ear, sense of hearing, the skin.

Mundane-The government, the authorities, status and ambition. Invalidation and domination tactics. Control and strategic confrontations.

House correlate-The Tenth/Status. The fully externalized self and physical experience.

Planetary lens or ruler- Saturn ♄ the most crystallized aspects of the self in physicality. The greatest fears of the identity. Where power is given to materiality. Limitation through acquiescence to the physical. Physical controls.

△ **Element**-Earth/The **Apex** of The trinity of physicality.

☐ **Mode**-Cardinal/The **Apex** of The quadruplicity of **Belief.**

Aquarius 11th house experience January 21- February 18

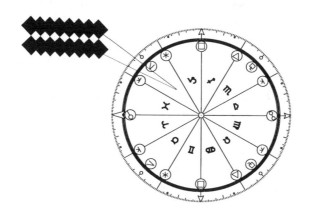

The Polarity of Extension (≈≈) *interaction* (♌)

Symbolism-The excitement of innovation, the electricity of revelation and inspiration is the water that is poured out by the water bearer when co-creators interact and dis-covery (the opposite of hell) results. Heaven is the place where constant discovery flows from co-created extension in interaction and harmony. The e-motion of the momentum of interacting beliefs creates synchronicity and everything flows like water (lines of least resistance) when excitement and vibrational equivalency is allowed full reign.

Aquarius reflects the recognition of choice in the creation of our reality. The equality between all beings as co-creators. It is the worth of the fully externalized 10th, and it is the 10th of the worth 2nd, the full externalization of our own values and worth are measured by the accolade, friendship, camaraderie and love received in 11, our love and worth appreciated and externalized.

Spiritual-Acknowledgement that the universe has no built-in meaning. The innovative mobility of mental creations in matter. The apex of energy motion manifestations of our beliefs and creativity. Destructurization of momentum.

Psychological-The need to have the individuality and uniqueness recognized and appreciated through creative interaction. Fears of not being appreciated for same.

Belief

+ The recognition of the unique and infinite ways that all that is has of expressing itself within the creation that it is. The recognition of the validity of all co-creators and their equality.

- Exhibiting bizarre or unusual behavior to attract attention because of a disbelief in the ability to express individuality effectively. Being different or rebellious for the sake of being different. De-structured and impractical. Procrastination.

Physiological-The ankles, calves and circulation.

Mundane-Electricity, mechanical inventions, technological advances, computers, the "New Age" innovation applied to humanitarian and inner self concerns. Extraterrestrial life and visitation. Space travel.

House correlate-Eleventh/Extension interaction. The **Apex** of the identity's creative applications and contributions. The synchronous accord between co-creators.

Lens or ruler- Uranus ♅ The symbol of unconscious forgotten knowledge and its awakening through creative interaction. Discovery that leads to heaven. The recognition of choice in the creation of reality. The falling asleep of the higher self. Rebellion against materiality.

△ **Element-**Air/The **apex** of the Trinity of idea interaction.

☐ **Mode-**Fixed/The **apex** of the Quadruplicity of **Emotion.**

Pisces 12th house experience February 19-March 20

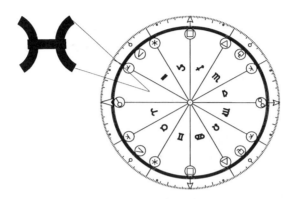

The Polarity of Perspective (♓) *interaction* (♍)

Symbolism-The polarized crescents of receptivity back to back and bound by the cross of physicality. Two fish swimming in opposite directions. The contradiction and expanded perspective as the effect of realization of paradox. The subconscious and its beliefs are discovered and internalization brings empathic recognition and response to others in need. The foundation of the psyche is found not to reside in ego definition but in the dissolution of it and a merging with "All That Is." The residuals of ego fade as the vastness of the consciousness energy sea allows for full trust and surrender. Psychological limitations to ego expression and introspective reward are found in the 12th and Pisces. The assimilation and review of the ego self's experiences as belief momentum are blended with the societal perspective and are rewarded with greater liberation or confines by the effect of its own definitions. The self's communication with the self is vital here.

Spiritual-The dissolution of the ego self to allow greater experience of the soul self, as the realization of the all being one, and the one being all.

Psychological-The empathic needs to be sensitive and compassionate. The need to consider the forest as a collective entity of trees. The fear of being taken advantage of because of this empathic accord with the all.

Belief

+ Full surrender, faith, trust in the greater self, higher self, the ideal. Self knowledge and the imagination as the key to doors to other levels.

- The escapist. The denial of limitations self imposed and the unwillingness to take responsibility for creations. The belief that the outer societal structure is cold and indifferent. The masking of pain and resistance through drug, alcohol or other addictions as an invalidation of the self and responsibility for its creations.

Physiological-The feet. Spinal fluids, lymph nodes and chemical balances in the body.

Mundane-The limiting effects, either physically or mentally of invalidating aspects of the identity's reality creation. Hospitals, prisons, and wards as the effect of that limiting efficacy. The entertainment industry and various mediums such as film, music or dance that allows the identity to break through the apparent confines of physicality via the imagination.

House correlate-The Twelfth/Perspective. The expanded perspective arising from the recognition of the illusion of boundaries in physicality. The societal perspective and collective thought.

Lens or ruler-Neptune ♆ The cross of matter receiving mind and spirit. The unseen, camouflage, the merging and blending with greater aspects of the self and ultimately "All That Is."

△ **Element-**Water/The **apex** of the Trinity of belief momentum.

□ **Mode-**Mutable/The **apex** of the paradoxical quadruplicity of **Thought.**

Summary

I.   The "Mask of Eternity" is the symbol for the ego's entrance into physicality and the loss of that transcendence as the effect of concept polarization into pairs-both masculine and feminine as the product of physical focus in materiality. The experiential template or natural Zodiac is the tool for understanding the diffraction like light of the spirit or soul in physicality through ***archetypal reference.***

II.   The "Christ" consciousness is the combined collective integration of these archetypes in this system as one consciousness. Transcendence is ***reintegration of it*** through developmental growth and being all that one can be in their bliss and excitement with integrity.

III.   DNA and other physical effects are the reflection of spiritual templates, or spirit in its physical version.

IV.   The natal or "birth" time horoscope is reflective of the artificial construct that is created by the oversoul as a choice in expression in physical life to "sound through."

V.   Time and space are effects of the physical dimension or 3D, and allows for the natural flow of any idea as the template reflects.

VI.   The persona is likened to a crystal structure composed of ***belief/emotion/thought***. These parameters are clearly defined and reflected through the experiential template or ***Zodiac***.

VII.   This Zodiac reveals 3 elemental modes of expression that are based on the 4 elements of being as ***Fire/Earth/Air/Water.*** They manifest as beliefs about reality with accompanying psychological modes of behavior and needs.

VIII.   The template is a hallway of experience that can be interpreted in many ways at different levels, either ***spiritually, psychologically, physiologically, mundanely.*** The duality of physicality also can be experienced either ***positively or negatively.*** Each archetype has a ***planetary lens or ruler that focuses and distributes the energy of that archetype in our solar system.***

IX.   All of these levels work together as one thing to bring

about personalities, events and experiences as
expressions within the mind of "All That Is." These
planets and signs are not outside of us they are us-one
level we view from another. All experiences in physical
reality, within this system, are definable by this
template.

Index of Terms and Concordance

Supplementary Reading list.

Anka, Darryl. The New Metaphysics.
California: Light & Sound Communications Inc.,
    1987
Anka, Darryl. Bashar: Blueprint for Change.
Seattle: New Solutions Publishing.
    1990
Arroyo, Stephen. Astrology, Karma and Transformation.
Washington: CRCS Publications.
    1978
Carlsberg, Kim, & Anka, Darryl. Contact Cards
New Mexico: Bear & Company
    1996
Goswami, Amit. The Self Aware Universe.
New York: G. P. Putnam's Sons
    1995
Haich, Elisabeth. Initiation.
California: Seed Center.
    1974
Holy Bible. Bible. With Apocrypha.
New York: Oxford University Press.
    1989
Lewi, Grant. Heaven Knows What.
Minnesota: Llewellyn Publications.
    1977
Lewi, Grant. Astrology For The Millions.
Minnesota: Llewellyn Publications. Bantam Edition
    1980
Ruperti, Alexander. Cycles Of Becoming.
Washington: CRCS Publications.
    1978

Sakoian, Frances & Acker, Louis. The Astrologers Handbook
New York: Harper & Row Inc.
        1989
Tyl, Noel. Astrology 1-2-3.
Minnesota: Llewellyn Publications.
        1980
        Holistic Astrology.
        1984
        Astrology 1-2-3.
        1991
        Prediction In Astrology.
        The Horoscope as Identity
        1974
Yott, Donald H.. Astrology and Reincarnation
York Beach Maine: Samuel Weiser Inc.
        1989

Chapter 4

Geometric Basics

'The non mathematician is seized
by a mysterious shuddering when
he hears of 'four dimensional' things,
by a feeling not unlike that awakened
by thoughts of the occult.
And yet there is no more commonplace statement
than that the world in which we live
is a four dimensional time/space continuum."
Albert Einstein

Symbology

Because 3D (referring to physicality) is the manifestation of spirit segregated in material terms, math delineates materiality. This manifestation takes form in terms of polarities through the template. Within our consciousness or circle of space surrounding us, planets and points form geometric figures and patterns within the circle. These figures are the physicalized representation of the matrix of energy between each of the points and a reference to the person and their world at the center.

There are 3 basic symbols that manifest in physicality-the circle, the square, and the triangle. Just looking at them from an aesthetic perspective we can sense the energy of them. The circle feels complete, contained, a "pool" of energy, a "sphere" of influence. Even in handwriting analysis, the circles are pools of emotion-energy-motion.[100]The circle is a holistic representation of the self sustaining enclosed and complete energy. There is no beginning and no end. It is smooth and unbroken. The planets are circular, stars, orbits (ellipses) and

---

100
  Amend, Karen and Ruin, Mary. *"Handwriting Analysis"*, California, Newcastle
Publishing.

hence the infinite sphere of the identity is also found within the circle as the horoscope. The circle reflects the immortality of the spirit. It also is the symbol for the complete arena of time and space. It is this division of the circle that we then interpret.

The seasons are the effect of the division of the circle by 4 as our planet orbits the sun with its tilted axis. Single lines-the *Cardinal Points* divides this space.

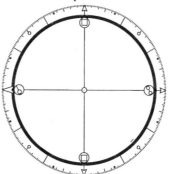

It is this division that initiates polarity and duality within the wholeness of the circle. As cells do, we divide and divide again.

The division or separation of things in physicality polarizes and energizes them. This is reflective of the ***segregative or negative energy*** we discussed in our definitions. The self encompassing circle divided gives us **hemispheres** that are now differentiated halves. The line through the circle gives it a beginning and the endless an end ***in time and space.***

The energy of "All That Is" seeks lines of least resistance, so while these separative energies divide upon manifestation (negative energy), they also seek reunification in development (positive energy). This basic conflicting premise generates ***developmental tension.*** The separated whole seeks the reunification of its energy. This back and forth energy is the sustaining force of the physical universe. It keeps the awareness of the self alive and ***conscious*** that way.

By halving the circle twice we create our second symbol the square or cross reflecting the idea of negative or segregative energy. Separated consciousness that seeks reunification and is in tension. The polarity and its counterpart polarization initiates the splaying out of the "Mask of Eternity", spirit in physical form.

The holistic aspect of the circle has now been interrupted and these lines must change direction to stay within the confines of the circle. The feeling is of rerouted energy every time it begins its trek forward. The square is the symbol of judgement and separating energy symbolically represented as the "knowledge of good and evil", or conscious interpretation of polarized energy. The separation of the "one" into different things. Time/space, self/others and inner/outer realities. This is a *view* of "All That Is" of itself. It remains all one thing despite this view. The forbidden fruit is the *perception* that their separation is the *only* "real" and that it is oppositional, rather than of service. The modes (3s) of the signs of the Zodiac are based on the square. These are the 3 Modes. On the right, the 4 Elements.

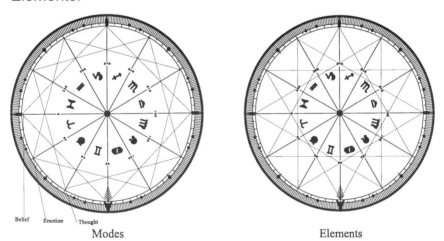

Belief   Emotion   Thought
Modes   Elements

Because energy takes the line of least resistance, a new symbol is formed to accommodate reunification efforts, one that is more "comfortable". This symbol is based on the division of 3. The holistic self divided by the *3D* of physicality creates the prism of persona. There are 3 primary colors, 3 basic forms, and the 3 primary aspects of personality we reviewed created by ***belief/emotion/thought.*** Linked equilibrium within the circle reflected through the equilateral triangle allows the divisional line of physicality to move within the confines of the circle with *ease.* Like a ball bouncing within the confines of the circle, the energy finds the least energy expression in the triangular motion. These trinary expressions are the 4 elements.

Within the circle of life then there is the trinary expressed 4 elements by the 3 quadruplicities of manifestation through belief/emotion and thought of squared modes. 3 squares or modes of 4 Elemental triangles.

The circle #1 ☉ Represents the non-physical unified higher self and consciousness, unconscious or superconscious integrity. The whole of the self.

The square #2 and **4** ▢ or cross + Represents the movement into and of physicality and material reality. Polarity and the ego and conscious mind. Separation, disintegration, contradiction and conflict. Paradox. The Christ consciousness is crucified on the cross of matter.

The equilateral triangle #3 Represents the integration of the two halves of the circle-or quadrants through the synthesization of all points at the apex. Equilibrium, integrity, unification, harmony balance and stability. The trinary integration of the identity in matter with its creative extensions and higher self.

The Zodiacal or experiential template signs and polarities are linked to each other through these geometric relationships. Everything in physicality is in relationship to everything else. A web or matrix of relationships.

The 4 Elements, are the collective belief manifestations in physicality (square reference) manifesting in 3 Modes of expression.

The **Elements** *Fire/Earth/Air/Water* represent the four basic belief pattern foundations or systems of approach through belief. Because the square represents the "movement into and of physicality," it reflects the initiation of these momentums into manifestation. The Elements (△) are the significators of the splaying out of the fundamental belief systems through the prism of different Modes (□) of expression. The format found in DNA patterning which is the *effect* and reflection of this universal geometric premise or template.

Elemental families are effortlessly unified by the commonality of their belief family.

The **Modes** of expression, or quadruplicities, *Cardinal/Fixed/Mutable,* are representative of the energy we discussed as the two halves of the circle. As opposites and polarities, the belief in separateness creates developmental conflict between the opposites, but in reality they are the same idea from polarized points of view. The second pair of opposites in square to the first polarity, creates a counter-polarity so that all 4 signs within the cross are all aspects of one idea as it manifests in materiality. I.e., Aries reflects the thrust of an idea into physicality and carries with it the idea of being first, separate, manifesting a psychological need for ego dominance or importance. The Elemental family is Fire; self motivating inspiration. The polarity of Aries, Libra shares the idea of separateness and identity definition, but from the polarized view acceptance is fulfilled by reception by others rather than distinguishing the self from others. Cooperation rather than separation to accomplish the same "identity" fulfillment. The counter-polarity of Aries/Libra is Cancer/Capricorn. In this case the identity's establishment automatically infers *Status.* How the self feels internally about their *identity* is reflected in Cancer and 4, and is manifested externally physically in Capricorn and 10. Therefore the idea of "who" one is, manifests as *identity/status* (Noel Tyl, Holistic Astrology, 1980) through the quadruplicity of Cardinal and the 1st, 4th, 7th, and 10th houses. It is one idea-*belief.* The "proof" of the belief in identity validity in the material world is seen through status and definition.

These quadruplicities can be broken up and applied from different sides easily. Supportive nurturing that reinforces identity validity, allows the self to feel emotionally secure (Cancer, 4), and the strategic manipulation of external reality (Capricorn, 10) are the *effects* of the self's belief in its own validity. Lack of social approval of identity validity (social rejection, Libra, 7) allows self to create emotional ***insecurity*** (Cancer, 4) and less than full externalization of the self in physical reality (Capricorn, 10). These all work hand in hand and it is important to learn them and look at them as schematic patterns or ***thematic profiles*** of aspects of the persona.

The first 6 signs of the template are the "parents" of the last 6 polarities. The first 6 internal and subjective, and the last 6 externalized and objectified. The first 4 reflective of physical life establishment and manifestation. The last 4 the culmination of self in physicality.

Non-physically we are one light, one color. Entrance into the physical world refracts that light into the horoscopic kaleidoscope of the natal chart configuration. The natural horoscope (the experiential template) is the "palette" of refracted light (spirit) in physical reality. We blend art and science. Instead of applying colors to create the picture, we "read" the colors to get the picture.

The Modes and the Elements, the triangle and the square, form the basis of all aspects and all relationships within the horoscope (circle). These patterns will be found in any horoscope either in their original formations, or derivatives and divisions thereof. They are essential to the understanding of the psychological, spiritual, or physical energy momentum and belief functioning within any horoscope.

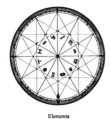

Elements

The Elements
120 degrees

△

The Elements are collective archetype belief systems that are fundamental to physicality and the product of the quadratic expression of belief/emotion and thought; the effect of the creation of the artificial construct we call personality. They are critical to the understanding of the background and foundation of the major belief systems in any horoscope.

A lack of a particular element within the chart is an immediate clue in the delineation of *the law of momentum flow.* Noel Tyl describes a similar idea in *The Principles and Practice of Astrology* called the law of naturalness. The law of momentum flow is a cumulative process wherein delineation factors are summed as the analyst goes through accumulating factors beginning with the elements to build a *profile* of the identity's belief systems. These beliefs reflect both karmic and psychological belief momentum and are one in the same.

If the elements are **lacking** representation, mistrust of that function is implied. If there is an **overabundance**, there is too much reliance on the element emphasized. This is usually found in an imbalance when one is overemphasized or when one is missing.

A point system is used to tally the representation; 1 point for each planet, the ascendant and Midheaven. 2 points for the luminaries, the Sun and Moon. Excessive is usually 7 or higher and 0-1 is considered low or lacking. When the belief system or element is over relied upon the count is high, when lacking or low there is little trust, use and belief in the element involved.

▸   "The four elements are ancient lore. Thales of Miletus (c. 610 bc) stated that all things were made of water. Anaximander criticised the cosmological theory of his predecessor by questioning the choice of one of the Elements over the others: if any one of the elements were the basic matter of things, it would long have since overcome the others. Anaximander ordered the theory: the boundless source of all endures stresses causing a separation of the Elements, wet and dry, hot and cold. Their mixtures form all things. *Change* was the strife of the *opposites*. Pythagoras (c. 532 bc) introduced the philosophic notions of harmony among things. Then Heraclitus developed a new theory from these ingredients: the real world consists of a balanced adjustment of opposing tendencies. Behind the strife between opposites, there lies a hidden harmony which is the world."[101]

It is important that the reader learn these trinities as groups and their relationships within the template. This is fundamental learning for proper astrological application.

Fire= 1)♈ Aries, 5)♌ Leo, 9) ♐ Sagittarius
The Trinity of Identity- The matrix of the self.
Excess- Fear of being ignored.
Balanced- Healthy sense of identity validity.
Low or Lacking- Mistrust of the self, natural birthright and aggression. Overcompensation with strategies and hesitation.
Psychological effect- Ego importance and defenses. Positive inspired expression.

This is the element of trust, inspiration, energetic application of the self. The belief in the identity's validity. The belief that if we act upon what it inspires and excites us to do, with integrity, that everything we need will be there to allow us to continue. The recognition that we deserve to express ourselves simply because we exist.

When this element is overemphasized, it implies that the individual is overcompensating with false trust, skipping over the obvious details out of a fear that it might be stopped or thwarted. A lack of belief in identity validity. When King Arthur could not defeat Lancelot in order that he might cross a bridge which Lancelot held, he became angry and wished to fight Lancelot to the death. Lancelot replied that it was not sensible to fight to the death over a stretch of road that he could easily go around. During the duel Lancelot held Arthur to the ground and declared "your rage has unbalanced you!"

The aspect of integrity and balance can easily disappear with too much fire. The zealot who in temperament seeks to prove the self loses his reasoned sense.

0-1 point in Fire suggests that the individual is very externally

101
Noel Tyl "Astrology 1-2-3", The Sun and the signs, pages 140, 141, Llewellyn Publications, 1984.

oriented and lacks internal trust and faith. They need to "see to believe." The doubting Thomas. Spontaneous application in experience is not relied upon and is avoided if possible. Insecurity and a lack of trust in the natural aspects of aggression and self promotion makes it laborious to assert the self and react.

Earth= 2) ♉ *Taurus, 6)* ♍ *Virgo, 10)* ♑ *Capricorn*
The Trinity of Physicality- The matrix of materiality.
Excess- Fear of functionality in the physical world.
Balanced- The recognition that the physical world is the material version of spirit. Comfort in physical applications.
Low or Lacking- The belief that material things and experiences are somehow less than ideal or spiritual. Avoidance of responsibility for ones material circumstances. Tries to look for "stable" things as an overcompensation.
Psychological effect- A lack of stability in dealing with the day-to-day functioning and material application. Positive; functional ease and feelings of efficacy. Tries to look for "stable" things as an overcompensation when low.

This trinity is the "next" trinity from the identity in house sequential reference. It is our success in the material world that validates the identity with our worth (2) work (6) and status (10). This trinity is the worth trinity of the identity. How we deal with physical or material reality (since we are that reality) reflects what we believe about our identity and hence its resources. Practicality, industriousness, and strategic effectiveness are the signatures of the Earth sign functions. Too much focus on materiality results from the idea of separateness and the belief in an external reality where we believe our fulfillment lies. Money and status are not the root of all evil, it is when these things become the driving force, or when our power is given to them that disintegration occurs. It is the addiction to the view that these things *determine* our status or power that negativity arises. The power is not in the reflection, but in ourselves to determine its meaning. (Refer to

the abundance definition).
Earth signifies the material manifestations of the self.

Air=3) ♊ Gemini, 7) ♎ Libra, 11) ♒ Aquarius
The Trinity of Idea Interaction- The matrix of ideation.

Excess-Fear of a lack of social or intellectual appreciation.

Balanced-Trust in the development, validity and contribution of the identity's ideas, expression, and the reflection of these ideas socially.

Low or Lacking-Difficulty in seeing the self or others with analytical discernment. Abbreviated abilities in abstract thinking. Does not believe that self reflection can come through social or intellectual interaction. Blinder effect. May overcompensate with cleverness and mental accomplishments to demonstrate the intellect.

Psychological effect- Positively; an appreciation of all the different ways that "All That Is" has of expressing itself. Social and intellectual diversity, interaction and vigor. Negative; preoccupation with the self and its perspectives. Overcompensatory communication and superficiality.

This is the element of the exchange of ideas and the quantum multiplication of information through social interaction. The identity seeks to express and share perspectives and beliefs. The reflection it receives from others, expands the recognition of self and its ideological significance. We gain perspective through the acknowledgement of the difference between our versions (projections) and the expression of another entity and idea altogether.

From the disempowered perspective, focusing heavily on approval from others, places the power outside the self. Not acknowledging the self through others as a mirror, leaves us with only versions. Either way the expansive discovery of the self and others is lost. The practical use of a mirror is indispensable, living only by the mirror leaves one empty and devoid of meaningful existence.

Water= 4) ♋ *Cancer, 8)* ♏ *Scorpio, 12)* ♓ *Pisces*
The Trinity of Belief Momentum- The matrix of the unconscious. e-motion

Excess- Fears of being taken advantage of through the sympathies.

Balanced- Sense of empathy and trust of the instincts.

Low or Lacking- Focus on the self-takes things personally. Difficulty empathizing with divergent views. Self defensive.

Psychological effect- Positive-empathic sensitivity and compassion. Negative-emotional self containment. Subconscious feelings (beliefs) predominate and intrude on conscious functions.

This element reflects the energy motion or e-motion of beliefs, primarily unconscious. The Water element is responsible for level changes of perspective by matching through vibrational pitch, allowing us to empathize with another's perspective and belief. Water flows in lines of least resistance, likewise the water element reflects the individuals ability to access the unconscious sea of the self through feeling in order to relate, change frequencies, and access information contained within the "wells" of psychic material.

When this element is balanced in the horoscope, the identity will demonstrate a naturally fluid capacity for compassion and understanding. They will not get "stuck" on their own perspectives.[102] When it is low or lacking the individual will have difficulty shifting perspective to another individuals beliefs and emotions, and will interpret them in their terms (projection). The only way things can then be understood is from their own perspective. There are no lines of empathic flow to take them anywhere else. They will be thoroughly convinced that *they* are misunderstood. Overcompensation usually takes the form of risk taking toward dramatic experiences in order to "feel" something.

---

[102] Of course full delineation may change some aspects of this analysis.

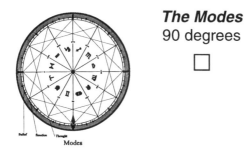

The Modes
90 degrees

□

Modes represent the *expression* of the elements of belief in physicality. As you can see in our figures, every element is represented in a different mode. **Cardinal** *(initiation)*, **Fixed** *(consolidation)*, **Mutable** *(dissemination).* This is the same idea we spoke of as the initiation of the personality in physicality. The artificial construct creation through **belief, emotion, and thought.**

Contradiction, conflict and paradox are the effect of modal expression because we now have elemental families interacting that are different views of the same issue. They will be in the cross or square and opposition relationship. Spiritually, these are the areas of the template and the horoscope that have been chosen by the higher self before incarnation to experience the dynamics of through developmental tension. The tension is felt because of the conflicting elemental interaction and the apparent conflict of polarities and concepts. The resolution of these issues and conflicts that register psychologically, is through the integration of the apparently separate functions, into one coherent **awareness.** It is not inherently negative, only its non-resolution, and maintenance of separateness of function is felt as conflict.

Cardinal
♈ *1st,-* ♋ *4th,-* ♎ *7th,-* ♑ *10th*
The quadruplicity of identity/status belief
As in the analysis of the elements, the same point system is used to identify definitions and beliefs that revolve around these modes.

The *Cardinal signs* and *angular houses* [103] represent the aspects and beliefs about the individuals *identity/status* issues. Motivation, action, and initiative signify the emphasis in these quadruplicities and houses.

In Aries-the motivation is to become (Fire).

In Cancer-the motivation is to nurture (Water).

In Libra-the motivation is to relate (Air).

In Capricorn-the motivation is to administer the self in physicality (Earth).

These are the primary functions of identity experiencing itself in materiality. All other descriptions arise from these basic functions.

Excess- Ego focus. An exaggerated emphasis on leadership to defend against the fear of identity invalidity.

Balanced- Belief conviction. Application of the self. Action.

Low or lacking- Believes efforts will not materialize desires. Invalidation of the self.

Psychological- The need to reinforce identity validity through action.

Fixed
♉ *2nd,-* ♌ *5th,-* ♏ *8th,-* ♒ *11th*
The quadruplicity of worth/extension emotion

The *Fixed signs* and *succeedent houses* reflect the beliefs one holds about the self's *worth/extension* issues. The consolidation of the resources of the self towards dissemination (Mutable always follows fixed). The accretion and attraction of energy motion (e-motion). The tools of reality creation. Stability, structurization and accumulation.

In Taurus-the consolidation of worth and values resources (Earth).

In Leo-the consolidation is of creative force and its expression (Fire).

In Scorpio-the consolidation is of energy motion or e-motion

---

[103] The 4 points of the compass, or horizon and meridian we described before. Each quadruplicity and corresponding houses have their own name.

itself, through the value interaction with others-significance (Water).

In Aquarius-the consolidation of co-created idea interaction (Air).

These are the primary resourcefulness beliefs the identity (or idea) maintains about itself and the momentums behind material creation.

Excess- Rigidity, as the effect of the fear of "risk".

Balanced- Spiritual and material resource-fullness. The belief in the abundance of the identity.

Low or lacking- Instability. Lack of diligence. Does not love the self. Believes in identity limitation of resource from the lack of validity (remember the identity quadruplicity will be the 12th house reference of this one-likewise this one will "limit" the next or indicate the beliefs that limit the next).

Psychological- The need to establish the self, maintain resourcefulness and leave remnants or established aspects of the identity through creations.

Mutable

♊ *3rd, -* ♍ *6th,-* ♐ *9th,-* ♓ *12th*

The quadruplicity of information/perspective thought

The *Mutable signs* and *Cadent houses* reflect the distributing and disseminating functions of the identity. The belief in resource distribution and sharing. The mental set that is held by the identity. The self reflective and mobilizing elements of a person or thing in polarity expression and idea interaction with the environment.

IN Gemini- The dissemination and interaction of conscious mind with its creations (the environment) (Air).

In Virgo- The dissemination of creations (5th) in the form of service and practical applications (Earth).

In Sagittarius- The dissemination of the beliefs and thinking of the self in interaction with others thinking. The dissemination of concepts through the higher self (Fire).

In Pisces- The distribution and dissemination of the emotional momentum and its final dissolution through the change of

perspective (Water) and the recognition of the all being one.
Excess- The scattering of energy and resources.
Balanced- Continuing growth in knowledge and vision. Awareness.
Low or lacking- Limited vision. Lack of discernment, dullness of perspective and inflexibility.
Psychological- The need to utilize, express, and distribute the self and its resources.

The experiential template, the elements and modes signify our relationship on earth to galactic or other consciousness. Perhaps a solar system situated differently relative to the galaxy would experience these basic template energy expressions differently. Our particular perspective renders the template as we experience it in this way. It is the relationship of the consciousness of the solar system to the consciousness of the galaxy that is experienced.

The infinite manifestation of these energies surrounding the solar system are filtered through the relationship of the planets of our solar system's consciousness in this order; **Nibiru** (hypothetical), **Pluto, Neptune, Uranus, Saturn, Jupiter, the asteroid belt, Mars, Venus, Mercury, Sun, moon, Earth.**

It is important to be reminded along our exploration that none of these delineations of our extraterrestrial environment affects or influences us except in the most obvious ways.

They are simply reflective of the personality constructs and formats of physicality which is in and of itself a creation on other levels. The planets act as lenses to focus the light of spirit into the world and reality we know. It is simply a matter of expression from the primordial to the temporal.

We must acknowledge that the elements and modes are not static. They are free flowing in almost infinite combinations (like DNA). As I have tried to show, their *derived* applications are valid in either direction because of the holographic nature of the universe. Because we are in 3D however, we can only read them in these directions.

Derivation
Aries is the 1st, it is also the 2nd of the 12th. It is also the 12th

of the 2nd and the 7th of the 7th. Taurus is the 2nd. It is also the 12th of the 3rd, the 10th of the 5th, the 3rd of the 12th, and around and around you can go. This derivative application must be learned and applied to become second nature intuitively.

What is important is that these templates are guides, they are not all inclusive nor should there be an attempt to make them so. They must be blended in practice.

The worth or value of analytical discernment (Virgo), is in the awareness we gain of ourselves through projection (Libra is the 2nd of the 6th). The projection (Libra) is the dissemination of our creations (Libra is the 3rd of the 5th). Don't worry if it is difficult at first. It is better to learn it this way and take a little longer but have a more holistic grasp.

An important observation of the template is the ***Apex points.*** The Apex is the pinnacle or paragon of the expression of the Element (Fire, Earth, Air, Water) in 4 ways. And the pinnacle or paragon of expression of the Modal function (Cardinal, Fixed, Mutable) in 3 ways. The integrated point of the first two points of the triangle, or most challenging point as the final point or corner of the square.

Sagittarius- Is the apex of the trinity of identity.

Capricorn- Is the apex of the trinity of physicality *and* the apex of the quadruplicity of status/identity belief.

Aquarius- Is the apex of the trinity of idea interaction *and* the apex of the worth/extension emotion quadruplicity.

Pisces- Is the apex of the trinity of belief momentum *and* the apex of the information/perspective thought quadruplicity.

The apex represents the pinnacle of integration and equilibrium. An accelerated point of reality interaction. The *all seeing eye* at the peak of the pyramid.[104]

The 4 apex points (Modes) of the trinities (3) of the Elements, resting on the *square* of physicality, reflects the

---

[104] Listed on US currency by its founding fathers. A subconscious remnant of the recognitions of Atlantis.

integrated combined consciousness awareness of our solar system and forms the ***Pyramid*** that was built as a testament and statement of this idea from ancient recognitions past.

Astrology not only mirrors the Pyramid, but the current model for the structure of DNA (4 nucleotide bases, and RNA expressions in 3's) but also the current standard model of the microcosmic atomic model.

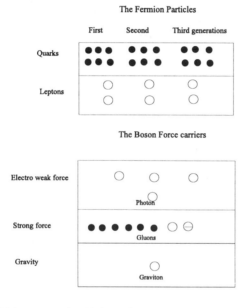

This is a very general model, please refer to the text cited for a complete explanation.

▸ "The standard model asserts that all matter is made of 12 fermions (signs) subdivided into 6 flavors of quarks (3 generations or modes) and 6 flavors of leptons (the template division). These particles of matter interact with one another via the 4 forces (Elements). There are 12 force carrying bosons; one photon; the W+, W-, Zo particles; and eight gluons. The bosons carry the electromagnetic, weak and strong forces, respectively."[105]

105
        Author's parenthetical emphasis. *"From Quarks to The Cosmos"*, Lenderman, Leon and Schramm, David. Scientific American Library. 1989

It is obvious to this writer that any unified field theory will be a derivation of these microcosmic and macrocosmic reflections of universal premise. Perhaps the irony will be that science ends up where metaphysics began.

Summary

I.   There are three basic symbols that manifest in physicality which all can be derived or represented by *the circle, the square or cross, and the triangle.*

II.   The seasons are the effect of the division of the circle by 4 (the Earth's tilted orbit), and division is represented by the single line running through the circle. This corresponds to the idea of negative energy discussed in previous chapters. This division gives us the *hemispheres or quadrants* of the horoscope and reflects the 4 dimensions template. It is the effect of time and space and creates *developmental tension.* The cross of matter creates the illusion of a soul separate from its source.

III.   The division of the circle by 4 three times, gives us the *Modes.* These modes express the division by 3 that gives us the *Elements,* the fundamental belief systems manifesting in physicality. This number 12 is the basis for the creation and expression of the personality in physical reality. This reflects *belief, emotion, and thought,* as the cornerstones of this construction of the persona.

IV.   These elements and modes initiate *the law of momentum flow*, that not only helps determine the belief systems of the individual chart being delineated, but helps us in profiling any idea within the Multiverse. These Elements and quadruplicities are counted using a point system to determine the identity's reliance in belief terms, upon them.

V.   The *Fire element* reflects the trinity of identity and is inspirational, *Earth* the trinity of materiality and is functional, *Air* the trinity of idea interaction and is social, and ***Water*** the trinity of belief momentum and is emotional.

VI. The ***Modes or quadruplicities*** are the way the elements are expressed through ***Cardinal=Identity/status belief, Fixed=Worth/extension emotion, Mutable=Information/perspective thought.*** They correspond to the Angular (1,4,7,10), Succeedent (2,5,8,11), and Cadent (3,6,9,12) houses respectively.

VII. The planetary lens vibrational order is from the least dense to the most; Pluto, Neptune, Uranus, Saturn, Jupiter, the asteroid belt, Mars, Venus, Mercury, Sun, Moon, Earth. This also reflects to some degree the flow of consciousness in the solar system in terms of most unconscious to most conscious. The ***Apex points*** reflect the culmination of the interaction of the self with its creations in physicality.

VIII. The Universal premise of the artificial construct is reflected through the ***Pyramid, DNA structure, subatomic particle model, the Bible and ancient sexagesimal systems reflecting the octa and tetrahedral structures discussed in chapter 1.*** The Pyramid suggests that man has known the structure of this universal premise first through the metaphysical premise, now scientific, back to metaphysical. A unified field theory seems feasible if derived from this premise.

Index of Terms and Concordance

Supplementary reading

Amend, Karen, and Ruin, Mary. Handwriting Analysis.
California: Newcastle Publishing.
    1980
Anka, Darryl. The New Metaphysics.
California: Light & Sound Communications Inc.,
    1987
Einstein, Albert. On The Generalized Theory of Gravitation.
Scientific American: Volume 182, No. 4,
    April 1950
Fix, William R. Pyramid Odyssey
Virginia: Mercury Media.
    1984
Goswami, Amit. The Self Aware Universe.
New York: G. P. Putnam's Sons
    1995
Lenderman, Leon and Schramm, David. From Quarks To The Cosmos.
New York: Scientific American Library.
    1989
Mader, Sylvia S.. Inquiry Into Life. Seventh edition.
Iowa: Wm. C. Brown Publishers.
    1994
Nemett, Barry. Images, Objects and Ideas. Viewing the Visual Arts.
San Diego: Harcourt Brace Jovanovich College Publishers.
    1992

Sakoian, Frances & Acker, Louis. The Astrologers Handbook
New York: Harper & Row Inc.
   1989
Thorne, Kip S.. Black Holes & Time Warps.
New York: W W Norton & Company.
   1994
Tyl, Noel. Astrology 1-2-3.
Minnesota: Llewellyn Publications.
   1980
   Holistic Astrology.
   1984
   Astrology 1-2-3.
   1991
   Prediction In Astrology.
   The Horoscope as Identity
   1974
Yott, Donald H.. Astrology and Reincarnation
York Beach Maine: Samuel Weiser Inc.
   1989

Chapter 5

Planetary Lenses

"Just as there is no such thing as color
without an eye to discern it,
so an instant or an hour or a day
is nothing without an event to mark it."
Lincoln Barnett

The experiential template is the backdrop and surrounding 360º "screen" upon which the path that we are is projected. The "light" of the other aspects of the self can be seen through the horoscope. The planets are the lenses through which this light is then focused down to earth. We absorb the unlimited aspects of the light and "All That Is" through these lenses. They color, focus, and refract that light into the life and illuminate the path we are. The "projector" of course is ourselves. The projectors of a 360 degree reality screen.

The solar system is an "identity" itself experiencing a particular path and version of the galactic template. This system is a type of consciousness as well. The planets are the types of lenses that focus the "light" from the template in varying degrees of focal length and quality, and "filter" it to Earth. They reflect the aspects of our identity and the particular archetypes of the consciousness we are. Archetypes permeate the solar system and the self from where they both emerge; deep in the unconscious. Inner and outer space, reaffirm the concept of the holographic nature of the universe and as

above so below.
The diagram below shows the relative size and orbits of the

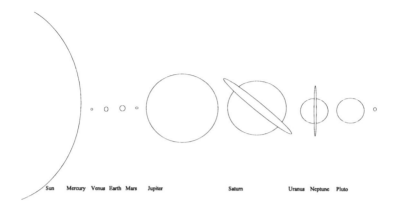

planets. It is important for the reader to learn them because forms follow archetypes. Although this book is astrologically oriented, it is always a good idea to keep up on new discoveries regarding the physical aspects of the planets to the best of our ability. This is the sign of a true seeker. All knowledge can be of service.

As an example of this physical=metaphorical correlation, Jupiter will have domain over largess, expansion, protection etc., all of which can be seen physically by its placement [106] and size etc.. Therefore astronomical knowledge can aid in philosophical and metaphoric recognitions. Why the "system" would express archetypal references may confuse the scientist, but makes perfect sense to the metaphysician, because they spring from consciousness.

 The further out from the sun center we go, the deeper and more expanded into aspects of self we go. At this time Pluto reflects the limits of identity definition that we experience because it is the boundary so to speak that we recognize of

---

[106]
     It has been postulated that Jupiter's Orbital placement inclines it to act as a sweeper up of comet material that falls into the system. With the impact of Schumacher/Levi's comet collision with Jupiter, we even observed it.

our system. It does not matter what the "real" boundaries are found to "be" later, it is our consciousness boundary that determines this, and is reflected in the one that we define and therefore see now. Until the 1700s, Saturn was considered to be the boundary, the end of the solar system.[107] That was when our consciousness did not allow us to perceive much beyond the "restrictions" of physical life and certain revelations in knowledge did not allow us to leave its confines (we now fly and have moved into space). This was when our submersion in physicality was at its peak. We have become the "masters of limitation." Saturn reflects that focus and limitation symbolically by its rings. We are focused on certain things at the exclusion of others. The levels of the outer planets (Uranus, Neptune, Pluto) are experienced personally after these limitations are recognized as self imposed. Until then they are experienced as collectively oriented perspectives and themes. This does not mean they cannot be experienced both ways, but it is the degree of self empowering perspective held by the individual that determines what end of this dimension is the primary spectrum of experience.

The bodies that weave new aspects of consciousness into the system periodically are called **comets.** They reflect level changes and shifts in the consciousness of the system. It has been proposed that a dark body nemesis of our sun periodically swings within gravitational range of our system and may trigger "rains" of comet material from the Oort cloud at the outer limits of the solar system.[108] We have seen by our exploration of the template that everything manifests in polarity in physicality. It would make sense then that the sun may indeed have some sort of counterpart. However, at this point, and from our view astrologically (within the constraints of time),

---

107
     This is debatable of course, especially in the lore of India and China where references are made symbolically to planets outside of Saturn's orbit.

108
     A theory favored by myself that explains perhaps the extinction of the dinosaurs from meteoric bombardment in one of these periods.

that counterpart, in a personal sense, is the moon.

Periodic comets tie together the various orbits (levels) and presage subtle changes in consciousness.

When we 'discovered' Uranus, Neptune and Pluto, the corresponding collective perspective was reflected in these discoveries. Primarily the 18th, 19th and 20th centuries respectively are what we are referring to as the periods and discoveries. Pluto was discovered January 21, 1930, after the depression and during the rise of the gangster, manipulative element, and collective ideological and economic power struggles. The bottom line end result was the alteration of perspective that results from systems of belief in conflict. It is rather obvious that as our collective perspective and awareness expands (inner space) we move further into outer space as well (outer awareness). Each orbit of a planet (from the Sun outward) "breaks" the limitation of perspective of the orbit that precedes it. By the same token, each orbit (level) inside another "limits" the consciousness of the next. The same interlocking system as was shown in the template (Zodiac) where the sign preceding limits the sign that follows.

Uranus' discovery coincided with the declaration of independence. Uranus is the "great awakener" and reflects the recognition of choice, unconscious knowledge, freedom, individuality and equality. It signaled the beginning of the demise of the "authority" and the beliefs that being earthbound was a "punishment."

Neptune was discovered in the 1840's. This discovery reflected the beginning of the dissolution of ego focus that had been expressed through the ruling class of dictators and kings. Neptune reflects a sea of consciousness blending and permeation. These changes lead us to the current transformational age and the ensuing dramatic shift of paradigm and perspective that will culminate in the recognition that we actually *are* the reality we thought we existed within. This will occur as a developmental change in the collective perspective reflected through Pluto as the age begins in earnest. [109]

This perspective alteration effect is reflected in the 17 degree incline (Mercury has a 7 degree tilt)[110] of Pluto's orbit that allows it to "view" the obits of the system from above and below the general planetary orbital plane. The metaphoric ability of Pluto to "view" the solar system; the observation of a "slice" of symbolic macrocosmic DNA. This altered view allows Pluto to be the pioneer into the other "levels" of the spiral ladder further up and down the "strand." If we were to "view" a strand of DNA from the top it may appear as a spiral galaxy of sorts. (see photo at right).

The "adjusted" perspective at Pluto from this incline, allows for the "otherworld" and underworld orientation. Pluto reveals the depth of mysterious secrets, fears and treasures of the unconscious. The persona or personality distinction begins to fade here and the dark reaches of space challenge the greatest fears of our identity and self definition; those of ***emotional significance.*** The full transformation of perspective that *brings this alteration* is the recognition that we are the

---

[109] Covered in the Paradigm Shift section of chapter 13.

[110] As the template reflects, these two planets rule the 6th (Mercury) and 8th (Pluto) and will be shown to be important in an aspectual way in chapter 6.

system and reality that we previously thought we existed within. When this in known beyond a shadow of a doubt by the collectivity (world populace) 3D will become 4D (fourth dimensional perspective) and movement in and out of the solar system will then be possible (please refer to threshold of believability, (Bashar) page 50). These transformations must begin taking place for the tremendous shift that begins in 2012 to 2015 as the Age of Aquarius dawns.

The spectrum of experiential levels from Sun to Pluto are the experiential arena we challenged ourselves to master in this solar system. This challenge is to integrate the conscious mind (Mercury) cognitive understanding with a full awareness of the validity of all functions, levels and aspects of the "self." "Adding" this cognitive conscious function to the oversoul's experiential "resume."

Therefore the vibrational "path" that the entity chooses as it enters the system (in non-physical soul form of course), will begin with Pluto and move inward toward Earth from the dark void of the unbroken wholeness where the intention to become physical arose (Nibiru or Transpluto?).

This adjusting aspect of ego and perspective is reflected in the relationship of Aries to Virgo (Mercury) and Aries to Scorpio (Pluto) in the experiential template called the Yod. This will be discussed further in the following chapters (see chapter 6 "Template Mechanics"). The constantly altering perspective of the identity (Aries) to its projections and reflections (Libra) is reflected in these two signs Virgo and Scorpio that lie on each side of Libra.

Wherever **Pluto** is placed in the horoscope either by sign and/or house, reflects the identity's *perspective* derived from beliefs about *emotional significance* with reference to the collective. This alteration emerges from plumbing the depths of beliefs about the apparently externalized reality and environment, be it personal, cultural, physical or societal.

Personalizing Pluto simply means the recognition that you are these environments. I say simply but it may be difficult if the individual is not willing to look at all aspects of the self which assist in the creation of it (Please review Chapter 1 vibrational levels). We are taught to believe in an external, uncontrollable reality. Although it may indeed be external, we are not separate from it and it is not uncontrollable. Science (empiricism) detracts from this perspective with its focus upon the externalized functions of physicality (Mercury/Virgo). Transformation is the recognition that you are the reality you previously thought you existed within (Bashar, 1986). When this perspective is reached the environment is experienced as the effect of belief orientation and attitudes toward it, not just the external impinging upon the self in an oppositional way.

Pluto rules this sense of personal empowerment and control and reflects self directed behavior through *trust of the environs* when positive. Fear of a loss of personal power is a negative manifestation. By its placement on the outer edges of the solar system and size, Pluto reflects this belief in the loss of power symbolically. Where it is placed in the horoscope reflects this belief in smallness or "struggling" for control (primarily if negatively aspected). How completely our psychological depths are known determines our belief in self empowered action.

Pluto is the lens of Scorpio and there are no dual rulers outside of Earth's orbit in this author's opinion.[111] The reasoning behind this is because the more focused we get as we move toward the sun, the more the illusion of polarity pairs is increased. At this "Pluto stage" the soul's entrance into this system requires transformations and crystallization into forms (establishing collective belief parameters) before any "splaying" or refraction ensues. Moving outward from the sun the "splaying" of the fragmented aspects of consciousness are re-integrated at Pluto.

Wherever **Neptune** is placed by sign and/or house is

---

[111]
    Since Pluto's discovery there has been much debate in the astrological community about whether Mars still (as it did in ancient times) rules Scorpio. In this author's opinion it may have been the closest lens (planet) that could be assigned then *because of our consciousness*, but Pluto's discovery relieves it of that and is more expanded and appropriate.

indicative of the self's co-fusion of non-physical aspects and concepts of the self (spirit or soul) with the conscious aspects of self. Thus its action is to dissolve the more focused aspects of the ego self (Aries/Mars). Co-fusion-not confusion. Confusion occurs when this blending or co-fusion is resisted from fear. Co-fusion is a blending and permeation of psychic levels. Doubt associated with Neptune, is a belief in and discounting of, the ability to manifest the ideal. Trust in a reality you *don't prefer* (Bashar).

We are the reality we believe we exist within, therefore the only type of deception that can occur with Neptune in the long run is self deception. This occurs when we disbelieve or invalidate portions of ourselves through extreme focus and reliance upon the matter portion of reality and discount the inspirational or idealistic recognition of things unseen. When we are dis-illusioned this is a sign that we are *ignoring* aspects of our reality that informs us that a situation is not a reflection of our ideal or what we prefer. Hence we ignore them (sacrifice them) because we do not wish to see things we believe are an invalidation of our preferences or our ideal. This is the effect of *expectation.* We then act surprised when this fact comes out into awareness and we feel disillusioned. Details that seem not to fit still must fit because we are a path not on one. Thus, disillusionment is the effect of expectancy and discounting. This is why critical thinking (Mercury/Virgo=focused analysis) and understanding the "All That Is" (Pisces/Neptune=broad perspective) need incorporation, blending and appropriate application. Focus on one to the exclusion of the other creates a perspective that is *capable of self delusion.* Intellect (Mercury/Virgo) and intuition (Pisces/Neptune) are two ends of the same perspective spectrum.

The camouflage aspect of Neptune, is the effect of the broader scope of "sight" the higher self has in determining what's best for the path we are. The focused ego self often misses the big picture and relies on immediate or obvious physical sense perceptions that may be distortions from being focused in space/time. The consciousness of Earth relies heavily on this physical perspective (Saturn). The paradox is that the unseen reality (spirit) may be the "real" reality and the seen reality (matter) the illusion-real while you are in it and experiencing it, but an illusion none-the-less. Therefore, the **dissolution of ego focus** is Neptune's primary signature and symbology. Neptune's fluidity broadens perspective (and hence compassion) and alerts us to our singularity as but a drop of water in the endless sea of dreams.

Neptune spiritualizes the house and sign it is found in by this dissolution of the status quo and allows for greater permeation of levels or the *co-fusion of them.*

Drugs, alcohol and other forms of escape are the negative expression of Neptune because they place the power in the external to satisfy internal development needs (see integrity definitions). The power is always in the self, and when negatively expressed, Neptunian escape is the attempt to sacrifice the self through the house and sign placement to the external reality. In this way Saturn and Neptune form a polarized pair in themselves.

The "great spots" of both Jupiter and Neptune reflect the vortices to higher levels of consciousness, co-fusion and expansion through the self directed assertion of self, without which stagnation sets in.

As spirit descends to the solar core (Sun), it now encounters aspects of its knowingness that will be held in abeyance in the physical experience. This restriction allows for physical focus and the creating of the illusion that the self we are is all we are. When unexpected events occur these unconscious aspects and knowledge are "dis-covered" by the conscious self. This occurs at **Uranus.** This sleeping aspect of the self is reflected by Uranus' axis tilt which is toward and away from the Sun and the consciousness center. Half of Uranus' orbit one side faces the Sun, and the other half faces out into darkness. The equality and validity of all co-creators is represented and symbolized by the lens of Uranus. Its placement by sign/house reflects the **uniqueness and expression of individual co-creatorhood.** Its placement signifies the unconscious and forgotten aspects of the individual and its co-creation with "All That Is." It is this forgetting that allows us to plunge into the focused realm of physicality (Saturn). We leave the multi-leveled and diffused Neptune. The awareness of the last two realms of consciousness are "tipped" into the unconscious state, hence the tilted axis of Uranus. At Uranus we forget our reality creating nature and ability to choose preference. Uranus' position and sign indicates where we need to wake it back up. We believe that the self we are is all that we are and enter the world of polarity and crystallized forms (Saturn). Uranus symbolizes the uniqueness of the form and the acceleration of its changing.

We are now in the transformational age. This age (Pluto made its closest approach to the Sun inside the orbit of Neptune or perihelion in 1989) begins the transition from the isolated ego perspective of "Earth" as the center of the Universe, to the other worldly expanded perspective and unification. Uranus, instead of Neptune (the self sacrificed) is now the level of our consciousness and the second coming (of the Christ consciousness) is this waking up and acceleration of it within each individual.

Wherever Uranus is placed in the horoscope we experience the "shock" and revelation of this unconscious knowledge surfacing through the props of physical reality or simple revelation. The re-membering of the other aspects of the self and the power we have as co-creators. Awakened is the recognition of choice in creating our physically focused persona and experiential reality. This awakening catalyses the concept of; "we find these truths to be self-evident, that all men" are equally valid co-creators as all the different ways that "All That Is" has of expressing itself within the infinite creation that it is (Bashar). Inalienable rights are the effect of co-creator responsibility and recognition in that choice. Full responsibility for one's reality=full freedom.

The concept of the "unexpected" often associated with Uranus arises from the lack of recognition that "accidents" are really denied and *resisted* unconscious creations. When events do not proceed as we think they "should", we are disappointed. This is because we are evaluating the scenario based on expectation. If it is unexpected could it not be a discovery? Might it serve us and not thwart us? Reveal insights into the unobserved and *unknown* aspects of the self created on another level of the psyche?

There is no planet more important in delineation of the natal chart then the planet **Saturn.** It reflects the material world-the physical dream, this level called physicality. Therefore, the dimension we *inhabit* is reflected in this focused, highly organized ringed planet. The archetype of the spiritual experience called physicality. Buying into Saturn and the illusion of external being the "real" reality alone is the limiting perspective that leads "us into temptation."

The superego, conscious mind and the ego self "deceive" us into "the survival of the fittest", 'no pain no gain," "striving, struggling" mental set or schema. Here at Saturn's orbit we encounter the first paradoxical issue of the belief in polarity and reality existence separate from the rest of the Multiverse *Deus ex machina" (or deity separate from the machine)* instead of the machine *being it (pantheistic).* Which is the "real" world? Saturn or Neptune? The further out the planet is the more encompassing the reality it represents, because it is more *expansive and unifying.* The more "real" (encompassing) therefore, is Neptune. But all realities are "real" while you are in them and therefore the point is rather moot except for the recognition of higher self choices and the thrust behind our understanding this point. Dream reality and physical reality are aspects of reality. The resolution to this paradox is the coherent integration and recognition by the *conscious self* of higher self choices being played out in this reality. What is the purpose of physical reality? This question when asked, leads to Neptunian or Uranian perspectives.

We will exist eternally in the Neptune reality (non-physical), temporarily in the physical. Therefore to gauge the temporal as the only real one, is to put the cart before the horse.

Saturn reflects ***strategic effectiveness in overcoming fears,*** in this plane, at this level in this world *alone.* It is the concept of learning the proper gear for the transmission; the reality of effective measures for survival of the organism in this world. Learning the functional interaction of the laws of the physical universe is the domain of Saturn. It has rule over science. Science can only measure this world. It cannot measure psychic material. And it cannot measure implied significance or qualitative preferences.

Fear, the effect of negative ego, strangles our recognition of choice in the creation of reality (Uranus). This is why in mythology Saturn castrates (renders impotent) Uranus.

We equate the manipulation of physicality with the locus of control, when in reality this is further from the truth. In an immediate sense of course we can manipulate physicality, but in an overall thematic sense, events have "higher" or more encompassing reasons for manifestation through the study of astrology.

Astrology allows us the recognition that the locus of control is obviously elsewhere and our actions are just reactions to the prescriptions or choices of the higher self since the horoscope exists as a set of probabilities AT birth.

In Matthew: 21 Christ explains that he must go to Jerusalem and there he will be put to death;

> ▸   "Then Peter took him, and began to rebuke him, saying, be it far from thee lord: this shall not be unto thee. But he turned and said unto Peter, get thee behind me *Satan*[112]: thou art an offense unto me: for thou savorest not the things that be of God (Neptune) but those that be of men (Saturn).

Wherever **Saturn** is placed by sign/house in the template or natal chart, indicates this giving away of power to the material world. Where we think like "men" instead of "Gods." This accumulated powerless perspective (crystallized) is the effect of fears of losing control in the material world. Thus, it is where we buy into the idea of a reality separate from us, that binds us

---

[112]
Author's Italics.

only to this realm and becomes our *only* locus of control. Saturn's rings are focused, wide and *crystallized* reflecting this self imposed limitation that leads to the knowledge of "Good and evil." We believe we need protection from this external reality, and this external reality determines our status. This is the judgment of paradise and an illusion of the material world, for no-thing is inherently "better" than another.

Jupiter, the second "vortex" planet is the largest in the solar system. This is because this archetype reflects the doorway to the higher self. Saturn's orbit (the limits of physicality) lies between that of the most expansive planet in the solar system (Jupiter), and the recognition of choice (Uranus). Our most abundant existence lies outside the orbit of the asteroid belt (the limits of conscious mind) and therefore outside the confines of ego justifications.

Jupiter reflects the expansiveness of awareness as we transform from specific focus to a more rarified and expanded consciousness mode. This comes as the effect of the interaction with other ideas and concepts that broaden the mind and the concept of self. The lens of ego focus (Mars) is **inflated and expanded** by Jupiter to greater levels of awareness. From the specific to the **conceptual.** Remember in the template Sagittarius (Jupiter) is the apex sign of the Fire trinity initiated with the ego self at Aries (Mars). All approaches in the Multiverse are first conceptual in nature. A philosophy is not just a "nice theory" **it is the foundation of all creation.**

Abundance follows as a Jupiter effect from the expanded recognition of **inclusiveness** of positive energy.

The attraction of abundance comes through trust of the Multiverse to support and provide the self, **with all it needs when it needs it.** This is the true meaning of abundance. By following your excitement, bliss and inspiration with integrity you allow the universe to manifest through this trust all the necessary items, events, or situations that are needed to support and lead to the fulfillment of the idea that you are. Therefore, the idea of attraction is what has allowed Jupiter to become so large as to be "on the verge" of becoming a star in its own right.

Where **Jupiter** is located by sign/house in the template or natal chart is where the identity's beliefs are sufficiently charged with this definition of attraction and expansion. This allows the energy of inspired bliss, and the identity free reign to create whatever it needs at any given moment; to create the abundance necessary to continue to follow and manifest that idea effortlessly and in synchronous accord; to expand the self to its fullest. When negative, artificial attempts to "inflate" lead to boasting and arrogance as the overcompensation to the belief implied of scarcity.

Jupiter reflects the trinity of identity Apex (Sagittarius), and the validation of identity and it's creations *automatically.* The ability to desire something, implies the ability to manifest it, when acted upon (Mars) with integrity and trust (Jupiter).

The lenses of the Persona

The asteroid belt marks the beginning of celestial objects that reflect the more *focused* functions of the artificial construct of the personality by their orbital locations.[113]

Mars, the "God of War," is the archetype of survival energy of the ego that manifests psychologically as the need to *prove and validate the self* (Noel Tyl). The need to prove is the ego's way to activate the identity definition and manifest the idea that you are, the path that you are through action. It is the *catalyst* of persona and the action required to defend and manifest it.

Action is the trigger that moves belief (Aries) into momentum and manifestation physically (Taurus). Therefore *action is the conviction of belief.*

The expansive excitement and bliss felt at Jupiter is then acted upon to attract to the identity all it needs to continue this acting and manifesting of the path that it is. It reflects the trust (Jupiter) that allows for action (Mars) that manifests materiality

---

113
    The asteroid belt it has been postulated, was the planet Maldek destroyed either by a collision or its inhabitants.

(Saturn). This action brings in all details required for the continued acting (through the attraction of Jupiter). So it is important indeed for Mars' position in the horoscope to be healthy, because any blocks to it, block the entire movement of reality creation (See "Perfection by Bashar and the "Stepping Stones" analogy). It is my belief that here is where life began and has moved inward to Earth as our focus increased. There may be remnants of civilizations that will be found there as we expand back out and explore its surface and our past.

Wherever **Mars** is by sign or house in the horoscope we find this action and energy application to prove the identity's validity. Also the bliss and excitement as the product of this need for path taking and acting. Mars leads the persona in the quest for its ultimate expression and manifestation. It is the masculine side of the "mask" of persona. In the female's chart the men in her life will be reflected through it as the reflection of her own masculine side manifesting in projected or shadow form. It will show her *versions* and creations of that side.

Aggression can be easily differentiated into two types (please refer to the psychological pendulum of repression presented earlier). Natural (positive) and unnatural (negative).

Natural aggression reflects the automatic and spontaneous expression of the self and it's needs, desires, feelings, opinions and preferences. Natural aggression is fearless and does not participate in repression (in the pure state of course there are going to be variations). This energy is the effect of the recognition and knowingness of integrity. Acting on all desires and needs for expression thwarts repression and frustration which promotes negative ego and *unnatural* aggression as an overcompensatory effect. If we believe we are empowered, actions are measured and self efficacy reinforced naturally. Acting without repression maintains the inherently positive intention and application of the self; health.

Unnatural aggression, is the effect of the belief in the powerlessness of the ego application and the need for protection. This is reflected in the early environmental structure where it was learned that repression was necessary to sublimate aggressive drives (please see "Learned Helplessness" in the definitions section). The denial of the instincts is based on this presumption of *inherently negative* behavior. But it is repression of natural instincts that is the reason for negative behavior from the ego feeling thwarted in its expression. Guilt is the invalidation of natural aggression and the effect of the belief in the need for protection. The belief in a "battle" to express implies the belief in attack (Saturnine externalism). But we experience our reality as the effect of our definitions that allow us to maintain a certain vibration or view, so what we hold as our vision of truth will manifest. The vibration that you are then becomes the reality you experience and express. You can only experience those you choose to, and be affected only by the ones you hold and believe to be true or *capable* of affecting you. No one can make anyone do anything or feel inferior without consent.

These two forms of aggression are the *effects* of positive or negative beliefs, intentions and the corresponding energies.

The father of the idea of repression, (sexual and otherwise) Sigmund Freud , himself had Mars in Libra (projections). This sign is 180 degrees from the natural placement of Aries, which of course from the psychological point of view, tells us more about Freud than about repression itself. It tells us that the power was given to the reflection and hence the disbelief in the positive and natural expression of aggression. Its retrograde condition (his chart is covered in Chapter 10) also reflects the idea of the pendulum of repression discussed earlier. It reflects his disbelief in the positiveness of *any* type of assertion or orientation of the ego. Hence the id, or what would equate to negative ego was the passion driven self that sought pacification. This idea of Freud's spurred his student Carl Jung to recognize the concept of projection and the idea of the mandala discussed earlier as well.

Mars reflects to us by sign and house beliefs the person holds of *identity validity and application.* It is at this point in the solar system "orbital" hierarchy that the persona makes itself clear and defined as a separate idea from the rest of the Multiverse. This is reflected in Mars' being the furthest out by orbit of the "rocky" planets.

The male side of the mask moves us to action and the pursuit of the path that we are.

Now that the separation of spirit into the separate self has been achieved it must have its counterpart polarity in the feminine; to be paired and polarized with the aspect NOT focused on by the ego portion of the mask. The mind/matter mirror, **Venus** embodies this archetype, this mirroring of the self is revealed in Venus' bright reflective surface of clouds. We experience the projected aspects of the self mirrored to us through others. We find our reflection therein. We seek to merge, harmonize with, own and *marry it.*

Wherever **Venus** is placed by sign or house indicates where and how this need for material and social reflection is sought and interpreted. It is the feminine and *reflective or receptive side* of the mask. The part of the self idealized but perhaps not expressed. The type of woman a man will be attracted to and attract. His *version* of the feminine function will be shown by Venus' placement.

The need to incorporate, integrate, and blend the masculine and feminine is the driving force of the "mask" towards transcendence.

The planetary pair of Mars and Venus reflect the self's relationship with itself in physicality. The signs and aspects of these planets between each other indicates the relative distance between the shadow self and the self we know and the relative security we feel with ourselves in relationship; The perceived distance between us and others. This perceived distance is equal; between the degree of our own self awareness and awareness of others.

The closest planet to the Sun is the antenna of conscious mind and acuity; **Mercury**. This planet's orbit (along with Pluto @ 17) is tilted to the plane of the ecliptic at 7 degrees. It is upon entrance (Mercury) and exit (Pluto) of the consciousness of this solar system that the greatest perspective alteration must take place. I will demonstrate in the chapter on aspects how this applies mechanistically. As with Pluto this orbital tilt allows Mercury to "view" the orbital plane of the other planets with a slightly different perspective. It's symbol is that of the perception of mind *in* matter (the crescent above the mirror). Because Pluto's tilt is greater (17) it implies a more encompassing perspective (non-physical), more inclusive.

   Logic, objectivity, discrimination and analysis-all reflect Mercury's symbology of perspective within the realm of the persona; the focussing of spirit in physical form as the self. Pluto-is the perspective of the expanded self (in outer orbit) with different "eyes."

   Mercury by sign and or house within the template indicates the self's ability to discern it's own experiences. Mercury embodies the ability to perceive, transmit, and categorize information in physical reality. Mercury defines the format or protocol in which the identity needs to express and think in psychological terms to assist the processing of physicality and it's mirrored images.

   The energies and corresponding planets discussed thus far are accumulated and expressed through the Sun/moon sign blend. This is where the light of the persona shines through, hence the luminaries are vital and are a focal point of the personality. They are themselves a polarized pair.

   The **Sun,** the light of the system and lens of Leo, consolidates the combination of planetary energies from Pluto through Mercury and shines it *outward* from the center of the system. It is the giver of life and transmits the energy of the solar system at every moment and brings it into **creation.** Thus reality is created from moment to moment through the creative power of the collective consciousness that creates the reality we inhabit. The vibrational frequency at any of these given moments is then reflected through the moon to the earth.

   Birth in astrological terms is defined as the first breath. We "breathe in" the vibration we are and the primal energy or vibration at this time. This creation and this moment "freezes" or crystallizes (Saturn) the vibration we are into physical form, into the body which then assumes the physical version of this spiritual vibration.

The **Moon** is the planetary lens of the personal unconscious. The matrix of the unconscious is reflected in the trinity of belief momentum (Water signs). The other two aspects (Scorpio/Pluto, Pisces/Neptune) of the unconscious are tied to the collective unconscious so that we may perceive a reality that appears congruent and "fixed" in its parameters. This is why science "works" and we all perceive the same external reality (relatively).

Pluto/Scorpio (8th house reference), and Neptune/Pisces (12th house reference) are above the horizon and represent the accelerated and exteriorized aspects of belief momentum in interaction with others. They reflect this binding of e-motion to the collectivity and consciousness.

The moon represents our unconscious, and the momentum of belief definitions we 'bring" from previous incarnations and other time tracks.[114] The Sun is the "light" of the vibration and the moon the prism that refracts that light into the consciousness of the personality. The Moon takes the light of the Sun and **nurtures** it through the unconscious by the need to imagine the self into-or visualize the self into actualization continually. What we image-in(e) ourselves to be is what we become.

Wherever the Sun and moon are by sign and house as well as their aspect relationship to each other, indicates the life energy (identity definition) and its artificial construct of imaging power (the personality) exist. This will be where these aspects of persona work together to manifest the aspects of the oversoul or entire self definition chosen as the hallway of experience in this incarnation. They are reflective of the method that the oversoul has agreed upon and chosen to express as a vibrational pattern of itself within the physical reality.

---

[114] Since there is really no linear or sequential movement so to speak the future and the past can be accessed from the present which is the only time we "really" exist.

The Sun and Moon are the symbolic references of the two sides of the mask the masculine (Sun-consciousness) and the feminine (Moon-unconscious) of the self physicalized (along with Mars and Venus).

Delineation

The law of momentum flow is the complete synthesizing and blending delineation of the chart as a whole idea in movement with implied *accumulation of effect.* The horoscope cannot be discerned without a thorough knowledge of the integrated delineation of Sun/Moon blends. Because the Sun/moon blends are the polarity aspects of the identity, they must be read together for a holistic and thorough understanding of the mask (the personality) and its workings.

The lunar cycle is based on the aspects between the Sun and the moon relative to the earth. All aspects between the planets and/or points within the horoscope are based on primary geometric structures discussed in chapter 4, and the relativity of the experiential template chapter 3.

The process of analysis and delineation is an application of art as well as a science, wherein the artist dissembles the applied medium to understand how the whole effect is achieved. This analogy will be employed because I am an artist and believe it the closest analog. I.e., when painting with oils, the background is laid down first. It is added upon, bringing the painting to the foreground and into detail. General to specific. This process must be followed in order to discern the law of momentum flow in the horoscope as well. Measurements and deductions confirm one another and are NOT to be treated as separated components. Only in the initial understanding as the astrologer is learning this archetypal reference for each position, placement, or point, are they considered in their singularity. This singularity changes dramatically when delineation is incorporated and interlocking beliefs and reference through planetary configurations and placements are taken as a whole.

Delineation Steps

1) First the element and mode count must be done. This determines the overall "shade" and tone of the backdrop of the "painting". The basic belief issues will be found here to be built upon.

2) What is discerned through the backdrop is then merged and compounded with the Sun/Moon blend which adds to our deduction of the identity's belief system, definitions about itself, and its approach through the ascendant or rising sign.

3) Aspects and their patterns are overlaid while continuing the discerned momentum through the first two steps. We must carry the idea forward overlaying one idea upon the other, changing its hue as we go. Indicators as to identity/status (belief), worth/extension (emotion) and information/perspective (thought) must be determined by patterns to determine which is the dependent or dominant relied upon function in the interpretation. The quadruplicity (by house or pattern) that holds the most conflict (negative aspects), will be where the *personality* focus will be.

4) The further refinement of deductions from this point forward are based first on Hemisphere emphasis, then dispositorship and rulerships (see astrological definitions). Other nuance will confirm deductions and at this point are usually quite clear with reference to momentum and belief. Planetoids and asteroids can add nuance only *after* primary functions are discerned and the level to some degree of integrity is understood (this aspect of delineation will be included in future volumes). This nuance can be gleaned from the "feel" of conflict (and actual measurement through developmental and aspect count) verses ease of expression. For now, it is essential that the student learn the basic premise of all factors which will spawn infinite possibilities of refracted blend of light, or its hue and color.

We must examine and define the lenses from furthest out to closest in; higher to lower; expanded to focused in the sequence of vibrational frequency and density.

The lens of Scorpio ♇ Pluto

Spiritual-The transformation of energy and focus into new forms. Hades.

Belief

+ Self empowerment and higher perspectives.

- The attempt to manipulate others or the environment from the fear of advantage.

Psychological-The need for emotional self significance and/or transcendence through the alteration of perspective and values interaction.

Mundane-Death, power struggles, race and national origin issues politics, religious structures and the collective consciousness.

The lens of Pisces ♆ Neptune

Spiritual-The co-fusion of greater or spiritual reality and worlds with physicality. Poseidon.

Belief

+ Manifestation of non-physical ideas and ideals through positive trust in the trigger of imagination and visualization, the realization of the one.

- The unwillingness to look at the beliefs of the self and invalidation of the unseen portions of the self through escapism.

Psychological-The fear of being taken advantage of. The need to find and trust the ideal.

Mundane-Any form of camouflage and sacrifice or escape.

The lens of Aquarius ♅ Uranus

Spiritual-The recognition of the choice in the creation of reality and the waking up of unconscious creations. Individuality as the effect of the need for awakening through revelation and acceleration. Sky god of Heaven.

Belief

+ Innovation-the avant garde or forward thought through the

tapping of unconscious knowledge.

- The need to emphasize the individuality simply for the sake of ego recognition for being different. Frustration with societal structures. Invalidation of creative abilities and their co-creative interaction.

Psychological-The need for individuality recognition and creative extension acceptance and appreciation.

Mundane-Invention, revelation, technological advancements, computer identity, and extraterrestrial visitation, discovery and interaction.

The lens of Capricorn ♄ Saturn

Spiritual-The experience of forgetting all other reality reference, in order to examine and experience limited focus. Cronus.

Belief

+ The enjoyment and exploration of physicality, through strategic effectiveness and conscious perception of the self in the mirror of mind, matter.

- The belief in the empirical existence of reality outside the self, and acquiescence to it. Fear. Power given to the mirror and "authority".

Psychological-The need for strategic effectiveness and defense against the perceived loss of control of physicality. The superego.

Mundane-External status; the complete physicalization of the identity definition, the authority, the governments. All forms of placing power outside the self.

The lens of Sagittarius ♃ Jupiter

Spiritual-The experience of the higher self in physicality and the apex of identity expression and manifestation as an idealogy. Zeus.

Belief

+ The recognition of the synchronicity and purpose behind everything as happening for a reason and a positive reason as the effect of definition-just because we exist.

- Exaggeration, extravagance and indulgence as the effect of the belief in scarcity.

Psychological-The need for the expansion, reward and opportunity for greater and more inclusive expression of the identity.

Mundane-Expansion of any form, abundance, the legal system and all those associated with it. Foreign interaction and international policy and exchange of ideas. Philosophical endeavors. Higher education.

The lens of Aries ♂ Mars
Spiritual-The specific idea focus of "All That Is". Ares.
Belief
+ Natural aggression.
- Unnatural aggression and accompanying repression.

Psychological-The need to prove the self and identity. Sexual energy application.

Mundane-Competition, sports, war, metals.

The lens of Taurus and Libra ♀ Venus
Spiritual-The mind/matter mirror. Aphrodite.
Belief
+ Seeing the self through others and reality reflection.
- Inferiority complex.

Psychological-The need for personal (Taurus) and social (Libra) reflection. (See Noel Tyl)

Mundane-Beauty, art and social grace. Money and possessions.

The lens of Gemini and Virgo ☿ Mercury
Spiritual-Perception of the mind/matter mirror. The messenger.
Belief
+ Objectivity through self analysis and/or critical thinking.
- Rationalization, trickery.

Psychological-The protocol or format with which the identity needs to use to think and communicate.

Mundane-Communication, travel, service, discrimination and dissemination.

The lens of Cancer ☽ Moon

Spiritual-The feminine and inner consciousness functions of "All That Is" in physicality. All moons (around any planet) are companions of support. The virgin goddess.

Belief

+ Emotional security, nurturing, sensitive and supportive.

- Lack of trust in the feminine functions, the dis-ease of needing to see to believe, before action is taken.

Psychological-The reigning need of the personality, the nurturance needs as overcompensation for deprivation (perceived or actual) or held as "issues" from maternal relationship. The parameters are defined by its position by sign and house. Inner fulfillment, spiritual home.

Mundane-The mother, restaurants, food, the home, the family. The ebb and flow of the tides and all rhythmic security inducing functions. Rocking.

The lens of Leo ☉ Sun

Spiritual-The outer and manifested physicalized version of spirit. The masculine functions of "All That Is." The driving force and creative force of the solar system, about which all revolves. The hero.

Belief

+ The self deserves expression and abundance, just because it exists. Self empowerment.

- Arrogance, egotism and dominance in the attempt to prove ego importance from fears of being ignored and creative impotence.

Psychological-The need to imbue with vitality, survive and create and perpetuate.

Mundane-The president, all forms of creative extension, drama and art. The children as creative extensions of the parents.

Summary

I.   The Solar system (all solar systems) is a "type" of consciousness and the planets within it are the "lenses" that focus the energies from outside and within the system.

II.   The planets and bodies in space are reflective of archetypal ideas or references in physical reality and their sizes and orbits determine the "level" of the psyche they reflect.

III. The boundaries of our system increases as our consciousness of ourselves collectively increases. Keeping abreast of other paradigms-astronomy especially-is important for the ever expanding understanding of our universe and astrology.

IV.   ***Comets*** reflect level changes and shifts in consciousness based on proximity, size, orbit, and other parameters and conditions.

V.   The outer planets of ***Uranus, Neptune and Pluto*** are reflective of collective perspectives and are only accessed on a personal basis when the negative aspects of ego focus are transformed and brought to resolution through awareness.

VI.   ***Uranus*** reflects the awakening of unconscious knowledge and freedom from the illusion of physicality. ***Neptune*** reflects co-fusing the "other worlds" and levels of consciousness as the ego dissolves through transformation and transcendence. ***Pluto*** reflects the alteration of perspective that occurs when we look at things from profound and altered views, and the resultant value structure changes. Emotional significance signifies its energy and affect. Pluto reveals the collective unconscious generational view.

VII. ***Saturn*** reflects the focus of the material world. It is the illusion of focus and strategy and the need to overcome fears are its signature. It is the format for testing one's ability to integrate aspects of the self through interacting with their crystallized versions in the material world.

VIII. *Jupiter* reflects expansion and awareness that is obtained through conceptual interaction with divergent views and ideas. Ideas and philosophies are the foundation of the Multiverse.

IX. *The lenses of the persona* begin at Mars and reflect the focused and personal-ized aspects of identity. *Mars*=action as the conviction of belief. There are two types of aggression, natural and unnatural. *Venus*=the reflective or receptive side of the mask of persona, and is the concept of marriage and union with other aspects of the self. *Mercury*=how the identity perceives and thinks about the interaction of the self and its environment. It is the eyes of understanding and critical thinking *about* physical reality. *Sun*=the "light" of the system or spirit that the planetary lenses focus into physical experience. It distills (by sign and house) the energy of "All That Is" and brings it into manifestation through the person. *Moon*=the personal unconscious habit patterns and beliefs that we believe we were deprived through nurturance (or focused on in the extreme), and overcompensate to image-in(e) ourselves to be.

X. Astrological delineation is an art as well as a science. There are specific delineation *sequences* that aid in recognizing the law of momentum flow of every horoscope. Asteroids, parts and other additions add only *nuance* to deductions already discerned through major delineation techniques, and must be regarded as such lest they confuse the understanding primacy. All planets manifest in infinite levels and this is determined by the persons resonance or level of awareness. Planets have basic thematic or archetypal symbology.

Index of Terms and concordance

Supplementary reading
Allen, Bem P. Personality Theories.
Massachusetts: Allyn & Bacon.
        1994
Anka, Darryl. The New Metaphysics.
California: Light & Sound Communications Inc.,
        1987

Anka, Darryl. Bashar: Blueprint for Change.
Seattle: New Solutions Publishing.
    1990
Arroyo, Stephen. Astrology, Karma and Transformation.
Washington: CRCS Publications.
    1978
Carlsberg, Kim, & Anka, Darryl. Contact Cards
New Mexico: Bear & Company
    1996
Cole, Sheila R., and Michael. The Development of Children. Second edition.
New York: Scientific American Books.
    1993
Davidson, Gerald C., and Neale John M.. Abnormal Psychology. Sixth edition.
New York: John Wiley and Sons, Inc.
    1996
Lewi, Grant. Heaven Knows What.
Minnesota: Llewellyn Publications.
    1977
Lewi, Grant. Astrology For The Millions.
Minnesota: Llewellyn Publications. Bantam Edition
    1980
Mischel, Walter. Introduction to Personality. Fifth edition.
Texas: Harcourt Brace Jovanovich Publishers
    1993
Roberts, Jane. The Nature Of Personal Reality, A Seth Book.
New Jersey: Prentice Hall.
    1974
Ruperti, Alexander. Cycles Of Becoming.
Washington: CRCS Publications.
    1978
Sakoian, Frances & Acker, Louis. The Astrologers Handbook
New York: Harper & Row Inc.
    1989
Sagan, Carl. Cosmos.
New York: Random House
    1980
Skinner, B. F., About Behaviorism.
New York: Vintage Books, A Division of Random House.
    1976

Tyl, Noel. Astrology 1-2-3.
Minnesota: Llewellyn Publications.
        1980
        Holistic Astrology.
        1984
        Astrology 1-2-3.
        1991
        Prediction In Astrology.
        The Horoscope as Identity
        1974
Yott, Donald H.. Astrology and Reincarnation
York Beach Maine: Samuel Weiser Inc.
        1989

Chapter 6
Template Mechanics
Part 1- Separated Aspects

> "I suffer nought against my will,
> I am not obedient to God, I am in accord with him,
> and the more so because I know that everything
> takes place in virtue of an immutable law proclaimed
> from all eternity."
> Saint Ignatius

The holistic integration of the horoscope's parts, produces more understanding than the sum of these parts can. The ability to bring together these apparently separate elements into a coherent whole that works flawlessly is a learned skill.

The goal of self-empowering perspectives, is to learn to assimilate these myriad aspects of the self, the life, the analysis, and allow them to flow into a picture of the whole. Life works when we let it, and the way to let it is to assume that because we create our reality, all of the "parts" must fit. Every moment is thus our own stepping stone to the next moment that contains all of the information we need to get on with the next step, and the next and the next.

Astrological mechanics reflect the idea(s) in development chosen by ourselves at some unconscious level, to be experienced and explored as a step. A life is a step. Most steps are forward some back. However, the ones back are usually so the forward ones can proceed more completely and in that sense really aren't "back." A willingness to be all that you can be in any given step, determines the quality of the next step. A fully explored and trusted step is a positive or integrative expression. A note of caution; A preponderance of positive aspects is not necessarily indicative of positive steps. Equilibrium or integral energies can translate into lethargy, defensive justification, elitism or just plain comfort with the status quo. This is not necessarily bad but it can limit awareness and drive to externalization; two very important reasons for living.

What we look for in the horoscope, as in life, is balance and expression that improves the quality of life. Positive and negative balance, no matter how many of each, leans holistically in the positive direction.

As an analogous example, disassembling a clock to rebuild it (negative energy) leads to the fulfillment of the repair and reassembly understanding (positive energy). Not only is the clock understood better through this process, but the repairman is prepared for further work should the clock need disassembly in the future. This analogy can be applied to the exploration of the self through time and space in the physical life.

A highly accelerative individual can have a high degree of developmental tension (squares and oppositions). This awareness is then "given out" or disseminated through the positive aspects (trines, sextiles) from planets that are a part of the same developmental network.

When we look at aspects and their patterns, we must realize that these are mathematical representations of vibrational frequencies. In the natal chart, they are the physical translation symbols for the energy that has been garnered from the moment during which they were formed. They do not *make* the person or situation a certain way. They reflect a potential or probable parameter of expression that the individual then in the conscious state can act upon and manifest through the will. They correspond to the vibrational frequency ideas discussed in chapter 1, and give us great insight into the negative or positive potential of a certain idea or framework being expressed in the chart. By choosing when to be born, they are created by the individual, to function as the parameters and prescription by their higher self choice before incarnation that facilitates the path they chose to be. However, because we are taught to ignore external reality having anything to do our creative self, this creates new definitions from this view that may further restrict the idea they have chosen to be in this life.

It is the astrologer/psychologist's job to help reflect back to the person, these unconscious or forgotten choices and assist in understanding why limitations may have been unknowingly created. This is done by corroborating and linking life events with self definitions brought to the client's awareness through dialogue. This allows the individual to re-evaluate their own (unconscious) choices and definitions and recreate them to preference if so desired.

The law of momentum flow[115] is very dependent upon aspect **networks**. These networks are the grouping of aspects into patterns which are much more revealing of beliefs than a single aspect alone. These ideas will be covered more later when we delineate them in sample horoscopes.

Many astrologers will go to great lengths to use mathematical aspects as a way to prove astrology to the scientific community. This is fallacious. Astrology's value is as a tool to lend insight. *Only* through application can we discern this. The "what" that makes it work is not known at this time. The fact that it does, is observationally obvious once application skills are acquired. The bottom line is that translating aspect factors into understanding and behavior is an art. It is learned. It produces an understanding of the whole, far more than an empirical sum of the parts can ever achieve. This is why computers *cannot* translate astrological factors into a profile of a human that through blended awareness and significance, is meaningful.

Following brief explanation, are abbreviated definitions of the mechanistic functions of the templates we have thus far presented. They represent the "clock" disassembly and its mechanical functions. Upon reassembly through delineation in chapters to follow, we will not only understand the clock and the measurements of its movements-but also how to tell time and when, how and why the clock is likely strike. We are the creators of the clock, the time and the experience of them.

---

[115]
This law will always correspond to Noel Tyl's *Law of Naturalness,* and/or Alfred Adler's *Laws of Movement* toward self created goals.

It is not my intention to be all inclusive in regard to aspects mathematically, to be picayune in analysis is reserved for final nuance or specific issue exploration. The conceptual understanding and blending is where meaningful empathic understanding comes into the observer's awareness. The structure is built and *then* adorned.

Aspects

The template reflects the relationship of the signs and defines all the major aspects possible between the planets. Minor aspects are derivatives of major aspects and will only add nuance to major delineations. Analogous to the number line, the derivatives are infinite. Therefore theoretically, the planets are in some aspect networks all the time. Some are of course more easily observable than others.

The planets in our solar system are in aspect to each other, the solar system is then in aspect with other solar systems, then in aspect relative to Galaxies, and Galaxies in aspect to each other and so on. It is for this reason that the sun as the center is irrelevant in astrology, although a meaningful discovery in astronomy and science.

Within our system we are concerned with the aspects between bodies within *it* relative to Earth, because this is where we are located. If we were located on another planet, (or begin to travel to them) the relative aspects of the planets to that viewpoint would then be considered, because location is an element of vibrational signature, a part of the "equation."

The geometric relationship field is a vibrational field and is determined by the relative aspect formation of bodies within that field. As we evolve it will be seen that perhaps heliocentric astrological measurements may take prominence over geocentric. This will be when our self definitions expand to encompass that greater reality. Since our incarnations at this point are on the Earth, then it follows that for now, Earth is our center.

Dots or circles will represent planets (except in certain cases) in our examples in order to keep delineations neutral as far as archetypal reference for now. This approach will allow the reader to get a feel of the different hours of the clock that aspects and patterns reflect. These aspects and patterns can occur anywhere in a person's horoscope and in any number of combinations of signs of the experiential template with the 10 basic astrological significators (planets). Others, such as points and asteroids will be incorporated in later volumes.

Simple geometric relationship in motion is what we will be exploring. Planets within the horoscope wheel will always be moving in counterclockwise fashion unless retrograde. So picture them in this way with the faster planet moving faster counterclockwise etc. Later we will add all of this together and see how easily it fits in delineation when we allow it to. The more coherently these templates are understood, the easier delineation will be in our future work.

Aspects-Opening/Closing and Applying and Separating

Every planet at any given moment, is either applying or separating to or from, aspect with another. They are either opening from an aspect that has just occurred, or are closing on another planet with an aspect about to occur. Since all planets move at different speeds, it is the planet of faster movement that is producing either the application of aspects or the separation of aspects. It is the relative motion of the planets that determines the timing (time) and movement (space), of events that the astrologer "projects" into the future. It is relativity that reflects the mechanics of and basis for, Astrological measurement.

The revolution (time it takes for the planet to traverse the Zodiacal template) or *motion* for each of the planets from the fastest to the slowest are as follows:

Moon-27.7 days

Mercury-88 days

Venus-224.7 days

EARTH- Our location on Earth makes it to appear that the *Sun* is travelling through the Zodiac at the speed of approximately 1 degree of the Zodiac per day, or 364.26 days to travel 360 degrees. Therefore the Sun (actually the Earth's orbit) would be the next in relative speed.

> ***Mars***- 1.88 years
> ***Jupiter***- 11.86 years
> ***Saturn***- 29.46 years
> ***Uranus***- 84.01 years
> ***Neptune***-164.8 years
> ***Pluto***- 247 years

The faster the motion, the "closer" it is to functions of the persona, conscious mind, and ego (all aspects of "focus").

In example 1, Mercury has a faster motion (orbit) than does Mars. Therefore, Mercury will "catch up" to complete it's trine aspect to Mars. After completion of the 120 degree aspect, it leaves or ***separates*** from the trine. This is what is meant by "applying" or "separating". It is analogous to waxing in strength, or waning in strength (in terms of the lunar cycles).

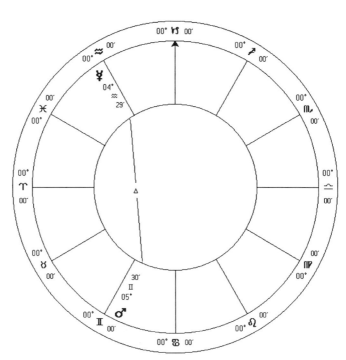

Example 1
Natal Chart (2)
Feb 8 1991
12:00 PM +8:00
La Jolla CA, USA
32N51 117W16
Geocentric
Tropical
0° Aries
True Node

Using the same example, the **ARC** of the aspect- the distance between the two bodies- determines whether it is an "opening" trine (120 degrees) or a "closing" trine (240 degrees). Once again the faster planet determines this. The arc in our example would be 240 degrees, because this trine would be **before** Mercury's **conjunction** with Mars, and **after** it's **opposition** had already occurred.

Example two demonstrates an opening trine to Mars. This would occur after conjunction, and before opposition.

Example 2
Natal Chart (3)
Feb 11 1997
12:00 PM +8:00
La Jolla CA, USA
32N51 117W16
Geocentric
Tropical
0°Aries
True Node

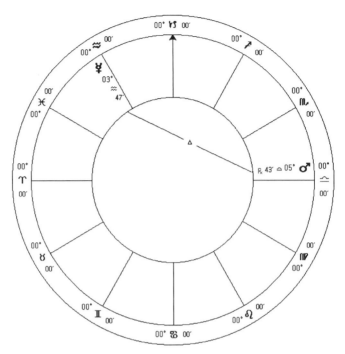

Opening and closing aspects reflect the natural order of the template, and indicate whether the energy between planets is being expressed is *subjective* (opening), or *objective* (closing). Internal reality experience, or external experience. Using the Zodiac or template signs, opening carries the connotation of initiation and establishment (Cancer). Closing carries the connotation of externalization and administration (Capricorn). A boomerang released at opening, is retrieved at closing. Opening is in anticipation of externalization (Virgo before Libra), and closing reflects the incorporation of externalization (Pisces before Aries).

In the second example Mars is also *retrograde* [116] (apparently moving backwards or clockwise) so that they are moving towards each other to the trine aspect, towards say 4 degrees where they may meet and make the 120 degree trine.

---

116 This is covered more in depth in chapters to follow.

This is called ***double applying*** (or separating if they are). The ***orb*** is the amount of degrees allowed on either side of the aspect from its point of exactness between each body.

Opening Aspects (subjective)

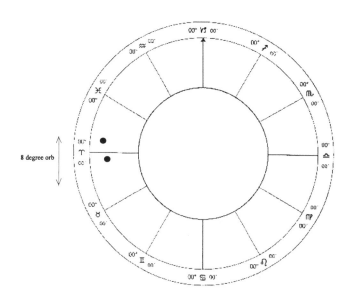

8 degree orb

Symbol- ♂

Aspect- Conjunction- 0 degrees between two or more planets.

Energy- Focus, neutral.

Spiritual- The focus and blending of one or more archetypes into expression.

Psychological- The integrated functioning of two or more aspects of personality and/or needs. One function colors the other. Applying conjunctions reflect the objectification of the energies and separating reflect the subjective experience of the energy permeation.

Connotation- Aries; Identity focus, emergence.

Orb- 8 degrees either side.

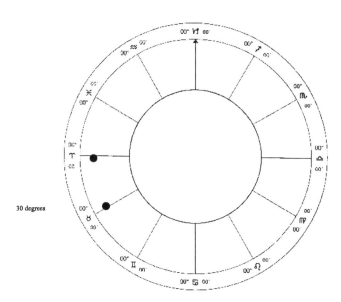

30 degrees

Symbol- ⊻

Aspect- Semisextile- 30 degrees between two or more planets.

Energy- Mildly supportive, positive.

Spiritual- The support of one or more archetypes to another.

Psychological- Minor support between beliefs.

Connotation- Taurus to Aries; consolidation of identity.

Orb- 3 degrees either side. Applying or separating.

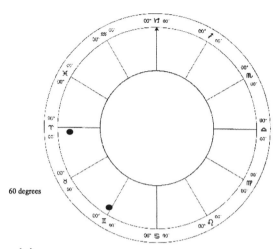

60 degrees

Symbol- ✳

Aspect- Sextile- 60 degrees between two or more planets.

Energy- Supports expression, positive.

Spiritual- The physical support of expression and expansion in physicality of one or more archetypes.

Psychological- Major support of beliefs within the identity of archetypal reference between two or more aspects of personality and/or needs. Positive expression. Diversification of the identity.

Connotation- Gemini to Aries; Reflective awareness and dissemination.

Orb- 6 degrees either side.

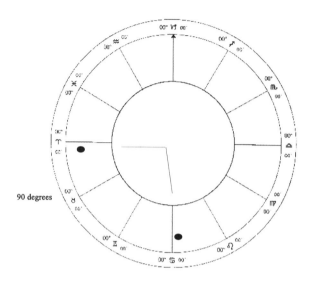

Symbol- ☐

Aspect- Square- 90 degrees between two or more planets.
Energy- The disintegration of archetypes. Negative, in conflict, and believed separate.[117]
Spiritual- "All That Is" or spirit separating into different foci.
Psychological- Archetypal belief conflict between functions that is determined by the planets involved. Developmental choice of application and exploration chosen for the life.
Connotation- Cancer to Aries; Unconscious creation and establishment of ideas and belief into physicality.
Orb- 8 degrees either side.

117
   This of course is BEFORE the person has integrated this aspect, which is the developmental purpose for having it. Until it is, it is felt as conflict. When it is integrated it is felt as excitement or inspired tension to take action or move in a certain direction.

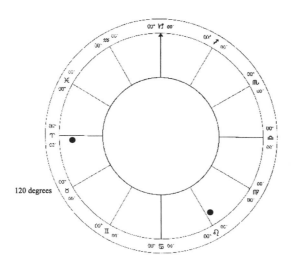

Symbol- △

Aspect- Trine- 120 degrees between two or more planets.

Energy- Positive integral energy, equilibrium. Intuited linking and expression.

Spiritual- Automatic creative extension and manifestation.

Psychological- The harmonious integration of archetypal reference. Routinized, trusted, relied upon, and reinforced behavior. The channel for the expression of the developmental aspects. Instinct.

Connotation- Leo to Aries; Trinity, the consolidation of identity through extension. All aspects from here on are externalized expressions of identity definitions.

Orb- 8 degrees either side. All major aspects will have this orb.

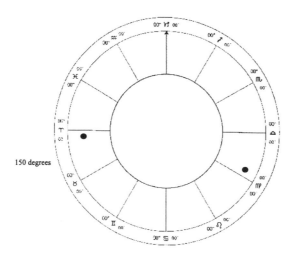

150 degrees

Symbol- ⊼

Aspect- Inconjunct- 150 degrees between two or more planets.

Energy- Negative and tension generating when transformational or adjusting energy is resisted. Positive when perspective expands and adjusts beyond simple ego focus.

Spiritual- The incorporation and consolidation of archetypal reference. Review of the ego self.

Psychological- Adjustment of archetypal symbols through reflection, refinement and alteration of perspectives. Conscious analysis of unconscious elements.

Connotation- Virgo to Aries; Analytical discrimination of perspective, dis-association and detachment.

Orb- 4 degrees either side.

Closing Aspects (objective)

As the template reflects, the first six aspects represent the subjective internalization between the planets through the aspects. These opening aspects were determined by the faster planet overtaking the slower planet as they approached the opposition phase (180 degrees).

The easiest way to visualize this and remember it is by reflecting upon the moon's phases with the full moon as the opposition point. The first six signs and aspects (sexagesimal) correspond to the phases of the moon from new to full. This is the ***sowing phase*** of momentum.

At full moon (opposition), the full illumination of the idea we are being (or any idea delineated astrologically), and the conscious projection of what has been sown, is experienced. After full moon and opposition we experience the ***reaping phase*** and incorporate, disseminate and interact with those creations either through others or the apparently external creations in reality. We encounter the horizon of awareness and process *there,* externally.

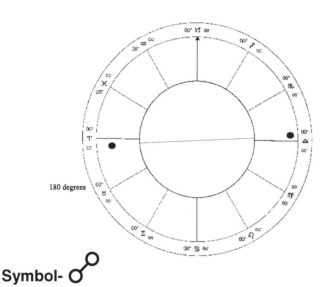

Symbol- ☍

Aspect- Opposition- 180 degrees between two or more planets.

Energy- Negative polarization and base pairing.

Spiritual- The single idea polarized and paired in manifestation. Mirroring.

Psychological- Tension awareness of archetypal symbols believed to be separate. A psychological manifestation of the need to resolve this apparent polarity contradiction and paradox. The belief that the pairs, whatever areas of the chart they represent or reflect, are "difficult" to reconcile. When judged in this manner the energy is felt as ***anxiety.*** When resolved and welcomed as ***developmental tension,*** it is felt as a motivating factor in the excitement of ***bliss and inspiration.*** It thus is ***resolved*** and ***integrated.***

This concept applies to the square aspect as well.

Connotation- Libra to Aries; AND from the "others" point of view, Aries to Libra. Illumination, the experiencing of the unconscious, and conscious definitions of the self and identity in physical reality.

Orb- 8 degrees either side. 10 for Sun or Moon.

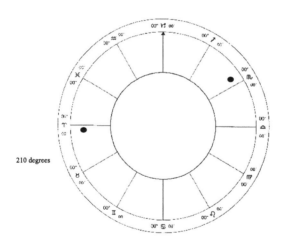

210 degrees

Symbol- ⊼

Aspect- Inconjunct- 210 degrees between two or more planets.

Energy- Negative and tension generating when transformational or adjusting energy is resisted. Positive when perspective expands and adjusts beyond simple ego focus.

Dependant upon the health of the ego.

Spiritual- The incorporation and consolidation of archetypal experience of the self at opposition that allows for relaxation and transcendence of negative ego.

Psychological- Adjustment of perspective and significance through internalization of unconscious experience of the self from the unconscious analysis at the previous (opening) inconjunct (Virgo).

Connotation- Scorpio to Aries; The consolidation of expanded perspective through projection. The waning of ego's focus on separateness.

Orb- 4 degrees either side.

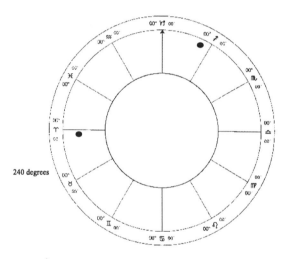

Symbol- △

Aspect- Apex trine- 240 degrees between two or more planets.

Energy- Positive integration, equilibrium.

Spiritual- The dissemination of the higher self in physicality.

Psychological- Through the integration of the base of the triangle, we see the effortless dissemination of the identity in interaction with other minds. Unless it is between the Sun and Moon it is not consciously applied but instinctually used. The ego need to have the beliefs reinforced and accepted by others.

Connotation- Sagittarius to Aries; The fruit from the integration and transformation to larger perspectives at closing inconjunct (Scorpio).

Orb- 8 degrees either side applying or separating.

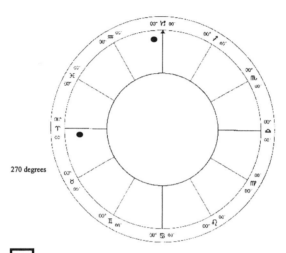

Symbol- ☐

Aspect- Apex square- 270 degrees between two or more planets.

Energy- Negative disintegration.

Spiritual- The culmination and concretization of the unconscious portions of self into physicality also reflected in the human gestation period (270 days).

Psychological- The portions of the self that began externalization at the opposition create a crisis in manifestation (if they have not been approached positively and resolved). If the owning of creations is practiced at opposition-transcendence occurred at inconjunct-and interaction with other ideas in the Multiverse seen as one at apex trine-*then* this aspect is the most powerful of all. It reflects the successful manifestation or culmination of the self in physicality (it always does anyway, but if positive, then psychological fulfillment of the identity and its "purpose" is seen here).

Connotation- Capricorn to Aries; The physical focus of identity material reality. The final quarter of the cycle (the moon) and the manifestation before dissolution and redefinition at new moon (new conjunction).

Orb- 8 degrees either side applying or separating.

At this "peak" of expression in physicality, the need for conviction and action creates effect. The planets involved, (the planet(s) applying or overtaking the slower planet(s)), are the archetypes requiring incorporation and externalization. This incorporation comes through the slower planet and its application in the life of the person.

Our "standing" or "status" is thus achieved as the effect of full manifestation of self, and responsibility to our environment as co-creator. Status is not externally "bestowed" upon us. We "bestow" it upon ourselves through the externalization of the "All That Is" that we are. Through the expanded state of higher self (closing apex trine) if approached with positive energy (inspiration, excitement, bliss). When approached with negative energy (anxiety, despair, judgment) the self perceived threat is having to "battle" all of the external creation in order to "survive," or "get ahead"; That we must endure "pain" in order to "gain," that it is a matter of the "survival of the fittest." These ideas are Saturnine views. If this is the view held, the next quadrant will shake us out of this delusion or confine us with it. If not and we are positive, we find the uniqueness of the idea we are reinforced by accolade and co-creator interaction distinction. Whether we are acknowledged for it or not.

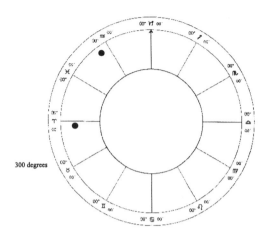

Symbol- ✶

Aspect- Sextile- 300 degrees between two or more planets.

Energy- Supports expansion, reinforcing.

Spiritual- The broadening of identity through the interaction and support of other co-creators.

Psychological- The need for social acknowledgement for uniqueness of physical manifestation and expression of the identity. The planet gaining on the slower planet brings diverse, supportive and innovative elements to the slower planet.

Connotation- Aquarius to Aries; Uniqueness supports the path the identity is.

Orb- 6 degrees either side applying or separating.

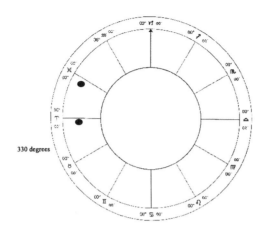

Symbol- ⊻

Aspect- Semisextile- 330 degrees between two or more planets.

Energy- Minor support.

Spiritual- Support of the self through interconnectedness.

Psychological- The limitations of the desire for singularity.

Connotation- Pisces to Aries; The reality of oneness limiting the reality of singularity.

Orb- 3 degrees either side applying or separating.

The following is a list of some commonly used aspects

Aspect	arc	meaning	orb	symbol
Conjunction	0	Focus, blending	8	☌
Semisextile	30	Growth, minor support	3	⊻
Novile	40	Completion	1	**N**

Semisquare	45	Initial separation, minor tension		
Septile	51.25	Consciousness expansion, insight	2	∠
			1	**S**
Sextile	60	Positive support	6	✳
Quintile	72	Creative application	1	**Q**
Square	90	Developmental tension	8	□
Trine	120	Equilibrium	8	△
Sesquiquadrate	135	Minor tension	3	⯐
Inconjunct	150	Perspective adjustment	4	⊼
Opposition	180	Physicalized awareness	8-10	☍

Index of Terms and Concordance

Supplementary Reading List

Anka, Darryl. The New Metaphysics.
California: Light & Sound Communications Inc.,
    1987
Anka, Darryl. Bashar: Blueprint for Change.
Seattle: New Solutions Publishing.
    1990
Arroyo, Stephen. Astrology, Karma and Transformation.
Washington: CRCS Publications.
    1978
Lewi, Grant. Heaven Knows What.
Minnesota: Llewellyn Publications.
    1977
Lewi, Grant. Astrology For The Millions.
Minnesota: Llewellyn Publications. Bantam Edition
    1980
Pelletier, Robert. Planets in Aspect.
Massachusetts: Para Research Inc.
    1974
Ruperti, Alexander. Cycles Of Becoming.
Washington: CRCS Publications.
    1978
Sakoian, Frances & Acker, Louis. The Astrologers Handbook
New York: Harper & Row Inc.
    1989
Tyl, Noel. Astrology 1-2-3.
Minnesota: Llewellyn Publications.
    1980
    Holistic Astrology.
    1984
    Astrology 1-2-3.
    1991
    Prediction In Astrology.
    The Horoscope as Identity
    1974

Part 2
Aspect Patterns

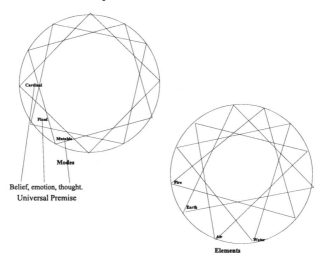

Planetary patterns reflect systems of belief. Psychologically, they reflect the complexity and the form in which the defenses and personality needs have taken to define, defend, and express the individuality. They reflect the interlocking functioning of the psyche (psychodynamics) and the probable behavior arising from it. Patterns are either developmentally charged (based on the square), physicalized effortlessly and instinctual routinized (based on the trinary form), blended and focussed upon heavily (based on the conjunction), or are expanded constantly (based on the inconjunct).

We will explore them in order of their power and significance with regard to the workings of the psyche. The ones discussed are just a few basic types. It is really not essential that they be memorized or used ritually in delineation. It is far more important to learn to translate the concepts outlined in this text into empathic awareness of the person who's chart we delineate as a guide to understanding and aid to service. How this is done evolves differently and individually with each astrologer.

Grand Cross

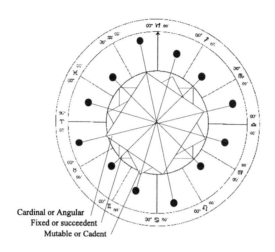

Cardinal or Angular
Fixed or succeedent
Mutable or Cadent

Basis- Square-modal quadruplicity

Delineation- Contradiction, conflict and paradox between the opposing functions of archetypal reference.

Psychological- The most acute awareness of developmental crisis and conflict.

In the first, fourth, seventh and tenth houses or in the ***Cardinal*** mode-Identity/status crisis and belief conflict. A crisis in motivation. Who am I? What is my status?

In the second, fifth, eighth, and eleventh houses or in the ***Fixed*** mode-resource/extension crisis. A crisis with habit patterning and structure. Conditional in love giving, defensive about worth and resources. Values developmental tension.

In the third, sixth, ninth or twelfth houses or in the ***Mutable*** mode-thinking/perspective crisis. A crisis with conflicting viewpoints, awareness and beliefs. Intellectual developmental tension.

T-square

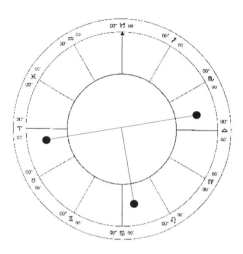

Basis- Square-modal quadruplicity

Delineation- Crisis, and conflict with the functions of archetypal reference (the houses and signs it falls in). The vacant house of the cross receives the developmental tension as an effect of this "bow and arrow" type of psychic tension.

Psychological- The acute awareness of developmental crisis and conflict. Overcompensation in an attempt to resolve conflict, especially in the vacant house. The tension is **applied** to the affairs of the vacant house.

In the first, fourth, seventh and tenth houses or in the **Cardinal** mode-Identity/status crisis and belief conflict. A crisis in motivation. Who am I? What inspires me to act on?

In the second, fifth, eighth, and eleventh houses or in the **Fixed** mode-resource/extension crisis. A crisis with habit patterning and structure. Conditional love, defensive about worth.

In the third, sixth, ninth or twelfth houses or in the **Mutable** mode-thinking/perspective crisis. A crisis with conflicting viewpoints, awareness and beliefs. Intellectual developmental tension.

Grand trine

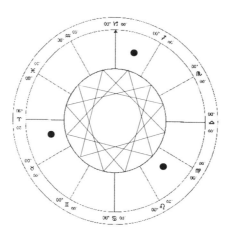

Basis- Triangle or trinary division.

Delineation- Self sufficient completeness, trust.

Psychological- The pattern usually occurs in a single element. Instability may accompany this configuration as it is a psychological defense against the fear of losing equilibrium.

In the first, fifth, or ninth houses or in the Element of **Fire-** A self-sufficient pattern of belief to defend or reinforce the stability of ego importance. The accompanying fear is of being ignored. Instincts need developmental aspects or remained unquestioned.

In the second, sixth, or tenth houses or in the Element of **Earth-** A self-sufficient pattern of belief to defend or reinforce the stability of functional or pragmatic control. The accompanying fear is of being out of control.

In the third, seventh, eleventh houses or in the Element of **Air-** A self-sufficient pattern of belief to defend or reinforce the stability of identity ideology validation. The accompanying fear is of being unappreciated or socially accepted (Noel Tyl, 1980).

In the fourth, eighth, twelfth houses or in the Element of **Water-** A self-sufficient pattern of belief to defend or reinforce the stability of e-motions or energy momentums. The accompanying fear is of losing that stability through advantage or manipulation.

Spiritual- Unquestioned trust of belief functioning.

Belief-

In Fire- In the fragility of identity. **In Earth-** In the manipulative effects of external reality. **In Air-** Invalidation of the power of ideas and individual expression of them. **In Water-** Invalidation of feelings as an accurate reflection of belief.

Hemisphere Emphasis

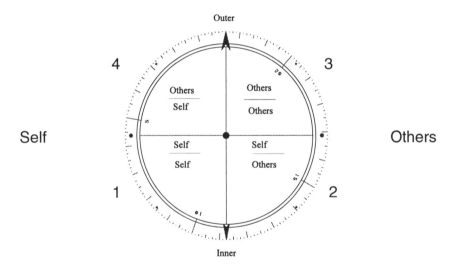

The four dimensions of experience we have been discussing, are **orientations** of perspective and correspond to the 4 Elements. Each of the angles acts as the four cornerstones of personality definition and these dimensions of orientation can tell us much about the individual's beliefs regarding **locus of control**. Hemisphere emphasis corresponds to the MPI (Maudsley Personality Inventory) of introversion/extroversion and ambivert determinations in psychology.[118] It can also be useful when used with the Keirsey Temperament Sorter (discussed in Chapter 1, page 31).

Upper and **western** hemisphere reflect **objective** and **external** determinations, and **below** the horizon and **eastern** reflect **subjective** and **introverted** determinations. Of course these are dimensions and no one is ever 100% anything, but falls somewhere on dimension scales. A person may be extroverted in an overcompensation for *below and eastern* emphasis for example. So it cannot by itself tell us what orientation the person has-although it may tell us *why*.

Each hemisphere **quadrant** reflects a psychological orientation by the clustering generally first, and aspect patterns second, that occur near the angles that we have defined thus far as Cardinal points. A planetary grouping by any angle indicates the belief in vulnerability psychologically and therefore the planets are grouped there as archetypal **defenders** of the angle. In other words the individual **invests** psychic energy in the orientation as a belief and accompanying defense.

The figure on the previous page reflects the orientation in terms of inner/outer and self/other orientation, that by now the reader should be becoming familiar with as an astrological key to delineation in many ways.

Stellium

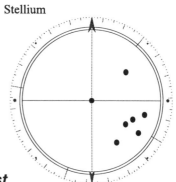

A grouping of four or more planets in proximity in just one house (usually) is called a **stellium** (based on conjunction).

When grouped in the **first**

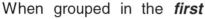

118
    Personality Theories, Bem P. Allen, Western Illinois University, 1994 Chapter 16, Raymond Cattell and Hans Eysenck, Objective Personality tests, page 444.

quadrant; *subjective self*, reflects the quadrant of ego development. Focus will be upon the identity's subjective experience of reality. There will be an emphasis on self development and personal efficacy in terms of self evaluation.

When they are grouped in the **second** quadrant; *subjective others*, the energy will be focused on the subjective experience of others for it's "feeling" (belief) about itself. There will be a focus on extensions as the determination of validation. I.e., I am valid because I give or create.

When the **third** quadrant is emphasized; This can represent either a very powerless belief or empowered-it is very dependent upon the planetary archetypes posited here. Either way projected versions of the self will be depended upon for self reflection strongly. There will be focus on seeking validation through *others* beliefs and values.

See-saw

When the **fourth** quadrant is emphasized; Provided it is balanced through other quadrants, it can reflect a high state of acceleration and awareness. If unbalanced exaggeration of identity. There will be emphasis placed on the person's place within societal structures.

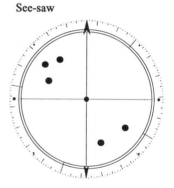

See-saw- (Based on opposition) Awareness and polarity conflict between hemispheres. If pronounced, paradoxical crisis.

Yod

Yod- (Based on inconjunct) Expansion of awareness and perspective. Indicator of a powerful awareness of the unconscious and/or the mystical. (I.e., Carl G. Jung).

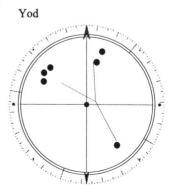

Mystic Rectangle- (Based on 2 trines, 2 sextiles, 2 oppositions. It usually occurs in all masculine or all feminine signs. The physicalized expression of higher self functioning and mystical prowess may be indicated. It is a highly integrated functioning of archetypes. Awareness and its expression blended.

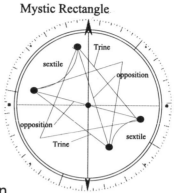

Mystic Rectangle

Splash- Usually planets in every quadrant in a splayed fashion is indicative of a conglomeration of smaller aspect patterns. It reflects diversity and balance.

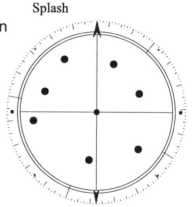

Splash

There are many other patterns we will explore as these volumes proceed, but for now, these are some of the more pronounced, common, and easily observed. Many of the companion texts recommended cover this area.

On the following page is what some computer programs can provide as far as identifying them within the horoscope for you. Ask your astrologer to provide you with a printout of them if this

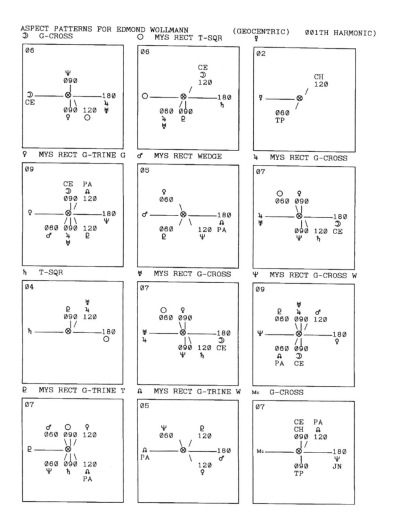

service is available. This one is from Matrix company's *Bluestar* program (for PC dos). They are also available in Winstar (Matrix) and Solar Fire (Astrolabe).

Retrogradation

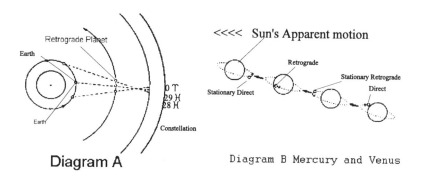

Diagram A   Diagram B Mercury and Venus

Diagram A depicts the mechanics of retrogradation of planets outside of Earth's orbit. As the Earth passes the planet farther out from it's orbit, it will appear that the planet it is passing is moving backwards through the constellation of the template behind it. Like a car leaving a stop before another next to it when viewed from the side, for a moment it appears to be rolling backwards because of the faster movement of the vehicle you are in. This appearance when involving planetary speed from the view of the Earth is called **retrograde**. The symbol Rx designates this condition when found next to the planet symbol in the printout of the horoscope.

Diagram B shows that the planets whose orbits are closer to the Sun than Earth, will almost appear to move through the template with the Sun as it moves through the sky in longitude. It is easy from this view to understand **why** they are considered indicative of conscious mind functions because they are **close** to the personal definitions core (Sun).

They appear to be retrograde when they reach the limits of their orbits to the left of the Sun, and begin to cross the front of the Sun from left to right as they continue in their orbit.

Therefore, they appear to be either ahead of the sun in the Zodiac (sky), or behind in it. When they reach the furthest point in front of the Sun (conscious expectations) and are returning to the furthest point behind it they are in this retrograde state or motion (the reassessment of these expectations).

The retrogradation of the *inner planets* represent the functions of the personality, and conscious mind. They are the archetypes that are the "closest" to the primary idea we chose to express in physical reality (the Sun) as opposed to the *outer planets* that are more unconscious and subconscious in meaning.

Retrogradation of either inner or outer planets reflect the judgement and repression of the planet involved. There is a reassessment of the idea (archetypical) that the planet retrograde represents. The sign of the template that the planet is in will reflect what the issues of reassessment will revolve around. The self believes it cannot "move forward" with the idea of the archetype that the planet represents. Rx is, psychologically speaking, a paradoxical conflict for the individual as they seek a balance in the expression of the archetype. There is much untangling to be done concerning the function and archetype of the planet and sign involved. Reflecting a "retake" through successive incarnations- it is as if "at first you don't succeed try try again." (see Reincarnation and Karma, Yott).

What will serve best as an analogy is the concept I have termed the *overcompensation pendulum* introduced in chapter 1 (page 25). We Will use Mars as our example.

In one life the identity may create scenarios wherein the attempt to prove the self gets out of hand. Insecurity may increase the behavior of the need to prove the self to compensate. Others may be "put off" by the pushiness that has been increasing. The identity may then feel alienation and push harder to prove the self to validate the identity. A vicious cycle is created of alienation followed by more belligerent pushing. This escalates perhaps to physical violence or even murder, "I will show them!" This unnatural aggression will create feelings of guilt (either in the life we are discussing or the next). The identity is out of integrity expressing negative energy (a negative spiral).

The effect of these defensive momentums, is the reincarnation of the individual with a repulsion for "aggressive people" out of guilt and judgement of the self and it's past behavior, now turned to projection. We teach best what we ourselves are learning. The reincarnation horoscope will then have Mars retrograde. Natural aggression in the previous life, turned to unnatural aggression in the present through judgement. Now in this life (through the pendulum swing) natural aggression is repressed from the fear that "aggression" is the root of all evil. Energy goes in before it goes out. This is not natural. The natural state is spontaneity. Projection of these beliefs ensues; "Other people always deny me my right to make my own decisions-to do what I want to do. I need to prove to myself and them that I can handle things."

These attitudes are the effect of the individual's own unwillingness to take naturally spontaneous actions in the life, because of their own inability to maintain integrity previously. When this person finally takes action after "they've had it with repression," their actions may once again be belligerent and individuals are hurt, here goes the pendulum again. The pendulum swings from rashness to repression. As the pendulum slows through the incorporation of responsibility for the creation of the scenario, the median point, the balanced point of natural aggression will resume. If the judgement of the self continues out of control Mars will not only be retrograde but increasingly developmental through aspects placement etc.. Until responsibility for creation of the scenarios connected with the archetype represented by the planet are acknowledged, the pendulum will continue to swing.

A parental structure will be chosen by the higher self upon incarnation that will be of a nature that allows the individual to reinforce it's own feelings of unnatural aggression and guilt. Or to set up developmental scenarios that bring them to light. In this particular case with Mars, perhaps through a rigid environment of moral or religious guilt "tripping."

The pendulum of retrograde planets reflect primarily the reassessment of actions taken. This is done in order to achieve a higher level of understanding, and a balance point of the archetypal function the planet represents. It is the assimilation of the "forward" experience that is being reassessed. Two steps forward, one back.

The retrogradation condition will represent an invalidation of the archetype of the planet involved. In the Mars example, the guilt from aggression in the previous life reflects the belief that aggression is "bad" and should be controlled. Therefore, a denial of energies in this life, will be unbalanced to the extreme in the next life. There will be resistance to spontaneous desire and aggression. It is always a factor in the early environment and the schema of attachment in some way.[119]

First and foremost, the retrograde condition is the effect of value judging the idea the planet reflects i.e. Mars= the need to prove the self. We all choose to incarnate to experience and express certain ideas. But it is this conscious mind judgement of "things" that creates the pendulum swing. The injection of values. The oversoul or higher self chooses scenarios (that may appear to be "fated") to assist the individual to learn to place the archetype function into proper perspective. The psychological, and often unconscious effect of the retrograde condition manifests as an extreme focus on the retrograde planet. The planet reflects an overcompensatory state.

There are other delineations in the chart that will confirm these deductions when traced. For example in the Mars Rx person's overcompensation, a further deduction of a negative belief about the archetype, would be the planet's placement in

---

[119]
Attachment schemas are covered well in the *Journal of Clinical and Consulting Psychology*, Volume 64, Number 4, 1996, February Issue.

the signs Libra (social acceptance) or Cancer (emotional security). It is the negative attitude, approach and the belief the person holds that causes the problems. When this changes so does the momentum.

Planets in Rx Delineation

MERCURY- Represents the conscious mind and perceptions. its' retrograde condition, indicates that the practical application of knowledge and information has been primarily used to prove intellectual superiority. The identity needs to balance the idea of conscious mind and the receptive or intuitive functions, which are both the polarity of one idea. There may be a "leap before you look" attitude, and an avoidance of intellectual demands. Defensiveness about how intelligent one is, will be an effect of the unconscious recognition of this avoidance. A fallacious notion may be held that one need not increase or exercise critical thinking with diligence.

VENUS- Is the reflection of mind, through the matter mirror. It's retrograde condition reflects overcompensation and preoccupation with reflections. It is very likely that other significators in the chart will signal a strong belief in dis-empowerment. A focus on the company one keeps or the possessions that one has as a way to gauge it's worth or value. It is a reflection of an inferiority complex. An alternate expression of the retrograde condition is one of reservedness and a "correct and proper" attitude toward relationships. Either way this condition, reflects the unwillingness or inability of the individual to see itself through the reflection of others. When we believe we are incomplete without another or the "one" person in our lives, then the Universe, acting on that energy we trust, will "send" us plenty of individuals that reflect this belief in our incompleteness. When you believe that you are complete as you are, then this belief will be reflected through the 'others' that you meet.

MARS- Reflecting the needs of the identity to validate itself, Mars is a powerful indicator of repression of that identity when retrograde. In any retrograde condition, the early environment and parental structure must be examined (the fourth and tenth houses, their rulers, the Moon's and Saturn's condition). However, this is especially so in the case of planets that represent the functions of ego and conscious mind. These elements (Sun-Moon=identity, Mercury=conscious mind function, Venus=personal and social reflection, Mars=the identity's beliefs about validity) depend on the actual physical circumstances of early environment, and the stability reflected within it (please refer to previous attachment schema note for more information).

Without the reinforcement of the identity's validity, other issues can never even be entertained or resolved. This is the issue with the Mars retrograde condition. There may have been strong judgements within the parental information/perspective patterns. Orthodox religious beliefs from the parental models, or strict disciplinary attitudes very often are reflected through children with Mars retrograde condition.

Mars retrogradation represents the invalidation and judgement of the identity itself. People who believe in the idea that they are "Born sinners," may believe that the identity is inherently negative. Actions must be guarded. Repression of instincts. Feelings of being denied. Overcompensation to "finally do something." Then a "bull in a China shop." Guilt, repression all over again. In terms of belief; judgement of natural assertion. Criminals react from despair, as an effect of continual repression, and lack of conflict resolution, finally exploding.

Anyone who acts on what they are capable of acting on, that it excites them to do, inspires them to do, with integrity, will never experience Mars retrograde. It results from a belief in the self's powerlessness.

JUPITER- Beginning with this planet, retrogradation will not be so apparent in it's reflection in personality terms. This is not to say that it's validity is lessened. However, it depends on the level or vibration of awareness an individual is functioning on, that determines that appearance. Jupiter retrograde indicates a lack of belief in deservability. The early environment may have had little in the way of reinforcement for the identity's capabilities or accomplishments. The person then forms a belief that reward or recognition for the expression of self is not easy to experience, or may not be there at all. The psychological effect may be an over amount of self reliance, or resistance to "tooting your own horn." Creations (if this stage is reached), are not "put on the table" for presentation. The invalidation of inspired expansion. The disbelief in abundant ease.

SATURN- The planet Saturn is the most important symbol in our system. It represents the idea behind the system; the experience of physical focus. Its rings are held in tight organization in very sharp focus. The purpose of living is simply to be all that you can be and to express all that you are. That's it. Saturn (physical focus) does not limit this. Saturn reflects to you, in sharp focus through the mirror of matter (your literal physical experiences) precisely what you ***believe*** about reality. It tests your ability to consciously perceive what your beliefs about reality create. There is nothing less important about physical experience relative to non-physical or spiritual experience. They are just two different ways to experience reality.

 Saturn's retrograde condition indicates that the individual is in the process of refocus. In the past life or lives the individual had been experiencing being enmeshed in physical reality too heavily. External reality was the determinant of motivation. Therefore now there may be hesitancy to "climb to the top." There are certain perspectives the person wants to re-view concerning the approach to material application of the self. Psychologically, the person may perceive a lack of fatherly concern or effectiveness.

A) The father was not present. B) The father died early in childhood and a step-father took his place. C) The parents separated early, and another father figure took his place. D) The father was an alcoholic, or in any of the above ways did not or could not instruct the child, or act as a model for physical reality efficacy. Therefore, there is reticence towards application, until the individual establishes their *own* philosophy and approach. Until this time the individual may express an inferiority complex from the feeling of something being missing. If the father was stable during childhood years, and Saturn is retrograde it indicates that the child is in a reorientation to a less materialistic physical experience, perhaps a more expanded one, that the generational perspective the father holds, doesn't allow. In belief terms; The contemplation that physical experience may be something other than conforming to accepted societal ambition. It may also represent a disbelief in the self's impacting importance and manifestability.

URANUS- The law of momentum flow throughout the horoscope will reflect a belief in the inability (from judgement) to feel a sense of choice in the creation of their experiences when Uranus is found retrograde. Most often, the planets of persona will be retrograde themselves, or in difficult interplanetary aspects with it. Where Uranus resides and its configurations tells where rigidity *needs* to be broken up.

Uranus represents the unconscious knowledge of our infinite creatorhood. This is why it is the next step (orbit) outside of Saturn. In mythology Uranus was the father of Saturn. The creator (or father) of the physical reality experience. However, Saturn through jealousy (Satan) castrated (rendered impotent) his father so that no other offspring would appear. Physical reality was considered the only reality (tipped into the unconscious awareness). Uranus' placement is where we (need to) "wake up" to this unconscious knowledge.

Its retrograde condition further complicates this idea. Retrogradation implies a contemplative mode. Innovative application held in suspension until we untangle the perspective of why we choose the creation of scenarios. Psychologically it symbolizes the need to have one's uniqueness recognized. The name Uranus means "Heavens," the discovery of the self's unique contributions is the step to it.

NEPTUNE- If Neptune is retrograde in the natal chart, it simply signifies by sign and house where the identity needs to co-fuse a more spiritual and altruistic version of the archetypes involved. Where the ideal needs review. In the past, a more Saturnine viewpoint has been adding to the powerlessness perspective. It represents the need to discover the "All That Is" that is within us and a reassessment of the mystical. Traditional texts may ascribe idealism to the planet Neptune. Nothing removes the darkness, like the light. This psychological effect allows us to stretch by envisioning ourselves to the "All That Is" and ideal that is already there. Choosing preference and the ideal in any situation or thing, this acts as a "carrot" that leads us away from Saturn of this world, to a more expanded one at Neptune. But remember, the ideal you find will always be you. Psychologically retrogradation of Neptune reflects a lack of trust that the ideal can be found. A continuing "search" does not allow the merging and blending to occur. There may be a preoccupation with ego issues that do not allow the barrier of negative ego to dissolve.

PLUTO- The ruler of the dead, the son of Saturn. A totally transformed perspective that represents the "birth" from physical reality to non-physical reality. When this planet is retrograde, perspective can turn into "tunnel vision." In the past personal perspective was the only perspective. Manipulation is the subtle coercion to force one's perspective upon another. Anyone who has to force an opinion or belief upon another, by any means, obviously does not believe in the power and validity of that opinion themselves or believe in it themselves. The individual with Pluto retrograde may meet with some powerful persons or situations that DEMAND alteration of perspective. Eventually, they will find that it is themselves and their own resistance that they are meeting. Personal power is in a reassessment mode to find its source, the self.

There is another condition dealing with the state of retrogradation that is called "stationary." Rx or Sd. When a planet is about to turn retrograde it will seem to "hover" for a few days (inner planets) to a few weeks (outer planets) on one or two degrees. This is called stationary retrograde. When it is about to resume forward motion it hovers again before it turns forward. This is called stationary direct. Stationary retrograde planets in the chart imply an accelerated unlocking from external focus, to the energy of reassessment (retrograde). When the planet is stationary direct there is an extreme focus of the expression of the energy of the planet. The implication in the birth chart in the case of stationary retrograde, is that the identity had "gone as far as it could go" with the external experience of the planet and it is time for reassessment. In the case of the stationary direct position, the individual has reviewed the archetype sufficiently, and it is time to take this insight, and apply it.

Astrological Definitions

"I don't want to 'be right'-
I only want to know
whether I am right."
Albert Einstein

The following is a glossary of Astrological definitions. It is not intended to be all inclusive. It represents terms and concepts necessary in using this book. There are many traditional concepts covered. However, they will be delineated in self-empowerment terms. Some are original in content and application stemming from my personal consulting experience during the last nineteen years. For a comprehensive Encyclopedic exploration see *The Astrology Encyclopedia*, by James R. Lewis, Invisible Ink Press, ISBN 1-57859-010-8, 1994, Detroit Mi.

The primary purpose of astrology is to increase awareness, it cannot give material advantage, (it can add to confidence for strategic advantage-but this is still dependent upon the strategy) nor can it save or protect anyone from themselves. The experience of living is the meeting of the self. The power is in each individual right now, not in the future not in the past, to create the reality we prefer. Now is the only time anyone actually exists. Therefore, we create the past and the future from the present. Astrology allows us to better understand the reasons for the present, and therefore alter the future. We can also estimate the effects of the changes in the present on the future. In these terms astrology can be of immense assistance. It allows us to become aware of the choices of developmental experiences. The path we chose to be. We are not on a path, we are the path. We cannot be "off" ourselves (Bashar). We can choose however, how we will go down our path.

These redefinitions are designed to assist in the experiencing of our path in the way we would prefer to.

Accidental dignity- The planet that is nearest the Midheaven in the horoscope is said to be accidentally dignified. Actually, it is because the archetype represented will be experienced in an accelerated projected form (upper hemisphere).

Air signs- The trinity of idea interaction. They reflect the concept of thought and idea exchange or sociability.

Angles- The cusps and houses of the 1st, 4th, 7th, and 10th They represent the identity/status concept of the Cardinal quadruplicity, and reflect the identity's definition of itself as a persona in physical reality. The initial cornerstone of the persona; Belief.

Apex- The uppermost part of the triangle or trinity (or final angle in the square). It reflects a state of effortless physicalization of the self, and the state of equilibrium (trine), and the culmination of materialization of belief (square). It also reflects the culmination of aspects in their finality of expression.

Apparent motion- The motion of any planet as it "appears" to be when viewed from the perspective of Earth.

Aquarian age- The Earth's polar axis wobbles in a circular motion, that allows it to appear that it is pointing at one constellation of the template for approximately 2,150 years This movement, called the precession;

The precession of the equinoxes is caused by the gravitational pull of bodies outside the earth on what is known as the equatorial "bulge" of the Earth. The diameter is 27 miles more than the polar diameter. The attraction is caused principally by the sun and moon that act upon this excess at the bulge and attempt to bring the Earth's equator into the plane of the ecliptic instead of the present angle of 23-1/2 Degrees from the plane. The gyroscopic effect of the Earth's rotation has the effect of resisting this pull and producing the compromise of the precession. As a result the poles then trace this circle against the backdrop of stars at about 47 degrees in diameter and then the equinoxes-the crossing of the planes of the equator and the ecliptic-then move westward, 45-50 seconds of arc a year-which when calculated comes to 25,800 years for a complete circle or precession through the signs. This precession was discovered by Hipparchus about 150 B.C.E.. Mathematically the expression is thus 50" .2564 + 0".0002 t per year, where t is the number of years after 1900. This precession corresponds to the proposed periods well-including the legend of Atlantis which would have appeared to have been in the Age of Leo 12,900 (approx) that we are now experiencing the polarity of in this present age as we approach 2150-the reaping phase or projected version (Aquarius is the externalized version of Leo) of our creative power and its use or misuse. That period allowed for the building of the Pyramidal structures still present on our planet. This creative force, however, was utilized by approximately one half of the population at that time. The energy was used in such a manner as to serve the domination desires of individual classes of people.[120] It remains to be seen whether our rediscovery of the creative force will remain in integrity or not. Aquarius symbolizes the recognition of choice in the creation of reality, as well as the recognition of the equality of all beings as co-creators with the "All That Is". The idea that every being is as powerful as they need to be, in order to create, whatever they desire to create, without having to hurt themselves or any one else, in order to create it (Bashar). This was the "fall" of Adam and Eve represented in Biblical literature. We are on the cusp of the age of Aquarius, which will be in full swing by 2150.

---

[120] Cayce, Edgar Evans. Edgar Cayce On Atlantis. New York: Paperback Library. 1968

It marks the beginning of our transition from 3rd density, to 4th density experience. When we fully realize that we are the reality, we previously thought we existed within.

Arc- The mathematical division of the circle, that reflects the relationship between planets or points within the template.

ARCTURUS- A star in the constellation Bootes;"the lofty" one, the one who rules, and the coming one by the Egyptians. This star is the center of many solar systems and represents the distribution and flow of information regarding agreements and contracts made by individuals in the higher state of consciousness Its energy reflects the idea of "the gatekeeper" that allows and/or controls the flow of awareness to this system. The Chalice is the recognition that "The King and the land are one in the same" (*Arthurian* philosophy), or "I and the father are one in the same" (*Christian* philosophy). ARCTURUS represents the gatekeeper of the chalice or the grail.

ARCTURUS. Bootis. - 23 Libra 7,. Notes. A golden-yellow star situated on the Left knee of Bootes. From Arktouros, the Bear Guard. Also called Arctophilax, the Bear Watcher; and Alchameth, Azimech, and other variants of Al Simak, the Lofty One. According to Bullinger Arcturus means "He Cometh," and was called Smat, One who rules, and Bau, the Coming One, by the Egyptians.[121]

Arcturus=known also as Alpha Bootis, an orange first magnitude star, the brightest in the constellation Bootes. Arcturus is the 6th brightest star in the sky and is 35 light years from Earth. Its diameter is 35 times that of the sun and an intrinsic luminosity 80 times that of the sun. Discovered by Halley in 1718 Visual Magnitude 0.2, Spectral type K, distance in light years 35-36.

According to *Burnham's Celestial Handbook* (Vol I, p 302-3):

---

[121] The Fixed Stars and Constellations in Astrology, Vivian E. Robson Bsc, Samuel Weiser, Ny, Ny, page 139.

Arcturus is the brightest star in the northern sky and 4th brightest over all. It was "formerly given 6th place, but shown by modern measurements to outshine both Vega & Capella". Magnitude -0.06, distance = about 37 LY, diameter = about 25 times greater than the sun, luminosity = 115 times that of the sun, color = usually described as topaz or golden yellow, occasionally as orange.

It's a population II star, a member of the great spherical halo which is centered on the galactic hub. "This explains the large apparent motion, and the rapid passage though our part of the heavens; Arcturus is moving in a highly inclined orbit around the center of the galaxy, and is currently cutting through the galactic plane ...".

Therefore;

▸   Here I present Bashar's response to a query of symbolic meaning to a dream I had of a picture of my own horoscope with this written in the corner "EM1 Arcturus" and an evaluation in the dream of the distance between the bodies of the Sun and the dark body that traverses our solar system in a very long trajectory (counterpart nemesis to the sun). I also asked of the meaning represented by the distance between our (perceived) conscious self and shadow self I was told; "You can recognize the electromagnetic vibration of Arcturus, to be the higher vibratory resonance plane that contains both the polarities of the bright star (sun) and the dark star (nemesis) represented in your system. And that if you can simply focus on the fundamental vibrational frequency of the tip of the triangle (Apex) you will then contain them both, and in containing them both, you can shorten any distance you perceive between them. For you are looking down-symbolically-from another plane of existence altogether, when you look through the eyes of Arcturus. A symbol that can be utilized that we have shared with many of you to help you focus on the vibratory plane of Arcturus energy and consciousness-is a white 12 pointed star, against an orange circle, against a black background.
Will this be of assistance?"
EW: "Yes, thank you."   March, 1987. "Southern Exposure"
Hence, the cover design for this text.

Ascendent- The sign of the zodiacal template that is rising on the eastern horizon at the time of any identity's or idea's birth. The definition chosen to be expressed in physical reality and the format of presentation.

Aspect- The arc of reference between planets or points to define their symbolic Archetypal relationship.

Balsamic moon- When the Moon is between 0 and 45 degrees behind the Sun. The dissolution of the idea initiated at New Moon, in preparation for the initiation of the next idea (next New moon).

Birth time- This shall be defined by the moment the infant takes it's first breath, because that is when it becomes a separate idea within the expression of "All That Is". The "vibrations" at the time then reflect what it *inspires* (to breath in!) the idea or person to be.

Cadent houses- The 3rd, 6th, 9th, and 12th cusps and houses within any horoscope, natural or natal. They represent the functions of information/perspective, the third cornerstone of the crystal of persona; thought.

Cardinal signs- Aries, Cancer, Libra and Capricorn, the quadruplicity of identity definition, which creates the effects of motivation, initiation and action. The movement into, and of physicality from belief.

Comet- Body that enters the orbital plane of the planets periodically, that represents the "tying together" of layers and levels of archetypal reference reflected by the planets. It also represents the hour hand of the clock, reflecting a "new hour" has come upon us. Since we have reached the life span reflected by comet Halley (76 years). It's archetypal reference will now be exceeded. Therefore it's return will not be necessary, and a new comet(s) will take it's place.

Composite chart- Two horoscopes are combined into one by defining the midpoint position between them on the shorter arc. The derived chart represents the vibrational pattern of the two, now acting as one. The chart then reflects the agreement and purpose for which the two are interacting.

Co-Ruler- Up until three hundred years ago, the outer planets Uranus, Neptune, and Pluto, were not known to exist. This of course reflected our state of consciousness previous to their "discovery". Saturn, Jupiter, and Mars carried the double rulership. Mars ruling Aries and Scorpio, Jupiter ruling

Sagittarius, and Pisces and Saturn ruling Capricorn and Aquarius which was the most accurate linking that could be done at the time. The planets inside the orbit of Earth- Venus and Mercury always carry the double rulership of Taurus and Libra (Venus), and Gemini and Virgo (Mercury).

Critical Degrees- Critical degrees in this book are defined as the last three degrees of any sign, and the first three degrees. A planet placed within the first three degrees of any sign indicates that the identity has difficulty in initiating the archetypes that the planet and the sign it is placed within represents. A planet (or point) placed within the last three degrees of a sign, reflects the inability of the identity to "wind up" the archetypal references delineated by the sign and planet, i.e. Venus at 29 degrees Capricorn, indicates the individual's preoccupation with establishing relationships for strategic gain, has been overdone and needs to be wound up so that the identity can get on with the next step of experience (using Placidus house system). In general either one indicates that the individual is resisting taking responsibility for the idea the archetypes represent, as well as the integration of them. In this way it also reflects a state of urgency.

Cusp- Imaginary line that separates the signs and houses of the experiential and horoscopic template.

Declination- A planet's measurement on the horizon in terms of degree, north or south of the equator When the planets are in the same degree together north or south, they are said to be parallel, which acts as a conjunction. When they are equal distance, one north the other south, they are contraparallel, which acts as an opposition.

Derivative house- The sequential progression of the horoscope's houses are derived from the ascendent being the first. Any house can take on the reference point as the "first" and the houses following; the second, third etc. For example with the sixth as the first, the second of the sixth, would be the seventh and would carry the symbology of the worth of the sixth. The "value" of objective analytical discernment, is through the perception of one's projection.

Descendent- The opposite point of the ascendent. It reflects the polarity or unconscious versions of self, that will be experienced through others.

Detriment- A planet is in its detriment when placed in the sign opposite the one it rules, i.e., Jupiter in Gemini; Higher self functioning is the antithesis, of conscious mind function. Much is dependent upon the awareness level of the identity as to the expression of the planet so placed.

Dispositor- The planet that rules the sign another planet is in, is said to be the dispositor of that planet.

Earth signs- The trinity of physicality Taurus, Virgo, and Capricorn, which reflect the trinary aspects of persona-belief, emotion and thought physicalized.

Eclipse- An eclipse of the Sun is called a Solar eclipse. The sign of the template in which it occurs reflects the archetype that needs looking at, that resides in the unconscious. The light of the Sun (physical reality) is blocked by the form of the Moon (unconscious). A lunar eclipse is when the light of the Sun reflected on the Moon is blocked by the Earth. This reflects a need to integrate habit patterns into conscious awareness.

Electional Astrology- Electing the timing of the initiation of an idea using astrological awareness.

Elements- The four (base) trinary (sides) elements of physical manifestation that are represented through the pyramidal structure- Fire, Earth, Air and Water. The pyramid reflects the "prism" of persona the artificial construct of the person-ality.

Event chart- A horoscope that is drawn for a specific happening or event. The life of the event can then be delineated.

Exaltation- The particular sign of the template, that most easily integrates the archetype of a planet when placed there The reflection of archetypal synchronous accord i.e., Venus is exalted in Pisces-empathic perception of projection.

Finger of God (Yod)- The configuration of two or more planets in sextile to each other, both inconjuncting a third point of two or more planets. It reflects a constantly adjusting perspective, and when positively integrated reflects a connection of higher self awareness with conscious mind function. An identity expressing a lower vibrational frequency will experience the aspect (will) of the higher self as seeming fated. Hence the title "Finger of God". It's integrated name is the Yod.

Fire signs- The trinity of identity Aries, Leo and Sagittarius. The expression of the cornerstones of the persona, belief emotion and thought as the conscious ego self.

Fixed signs- The quadruplicity of worth extension. The movement into and of emotional consolidation of the identity in physical reality. The signs Taurus, Leo, Scorpio and Aquarius.

Full Moon- Every 28 days the cycle of the Moon places the Earth between the Sun and Moon so that we see the lit up face of the moon. An opposition between the Sun and the Moon, that "illuminates" a polarity of archetypes, dependent upon which signs of the template it should fall.

Galactic center- The 26th degree of Sagittarius (higher self reference) coincidentally is the center of the consciousness of our galaxy. The point that the entire solar system, along with other systems, orbit.

Gibbous Moon- 135 to 180 degrees between the moon and Sun that reflects the idea inherent in the template sign Virgo The anticipation and preparation for full harvest at the full moon about to culminate.

Higher octaves- The outer planets represent the higher self. Specifically, Uranus is the higher octave of Mercury, Neptune the higher octave of Venus, Pluto the higher octave of Mars. Once the self imposed limitations of Saturn are dissolved, (Saturn is the higher octave of Earth) though the recognition of choice in the creation of reality (Uranus), a whole new dimension opens to the senses, as well as an infinitely expanded set of senses.

Horary Astrology- A horoscope is drawn for the timing of a question-if it has momentum behind it and a strong need to ask it, then the answer will be found within the timing of the question through the Horary chart.

House rulership- As discussed before the planetary lens of a sign is said to "rule" that sign. If you have a Leo ascendant, then the Sun rules the ascendent, even if it is placed in the sign of Aries. Or the moon would rule whatever house or houses in your horoscope, that have Cancer on their cusp This is what is meant by house rulership.

Imum coeli - The fourth house cusp. The point in the horoscope that represents the furthermost depth of the unconscious is the path to the higher self. Jupiter is exalted in Cancer. (See exaltations)

Inferior planets- The planets that deal with conscious mind functions. No planet is inferior to any other. They are equal.

Interception- Interception occurs when, because of latitudinal difference closer to the poles of the Earth, the curvature causes the houses of the horoscope to be of varying sizes. The effect is that an entire sign of the template may fall in between two house cusps. For example Aries on the eleventh house cusp, Taurus intercepted in the eleventh, and the Gemini would be on the twelfth house cusp. The polarity of signs (Scorpio would be intercepted in the fifth house) that are intercepted reflect the archetypal concept by sign and house, that the identity needs to incorporate in an integrative way with the rest of the horoscope's momentum flow. Usually we will find retrograde planets within the intercepted house, which, further reinforces a concept of review or reassessment of the interception as well as the retrograde planet within its missing in reference cuspal arrangement.

Light- The physically detectable (without instruments) and undetectable vibrations of the electromagnetic spectrum, of which everything in the Multiverse is made.

Lunation- A new moon. The initiation of a 28 day cycle of unconscious archetypal reflection. The lining up of the moon between the Sun and the Earth.

Medium coeli- The Midheaven or 10th house cusp. It represents the highest point in the horoscope, and reflects the point of deepest immersion and experience of physical reality.

Midpoint- The shorter halfway point in arc (distance) between two or more planets. It is a sensitive point in the triggering of the aspect between the planets involved, by transit, a planet by progression, or a point of the same degree from another individual's chart.

Mundane Astrology- The study of material affairs and of countries and places through the use of astrology.

Mutable signs- The information/perspective quadruplicity, that reflects the identity's ability for objectification, reflection and self awareness. The third point in the cornerstone of the creation of persona; thought. The signs Gemini, Virgo Sagittarius and Pisces.

Mutual reception- When one planet rules the sign another planet is in and that planet rules the sign the planet that disposes of it is in, i.e., Jupiter in Virgo would be in mutual reception with Mercury in Sagittarius. It reflects a very close tie between the two archetypes represented, and that the functioning of each may be dependent upon the other.

Node- We will deal only with the moon's nodes, as the movement of the planet's nodes are negligible except over long periods. The point at which the Moon crosses the apparent path of the Sun is the point at which the north node would be located. The polarity node, the south node, would be located exactly opposite the north node. They represent unconscious habit patterning and especially relate to the relationship with the mother. A planet aspecting, or notably conjuncting the nodal position, indicates that the mother had a very strong effect on the identity's attitude and beliefs concerning the archetype involved. In spiritual terms, the nodal axis represents the overall direction the higher self has chosen as the new direction (North node) to be taken in this life which is the polarity of the direction (or focus) taken in the past life (south node). Since polarities are simply different viewpoints of the same idea, it is simply a polarized REaction to the focus on one viewpoint of it.

Occultation- Hidden from view.

Outer planets- The planetary archetypes which represent the functions of the higher self. In this book they are the planets past the Asteroid belt.

Part of Fortune- A point in the horoscope which is the same distance in aspect from the ascendant, as the moon is from the Sun in the same horoscope. It reflects the overall benefit or extrapolation of archetypal concept that any chart was incarnated for. The overall reason for the physical manifestation of any idea, and it's apex of potential.

For those so inclined here are some of the parts and their formulas. They will be used intermittently but are ALWAYS secondary and minor in delineation terms.

Part of:

    ABANDONMENT = Asc + Neptune - Pluto

    ADDICTION 1 = Asc + Neptune - Pluto

    ADDICTION 2 = Asc + Pluto - Neptune

    ANXIETY = Asc + Pluto - Uranus

    ASSASSINATION 1 = Mars + Neptune - Uranus

    ASSASSINATION 2 = Mars + Uranus - Neptune

    ASSAULT 1 = Moon + Saturn - MC

    ASSAULT 2 = Mars + Uranus - Venus

    ASTROLOGY = Asc + Mercury - Uranus (***)

    BANKRUPTCY = Jupiter + Jupiter - Uranus

    BRETHREN = Asc + Saturn - Jupiter (***)

    BRUTALITY 1 = Mars + Pluto - Saturn

    BRUTALITY 2 = Mars + Saturn - Pluto

    CANCER MALIGN.= Asc + Neptune - Jupiter

    CATASTROPHE = Asc + Uranus - Sun

    CHANGE-RADICAL = Asc + Pluto - Uranus

    CHILD, FEMALE = Asc + Venus - Moon (***)

    CHILD, MALE = Asc + Jupiter - Moon (***)

    COMMERCE = Asc + Mercury - Sun

    DEATH = Asc + House 8 - Moon (***)

    DEATH PARENTS = Asc + Jupiter - Saturn

    DEATH, POINT = Mars + Saturn - MC

    DEATH/SEP.= Asc + Saturn - Mars

    DEATH SIBLING = Asc + (10 Gemini) - Sun

    DECEIT = Asc + Venus - Neptune

    DECEIT (LOVE) = Asc + Neptune - Venus

    DEGRADATION = Asc + Sun - Neptune

    DEPENDENCY = Asc + Neptune - Moon

DEPRESSION = Asc + Neptune - Mars
DESTINY = MC + Sun - Moon (***)
DISASTER 1 = Asc + Pluto - Mars
DISASTER 2 = Asc + Mars - Pluto
DISASTER 3 = Uranus + Pluto - Mars
DISCORD = Asc + Jupiter - Mars
DIVORCE = Asc + Venus - House 7 (***)
FAITH & TRUST = Asc + Mercury - Moon
FAME/MONEY 1 = Asc + Jupiter - Sun
FAME/MONEY 2 = Asc + Sun - Jupiter
FASCINATION = Asc + Venus - Uranus
FATHER = Asc + Sun - Saturn (***)
FORCE 1 = Mars + Pluto - Uranus
FORCE 2 = Mars + Uranus - Pluto
FORTUNE, day = Asc + Moon - Sun
FORTUNE, night = Asc + Sun - Moon
FRAUD = Asc + Neptune - Mercury
FRIENDS = Asc + Moon - Uranus
FRIENDSHIP = Asc + PartSpirit - PartFortune (***)
FRUGALITY = Asc + Saturn - Venus
HAPPINESS = Asc + Uranus - Jupiter
HEAD INJURY 1 = House 8 + Mars - Moon
HEAD INJURY 2 = House 8 + Moon - Mars
HOMOSEXUAL = Asc + Mars - Uranus
HONOR = Asc + (19 Aries) - Sun
ILLUMINATION 1 = MC + Uranus - Neptune
ILLUMINATION 2 = Asc + Uranus - Neptune
ILLUMINATION 3 = MC + Neptune - Uranus
ILLUMINATION 4 = Asc + Neptune - Uranus
IMPRISONMENT = Asc + PartFortune - Saturn
INDIVIDUALITY = Asc + Sun - Uranus
INHERITANCE = Asc + Moon - Saturn
JEALOUSY = Venus + Saturn - Mars
KARMA = Asc + Saturn - Sun (***)
LAWSUITS = Asc + Mercury - Mars
LEGAL AFFAIRS = House 3 + House 9 - Venus
LOVE = Asc + Venus - Sun (***)

LOVERS = Mars + Venus - House 5
LUCK 1 = Asc + Moon - Jupiter
LUCK 2 = Asc + Jupiter - Uranus
MARRIAGE = Asc + House 7 - Venus (***)
MARRIAGE, MAN = Asc + Venus - Saturn
MARRIAGE, WOMAN = Asc + Saturn - Venus
MOTHER = Asc + Moon - Venus (***)
MOTHER/FAMILY = Asc + Jupiter - Venus
OBSESSION = Venus + Mars - Uranus
OPPRESSED = Asc + Uranus - Saturn
ORGANIZATION = Asc + Pluto - Sun
PASSION = Asc + Mars - Venus (***)
PERVERSION = Venus + Mars - Neptune
PLAY = Asc + Venus - Mars
POLICE = Asc + Saturn - Mars
PRFL. FRIENDS = Asc + Sun - PartFortune
QUAKE 1a = Mars + Pluto - Saturn
QUAKE 1b = Mars + Saturn - Pluto
QUAKE 1c = Saturn + Pluto - Mars
QUAKE 2a = Mars + Pluto - Uranus
QUAKE 2b = Mars + Uranus - Pluto
QUAKE 2c = Uranus + Pluto - Mars
QUAKE 3a = MC + Saturn - Moon
QUAKE 3b = MC + Moon - Saturn
QUAKE 3c = Moon + Saturn - MC
QUAKE 4a = Asc + Pluto - Saturn
QUAKE 4b = Asc + Saturn - Pluto
QUAKE 4c = Saturn + Pluto - Asc
RAGE/MURDER 1 = Asc + Pluto - Saturn
RAGE/MURDER 2 = Asc + Saturn - Pluto
RAPE 1 = Mars + Pluto - Venus
RAPE 2 = Venus + Mars - Pluto
SELF-UNDOING = Asc + House 12 - Neptune
SEX DRIVE = Asc + Pluto - Venus
SICKNESS = Asc + Mars - Saturn
SLANDER = Asc + Saturn - Neptune
SORROW 1 = Asc + (Asc + Moon - Sun) - Neptune

SORROW 2 = Asc + (Asc + Sun - Moon) - Neptune
SOUL = House 4 + Moon - Sun (***)
SPECULATION = Asc + House 5 - Jupiter
SPIRIT, day = Asc + Sun - Moon
SPIRIT, night = Asc + Moon - Sun
SUCCESS, day = Jupiter + Sun - Moon
SUCCESS, night = Jupiter + Moon - Sun
SUDDEN ADVANCE = Asc + PartFortune - Saturn
SUDDEN PART = Asc + Saturn - Uranus
SUFFERING 1 = Asc + Neptune - Saturn
SUFFERING 2 = Asc + Saturn - Neptune
SUICIDE 1 = Asc + House 8 - Neptune
SUICIDE 2 = Asc + Neptune - House 8
SURGERY = Asc + Saturn - Mars
TERMINATION = Asc + Uranus - Neptune
TORTURE 1 = MC + Saturn - Moon
TORTURE 2 = MC + Moon - Saturn
TRANSFORM 1 = Asc + Pluto - Uranus
TRANSFORM 2 = Asc + Uranus - Pluto
TREACHERY = Asc + Neptune - Sun
UNDERSTANDING = Asc + Mars - Mercury
VICTORY/AID = Asc + Jupiter - PartSpirit (***)
VIOLENCE = Mars + Uranus - Saturn
WIDOWHOOD = Asc + (09 Libra 48) - Neptune

NOTES: Any Part with a (***) following means that the last two terms are reversed in a night chart.

PartFortune = (FORTUNE, day) in a day chart and (FORTUNE, night) in a night chart. PartSpirit = (SPIRIT, day) in a day chart and (SPIRIT, night) in a night chart.[122]

Polarity- The version that "All That Is" is, upon expression within physical reality. The extreme opposite views inherent within one idea.

Progression- We will be using two types in this book Solar

---

[122]
For further explanation and application please refer to Robert Zoller's book 'The Arabic Parts in Astrology - A Lost Key To Prediction', Inner Traditions International, Ltd., One Park Street, Rochester, VT 05767, ISBN 0-89281-250-8.

arc, and secondary progression. They are both ways to move the horoscope from birth, through time. Solar arc is exceedingly simple.[123] Since the Sun moves approximately 1 degree per day. We simply count one degree to equal one year. Just add one degree to each planet in your natal chart to represent one year of life. If you're 23, add 23 degrees to all planets. This would be the approximate progressed solar arcs (directions) for your 23rd year. Secondary progressions are the equating of planetary positions 1 day after birth, to reflect 1 year after birth (planetary positions listed in the ephemeris). For example, since the moon moves an average 13 degrees per day, then your secondary progressed Moon 1 year after birth would be moved 13 degrees forward. The new location would be the secondary progressed position of the moon. As you move forward in days (years), however, accuracy would be lost. It is drawn for the same time for any day (equaling one year) after birth. A secondary progressed chart is much more easily acquired from an astrological computer service and are only a couple of dollars. Progressions represent the unconscious integration of the birth planetary pattern and serve only as a backdrop to delineation.

Quadrature- The developmental aspects of the opening square, opposition, and closing square. The 4th harmonic of physicality.

Regulus- A star in the constellation Leo that reflects regality and self empowerment. The 28th degree of Leo.

Return or Revolution- A revolution is one complete orbit of any body in the solar system. A chart drawn for the return of any planet, including the Sun or Moon, acts as a lunation, a new beginning or cycle of that planet's expression within it's next cycle. I.e., a solar return (usually occurs the day of your birthday or the day before or after) reflects the ideas and experiences (only in the thematic sense) an individual has

---

[123] To be more precise one can use the actual motion of the sun, since over time the differences can increase and create errors in prediction. Computer programs do this automatically.

chosen though higher self will to experience within the next yearly cycle. Conscious awareness of these ideas can allow the conscious mind to begin to understand the significance of the events and developmental potential and experiences. This will allow an integration of the beliefs about to be experienced to enhance developmental resolution through conscious understanding. There is no such thing as a prediction of THE future. All probable futures are just as capable of manifesting. However, what we are sensing when we look at projections of the future, is the momentum reflected through astrological significators, of the *most likely* events to occur should the energy *not* change. Becoming aware of the most likely momentum to occur through astrological significators can itself change the momentum. This is one purpose of astrology; To allow us to look at our beliefs and the momentum connected with them to change them if we don't prefer them. Change our beliefs and view, change our experiences.

Succeedent houses- The 2nd, 5th, 8th, and 11th cusps and houses. They reflect the self's beliefs about self worth and creative extension (giving and receiving love). They symbolize the second cornerstone of persona manifesting as the momentum of belief or e-motion.

Transit- The continuing or current movement of the planets in outer space and their relationship though aspects to the planets or points of the birth chart or natal horoscope.

Trigger- The planet or planets (usually the moon) that sets off major aspects that have been culminating (increasing) in aspect or power.

Vertex- Calculated by subtracting the birth latitude, from 90 degrees to find the co-latitude, noting the degree and sign upon the fourth natal cusp, and regarding it as a Midheaven reference in the table of houses; finding this reference under the Midheaven column in the tables at the co-latitude and the ascendent listed. The ascendent degree and sign is the degree and sign of the vertex (see parts).

The vertex represents the type of shadow self or unconscious polarity that we attract (usually of the opposite sex). It represents the law of momentum flow of our hidden beliefs (hidden to ourselves).

Void-of-course- Any planet (usually the moon), is void of course when it will not make any more major aspects (major meaning conjunction, sextile, square, trine or opposition) before it leaves the sign of the template it is in to enter the next. It signals the probability that nothing more will come of this momentum-or that it is impotent. (refer to critical degrees).

Summary

I.   The whole surpasses the sum of the parts. Integration is the blending of the parts into a functional integral whole. Aspects reflect the idea of positive and negative energy discussed in previous chapters.

II.   Balance is far more important than types or numbers of aspects. Aspects reflect psychological workings and energies to defend or establish the identity.

III.   The *law of momentum flow* is determined by aspect networks in delineation sequence.

IV.   The aspects are derived from the Experiential template and are made up of all possible relationships geometrically within the circle, the whole of life. Everything in the Multiverse is in some form of aspect arrangement.

V.   Aspects can be applying or separating and opening or closing. This is determined by the *arc* of the aspect and the *motion* of the planet. Double applying or separating occurs when one of the bodies is forward and the other retrograde.

VI.   Subjectivity and objectivity is reflected in both the form of the aspect and its opening or closing condition.

VII.   Planetary patterns reflect belief systems and psychological networks. The major ones are *Grand Cross, T-square, Grand Trine.*

VIII.   Hemisphere emphasis reflects beliefs about locus of control. They correspond with the ideas put forth by Carl Jung of *introversion/extroversion* and indicates where the person invests psychic energy.

IX.   *Retrogradation* reflects a person's repression and reassessment of the archetypal symbols involved both of the planet and/or house and sign. The *inner planets* correspond to the more focused aspects of conscious mind and ego. The *outer planets* correspond to more unconscious and subconscious aspects of the personality. The Overcompensation Pendulum accounts for repression and reassessment of archetypes over lifetimes.

X.   Each planet reflects a different type of energy reassessment and is very revealing when used in conjunction with the steps of delineation to determine the law of momentum flow.

Index of Terms and Concordance

Supplementary reading

Allen, Bem P. Personality Theories.
Massachusetts: Allyn & Bacon.
    1994
Arroyo, Stephen. Astrology, Karma and Transformation.
Washington: CRCS Publications.
    1978
Cayce, Edgar Evans. Edgar Cayce On Atlantis.
New York: Paperback Library.
    1968
Cerminara, Gina. Many Mansions, The Edgar Cayce Story on Reincarnation.
New York: William Morrow and Company.
    1978

Cole, Sheila R., and Michael. The Development of Children. Second edition.
New York: Scientific American Books.
        1993
Keirsey David, and Bates, Marilyn. Please Understand Me.
San Diego: Promtheus/Nemesis Book Co.
        1978
Lewi, Grant. Heaven Knows What.
Minnesota: Llewellyn Publications.
        1977
Lewi, Grant. Astrology For The Millions.
Minnesota: Llewellyn Publications. Bantam Edition
        1980
Lewis, James R. The Astrology Encyclopedia.
Michigan: Invisible Ink Press.
        1994
Pelletier, Robert. Planets in Aspect.
Massachusetts: Para Research Inc.
        1974
Ruperti, Alexander. Cycles Of Becoming.
Washington: CRCS Publications.
        1978
Sakoian, Frances & Acker, Louis. The Astrologers Handbook
New York: Harper & Row Inc.
        1989
Sagan, Carl. Cosmos.
New York: Random House
        1980
Tyl, Noel. Astrology 1-2-3.
Minnesota: Llewellyn Publications.
        1980
        Holistic Astrology.
        1984
        Astrology 1-2-3.
        1991
        Prediction In Astrology.
        The Horoscope as Identity
        1974
Yott, Donald H.. Astrology and Reincarnation
York Beach Maine: Samuel Weiser Inc.
        1989

Planetary Dignities

Planet	Ruler	Detriment	Exaltation	Fall
Sun	Leo	Aquarius	Aries	Libra
Moon	Cancer	Capricorn	Taurus	Scorpio
Mercury	Gemini Virgo	Sagittarius Pisces	Virgo	Pisces
Venus	Taurus Libra	Scorpio Aries	Pisces	Virgo
Mars	Aries	Libra	Capricorn	Cancer
Jupiter	Sagittarius	Gemini	Cancer	Capricorn
Saturn	Capricorn	Cancer	Libra	Aries
Uranus	Aquarius	Leo	Scorpio	Taurus
Neptune	Pisces	Virgo	Leo	Aquarius
Pluto	Scorpio	Taurus	Leo	Aquarius

Chapter 7

Archetypal Merging

> "Weep no more for treasures
> you've been searching for in
> vain 'cause the truth is gently
> falling with the rain; high
> above the forest lie
> the pastures of the Sun
> Where the two that learned the
> secret now are one."
> The Moody Blues
> "Every Good Boy Deserves Favour"

LIVING LIGHT-THE PERSONA

It has been theorized that there exists many alternate and parallel realities. In order to participate in the focused dream of physical reality, we must continually act our "parts." Carl Jung referred to these parts as personae. The word is derived from the Latin word persona, meaning; "mask or false face." The mask worn by the actor on the Roman stage, would announce "personare!" meaning; "to sound through." The trinary aspects of Sun/Moon blend + Ascendent of any horoscope reflects this persona.

This mask or false face, has been referred to in this book as the artificial construct of the person-ality. This artificial construct is "worn" by the oversoul to experience or "to sound through" while experiencing the focused dream of physical reality.

The Sun and Moon, are the "lights" of the personality, we call them luminaries. In Chapter 5 we discussed the vibrational frequency of these aspects of consciousness symbolized by the planets and their orbits. We began crystallization into physical reality at the vibration of Pluto as the soul "descends" into materiality. Symbolically speaking of course, because the concept of time or its counterpart space are not experienced sequentially or spatially in non-physical reality. As the non-physical "light" of the identity projected by the oversoul "makes it's way" through the levels of oversoul projection, it will "descend" from Pluto through the planets toward the Sun. The vibrational frequency is then "lit up" and shines back through the solar system, back through the planets of Mercury and Venus to Earth. Hence the double sign rulership of these two planets. Finally, the combination of light from the Sun (sign), is reflected through the moon (sign), and together these two lights focus their combined vibrational frequency, and converge into what we perceive in the individual, as the personality. This personality forms the artificial construct necessary to deal with the particular focus or "dream" of physical reality. The final "face" that is then put on this persona is the rising sign or ascendant, the sign of the template ascending at birth. In this way we express a specific aspect of the unbroken wholeness of "All That Is."

The journey "back to Pluto", or the ascension of consciousness to the higher self, is then experienced on Earth as a *physical being* with full conscious commandment. The purpose of living is to express as this artificial construct, one of the ways that the "All That Is" has of dreaming itself into physicality. In order to play the game of forgetting and to exclude peripheral information from distracting us from this focus, we create the persona we are and convince ourselves that is all that we are. Now in this age it is the time to re-member our selves back together. The reintegration of the "waters of life" and their co-creative application is the thrust of the Aquarian age.

The prism of the persona (Sun, Moon, Ascendant) is the vehicle which allows the shining through of the light of "All That Is" in materiality through each and every being (and idea). It consists of the trinary expressions of belief, emotion, and thought, again reflecting the trinary aspects of the personality. It is based on the house flow Aries, Taurus, and Gemini, and their extensions by Element (trinary) and Mode (quadruplicity).

The manifestation of an identity from this format is from trust, belief definition (Aries) and intention. The consolidation of the momentum is from e-motion or energy motion (Taurus). Thought (Gemini) is the reaction to the manifestation of the self and it's momentum(s) disseminated as behavior in the world of duality.

Because the Moon "collects" the light of the Sun, it acts as a reservoir or pool (archetype) of the personal unconscious. Although they may be unconscious, the moon represents the reigning needs of the persona. What we imag-in(e) ourselves to be, what we most need to be and nurture as the primary aspect of the persona (Noel Tyl, *"The Principles and Practice of Astrology"*, vol. 5 Needs, Tyl, *"Holistic Astrology"*). These reigning needs are internalized through the relationship with the first symbol that reflects emotional nurturing, the mother. Curiously, the reigning need typically implies the aspects of nurturing not believed fulfilled through interaction with the mother (this depends on the whole chart of course often it is the reverse).

For example, when the moon is placed in Leo, it implies that obtaining dramatic ego reinforcement, allows the identity to feel emotionally secure and efficacious. It implies that from the perceptual perspective of the individual with the moon so placed, the mother did not fulfill these needs in the early environment, or that her behavior was such as to reinforce this need in the child with the moon in this position as an issue (see anaclitic identification pages 27, 28).

Because children are born with different moon placements, these differing needs by each child reveals more about the child's beliefs than it does about the mother. Remember, I assert that the child brings a "something" with it in that defines personality and is *not* a programmable blank slate. The **feeling** of emotional insecurity, reflects fears and **beliefs** of the identity if the need for dramatic ego importance not be fulfilled. This idea corresponds to *The response deprivation theory* of reinforcement proposed by William Timberlake and James

Allison (1974: Timberlake 1980) in psychology. That behavior becomes reinforcing when the organism is prevented from engaging in it. The identity then carries these needs for nurturing as the primary component to fulfill the life path. The mother then acts as a sounding board or catalyst to establish needs for fulfillment and manifestations of *themes* to be explored in the life.

The general thematic reigning needs of the Moon, reflected by template placement, are as follows;[124]

THE REIGNING NEED OF THE PERSONA

MOON IN ARIES- The reigning need is to experience validation of the ego through self direction, to be first, to prove the self. Fear of being ignored. Belief.

MOON IN TAURUS- To find stability, form, and establish the personality worth and resource base. Maintain the status quo. The fear of losing control. Emotion.

MOON IN GEMINI- The need to experience appreciation for the diversity, intelligence and communication abilities. The diversification of the self and dissemination of resources. Fear of not being appreciated. Thought.

MOON IN CANCER- Need for emotional security and to nurture the inner emotional base. Fear of being taken advantage of. Belief.

MOON IN LEO- The need for dramatic ego reinforcement for creativity and directed extension. Applause. Fear of being ignored. Emotion.

MOON IN VIRGO- The need to be analytically correct, discern or judge pragmatic efficacy and discrimination. Fear of losing control. Thought.

MOON IN LIBRA- To validate the identity through social acceptance and social mirroring. Fear of not being appreciated. Belief.

MOON IN SCORPIO- To be impactual and emotionally

---

[124]
        Please refer to all Noel Tyl references listed as supplemental texts. It is extremely important that the student learn these well.

significant. Transcendence of ego limits Strong fear of being taken advantage of. Emotion.

MOON IN SAGITTARIUS- To have the intellect respected and ego reinforced through intellectual exchange. To have the beliefs and ego validated through the acceptance of one's opinions by others. Fear of being ignored. Thought.

MOON IN CAPRICORN- To control one's own security in physical reality and fully manifest the self. Functional pragmatic efficacy. Strategic effectiveness. Fear of losing control. Belief.

MOON IN AQUARIUS- To be recognized for one's uniqueness through co-creative interaction and abstract or ideological social exchange. Fear of not being appreciated. Emotion.

MOON IN PISCES- Need to be compassionate, sensitive and empathetic through the recognition of the all as one. The fear of being taken advantage of. Thought.

The primary cornerstone of the artificial construct, the Moon, represents the second point, emotion. All of the planetary archetypes reflect different levels of these cornerstones; belief, emotion and thought (following the pattern outlined in the template).

The Sun-belief, Moon-emotion and Mercury- thought. These planets reflect the most focused aspects of the personality construct. They must be delineated as being the two focal points that channel all of the remaining energy in the horoscope. The others in order from lowest to highest vibration (meaning level of focus) are as follows; Mars-belief, Venus-emotion, Jupiter-thought. Then Saturn-belief, Neptune-emotion, Uranus-thought. Pluto represents the knowingness associated with an entirely different dimension-4th density-which is the integration of all levels in this system before it can be left or physicality transcended.

► "In this same archetypical manner you have described the myth you call the crossing of the River Styx. This puts you in touch with what you previously assumed to be the darker regions of your consciousness. It is another way of saying that you enter the blending of your positive and negative polarities, and therefore allow yourselves, in the crossing of that threshold, to glean only a positive effect out of the blending of the positive and the negative. This is why you have intuitively labeled Pluto's moon with the same name as the ferryboat driver that drives you across the mythological river Styx . . . Charon. Bashar "Blueprint for Change"

This also reflects the idea of the resurrection as the orbit of Charon is approximately 3 days. The blending of all is the expression of the Christ consciousness.

Psychologically speaking, there are no significators more important in reflecting identity definition, than the Sun/Moon blend + ascendent. The Sun/Moon blend indicates the masculine and feminine aspects of the persona combined. Developmental aspects between these luminaries in the horoscope, reveals beliefs regarding the dis-integration of the masculine and feminine aspects within the identity. There will have likely been developmental issues with the parental structure when they are in developmental tension (quadrature). As a coping mechanism, one function may become dominant; if the Sun; masculine-conscious self, or Moon; the feminine unconscious self. The opposition aspect between the sun/moon at birth, reflects a powerful tug-of-war (full Moon) between the masculine and feminine within the psyche of the person with reference to the archetype or polarity of signs in which it falls. An "illumination" of the polarized aspects of the sign axis. Belief and emotion at odds. If they are integrated, an illuminating insight into the concept the polarity represents.

All forms of developmental tension (refer to aspect types) are the effect of the judgement of the archetypes involved. In example; Aids is the dis-ease reflecting the inability or unwillingness of the person to integrate the aspects of the feminine and the masculine. The effect of lowering barriers to interaction, without transformation of perspective to higher self functioning (symbolically). All dis-ease is the effect of separation, resistance to growth and the imbalance of the rest or natural state. The Sun/Moon blend reflects the vibrational frequency of the core of the identity, *congealed.*

The keys presented in this book are presented in basic terms because the complete picture unfolds as we take the keys and blend them with other indicators. For this reason, there really is no reason to build a giant interpretation from one indicator. The whole thrust of identity direction and momentum is clear with our keys blending holistically as we are guided to understanding.

The keys are delineated with a middle ground approach or level as *basic operations*. They can manifest higher and more integrated and noble-or lower and more base. The aspects covered in the previous chapter can be referred to for more insight into meaning. For aspect relationships of the Sun/Moon blend, refer to aspects and orbs because this relationship is measured by degree closeness.

The key thematic interpretations for the Sun/Moon blend possibilities are as follows;

SUN-MOON BLENDS

SUN IN ARIES- The need to validate and experience identity definition. Action as the conviction of belief. These attributes are channeled through the Moon and it's relationship to the Sun.

☽ in

MOON in Aries- Conjunction. A powerful focus upon the self. The reigning need serves the physical expression. Drive, desire, and ego are very important. The placement of Mars is very significant in further delineation.

MOON in Taurus- The urge to become is stabilized. Energy economized. There can be fixation with the Moon placed here and obvious self orientation.

MOON in Gemini- The sextile relationship supports the life energy. Quickness of wit. The Moon in Gemini would need anchoring through squares or oppositions to direct the energy.

MOON in Cancer- Opening square. This can represent a balanced identity when integrated. Disruption in the parental structure. The ego can get out of hand because of sensitivity. Insecurity. The Moon in Cancer always reflects powerful maternal influence. Nurturing and ego importance at odds. A strong need to establish identity.

MOON in Leo- Opening trine. Ego projection is dramatic and fiery. Expects success to gratify ego importance. Needs softening by more sensitive positions. Easy expression.

MOON in Virgo- The reigning need imposes strictures upon the expression of the Sun's energy. Judgement can accelerate. With positive aspects to the Moon-aggressive discernment.

MOON in Libra- A conflict between aggressive self assertion, and toning down ego for social acceptance. This can result in a back and forth effect upon relationships. The balance point is to recognize that others reflect the self, not determine it. The Full Moon positions in any sign suggest a need to resolve the belief in inner verses outer dynamics.

MOON in Scorpio- The self presentation can be overdone. Power needs hide the insecurity that the self will not be important. If negative ego is not transcended, the personality may only reflect pushiness and arrogance.

MOON in Sagittarius- The apex trine between the luminaries, is always reflective of the possibility of great integrity-as long as energy and intention remain focused. This is an aspect of the expression of honesty and integrity. Following your excitement is easy. Mental influence.

MOON in Capricorn- The apex of developmental aspects reflect an accelerated need to resolve conflicts. Without spiritual direction this position tends to "gaining the world, and losing your soul". There is a tremendous drive to achieve based upon the early environmental conflicts with the parents or home environment. "No pain, no gain" belief system.

MOON in Aquarius- The reigning needs soften the focus upon the self. This position needs social outlets to validate identity. Stability is needed through other significators in the horoscope. Impulsivity possible.

MOON in Pisces- This position can present difficulties if stability is lacking. The idealism of Pisces, can put out the fire of the sun-if the life energy is not directed and expressed with integrity and trust. (see definitions under integrity) .

SUN IN TAURUS- The reigning needs of the Moon will reflect the Sun's energy of self worth, and value establishment. The Taurean idea is the structuring of identity, giving it value and meaning. Resourcefulness.

MOON in Aries- As with the Sun in Aries Moon in Taurus, there can be a fixation upon the self. The Moon in Aries however, adapts more easily to change. Things, rather than values can be forcefully pursued to establish worth.

MOON in Taurus- The conjunction. There can be a balanced view of one's worth. A calmness and patience in the experience of life. If in developmentally tense aspects, there needs to be changes in the structure of the identity that may be unsettling. Insecurity so great, that the heels are dug in.

MOON in Gemini- Application of the self must be in diverse terms, otherwise indecisiveness and change-ability dissipate the identity and a loss of direction will occur. The conscious and unconscious are contradictory in definition. But only if there is not expression of diversity within a structured format.

MOON in Cancer- There is a tremendous focus upon security needs. These positions are the symbol of a persona that is comfortable with physical reality. The builder of security. The mother will be very supportive. The sextile.

MOON in Leo- Opening square. The personal needs and expression are established to display worth. Dramatic display of the will. Creativity can be enormous. If the reigning need is not fulfilled dominance can replace the self empowered approach.

MOON in Virgo- Opening trine. Expression comes easily. Analytical discernment can be well developed. Action is needed to further development. Creativity is the key.

MOON in Libra- A preoccupation with social graces can make a stand of opinion elusive. Harmony at all costs. Sometimes integrity is the cost. Perspective needs adjustment.

MOON in Scorpio- A powerful momentum of rigidity. Full illumination of subjective value judgements that need transforming. Insecurity may not allow interaction with others, or sharing not possible. The parental structure is extremely important in analysis.

MOON in Sagittarius- Gives a lift to the Sun's materialistic perspective. it also can reflect an identity that may be preoccupied with seeking the good opinion of others. There can be a stubborn presentation of beliefs. Inconjuncts require adjustment and blending of personality functions.

MOON in Capricorn- Because of the Moon's placement in apex trine, this is one of the more integrative expressions of a Capricorn Moon. Discernment is accurate. Responsibility is inherent. The higher self easily manifests the values of the life energy (Sun). The wedding of the ideal, with physical reality.

MOON in Aquarius- Apex square. Developmental tension to fulfill the self worth through innovative application. Success is based on welcoming change to allow innovation to grow. If not integrated, being different for the sake of being different amounts to annoyance.

MOON in Pisces- Sensitivity supports the self worth. There may be shyness in expression. More confident positions are needed to externalize the constructive or creative aspects of this configuration.

☉ ♊

SUN IN GEMINI- The energy of communication, diversity, and mobility are reflected by the Moon's position and distributed through the reigning need.

 ☽ in

MOON in Aries- There is a confident cerebration with the Moon in this position. The water balance of the elements will be needed to take the edge off mentality. Humor and vivaciousness. The assertive needs of the Moon easily express the life energy.

MOON in Taurus- The reigning needs of the Moon stabilize and calm the nervousness of the life energy. Easy going, generous, a good friend. All Moon in Taurus positions reflect a need to evaluate early environmental security. There is a psychological reason for such a need to maintain the status quo.

MOON in Gemini- Diversity may be rampant. There must be focused aspects or positions to balance this blend. Ingenuity will profit the identity, as well as being a fountain of knowledge. Try to find somewhere to apply it in service.

MOON in Cancer- The Earth element will need to be represented strongly in the horoscope where this blend is found. The sense impressions are acute. If there is an insecurity reflected elsewhere in the chart, emotional or psychological understanding must be cultivated.

MOON in Leo- This sextile helps to tone down the dissipation of the sun's energy. There is usually a need for a dramatic show of diversity, preferably in communication of some type. Artistic or romantic inclination.

MOON in Virgo- Opening square. There is a developmental tension to categorize information based on some sort of value structure, applying the self with natural aggression will solve the indecision problems. Act on convicted beliefs that you are capable of acting on. Things will fall into place.

MOON in Libra- The reigning need of the Moon in opening trine reflects social ease and adaptability. There needs to be a practical anchor or superficiality patterns allow the identity to give power to the social mirror.

MOON in Scorpio- Unless there is some serious focus through other positions or aspects, the mentality may be controlled by the passions. The inconjunct aspect, especially the opening one, reflects the need for perspective alteration and adjustment. If the mind is applied to the metaphysical, great insights could be garnered.

MOON in Sagittarius- A full Moon in the information and mental signs equals a thinking conflict. There is a strong need to prove the intelligence. Talking about ideas replaces action with them. All oppositions need resolution. A blending of this polarity through aspects, could result in mental prowess.

MOON in Capricorn- Closing inconjunct. The Sun energy may not be able to serve the ambitions of the reigning need. Again we have talking replacing action. There could be a tyrannical attitude that develops, unless self empowerment principles transform perspective.

MOON in Aquarius- Apex trine. Here the intelligence is served well by innovation and a genuine need to share ideas and concepts. Intuition is well developed. A strong Earth and Water element distribution would reflect the facile and empathic humanitarian.

MOON in Pisces- Apex square. There may be some difficulty reconciling the intuition (Moon) and the intellect (Sun). What needs to be fulfilled is the recognition that these two ideas are the polarity of one idea. Lack of trust and being fearful are always the reasons for anxiety.

☉ ♋

SUN IN CANCER- The dimension of inner self, emotional security, and nurturing will be distributed by the reigning need of the Moon. The Moon sign gains a more powerful significance when the Sun is in Cancer because the Moon will be the dispositor (or ruler) of the Sun position. Cancer is impressionable and reflective.

 ☽ in

MOON in Aries- Apex square. When the developmental issue of security through projection is resolved, the balance of sensitivity and ego assertion will fulfill the purpose of living. Inner self manifested through identity focus.

MOON in Taurus- Sextile. As with Sun in Taurus, Moon in Cancer, there is genuine warmth and appreciation for the aesthetic. A gentle soul. The reigning need is in harmony with the inner self dimensions. Some developmental aspects are needed for balance.

MOON in Gemini- This position may be a little too impressionable and a little too flexible. The reigning need may not find serious fulfillment unless concentration is found elsewhere in the horoscope.

MOON in Cancer- This is such a reflective combination that much of the remaining frequencies in the horoscope will determine the effect. If there are strong representations in the remainder, great emotional insight could be expressed. If not timidity needs to be looked at and the reason for insecurities discovered.

MOON in Leo- This blend offers more strength to the life energy. The sensitivity is best expressed creatively. The Sun and Moon would be in mutual reception. The ego seems to have just the right expression.

MOON in Virgo- The sensitivity of the life energy, is tied to analysis and the practical application of knowledge. If the fire element is well represented in the rest of the chart, this sextile supports the expression of the inner self with conscious mind functions.

MOON in Libra- Opening square. The social needs of the Moon may express themselves defensively until there is a recognition of the sensitivity in others. There is a lot of insecurity here. The parental structure may be where insecurity beliefs were triggered.

MOON in Scorpio- Opening trine. There is an ease in perspective alteration- and in indulgence. This combination needs breadth of vision to carry the depth of emotion into spiritual application. The reigning need (the unconscious) may have a stronger momentum than the security needs of the life energy will want to deal with. In other words a lot of psychic energy.

MOON in Sagittarius- There is a heightening of the perspective. Spiritual goals are the security need. This blend can manifest the inner self altruistically.

MOON in Capricorn- Full Moon-opposition. This position is indicative of a definite need to recognize that you create your reality by the beliefs you harbor. Conscious strategic application and the flow of inner self are at odds. This is THE reflection of the belief in reality existence outside the self. The inner momentum IS the outer self in physical terms. If resolved, a wisdom regarding this idea develops.

MOON in Aquarius- The Sun/Moon blend of the United States. Security is sought through innovations that liberate the self from confining structures. The self believes that it is practical, others may see a little more theory than practice.

MOON in Pisces- Apex trine. The emotions find their home through merging and blending with "All That Is". Emotional sensitivity. The helping professions will allow full expression. Water follows the lines of least resistance. There must be developmental aspects to generate desire and action.

SUN IN LEO- Dramatic expression of the identity is the energy of the sun in this position. The sun is the lens of Leo, and Leo expresses the masculine energy of drive, love giving, creativity and the heart of the persona. This energy will be used to fulfill the reigning need of the personal unconscious.

☽ **in**

MOON in Aries- Apex trine. Confidence, courage and trust best express the energy of this fiery combination. The energy of assertiveness of the personal unconscious instinctively brings out the leadership aspects of identity. If the Earth element is balanced, accomplishments are limitless.

MOON in Taurus- Apex square. The security needs of the unconscious can manifest as obstinacy when external reality challenges the fire of the life energy. Fixed sign developmental aspects indicate a lot of energy motion (e-motion), and an apex square the culmination of that energy. Perspective and integrity are needed to apply this energy constructively.

MOON in Gemini- Sextile. The light of the sun is distributed diversely. Dramatic expression serves to reinforce the reigning needs as easily as possible. Ideas and action in harmony.

MOON in Cancer- Mutual reception. The sensitive needs of the personal unconscious soften the ego needs of the persona. Self worth is assumed, overcompensation is not necessary.

MOON in Leo- Conjunction. Much depends on the aspects to this blend. Positive aspects reinforce a dramatic and forceful expression of the creativity. Negative, pride and vanity are overdone.

MOON in Virgo- The mental dimensions of the unconscious needs narrow the grand expression of the life energy so that analysis replaces drama. Self confidence is only an outer show.

MOON In Libra- The needs for acceptance socially may put a damper on the life energy bravado. The effect may be a denial of the recognition of personal truths. With confidence and self empowering perspectives a grand acceptance of these personal truths can be realized. Idealism.

MOON in Scorpio- Opening square. The momentum of the insecurity of the identity may be so great that the passions may get out of control. Everything is bound up in the personal perspective. The mother may have been perceived as very manipulative. Control comes with the belief in self empowerment.

MOON in Sagittarius- An easy manifestation of the higher self. The reigning need serves the identity through travel, new ideas and an expanded perspective. Excitement can be easily followed-fulfillment assured with trust.

MOON in Capricorn- The reigning need for physical manifestation plus life energy of creativity, makes for an administration of the will that is very competent. There definitely needs to be softening aspects and placements or tyranny can replace self empowerment.

MOON in Aquarius- Opposition, Full Moon. The integration of this blend can reflect a very active humanitarianism. The challenge is to compliment through creative extension, not compete with others for it.

MOON in Pisces- The power of the Sun's energy finds a moral and sensitive application through the reigning needs of the Moon.

SUN IN VIRGO- The self seeks to categorize, analyze, and disseminate information and apply it to practical considerations when the horoscope contains the Sun in Virgo. The energy of discernment is filtered through the personal unconscious.

MOON in Aries- Aries reflects instinctive assertion. Virgo, focused dissection. The effect rendered is the identity's censorship of reigning needs. There may be ego insecurity stemming from the relationship with the mother. Action speaks louder than words and will build needed confidence.

MOON in Taurus- Apex trine. Positive manifestation of the identity in the material world. An understanding of the need to be of service brings abundant rewards. An expanded viewpoint and developmental aspects are needed to awaken the identity to higher self motivations.

MOON in Gemini- Apex square. There can be a preoccupation with conscious mind functions. This blend reflects the belief that the conscious mind is in "control" of the security of the identity. There is little trust in the instincts and emotions. Life will be difficult and challenging as long as the identity believes it is living by it's wits. He who lives by this sword, must also die by it.

MOON in Cancer- Sensitive service is the best form of fulfillment for this blend. Reticence can manifest as reluctance unless there are stronger self projection aspects in the birth chart. Insecurity. Good sense of humor.

MOON in Leo- There is a devotion to duty with this blend. A contentment with being of service. However, if anxiety is felt from the lack of fulfillment of the reigning need then perhaps more creative extension of the identity can solve the habit of hiding your light.

MOON in Virgo- The need for analytical accuracy can blind the identity to wider horizons. The conjunction of such focused energy of detail and refinement, implies a severe lack of trust in the self. If other components of the horoscope point to broader perspectives, then the power of the focus will be an asset.

MOON in Libra- The need of the persona to be socially accepted can place expectations and judgements on what type of acceptance one "should" receive. This can lead to isolation and snobbery. Developmental focus and self direction may be needed.

MOON in Scorpio- The need for emotional significance with this Moon position relays the Sun's flamboyant energy and seeks intellectual impact as well. An over exaggeration of the self's importance can destroy analytical discernment. Incisive, indulgent.

MOON in Sagittarius- Opening square. The establishment of analytical discernment may be at odds with large concepts. Floating along with big ideas and never applying or bridging the gap between them and day to day reality. Incorporation of realism and blending it with idealism is necessary.

MOON in Capricorn- Opening trine. The personal unconscious serves the life energy well. The practical application of the intellect is administrated comfortably, strategically, and confidently. In combination with broader perspectives and inspiration, a higher self integrity can be expressed.

MOON in Aquarius- The innovative aspects of the personal unconscious adds a breadth of vision to objectivity. This coolness can be a defense against personal involvement. Sensitivity and empathy may need cultivation.

MOON in Pisces- Full Moon, opposition. The awareness in this blend registers in perspective, which is the area of experience that needs resolution. The resolution is in the recognition that intuition and intellect are the polarized components of a single idea. Once integration takes place, enhanced perspective can be applied to service to man instinctually.

SUN IN LIBRA- The need for social acceptance-or in spiritual terms-the need to merge with the projections of self through social interaction, are represented in the life energy of the Sun in Libra. The personal unconscious then "colors" this need for interaction with the "other" portions of the self.

 in

MOON in Aries- Full Moon, opposition. This is the blend of identity crisis. The unconscious needs are to be an individualistic pioneer, the life energy seeks to blend and harmonize. There may be eccentric expressions of the identity in seeking to find it`s place as an individual. The path to the alleviation of conflicts is to recognize that the identity contains both polarities.

MOON in Taurus- There is a strong desire to see the self through social (Libra) and personal (Taurus) reflections. This can manifest as a desire for harmony on all levels. There may be a resistance to looking at the more unpleasant aspects of the self through others.

MOON in Gemini- Apex trine. This blend reflects an extremely easy social nature. There must be a grounding aspect or placement to bring these negotiating abilities into practical application, otherwise the reigning needs may be only superficially fulfilled.

MOON in Cancer- Apex square. Specific goals will need to be defined in order for this blend to be integrated. The desire to please for security needs of the persona can be overdone. Bringing the inner self to external fruition is the challenge.

MOON in Leo- There is a lot of idealism reflected in this blend, so much so that the self may not see the difficult experiences as it's creations. We cannot experience things that are not a part of us on some level.

MOON in Virgo- There may be an excess of judgement of what is deemed correct and proper socially. There may be fears associated with boldness which is sometimes required to be analytically correct. Repression of the self for social acceptance.

MOON in Libra- Conjunctions carry neither positive nor negative meanings within themselves. This blend if integrative can reflect the recognition of the self through others in relationship. If negative, social and romantic needs deny self definition. The planet Venus will be very important in analysis.

MOON in Scorpio- The perspective of others determines the actions of the self. Emotional significance is based upon social acceptance. Transcendence could manifest when the identity takes responsibility for it's creations.

MOON in Sagittarius- There is a strong desire to have the personal philosophies accepted by others. In order to accomplish this there definitely must be practical grounding through the Earth element, otherwise the ideals and the reality of experience separate.

MOON in Capricorn- Opening square. The establishment of self is perceived to be accomplished through the manipulation and management of others. There is insecurity if the good opinion of others is not achieved. A belief in powerlessness can be the reason for this need to prove the self. The parental structure will be very important in analysis.

MOON in Aquarius- Innovation can run rampant in an attempt to be socially accepted as unique. With stabilization, the artistic expression will help to raise consciousness through humanitarian ideologies. The romantic with a message.

MOON in Pisces- Perception of others through empathy can allow for a good amount of psychological understanding. This is the blend of a good listener, counselor, therapist. Absorption of others energy alleviates any threat so that sharing comes easily.

SUN IN SCORPIO- The life energy of the Sun in Scorpio manifests as a strong desire to be emotionally significant in some way, shape or form. Transcendence is the effect of the recognition of the differing values between people and relinquishment of negative ego. The e-motion of expanded experience and personal power is distributed by the light of the Moon.

☽ in

MOON in Aries- This blend signifies the need for the transformation of the ego self to more conceptual levels. The personal needs of the unconscious must be fulfilled. When a feeling of personal significance is achieved perhaps more of a consideration for others can be cultivated. Opening inconjunct.

MOON in Taurus- Full Moon opposition. The opportunistic aspect of this blend implies that the value structure of the identity has accelerated to the point where there must be transformation. There has been a heavy focus upon sustenance physically. Resources must be found in the higher levels as well. The ego may struggle to stabilize itself by ignoring weaknesses.

MOON in Gemini- The self may fool itself into believing that intellectual significance can be achieved without diligence. Conscious mind function tries to justify emotional reactions. Introspection is needed. Insight is acute if positive.

MOON in Cancer- Apex trine. The important aspect of this blend is that if security is found, it will be found through the realization that no one can take advantage of the self. Once this is integrated the emotional perceptivity can be applied to self awareness and assisting others. Defensiveness is the signal of a dis-empowering perspective.

MOON in Leo- Apex square. This will be a very difficult blend until the identity realizes that it's great expectations and demands on others stem from the belief in striving and struggling to impact the environment with the self. What can be done as a service to others will allow impact as a bi-product or effect of integrative thinking. Emotions can run away with the self.

MOON in Virgo- When balanced, the intellect can reveal an accurate insight into others. The danger is in a tunnel vision that makes the self's perspective, the only one. These two possibilities can be expressed depending upon the sense of security the ego feels. If secure, insight; insecure, tunnel vision.

MOON in Libra- The intensity of the life energy may conflict with the desire to be socially accepted. The value of the self must be put into perspective, so that breadth of vision is cultivated. Everyone is significant, and everyone thinks differently.

MOON in Scorpio- Conjunction, New Moon. There is an extreme focus upon the desires, opinions and demands of the self. Significance is assumed. Sensitivity and sharing are believed to be weakness. Transformation to a loftier level is definitely implied, whether this can be accomplished or not depends upon awareness reflected through the rest of the horoscope and the person's approach.

MOON in Sagittarius- With practical application, this blend can take the life energy intensity and transform it into spiritual awareness. Ethical service and integrity will fulfill potential.

MOON in Capricorn- The power needs of this sextile are great. If the perspective is oriented to self empowerment, fulfillment will be great as well. Strategy is very important. If the self believes it is in control, then sensitivity replaces domination. The reigning need for strategy serves the impacting needs of the life energy.

MOON in Aquarius- Opening square, the establishment of identity may have experienced disruption in the early environment. An intense need to have uniqueness respected. A worthy goal needs to be defined early to apply vision in an altruistic manner. If insecurity mounts, there is the possibility of a powerfully disruptive identity expression.

MOON in Pisces- Refinement of the emotional responses, takes the edge off intensity of the life energy. The intuition and intellect are well blended. Instincts are accurate. The identity must be aware however, that the outer is always a reflection of the inner. The inner is not a hiding place, from the outer.

SUN IN SAGITTARIUS- Philosophy and any type of expansive expression and/or conceptual expression of the self, reflects the life energy needs of Sagittarius. A "freeing up" of the identity in terms of mobility either physically or mentally is sought. Noble and broad.

 in

MOON in Aries- Opening trine. The expansive pioneer. The reigning need of the moon allows the identity to personalize the conceptual aspects of the life energy. Honor and integrity allow the ego self comfortable expression. An active mind, body, and spirit. The physical expression of higher self functioning.

MOON in Taurus- An adjustment of perspective. Either the unconscious needs will put a damper on the life energy, or ideals detract from security needs. When these two energies are integrated, we again have realism and idealism working hand in hand.

MOON in Gemini- Full illumination of the mental axis. Information, movement, diversity, and travel are outlets necessary to resolve the sense of contradiction and paradox that may accompany this position. Organizational functions will need to be reflected elsewhere in the horoscope to funnel this energy and allow it to be applicable to a goal.

MOON in Cancer- The inner self can find expression in this blend, if the security is founded upon a rock. This rock must be the recognition of the power of the self. If not, gullibility is a possibility.

MOON in Leo- The successful integration of the higher self and creativity allow this apex trine to reflect loyalty, honor and ethics to be the rule of the day. Imagination is unbounded. Reality is created by what you imagine it to be, therefore the reality experience of this configuration can have no bounds.

MOON in Virgo- Apex square. The identity experiences the conflict of missing the trees for the forest, or the forest for the trees. The mental resolution provides for the application of concepts in practical terms. Anxiety in communication can be soothed if righteousness is curbed.

MOON in Libra- Expansiveness is expressed through the social mirror. A practical anchor is needed to bring ideals down to earth. A need for eternal change, places the power outside the self and may deny opportunity for self exploration inwardly.

MOON in Scorpio- Events become opportunities and avenues for emotional significance. A belief in powerlessness can promote opportunism without regard for consequences. Obsession is always a possibility with the Moon in Scorpio.

MOON in Sagittarius- New Moon conjunction. The intellectual focus may be too great. The organization and diligence needed to interlink philosophy with a personal transformation will not come about unless practical developmental issues demand it.

MOON in Capricorn- The higher self finds strategic application. The fire of the life energy manifests as leadership. If self empowerment is not employed, self righteous judgements of others is entirely possible.

MOON in Aquarius- Idealism is applied in humanistic terms. Being too comfortable with the self may lead to a justification of laziness as the self's needs to be unique. The application to service in practical terms is necessary for full deployment of the identity.

MOON in Pisces- Opening square. The establishment of the life energy meets the apparent illusion of the dream. When integrated the mystic appears. Reality is formed into understanding of significance. When disintegrated the self believes it has been victimized.

SUN IN CAPRICORN- The physical application of the identity through strategy, and the maximization of expression of the self in materiality. The concretization of belief momentum in their applicable physical versions is the life energy represented by the Sun in this position. Administration of the self.

in

MOON in Aries- Opening square. There is a strong application of self to the environment for personal gain. The ego (Aries) and the superego (Capricorn) combination implies a preoccupation with the self and it's censoring structures. Insecurity is masked with aggressive application.

MOON in Taurus- Opening trine. This is the blend of practical management. If people or aesthetics are involved so much the better. The structure of the Taurus Moon finds more comfort in dealing with the physical manifestation of identity. The leadership aspect can become an end in itself.

MOON in Gemini- The diversity aspect of the intelligence needs of the Moon can undermine diligent application. Talking about application options can replace the actualization of them.

MOON in Cancer- Full Moon opposition. There is the belief of inner and outer realities in conflict. If allowed to, sensitivity can detract from "realistic" application of the self. Without an emotional base, life is too cold and hard. The polarities are dissolved by removing the solid definitions of what they are-or are not-and replacing them with the idea that the inner and outer reflect the same definitions and are not contradictory.

MOON in Leo- The need to impress the identity upon the physical reality is dramatized. Power motives are not easily concealed. The transformation of perspective required here (closing inconjunct) may be difficult for the identity to accept, since precision and forceful application of the self bring so many rewards. Power comes in many forms, even though it may not fit your prescription of proper application.

MOON in Virgo- Apex trine. Convention allows for a pillar of society. When it comes to a bold presentation of the self however, confidence may be lacking. There needs to be developmental tension with individuality to get the most out of the combination of practical application and the intellect. Convention is the easy way out of confrontation.

MOON in Libra- Apex Square. The identity may feel the contradiction between being all you can be, and living up to "social demands." There is the belief in the harshness and superficiality involved in the experience of relationship. Realizing that it is only the self's projections that are threatening can assist in lowering defenses to interaction. A perceived threat.

MOON in Scorpio- The sense of enormous importance needs tempering through sensitivity. Changes may be made, but only to gain greater advantage. The identity would rather "fight than switch." If perspective does not take others into consideration existence may be lonely indeed.

MOON in Sagittarius- The mental energy of the reigning need softens and heightens the focused application of the life energy. Philosophical organization or applying structure to beliefs about living could be the primary expression.

MOON in Capricorn- Conjunction. The focus of strategic application implies a powerful belief in an external battle. Insecurity may be related to the early environmental difficulties. Power motives and selfishness are possible. To be the authority ensures control.

MOON in Aquarius- Humanitarianism displaces strategic control. A unique application of the ambition serves humanity. Social status may be important to you.

MOON in Pisces- This blend invites popularity. The sensitivity of the reigning need channels the ambition into humanitarian avenues. Responsibility is assumed easily. The ability to respond to the environment should be based on the identity's sense of integrity, not by the demands of others.

SUN IN AQUARIUS- The sharing of creative extension is the thrust of the Aquarian idea. The equality and the uniqueness of the expression of the individuality. The sharing of innovation between beings. Sharing like minded interests and social activities in progressive ways.

☽ **in**

MOON in Aries- The ego needs of the personal unconscious place an excessive amount of attention on ego reinforcement for unique recognition. The apparent superiority complex is a smoke screen for defending against a possibility of the lack of recognition.

MOON in Taurus- Opening square. Here the individuality seems to be concretely established. The physicalization of innovation. The identity wants to see the fruition of creative extension. There is the danger of a fixed and stubborn presentation to defend against the de-structurization of the persona.

MOON in Gemini- Opening trines always reflect the subjective experience of the integrated energy. Idle chit-chat undermines innovation. The temporary social reinforcement of superficial communication replaces focused application of the intelligence to fulfill reigning needs. Needs the focus of developmental aspects to perform with any diligence.

MOON in Cancer- Opening inconjunct. Intuition is highly developed and is applied to personal interaction. Generosity with the emotions is the greatest strength and the greatest weakness. The adjustment of perspective is the recognition that you cannot protect people from themselves.

MOON in Leo- Full Moon opposition. There is a strong momentum in the intellect and emotions. They compete for the identity's attention. The resolution to developmental awareness is integration of the perspective that love given and love received are one in the same thing. Creative powers need confirmation.

MOON in Virgo- The personal unconscious is caught up in the thinking process. Innovation combined with analytical discernment make for a very insightful critical analysis. The emotional perspective may be lacking integration within the entire personality. The alteration of the perspective involved in this closing inconjunct, is the incorporation of emotional synthesis from diverse levels of the psyche.

MOON in Libra- Apex trine. The personality may be so socially oriented as to direct the life goals based on the support of others. Working alone may be difficult. The higher self incorporation in this blend is the recognition that others only reflect the beliefs of the self, and do not direct it.

MOON in Scorpio- Apex square. Perspective transformation has a powerful momentum (Fixed signs, closing square). The self has such a need for emotional significance, that it perceives itself as uniquely significant. This assumption however, is a smoke screen to conceal the tremendous fear of identity invalidity. The integrative resolution is through the application of self to establish this identity, so that significance will not need to be forced from a scarcity view but with confidence.

MOON in Sagittarius- The expansive needs of the personal unconscious support the need for innovation of the life energy. A practical anchor will be necessary to bring talents into service. A diverse range of social contacts promotes the publicity the self enjoys.

MOON in Capricorn- The administration of humanitarian principles. The broad social concerns of the life energy are focused and applied by the reigning needs of the persona. Facts and an understanding of human nature can present a powerful and just persona.

MOON in Aquarius- The objectified creator. The scientist. Innovation is the key to personal fulfillment, as well as the sharing of these innovations socially.

MOON in Pisces- This is the blend of the natural metaphysician. Innovation is served by empathic sensitivity. The blending of science and art. Earth sign representation must be balanced to avoid self delusion.

SUN IN PISCES- The life energy represented in Pisces is one of fluid motion, sensitivity, compassion, empathy, and when disintegrated-disillusionment. The energy necessary to the dissolution of negative ego energy, to merge and blend with "All That Is." The desire to be a part of the forest, not the trees.

in

MOON in Aries- Contradiction. The life energy (Sun) has the momentum of dissolution of ego focus, however, the reigning need of the persona is to be ego important. The personal unconscious in this case represents insecurities internalized through the mother in the early environment. If these energies are co-fused (blended), energy can be directed to assertive presentation of mystical premise.

MOON in Taurus- The mystical energy gains a practical anchor. A genuinely sincere persona. The expression of unconditional love comes easily. Conscious mind functions will need strength of will to apply unconscious understanding fully.

Moon in Gemini- Opening square. The identity experiences the apparent separation of conscious and unconscious mind functions. The developmental tension is to integrate functions into coherency with consistency rather than quick fixes. Vacillation undermines action. Whims are enforced to save face.

MOON in Cancer- Opening trine. The subjective experience of the self's momentums. There needs to be some practical realism reflected elsewhere in the horoscope, lest emotional hurts turn into martyrdom.

MOON in Leo- The outer bravado reflected by the personal unconscious, is more bark than bite. If diligent application of self is to be practiced by starting with small accomplishments, this will lead to strength of character. The life energy has difficulty fulfilling the reigning needs.

MOON in Virgo- Full Moon opposition. The resolution to developmental awareness tension is the recognition that intuition and intellect are polarities of a single idea. Until this occurs, the persona may feel sorry for itself, lonely and carry the belief that it's perspective will never be understood.

MOON in Libra- The person may be lead by the nose through the expectations of social situations. The life energy would find it's best expressions through the arts. Practical incorporation and application is an absolute necessity.

MOON in Scorpio- Apex trine. This can be one of the more integrative positions of the Scorpio Moon. The emotional significance needs are given more depth and meaning. The spiritual can gain a hold on the identity. Analytical discernment abilities shown through other aspects in the chart will be necessary to counteract the indulgent potential of this blend.

MOON in Sagittarius- Apex square. The identity experiences the conflict of analytical understanding with the application of the intellect to intuitive recognitions. The integrative energy of these two principles represents grand intellectual awareness married to mystical awareness. The resolution is application with focus.

MOON in Capricorn- The reigning needs of the personal unconscious strengthen the application of sensitivity of the Sun's energy. Idealism distributed realistically. Business serves compassion.

MOON in Aquarius- The reigning needs distribute sensitivity in humanitarian ways. The missionary. An affinity for world reforms. Again practical application determines the extent of fulfillment and effectiveness.

MOON in Pisces- New Moon conjunction. Intuition needs a balance. There is an extreme focus upon the feeling aspect. A conscious mind focus represented elsewhere, can reflect strong empathetic understanding. The danger is in not applying it and falling under a self delusional trance.

These then are the possible Sun/Moon blends that reflect the quality of the prism or crystal of the persona. These are but extremely abbreviated suggestions because the expression possibilities from them is great (for a more comprehensive behavioral understanding see *"Heaven Knows What"*, by Grant Lewi, and/or Noel Tyl, Astrology 1-2-3). The blends reflect the masculine and feminine aspects inherent in every individual, and the inner relationship between them. In analysis, the Sun/Moon blend is the second "medium" applied to our portrait.

LIGHT BEAMS

"Monks and scholars should
accept my word not out of
respect, but upon analyzing
it as a goldsmith analyzes gold;
through cutting melting, scraping and rubbing it."

Buddha

As the Earth spins on it's axis, it is constantly turning into a different segment of the experiential template on the eastern horizon. We see the major star of our system; the Sun, rising on the eastern horizon morning. The constellations of the template rise continually as well. The constellation rising at the time of our first breath at birth is called the *rising sign*, or *ascending sign*. The framework of each individual's horoscope is constructed beginning with the sign ascending at birth. It marks the beginning of the first house and self projection.

The rising sign indicates the specific definition an identity has chosen through the higher self will to express. The personality now finds it's specific approach to expression through the rising constellation at birth and the corresponding house flow. For example, let's take the Sun/Moon blend energy focused through the sign Leo on the ascendant. The corresponding house arrangement would be thus; Leo on the first house cusp; Virgo on the second; Libra on the third. Around the template would we go, until we ended at Cancer on the 12th.

Because the rising sign is based on the *moment* of birth, it reflects a very specific definition of the identity. It reflects the point of entry and exit of the Sun/Moon blend and the interaction point for the remainder of the horoscope's configurations. It indicates the definition the identity *BELIEVES* it needs in order to express the idea that has been chosen to be expressed as the overall "path". It is the "Mask" the persona will wear while acting it's part in physical reality. Therefore, the light of the persona will be shown and seen through the filter of the ascendant. The planetary ruler of the ascendant (i.e. Aries ascendant would be ruled by Mars) and it's sign and house placement, describes the area of life (house); corroborating template focus (the sign placement of ascendent ruler); and ease or dis-ease in it's blend with other areas of functioning that are represented in the remainder of the birth chart (aspects).

The physical appearance of the identity is made up of the trinity of persona; Sun+Moon+Ascendant. Planets near the ascendant or in the house also color this projection, self definition, and physical appearance.

THE ASCENDANT
LIGHT PROJECTOR

A_S

ARIES- Unless Mars is in a difficult or repressive condition (retrograde), the expression of this identity definition is ardent, direct, vital, naturally aggressive and has a very strong need to project the self as quickly and spontaneously as possible. Identity in the act of becoming. The personality- no matter what other configurations- will present itself through action and impulse. Possibility of recklessness.

TAURUS- The self projection and definition seeks stability and establishment. The presentation of the self is calm and focused. The identity definition and self projection revolves around issues of worth. Venus' position corroborates further identity definition indices.

GEMINI- Mutable signs on the angles(1st, 4th, 7th, and 10th), reflect dissipated energy application. Physical focus is weak, mental focus and flexibility is strong. This ascendant will define an identity that is expressive, articulate, diverse and needs to be seen as intelligent.

CANCER- Cancer is a very reflective and impressionable sign. As a form of identity projection, this sensitivity will be shown by an individual who absorbs, then reflects whatever environment they may find themselves in. The personal projection will exude kindness, and may be rather reserved in definition. The Sun/Moon blend will be especially important in analysis, particularly the Moon, as this body will be the lens of the ascendant.

LEO- Extroversion would best describe the energy of this ascendant. The need to project a dramatic version of whatever energies are inherent within the birth chart will be evident. Magnanimity and a breadth of vision shun petty issues. Unless more down to earth energies are reflected through the remainder of the horoscope, the identity may be manipulatable through appeals to ego reinforcement or "flashy" without substance.

VIRGO- There is a strong sense of service towards an ideal. Self projection may be limited and focused unless the Fire element is well represented. There is also a strong need to be analytically correct, to say and do the "right" things. Change-ability is toned down in this mutable ascendant because of the Earth element.

LIBRA- Amiability. The need to be socially accepted will be very apparent. Also a strong concern about the physical appearance. On the positive side, the reflective tendencies take focus off of the self and increase sharing. On the negative side, acquiescence makes the self`s true stand of opinion or loyalty, elusive.

SCORPIO- The definition will be reserved, cautious, and secretive based on an extreme fear of being taken advantage of. The empowered Scorpio ascendant will be fearless and emotional insight keen. Depth of feeling. Confrontation welcomed. The dis-empowered will exhibit manipulation and little objective perception of the self. As an analogy of manipulation fears, the game of poker serves well. The identity would need to know all the opponent's cards (and would use any tactic to ascertain them), and not allow anyone to know theirs, just to feel equal to the game.

SAGITTARIUS- A definition of personal freedom. Travel as an effect of the need to expand the identity, or it's mental influence. As long as stability is shown elsewhere, integrity is usually the mode of operation. Beliefs and intellectual property issues, honesty or ethics and breadth of vision may be issues of self definition.

CAPRICORN- The identity definition is very down to earth, and not likely to indulge in speculation. The here and now is the immediate concern. Practical and organized. A very strong belief that physical reality exists outside the individual. Saturn's placement will be very important in analysis.

AQUARIUS- There is a brightness of individuality expression. Being defined differently is very important. Creativity must be applied or the identity will find anything to "rebel" against. Uranus' position will define what ideas and issues the identity believes it must break free from.

PISCES- A non-threatening posture. The identity unconsciously recognizes itself as a part or "All That Is" and may find projection in terms of *I* distasteful. Unless strength is shown in other configurations the definition of self may be elusive and problematic. A very sensitive and idealistic and perhaps sentimental ascendant.

The self has been "crystallized" as the persona through the Sun/Moon blend and clarified the definition of projection form through the ascendant. The following definitions of the inner planets reflect the identity's methods of interaction with the projected versions and counterparts of itself through the mind-matter mirror of the physical life.

The inner planets- Mercury, Venus, and Mars, represent the effects of identity definition choices and the corresponding psychological functions required to interpret and interact with physical reality. They are the lenses as well as the refracted light of "All That Is" manifesting itself in the apparently separated colors (types or versions of planets and positions). They don't affect us, they reflect us-because they are us in another version or expression. Life happens through us not to us.

REFRACTED LIGHT

The planet **Mercury** indicates conscious mind function as an effect of ego or persona definition. The identity sees itself, others, and life through the lens of Mercury and it's placement. The symbol for Mercury is the dish (crescent) on the circle of spirit, over the cross of matter. Venus; the circle of spirit on the cross of matter, or the mind-matter mirror. With the dish on top, Mercury becomes the receiver or perceiver of the mind-matter mirror, which is what physical reality is; the mirror of mind as physical matter.

Mercury is never more than 28 degrees away from the Sun in the horoscope. Venus is never more than 46 degrees away from the Sun. This symbolically reflects the idea that they are components and aspects of personality definition functioning in the realm of the conscious level or bank of material. Conscious mind and its functions (Mercury) either leads the life energy (ahead of the Sun) or is secondary to life expression (behind the Sun). Reflections and relationships (Venus) either alter external expression of the life energy by seeking approval first (ahead of the Sun) or relationships are internalized and made a part of the life energy (behind the Sun in sign and/or degree).

The following brief definitions of the sign placement of Mercury is all that is needed to begin to understand the way the identity believes it needs to interact in awake conscious terms with physical reality. The thinking needs and mental profile.

MERCURY IN

ARIES- The ego is bound up in the thinking process. An extreme conscious mind focus. Impulse, assertion, and the need to think, where no man has thought before. The pioneering thinker. Self assertion thoughts.

TAURUS- Plodding, stable and structured approach to thinking, planning and communicating. Methodical. The need to keep things as they are implies that there is the belief that the "something else" that comes along will be threatening to the identity. A belief in the need for patience, implies the belief that something "better" will come along. Nothing "better" will come along because this is a subjective value judgement. Things will always change, and they will always reflect perfectly the idea you are being at any given moment. Instability.

Change is the only constant in the Multiverse.

GEMINI- The lens of Gemini is Mercury. The mind is quick, facile, diverse, and communication fluent. This position reflects an accelerated functioning of the conscious mind. Unbiased, objective and logical-or clever, slick, superficial. The perception of the mind-matter mirror (unless in extremely developmental aspect networks) functions at it's highest speed and can manage many ideas at once.

CANCER- The impressionability can serve as an asset toward perception, and also as a liability in affecting it. Thinking may be caught up in emotional security or domestic/family concerns. Fear of ridicule. Reflective.

LEO- There are big bold and colorful ideas about life that are dramatized, also in reference to the self. Here self importance and dramatization can create bias. If the mind is applied to creative endeavors or the arts, then these traits will be an asset. Warm and/or egoistic thinking.

VIRGO- Again the lens of Virgo is Mercury. With this placement however, the focus upon the Earth element may not allow the identity to discern abstract aspects of thought as easily as the material aspects of experiences. An accelerated functioning with regard to material manipulation is a different type of "intelligence." If broader understanding is found elsewhere in the horoscope, then the categorizational characteristics of this placement will reflect strength in objective logic.

LIBRA- Unless the identity recognizes the self through social interaction, this placement tends to place the power of decision making upon others. When integrative, a finely balanced ability to weigh pros and cons enhances abstract reasoning.

SCORPIO- When positive, depth of understanding and significance real or implied. When negative, the fears of being taken advantage of obsess the thinking and perceptive functions. A need to find mental significance.

SAGITTARIUS- Positively, this placement can reflect a trusting and inspirational mental set with broad understanding. Negatively, an avoidance of facts or details so the identity will not have to take responsibility for it's creations. Viewing things with a broad brush may bias the person to see a "different forest" than the trees indicate.

CAPRICORN- Within more spiritual configurations, perception can be great. An understanding of physical reality and strategies within it. Disintegrated; a preoccupation with concerns of the physical world and it's "demands." Saturnine thinking replaces awareness.

AQUARIUS- When well aspected, the capability of innovative and scientific perspectives is enhanced. Logic and intuition blend. Negative; a preoccupation with the ego and it's innovations or uniqueness. A need to think "differently" may be to avoid boring facts.

PISCES- The thinking is blended with feeling. A feeling is a reaction to a belief. Therefore, all one may be re-acting to is the subjectivity of the self and it's unconscious projections. The mental set is best suited to inspirational or artistic endeavors where the identity may more easily see itself reflected. Objectivity needs expanding. When positive, intuition supports the correct answer and inspired desired effect.

Whereas Mercury represents cognition of the identity and it's reflections, **Venus** represents the reflections themselves. The mirrored polarity of the identity in physical versions. It rules the relationships of the identity to aspects of itself that may not be focused on within physical experience (as the self) but shadow aspects (outside the self). Venus represents femininity. Notice that the feminine signs of the template are Earth and Water. Physical reality (Earth) and it's accompanying momentums (Water). Physical reality reflects the feminine aspect of "All That Is." The feminine energy receives the energy of mind (Air) and spirit (Fire). (see chapter 1, Spirit).

Venus by sign, house and aspects represents psychologically, the needs for personal and social reflection (Tyl, Principles and Practice of Astrology, 1972).

The physicalized versions of the identity's beliefs about itself, are reflected through relationship with others and the physical "props" of material experience.

♀

VENUS IN

ARIES- The aspects of ego focus are explored through relationship. Exploration of things and people to reinforce ego importance. The hunt is more important than the kill. If the ego is secure, it is easy for the individual with this placement to see the self through relationship reflections and trust they support it's continued exploration. If insecure (dis-empowering beliefs), people and things are sought to enhance the ego's image.

TAURUS- High self esteem. Needs for personal and social reflection are fulfilled easily. The recognition that abundance is deserved just because the identity exists. If negative, the idea of possession becomes the end in itself.

GEMINI- The needs for reflection are cerebrated, mental and based on communication. The exchange of information colors relationship. A need to have a "meeting of the minds." When negative, thinking about relationship replaces the experience of it.

CANCER- Relationships and possessions reflect the identity's sense of nurturing and security. Sensitive and maternal. When negative reflections are pursued for the sake of emotional security. A need to protect the reflection.

LEO- The self needs dramatic reinforcement through relationship. Warmth and generosity are exuded. Pettiness is excluded. If negative, flamboyancy replaces sincerity.

VIRGO- Relationships for the sake of efficiency. Thinking the self through feeling. This can be an excellent position for analytical discernment of self beliefs through reflection. When negative analyzing emotions displaces getting in touch with them.

LIBRA- The need for reflection is strong. There is a strong desire for harmony. If positive this harmony is based upon the identity's recognition of itself in relationship. If negative, the identity loses identity clarity through acquiescence.

SCORPIO- The self seeks significance through relationship. If positive, transcendence is possible through ego transformation (emotional depth, and psychological insight). When negative, the self's paranoia to achieve emotional significance leads to indulgence in physical orientation, sex being paramount. Secretive.

SAGITTARIUS- This can be an excellent placement for higher self connection. Mental and intellectual concepts attract. However, there must be an extremely secure personality shown through the rest of the chart. There needs to be practical focus shown elsewhere also or conceptual idealization replaces personal sharing.

CAPRICORN- Emotional strategies. This is one of the more limiting positions of Venus. The individual may be so immersed in status issues, that relationships are chosen or initiated based on material considerations or advantage. Emotions have fallen in importance. There may be little perception of the self in others. Positively, there will be a down to earth reliability-a companion who is content to deal with everyday aspects of "getting ahead." The early environment needs to be inspected to find the reasons for emotional fear or perhaps lack of belief in deserve-ability. If integrated, emotional wisdom is possible.

AQUARIUS- This position can translate into unconditional love if self empowerment is exercised. An appreciation for all the different ways that infinite creation has of expressing itself is inherent. Intuition can be well developed. Friends are made easily. A need for humanitarian expression socially. If negative, the need for independence and the avant garde can cause difficulty in relationship. Seeking the "different" can amount to poor judgment.

PISCES- There is a very soft expression, and sentimentality is high. When positive the identity will express unconditional love and compassion for all living things. When negative the ideal becomes something tucked away, and illusions replace the experience of self reflection.

Mars represents the persona or ego's health as a whole. The physically evident aspects of the ego, conscious mind, and action as the expression of that persona in physical terms. The movement into and of the persona in physical reality.

On the psychological level, this translates into the need of the persona to validate the idea the oversoul chose as a general path to express in this life. The self definitions. It is the activating principle of becoming. Mars' orbit outside the Earth reflects the direction the personality's actions will lead; to the outer planets, the symbols of the experience of higher or deeper self in physical reality. Mars is the catalyst to propel the self "upstairs" (higher self). Its symbol is the circle of spirit activated by the arrow or motion of physical reality. Mars' position, sign, and aspects are very important in determining the integrity of the persona and health of the ego. Negative aspects reflect the disbelief in self power or ability for self directed action. Positive; the incorporation of the archetypes represented into the workings of the artificial construct called personality and natural expression.

MARS IN

ARIES- This is the natural position for Mars. When positive it is the symbol of the expression of natural aggression. A strong persona with fire behind it. When negative, temperament is the effect of the belief in a "battle between good and evil" or with the "difficulty" of self expression. Recklessness as the over-compensatory effect of believing the identity is restrained. Tactical.

TAURUS- There will be reflected in the personality, the need for security and a proving of the value structure. If positive, the security needs are perceived as fulfilled, which allows the identity to believe they will always be fulfilled abundantly. There is a methodology to applying energy and proving the self. Insecurity works against more spontaneous application of the self.

GEMINI- The identity needs to prove the self through the intelligence and the communication abilities. When positive sense perceptions are swift and accurate. Diversity in the physical and mental are necessary for balance and health. When negative, the identity will argue and attack mentally to try to establish intellectual domination.

CANCER- This position of Mars reflects that the identity believes it is at a disadvantage. That it is inherently powerless and must "plan to make sure" that it has the "insurance" of something to "fall back on" should what it pursue, "fail". These are all reflections of the belief in the invalidity of the identity. Doubt. By implication, if the identity makes a mountain out of a molehill it is reinforcing that it **must be** a mountain, and therefore will experience it as such. Emotional security considerations are tied to the action and expression of the persona. If positive, the identity will be able to find ego reinforcement through the nurture of others.

LEO- This placement needs and assumes that the persona must be dramatically ego reinforced. If positive, the identity will probably find this reinforcement through creative extension. This will allow the application of the self to more expanded endeavors. If negative, the feelings of dis-empowerment will manifest as a person who tries to run everyone else's life because this is easier than taking responsibility for their own and are looking for reinforcement for a frail ego.

VIRGO- The need to prove the self as analytically correct. With breadth of vision, discernment is a powerful asset. When negative, value judgements of others reflect how much the self judges the self and criticizes the ego.

LIBRA- This placement is similar to Cancer. The spontaneity of self assertion is censored by the need for social acceptance by others. The validity of the self is tied to "proper" social behavior. If integrated, the self will begin to realize that it can't hide from itself and take self directed action regardless of popularity concerns to better social conditions.

SCORPIO- The need to prove the significance and deep psychological meaning of the persona can result in the transcendence of the self when positive. Intensity. If negative, we have a very volatile temperament as passion takes over the persona as an effect of paranoia and belief in powerlessness.

This position reflects a very strong momentum of the identity either way.

SAGITTARIUS- Here we have the need of the identity to prove validity through acceptance of the intellect. To sway others through validation of opinions. To advise. If positive, this energy will be applied to assisting others to higher self paths. When negative, a lack of objectivity leads to arguing and the attempt to force opinions upon others. If they have to be forced, the identity does not obviously believe them itself.

CAPRICORN- As long as strategy does not overwhelm spontaneity, this placement reflects the willingness and diligence to see the self manifested in physical reality. Focused application. Healthy ego orientation.

AQUARIUS- The fixed signs are not conducive to natural aggression as structure seeks accumulation of power rather than its expression. If positive, this placement indicates that invention and humanitarianism will be the area of experience that the self will find it's best application. If negative, the temperament is extremely touchy about the identity's uniqueness. Being different for the sake of being different.

PISCES- Unless the identity applies itself to spiritual work or the helping professions, the expression of identity will find it difficult to compete with egos that find natural assertion not so complex.

LIGHT SOURCE

As the solid and rocky spheres represent aspects of the physical self and conscious mind, so the outer and gaseous planets represent the aspects and functions of the higher self. They are the representations or conceptual aspects of existence within the Christ consciousness (solar system) on a thematic level.

Jupiter; the concept of the experience and expansion of concepts themselves. **Saturn**; the concept of the physically focused dream (material world) that apparently limits expression. **Uranus**; the concept of awakening unconscious awareness of the "All That Is" into the dream of physical focus. **Neptune**; the concept of experiencing ourselves AS the "All

That Is". **Pluto**; the concept of the Christ consciousness, wherein we realize that we are the consciousness we thought we existed within, transcend the system altogether, and view the system from the fourth dimensional perspective (referencing the orbital tilt).

The *effects* of Pluto and Neptune are basically the same; to change levels. This is why they share a similar orbit often (sometimes Neptune is actually closer in than Pluto).

The outer planets are "whence we came from" before incarnation, and "whither we go" as a person in the focused dream of physical reality. The stepping stones that lead back to "All That Is."

Definitions of the outer planet placements will be brief because much depends on the integrity of the person with regard to the incorporation and experience of the higher self and unconscious functions and themes.

Through **JUPITER**

Jupiter, the first planet outside the orbit of Mars, reflects the fruit of natural aggression, the opportunities from integration of positive ego (understanding the self). The "fruit" is the experience of abundant opportunities that are presented through the conviction of trust and action. Jupiter by template placement reflects the person's belief in the higher self. The unseen helping hands that manifest all the opportunities the self will need to continue to follow what it excites it to do (with integrity) as an effect of that trust. Jupiter reflects the overall concept of that bliss by house, sign and aspect network. It inflates and expands the archetype and house, either positively or negatively.

JUPITER IN

ARIES- The concept and experience of trust in the persona and self validation.

TAURUS- The concept and experience of trust in the self's values, resources and worth. The trust in stability.

GEMINI- To trust in the experiences of conscious mind and the accompanying diversity and appreciation of knowledge.

CANCER- Jupiter is exalted in Cancer. Trust in the inner self, and the experience of emotional security by always being in the "right" place emotionally.

LEO- The concept and trust in the ability to create, and enjoy creations, drama and love; re-creation or fun.

VIRGO- The concept of enjoying the details of physical focus. Specificity limits expanded awareness. Contradiction.

LIBRA- Trust in the concept, that you cannot experience a relationship to anything that is not a part of you on some level.

SCORPIO- Trust in the significance of the person's resources so that it is not more than, but equal to the higher self. Significance transcends death.

SAGITTARIUS- Trust in the concept of a higher power or higher self through knowledge, intellect and wisdom.

CAPRICORN- The most limited and focused position for Jupiter. Contradiction. Expansive concepts cannot be found through strategic implementation. Trust may be the problem.

AQUARIUS- Trust in the breadth and width of the application of individuality and co-creative interaction.

PISCES- Trust in the meeting of the concept of "All That Is," through selflessness in the physical dream. Empathic.

THROUGH SATURN

There is no planet more important in discerning an individual's momentum (accumulated beliefs), fears, and/or any limiting definitions that may be experienced in physical reality, than **Saturn**.

Saturn reflects the embodiment of the concept of the experience of physical reality. Saturn's placement by sign, house, and aspect network reveals with powerful sharpness, the individual's beliefs about reality that create experiences in the mirror of mind, matter.

Saturn's revolution, one complete orbit, takes approximately 29 years. It's quadratures by transit opening square, opposition, closing square, and return to birth sign and degree), occur at 7 years of age (opening square), 14 years of age (opposition-externalization) 21 years of age (closing square) and conjunction to it's place at birth at 28-29 years of age. These quadratures reflect critical developmental periods of belief (or fear) externalization into the physical experiences. Through it's birth position and corroborating life experiences, it DEMONSTRATES beyond a shadow of a doubt, that each and every individual creates the reality that they experience, LITERALLY. Fears *become scenarios.*

► "When an inner situation is not made conscious, it appears outside as fate." C.G. Jung

At 7 years of age, the beliefs inherent in the reflection of the birth chart configuration are internalized and established in physical reality through the experience of the beliefs/fears in the externalized reality. The registration of it may be unconscious. Never-the-less it will be experienced in full awareness (opposition) through events in the individual's life at or around age 14 (in varying degrees dependent upon awareness as always). This is the age of puberty, when full conscious commandment is *capable* of perceiving it's reality creations appearing as events outside the self. The opposition requires resolution. The resolution is in the owning of the experience as the effect of belief definition momentum manifestation that has accumulated through successive lives. In our analysis of life experiences in chapters that follow, this will be demonstrated as a discernment when we match life scenarios with the fears implied in Saturn's birth position.

How much difficulty in the world would have been avoided had every individual upon this planet taken responsibility for their creations rather than blaming the environment, the parents, "natural forces," the planets, the other person, the government? That is the nature of the beast; how to change behavior is the question. The world will only change when each individual takes responsibility for themselves and their co-creation participation as either *part of the solution or problem*. Before collectivities can change, individuals must change.

The "government"(s) is a reflection of Saturn (Satan)! Science is also a Saturnine affair (placing all power outside of the self, focus and exclusionary applications). This is neither good or bad, it is simply a locus of control issue.

There would be no need for government if every individual took responsibility for their own actions. It is created from fear of facing our own creations, so we create a "shell" identity to take responsibility for things we don't believe we can or are not willing to. It can only be sustained by fear. We create our own reality, therefore what do we need defense from? Of course this is utopian in nature to think this way (or is it?). But perhaps raising our children would be entirely different if this was understood and trusted by parents and a popular notion. When the power is placed outside the self we believe we need a defense against an external and oppositional environment.

Because focus is an aspect of physical reality, we forgot our natural state as co-creators and that we were created in the "image" of "All That Is." Saturn's placement reflects the self's individual "fall" from grace, buying into "Satan," "thinking with the mind of men, rather than of God," where we place the power in the external and believe we need protection from "the forces of nature," that everything can be "scientifically explained as natural phenomena." It's placement reflects where we do not believe that Godhood is the natural state.

The experience of limitation is not "the way it is," evidenced by the expanse of the universe, it is the *exception* to the way it is within the Multiverse. This view is not so utopian if we look at nature from this view replacing the striving view (survival of the fittest) with natural abundance.

Saturn's placement translates psychologically into the identity's greatest fears about the experience of physical reality. Therefore, it represents the strongest momentum of belief overall likely to manifest physically from fear, which is a belief. It represents the archetype of the father figure. The relationship with the father or father figure, will be a prominent issue in connection with the belief represented. Replacing fear with trust (Jupiter) is the resolution to Saturn.

Tremendous overcompensation occurs psychologically (within the archetype sign) and house placement of Saturn.

Through overdoing, over-strategizing, and over-control of the experiences connected with these placements, the person becomes a physical reality "expert." Through the integration of fears, one can transcend them and take back power from the apparently external and oppositional reality (the completed and fulfilled action of course-please see actualization).

♄

SATURN IN-

ARIES- The fear that the identity itself is under attack from the environment or "others." The greatest fear is that the ego self will not receive validation from the environment. Assertion will then be the "overcompensation."

TAURUS- The lack of self worth manifestation (resourcefulness), either materially or personally are the persona's greatest fears. Dependency on material forms as being the signature of worth.

GEMINI- The fear that the intelligence must be validated. Living by ones wits, translates into conscious mind function as the "real" experience.

CANCER- The emotional insecurity is so great with this placement, that the persona will have to have big accomplishments to replace the insignificant feelings that this position reflects. The parental structure has much to reveal.

LEO- Self extension is overdone to get attention. The ego structure is very insecure. This reflects a disbelief in the validity of identity and effortless creation as a natural consequence.

VIRGO- This placement reflects a tremendous belief in physical reality as something outside the self that can only be wrestled into submission through strict adherence to methods and procedures. The trees are far overdone, to the point that the forest may never be seen.

LIBRA- Fear of not being accepted by others leads to possibly being untrue to the self-or even awareness of what the self's true position is. Natural aggression is a must with this placement.

SCORPIO- The doom of the personal significance is keenly felt. The momentum of incarnations demands transformation of negative ego to higher self experience.

SAGITTARIUS- Tremendous intellectual overcompensation stemming from the fear that mental competence may be wanton. The higher self is believed to have been trampled under foot.

CAPRICORN- This is THE placement of dis-empowerment. The momentum of the ego structure is so enmeshed in seeing is believing and that external status determines true worth, that it will take many contradictory aspects and placements to change this discernment. A powerful player in the destruction of Atlantis.

AQUARIUS- The fear that society does not allow the individuality expression. Overcompensation to get "the good opinion" of others with regard to the self's contributions. The fear of the automatic invalidation of creative extension, if this acknowledgment is left to others.

PISCES- The momentum of fear of this position, is fear itself. Fear is always the effect of believing in the physical self and its separateness from life-or as all there is to life. Introspection has been neglected and now may be overdone. A perspective needs to be maintained regarding futility and powerless views, lest self pity replace self understanding. When positive, responsible holistic views develop.

THROUGH URANUS

Uranus symbolically represents the recognition of choice in the creation of our reality. This recognition comes about through the waking up from the dream of physical focus, to the dream of non-physical expanded awareness from a new way of *thinking*. The unconscious knowledge of our co-creatorship with "All That Is" that has fallen asleep while in the dream of physical focus. The orbit of Uranus lies between the orbit of Saturn (Satan) and the orbit of Neptune (the merging with "All That Is").

Psychologically, Uranus' placement reflects where the identity needs to awaken ideas connected to the sign (archetype) it is in. Dis-covery (uncovering aspects of the psyche) through the expression of the individuality and acting on what it excites the identity to do with integrity is how this awakening comes about. Aspects between it and other planets reflect how difficult or easy the self believes this archetype awakening will be. Rigidity may be implied in a planet in relationship with Uranus if the aspects are negative.

URANUS IN-
ARIES- The awakening of natural aggression, and the trusting of instincts.
TAURUS- Needs to wake up and recognize the choice of positive or negative self worth definitions, and access to resources.
GEMINI- The awakening of the limitless functions of the conscious mind and the exploration of duality.
CANCER- The recognition of inner self infinity. Emotional security awakened through the recognition of security as a definition choice.
LEO- The need to recognize the identity as the infinite creator; a need to awaken creative extension and giving love without condition.
VIRGO- The need to awaken application of innovation to practical service. The recognition of the capability to choose discernment instead of judgement.
LIBRA- The need to wake up to the recognition that anything or anyone you experience must be a part of the identity on some level. So which self do you choose to define yourself to be? New ways to relate.
SCORPIO- The awakening of the higher self, through transcendence of negative ego.
SAGITTARIUS- The need to recognize a choice in conceptual definition and the validity of all opinions.
CAPRICORN- The recognition of the choice in the creation of the physical reality and one's own status.

AQUARIUS- The need to wake up as one of the equal but unique ways that infinite creation has of expressing itself.

PISCES- The need to recognize the choice and the ability to wake up and dream the dream you prefer to dream and that compassion stems from the recognition of the all as one.

THROUGH NEPTUNE

Neptune indicates by house, sign, and aspect network, where the "All That Is" will be made manifest through the unconscious choice by dissolving ego focus. Neptune reflects where the non-physical dream, merges with the physical dream. Where co-fusion takes place and the apparent separation of the self from its reality no longer exists.

The imagination is the door to other worldliness. Whatever you can imagine, *must* exist on some level, otherwise it's conceivability would not exist. Neptune is the "antithesis" of Saturn. For in non-physical or dream reality it is *physical* reality that is the dream and the illusion. The illusion of the Saturnine fear dissolves with the recognition of the eternity and indestructibility of the soul. A lack of trust in the non-physical reality and the imagination as the door that can serve, is the reason for dis-illusionment.

We cannot "serve two masters," one reality will always be "an illusion." It makes sense then to allow the one that is eternal, to be the one we image-in(e) is the "real" one.

All forms of sacrifice are the effect of this unconscious recognition of the transitory experience of the physical dream. The ideal-our God and a more encompassing reality will be explored and learned wherever Neptune resides.

NEPTUNE IN-

ARIES- Ego focus needs to be dissolved. Reluctance to do so results in self deception or invalidation of identity.

TAURUS- The power is placed outside the self and security is sought in material forms. The need to recognize the unseen support of infinite creation.

GEMINI- The need to dissolve the boundaries of conscious

mind function. This may result in the need to mentally experience all other than is easily perceptible or conceivable.

CANCER- The need to expand the boundaries of the psyche and personal unconscious past the simple need for physical emotional security.

LEO- The dissolution of the idea of having to do something special in order to deserve love and the "right" to exist. Conditional love transcended to the unconditional. Spiritual creativity.

VIRGO- The need to dissolve the subjective perception of self. The recognition of self-less service. Understanding of the trees, must be incorporated into the understanding of the forest.

LIBRA- The dissolution of the boundaries of identity distinction. The recognition of the unconscious levels of self through others who act in service as that reflection.

SCORPIO- The shedding of the ego structure brings the recognition of the perspective of resurrection. Like the serpent or snake, the self sheds it's skin and shakes off death. A plant dies and its seeds spring up elsewhere.

SAGITTARIUS- The dissolution of the barriers to higher self functioning which is represented by the Centaur's lower animal half, the physical and the sensual.

CAPRICORN- The dissolution of Satan (Saturn). The dissolution of the apparent boundaries between the physical dream, and the non-physical dream. Material made God.

AQUARIUS- The messiah that brings the message that all individuals are co-creators with the infinite-and therefore *are* the infinite. That all beings reflect all the different ways that "All That Is" has of dreaming itself into existence. Alien.

PISCES- The dissolution of selfish desires allowing the merging and blending of the identity back into the "All That Is," without the "loss" of self.

THROUGH PLUTO

The planets of Neptune and Pluto remain in one sign of the template for very long periods (approx. 15 yrs to 24 yrs). These time periods may vary depending on sign placement, some shorter, some longer. The length of their transits reflect mass consciousness and collective archetypal experience and changes. The transformation of perspective as it evolves generationally, is revealed through these cycles. Within this collectivity of archetypal perspective alteration, each individual reflects a specific aspect of the overall consciousness through the natal birth placement by house, sign, and aspect network of Pluto or the "outer" planets. The recognition of the environment as the self, is the transformation of perspective reflected by Pluto. It embodies the Christ consciousness in every individual that remains latent until activated through the recognition of self-empowerment.

Through the death of Satan (Saturn) we awaken unconscious re-membering of our godhood (Uranus), dissolve the boundaries of confining ego definitions (Neptune), and are "born again" to the *perspective* of eternal life. That we are the external (Saturn), that we self-deceived (the "fall" of Adam and Eve) ourselves into believing we existed within. The second "coming" will be through the tapping into the Christ consciousness by each and every individual upon the planet. It may come at once, in waves, or a single person at a time. This is what is meant by "the Christ gave his life, so that we may be saved." *Every* individual that taps into the Christ consciousness, makes it that much easier for others to do the same. This is accomplished only through acknowledging complete responsibility for our reality, and the creations therein.

The Christ "broke ground" so that the path to Pluto, would be that much easier, that's all; by *expressing Neptune*.

The combination of Pluto and Uranus energy is physically reflected in the geophysical phenomena known as earthquakes. The more we chose to wake up on the conscious level, the less need will there to be "shaken" awake through the level of the collective unconscious.

PLUTO IN-

ARIES- Self-empowerment through the recognition of the ego self *as* the higher self. Perspective alteration through identity redefinition.

TAURUS- Self-empowerment through the recognition of the unlimited access of abundance from the infinite. Perspective alteration of values.

GEMINI- The conscious mind finds strength if self empowered. Redefinition of ego focused thinking that must be altered. Propaganda.

CANCER- The transformation of the boundaries of sources of emotional security and nurturing. Not within the confines of identity, family, country, but of infinite dimensions.

LEO- The transformation of perspectives with regard to personal self empowerment and the full use of creative powers-unconditionally. This is believed by some to be Pluto's exaltation sign.

VIRGO- Perspectives of focused application need alteration to include broader awareness. The need to recognize dis-ease, for what it is.

LIBRA- Self-empowerment comes through the altered perspective that the mind-matter mirror serves instead of challenges. Relationship perspectives and their significance change dramatically.

SCORPIO- We recently experienced this transit. The great Astrologer Grant Lewi delineated this position 40 years ago "Psychic research and education allow more people to become aware of their inner natures. Psychic talents are developed among many more people as spiritual awareness, peak experiences and ego loss become more common." This is the age and placement of transformation. The children born-in this time period, reflect the quantum leap of accelerated

perspective.[125] The beginning of the second coming of Christ.
SAGITTARIUS- The collective experience of the higher self manifested in the physical dream. The perspective alteration of the higher self as "real." All truths begin to blend into one. Propaganda and "spin" rampant.

CAPRICORN- The political, economic, the external in general transform to reflect inner knowingness of a self-empowered populace. Material prowess as a weapon.

AQUARIUS- Spiritual and scientific knowledge become one. The association of worlds becomes commonplace (extraterrestrial interaction).

PISCES- Mind and matter reflect the oneness of the "All That Is." Personal perspective alteration allows thinking as the only necessary element to travel. Understanding displaces power motives.

The experience of the Pluto positions past our present will be determined by the integration of the current concepts of self-empowerment.

In the following chapters we will apply the awareness and understanding of Astrological premise to the life experiences of some well known persons and some personal clientele. We will begin to use some of the methods outlined as we get a feel for their application. It is strongly recommended that the astrological texts recommended be explored in conjunction with this text for those beginning the study of astrology. This text is broad in scope and application. Specifics have been written and rewritten by some very talented astrologers and add to this text details that may allow some a more comfortable understanding of the chapters to follow (particularly the Noel Tyl and Robert Pelletier texts recommended).

Summary
I.   The horoscope reflects the *living light* that we are. The

---

[125]
        Pluto positions set the tone as the younger generation between 20 and 30 years of maturity exert their perspective.

sun/moon blend and the ascendent reflect the trinary aspects of the persona or personality form that we "sound through" in physical reality.

II.   Feelings are reactions to beliefs. The moon represents the reigning need of the personality and what is believed needs nurturing and the image we visualize ourselves to become.

III.   The sun/moon blend acts as the basic and most important key in delineating personality.

IV.   The rising sign is then the mask that the personality wears to project the personality through. The face presented to the world and the way the identity specifically defines the idea that it is.

V.   *Mercury* is conscious mind functioning and the thinking profile.

VI.   *Venus* is the need for personal and social reflection and the relating profile.

VII.   *Mars* is the natural aggression instincts and need to prove the self and the ego profile.

VIII.   *Jupiter* is conceptual experience and higher self recognition and reflects the idea of expansion.

IX.   *Saturn* reflects the actualization of belief into physical reality. It is the fear profile and where power is placed outside the self.

X.   *Uranus* is where the aspects of power given away that have been crystallized at Saturn are awakened. It is the individuation profile.

XI.   *Neptune* is where ideals and versions of God are found in the profile of beliefs (horoscopic gestalt) and where sacrifice may be made as the disbelief in the ability to manifest it. Where Neptune is ideas are co-fused into a greater reality and identity is feared lost and where ideals need to be found. It is the escape and dissolution profile (as the defense against physicality).

XII.   *Pluto* is where transformation of petty ego focus is transformed through value interaction and destructurization of subjective value judgements. This allows us to see the perspective profile. It is the transcendence profile as well.

Index of terms and Concordance

Supplementary reading list

Allen, Bem P. Personality Theories.
Massachusetts: Allyn & Bacon.
        1994
Anka, Darryl. The New Metaphysics.
California: Light & Sound Communications Inc.,
        1987
Arroyo, Stephen. Astrology, Karma and Transformation.
Washington: CRCS Publications.
        1978
Campbell, Joseph. The Power Of The Myth, W/Bill Moyers.
New York: Doubleday.
        1988
Pelletier, Robert. Planets in Aspect.
Massachusetts: Para Research Inc.
        1974
Lewi, Grant. Heaven Knows What.
Minnesota: Llewellyn Publications.
        1977
Lewi, Grant. Astrology For The Millions.
Minnesota: Llewellyn Publications. Bantam Edition
        1980
Ruperti, Alexander. Cycles Of Becoming.
Washington: CRCS Publications.
        1978
Sakoian, Frances & Acker, Louis. The Astrologers Handbook
New York: Harper & Row Inc.
        1989
Tyl, Noel. Astrology 1-2-3.
Minnesota: Llewellyn Publications.
        1980
        Holistic Astrology.
        1984
        Astrology 1-2-3.
        1991
        Prediction In Astrology.
        The Horoscope as Identity
        1974
Yott, Donald H.. Astrology and Reincarnation
York Beach Maine: Samuel Weiser Inc.
        1989

Chapter 8

The Identity Experience
Belief

> "The senses turn outward;
> Man, therefore, looks toward what
> is outside, and sees not the inward being.
> Rare is the wise man who shuts his
> eyes to outward things and so beholds
> the glory of the Atman within."
> The Upanishads

Every natal horoscope becomes active through the triggering of the early environment. The unconscious is not an empty "blank slate." Momentum of belief is carried into the birth chart. The horoscope becomes active at birth. The horoscope exists before the early environment. The parental structure is chosen by the oversoul previous to incarnation, as the "hallway of experience" containing the most compatible momentum necessary to trigger beliefs and concepts that will best serve in accelerating the awareness of the identity involved. The horoscope reflects the themes that will best accomplish agreements made prior to the physical life.

The early environment does not pattern a "blank slate" unconscious, but acts as a catalyst to assist in the acceleration of unconscious identity definition already *primed* with belief. Recognition of this premise alleviates the dis-empowering perspective of parental "blame."

How willing any person is to know themselves utterly determines the effects of the life thereafter. Self knowledge is the key to proactive as opposed to reactive behavior.

- "...memory does not so much PRODUCE as DISCOVER personal identity, by shewing us the relation of cause and effect among our different perceptions." David Hume on personal identity.

  "The demand that he should see only objectively is quite out of the question, for it is impossible. We must be satisfied if he does not see too subjectively. That the subjective observation and interpretation accord with the objective facts proves the truth of the interpretation only in so far as the latter makes no pretense to be generally valid, but valid only for that area of the object which is being considered. To this extent it is just the beam in one's own eye that enables one to detect the mote in one's brother's eye. The beam in one's own eye, as we have said, does not prove that one's brother has no mote in his. But the impairment of one's own vision might easily give rise to the general theory that all motes are beams. Carl Gustave Jung Collected Works Vol 6.

The identity is established in the earliest environment when perceived patterns of "the way life is" are encoded as a schema then reflected in the chart. Understanding this schema is the most valuable offering I believe astrology to supply. Because if we can own this schema and definition as the product of choice-it is far easier to change.

▸   Research on what leads to variations in patterns of attachment has focused on several likely factors: The behavior of the mother toward the child, the capacities and temperamental disposition of the child, and the child-rearing patterns of the cultural group to which the mother and child belong. The Development of Children, Chapter 6 *The End of Infancy* "The Causes of Various Patterns of Attachment", Michael Cole & Sheila R. Cole, 1993, page 232.

The analysis of the early environment is as much a benefit to the analyst, as to the analyzed, for it allows us an empathic understanding of the whys and wherefore's of the encoded schemas reflected in these patterns. And because of this, its possible to understand the most likely events to be created and experienced in later life when these patterns are triggered by future planetary configurations.

The Universe does not contain built in meaning. The purpose of astrological analysis is the discernment of the meanings *given* it by the owner of the chart. The counselor brings their own sensibilities acquired through self understanding, and introspective awareness into the analysis. The meanings given to reality are established in the early environment as a *template* of foundational perspective that the person then extracts experience from as their life evolves.

We are taught that physical reality and experience exists

separate from us. Is it any wonder that physical appearance is so important in most societies? Nor is it any revelation that reasons for limitation or difficulty are rarely seen as the *total* effect of perspective. Science reinforces this, assigning "cause" to genetics that removes personal connection and responsibility-the *ability* to respond. If we get Cancer, it must be in some dietary pattern of intake, or ecological substance. Attitude, it is believed, has very little to do with it. Attitude has *everything* do with it.

Therefore in line with my previous assertions, the following life paths are not the effect of astrological "influences." Nor are they the effect of parental influences. The horoscope is the hallway of choice. Therefore, these charts are reflective of certain "hallways" of experience chosen by spirit. This hallway of choice is then acted upon by the free will of the physical self. So any way we spin it, it remains free will. It is the conscious commandment or awareness of the physical self that utterly determines the quality of the trip down that hall.

There is no *one* way to go down a "hallway." It can be an exceedingly horrid experience, or it can be the most ecstatic experience ever. But we *willed* ourselves down that hallway.

As discussed in previous chapters, it is conscious mind value judgements that determine this. However, to introduce astrological procedure is the main goal at this point. To lead towards an understanding of the significance of precisely how we create our reality, and how astrology allows us to understand our specific journey. Astrology is the most powerful tool in the expansion of this recognition.

Identity is viewed through the condition and placement of the 1st and 7th axis. This axis reflects what sort of polarity from the experiential template the person deems most reflective of their specific self definition.

The 4th and 10th houses reflect aspects of identity's beliefs about status and the internalized parental schema the person *creates*. Identity and status are co-created and formed together. Self definition allows status considerations to be derived from these definitions. The parental structure acts as a catalyst (being a part of identity/status quadruplicity) in the formation of belief patterning through the aspects etc.. These aspects then act as a base or springboard for personal unconscious "hallway" creation.

The horoscope of Marilyn Monroe[126] on the following page reflects tremendous insecurity. By using the methods outlined in chapter 4, the element count shows a conspicuous lack of the Earth element. The belief that the physical is something "less" than ideal. It reveals the disbelief that the ideal *can* be found in physicality. Physicality is cruel and difficult, and the self believes that it's ideals are of the finer realms. Her difficulties with responsibility is well known; a reflection of this distaste for physicality.

The Fixed Mode count is also extremely high, a strong need for structure, and a very powerful emotional energy or momentum. Habits would be difficult to break.

The Sun is in Gemini, Moon in Aquarius; A strong need to share ideas and concepts, the practical expression or implementation of them however is missing (Earth) (page 250).

The ascendant is in Leo; Unless more down to earth energies are reflected through the remainder of the horoscope, the identity may be manipulatable through appeals to ego reinforcement. From the life we know she lived, it seems that physical appearance *was* this reinforcement. The reinforcement that kept the ideals to share ideas and concepts as a *secondary* need. She was not known as the definition required by the reigning need reflected in the Sun/Moon blend. Therefore, there was no *fulfillment* of the reigning need, no matter how famous or admired. The Moon in Aquarius needs to be recognized for its uniqueness. There can be no respect engendered as to ideas and concepts expressed, if the definition is a "dumb blonde" sex symbol.

The Moon, the symbol of the mother, opposes Neptune (dissolution) and squares Saturn (focus and fear). The reigning

---

[126] All chart data sources are from Noel Tyl, Marc E. Jones, or personal communication with the individuals under analysis unless otherwise noted.

need is believed to be separate from physical reality (Saturn) and that nurturing emotional security will not be found in the physical (Saturn). The ideal needs incorporation and resolution with the self image (Moon opposition Neptune).

The physical early environment reflected these beliefs through the mother's inability to care for her. Numerous foster homes, and early sexual violation-presumably with one or more of the "father figures"-was obviously devastating to identity validity and emotional security (Saturn in Scorpio Rx in the 4th house).

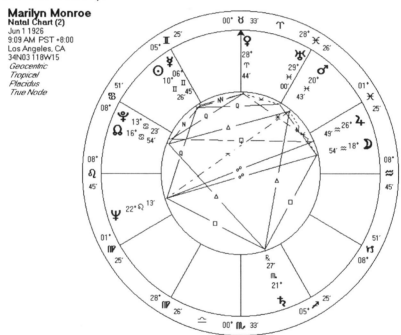

Marilyn Monroe
Natal Chart (2)
Jun 1 1926
9:09 AM PST +8:00
Los Angeles, CA
34N03 118W15
Geocentric
Tropical
Placidus
True Node

The reasons for incarnation are reflected through the 12th house and it's ruler and configurations. This house and the others that reflect the unconscious (4th and 8th) tell us much about unconscious momentum (beliefs).

Cancer is on 12, ruled by the Moon in the 7th; The need to wake up the unconscious with regard to co-creating interaction (Aquarius) through the projected aspects of self (through others in the 7th).

Pluto, the ruler of the 4th and dispositor of Saturn, is *in* the 12th, protecting from the intrusion of the unconscious and perspective through the Grand trine, and is disposed of by the Moon. This reflects the strong fear of being taken advantage of through vulnerability.

Saturn (physical focus) needs to be integrated into the personal unconscious aspect of the persona (base of the T-square and the grand trine). Saturn is in the 4th house in Scorpio; The doom of personal significance (Scorpio) is keenly felt-was keenly felt through the early environment. The lack of belief in the Earth element was reflected in the early environment, and is corroborated by the placement of Saturn (greatest fears). The lack of physical security in her early environment did not influence her to believe that physical reality would not reinforce her definition, it reflected her *belief* that it would not.

The experience then of the early environment being insecure, may have re-inforced the already existent belief (that fit the thematic definition is what is meant) at birth. The mother was institutionalized and the father was no nowhere to be found. She spent most of her childhood in numerous foster homes. Spiritually, this refection of inner dynamics of the personal unconscious beliefs (Moon, and the 4th house) was not created to reinforce the existing beliefs, but to reflect them back to the identity, so that a preference of definition can take place consciously. But when we believe that reality is outside of us, this experiencing of the reality as the effect of our definitions then becomes a reinforcer of them as well.

The Moon is in the T-square from the 7th to the 1st and 4th. An identity/status crisis to accelerate perspective and thinking (Saturn rules the 6th. Moon rules the 12th, and Neptune rules the 9th). The sun rules the ascendant (identity definition) and is the "way out" of the crisis (trines the Moon in the 7th). This reinforces the idea we already established as a possible momentum with regard to appearance and Leo ascendant. Saturn also forms a grand trine with the Mars/Uranus conjunction in 8 (9th cusp), and the node and Pluto in 12. A self sufficient containment of the emotions to defend against the fear of being taken advantage of.

These significators are all strong signatures of the belief in vulnerability and powerlessness. The grand trine protects the unconscious from intrusion 4th, 8th, and 12th houses). Neptune in the 1st house square Saturn in 4 reflects this powerful belief in the separation of the ideal and non-physical reality, and the concretization of identity in physical focus.

Saturn is also retrograde. A signature that the identity is in a state of reassessment about physical focus, and a repression of this function (through the belief in the need to re-align its significance).

Jupiter in the 7th house is also square Saturn, expansion and contraction (or control) are believed in conflict and are in need of fulfillment. Saturn rules the 6th of discernment, and Jupiter rules the 5th, creative extension and love giving. These archetypes were chosen by the higher self to be integrated through the life experience, to recognize them as polarities of single ideas-not the real vs the ideal. Power is placed outside the self (the 7th as the mirror) in hopes of the environment providing stimulus to transform perspective through the Saturn in Scorpio, where it is the inner self and unconscious that needs to be transformed (4th house, Moon aspects). The T-square arrow (Saturn in 4) is released and "affects" the affairs of the 10th (life direction, externalized beliefs as status).

This law of momentum flow is also reflected throughout the chart; Mars/Uranus conjunction in 8, the need to wake up (Uranus) the persona (Mars) through introspection and ego dissolution (Pisces) and transform perspective (8th) to higher self functioning (Mars rules 9th and disposes of Venus ruler of the 3rd).

Neptune in the 1st *also* reflects a need to dissolve ego focus for redefinition. The planets reflecting persona (inner and personal) are all in conscious-mind ego focused signs-except Mars in Pisces and the Moon in Aquarius. They are involved in the grand trine and t-square networks. This effectively cuts off and separates the conscious from the unconscious moon (personal unconscious and rules 12, also Mars is in Pisces in the Water grand trine in the matrix of the unconscious).

The next chart has the transiting planets outside the natal horoscope and are the transiting positions at the time of her death during the filming of the movie co-incidentally entitled, "Something's Got To Give"! Her repeated failures to show up on the set during the filming, were reportedly because of illness (dis-ease). T-Saturn, the physicalization of beliefs (or fears), is in the 6th (analytical discernment in preparation for the meeting of the self in 7, opposing the ascendant identity definition).

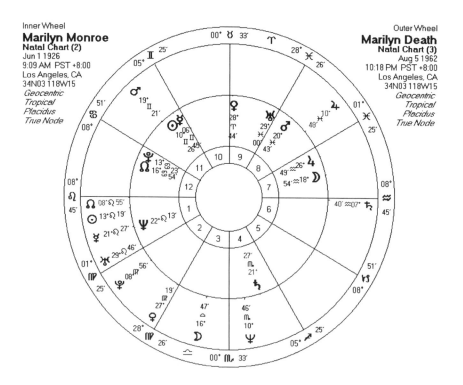

Inner Wheel

Marilyn Monroe
Natal Chart (2)
Jun 1 1926
9:09 AM PST +8:00
Los Angeles, CA
34N03 118W15
Geocentric
Tropical
Placidus
True Node

Outer Wheel

Marilyn Death
Natal Chart (3)
Aug 5 1962
10:18 PM PST +8:00
Los Angeles, CA
34N03 118W15
Geocentric
Tropical
Placidus
True Node

Jupiter is in 8 (death), ruling 5 (creativity as an extension of identity definition), and is exactly square the Sun, ruler of the ascendant! Venus rules the 3rd (conscious mind), and the 10th (external status), and opposes the natal Uranus from the 2nd house (sense of resourcefulness) and 3rd/9th axis (thinking profile). Transiting Uranus is in the first house at 29 degrees Leo (need to accelerate waking up to "get off" this momentum), and opposes natal Jupiter in the 7th, ruler of the 5th. Since Uranus rules the 7th (the public and relationships or "reaping") there were obviously intense relationship issues on her mind.

We can easily see that measurements continually reinforce problematic initial deductions. The value judgements of early environmental experience could not be shaken and transformed. The identity was waiting for the dramatic role that would allow her the respect that she believed she needed to be regarded as someone whose "status" would be significant enough to be taken seriously in the expression and sharing of ideas and concepts, the **primary** definition needs of the persona.

Venus in the 9th (other's opinions) is also in critical degree acceleration and opposes the critical Uranus-a need to awaken the recognition of choice in these scenarios.

Transit Mercury is conjunct the Neptune discussed earlier and exactly square Saturn! Mercury rules the 11th (love received and creative interaction) and 2nd and 3rd (the worth profile) and Saturn rules 6 (work and the practical application of knowledge-remember we established her lack of trust and reference in these areas at the beginning of our analysis. Transit Saturn is square transit Neptune, and transit Mars is square Natal Mars. There just wasn't enough trust to overcome doubts. Pluto square (ruling 4) Sun (1) confirms our deduction.

In conclusion, the beliefs inherent as a momentum at birth, were reflected in the early environment to "set the stage" of the reigning needs to seek fulfillment. The conscious self free will chose to continue the beliefs in powerlessness in terms of sacrificing these needs (obviously through the belief that "this is the way things are"). In order to achieve external security, the mirror replaced sharing ideas and concepts. After this "substitute" was realized, identity crisis began all over again. It was the dis-ease with this recognition that accelerated the identity to the ultimate dissolution, death. In the drastic need for love and acceptance, "something had to give."

The next chart is a private case of a female. The element and mode count, shows moderately high Earth, definitely high Mutability. Low Water with Neptune, an outer and collective orientation, the only water planet point. Emotions sacrificed or dissolved somehow? Flexibility would be high as a defense against strong definition.

Female
Natal Chart (4)

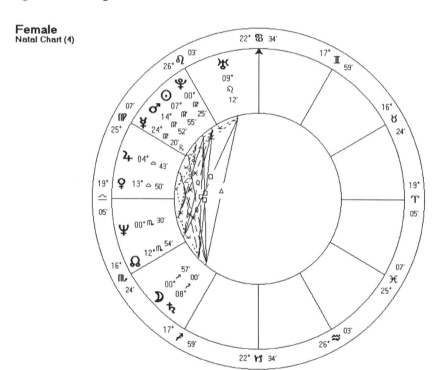

The Sun/Moon blend reads; The establishment of analytical discernment may be at odds with large concepts. Floating along with big ideas and never applying or bridging the gap between them and day-to-day reality. Incorporation of realism and blending it with idealism is necessary (page 255). We have much corroboration at this point already to indicate a possible lack of decisiveness and clear identity definition.

The ascendant is in Libra; Amiability. The need to be socially accepted will be very apparent. Also a strong concern about the physical appearance. However, the ascendant ruler, Venus is in the 12th house. We get the sense of identity dissolution with regard to the Libran idea from this placement. A law of momentum is already established. Further deductions will reflect this momentum. The hemisphere emphasis shows a decidedly eastern orientation. The "army" of planetary archetypes surrounding the ascendant definition to defend self projection (psychic investment page 204). There are no oppositions at all in the chart (externalized awareness or centralized focus). The reigning need (moon) is conjunct the greatest fears (Saturn). This conjunction is square (believed separate) the Sun, ruler of the 11th of creative interaction (or love received). The self worth (Saturn/Moon conjunction in 2) relies upon acceptance and respect for the intellect (Sagittarius), but in contradiction does not believe in it's manifest-ability (Saturn conjunct Moon, square the Sun).

Where would these beliefs about reality be most powerfully reflected and established? Saturn rules the 4th (early emotional security establishment), and the Moon rules the 10th (Saturn as well as the 10th house represent the father figure), the axis reflecting interaction with the parental structure.

The concept of relationship and the social mirror is the identity's definition and reason for incarnation; To look at the limiting effects of placing the power outside the self; to be accepted by others (Venus rules the ascendant and is in it's own sign in Libra in the 12th). The psychological effect in behavioral terms, would be an isolation or idealistic fantasy of the "perfect" relationship perhaps believed "not possible on the Earth plane." This is in effect a judgment of physicality as not being conducive to the real-ization of this desire and preference.

Mercury, the ruler of the 12th (self created limitations), is retrograde in Virgo; Reassessment of objective analytical discernment regarding "love received" from others, is another reason for incarnation.

In order to understand with clarity the possible physical manifestations of belief momentum, we find the placements of planetary positions at the time of most powerful externalization into physical reality of belief, *Saturn opposition it's birth placement* at or around age 14 years. This method of understanding the greatest fears and the materialization of them is used often in my practice (see Tyl volume VII *"Integrated Transits"*).

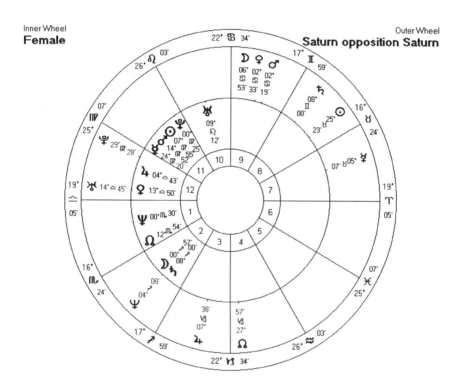

The planets outside the natal wheel are the transiting positions at the Saturn opposition Saturn.

The opposition of course, occurs in the polarity placement opposite natal Saturn. The fear of the intellect not being respected, would be real-ized through the early environment and disrupt the identity emotional security (Saturn ruling the 4th). The challenge to perspective through value interaction would be experienced (opposition from 8 to 2). Love received would be the casualty (the opposition squares the Sun in the 11th).

Transiting Uranus (ruling 5) is exactly conjunct the natal Venus in the 12th. The waking up of unconscious knowledge regarding the limiting perspectives of identity definition, and relationship beliefs. The natal planets of Pluto, Neptune, and the Moon, are all at 0 degrees, reflecting difficulty in initiating new perspectives, dissolving the boundaries of identity definition, and gaining respect for the intellect as a persona definition respectively. Transit Venus and Mars *both ruling the horizon line of identity* are conjunct in 9 (others opinions again!) opposing transit Jupiter and square the natal Jupiter in 12 (ruling her 3rd and is *the archetype of others opinions and thinking!*). They are square transit Pluto ruling the natal 2nd (worth) which is in the accelerated urgent need for clarity 29 degree Virgo placement in 12. Transit Neptune (dissolution) is at the Moon/Saturn midpoint ....transit Mercury opposes natal Neptune-all confirmations of the challenge to the *birth premise and definition.*

Upon her arrival, we discussed the aspects of creating our own reality, and that the consultation would be more of a sharing or discussion rather than a "reading." I conveyed to her what types of energy and beliefs I perceived reflected through her horoscope and the corresponding "feelings" or personal orientation of her personality as the effect of them. She acknowledged these and felt the identification empathically by myself were very accurate.

I immediately said that I would like to discuss the period around age 14, and gave her the specific date of the transits at Saturn opposition Saturn. I said that I believed at this time the issues we just outlined may have been "triggered" and there may have been sexual abuse from the father figure (she had already stated a stepfather situation), and that her need to be respected for her intellect to ensure her worth, obviously was crushed by this experience. She said "no one knows this except my stepfather and myself." Intercourse had apparently continued for some time, and she was afraid her mother had found out (Moon aspects).

She came to me initially to discuss her plans to marry her fiance. After realizing how these scenario's were created however, and that she felt there may be unresolved issues-she decided that perhaps an incorporation of self introspection to find resolution and to feel complete as she was, was perhaps what she really needed at this time.

In conclusion, the identity experienced it's greatest fears through the early environment, through the parental structure. This is not meant to imply that they *must* be experienced in this way. It is awareness of course that determines much, and we must find ways to allow ways for these clients to convey experience without feeling as if they are the perpetrators. Judgment and value structures must be carefully discerned so as to not perpetuate any direction for blame. But the implications of astrological discernment and measurement-at the very least-are indicative of a plan of some sort from other realms and the higher self.

However, if and when they are experienced in this way (painfully), the only way they will change, is by recognizing how events can serve the identity by showing it its part in their creation. Not in an accusatory way, but as an effect of identity definition. Whatever the parents (or other perpetrators) experience or derive from their dis-integrating and powerless acts is their responsibility and will be met. Either in the present, in the future, or in another life, but it will be met.[127] We cannot be responsible **for** anyone, we can only be responsible **to** them, by being as much as we can be in reflective example. (Of course parents **are literally, through being physically**

---

[127] Of course there are laws and external controls to ensure the safety of individuals, I am not addressing that issue here.

responsible for the child's welfare).

Whatever meaning is put into a scenario, will determine the effect extracted from it, as we will see through our next example.

Horoscope number three is the horoscope of Charles Manson, convicted murderer. Once again we see tremendous insecurity. Our element count shows only one point in Fire, and is represented by Uranus in the 12th retrograde! The only Fire reference is repressed (retrograde) perhaps limited (12th house) and reflects a need to seek awareness of self limiting perspectives. There would be extreme difficulty in entering into experience with faith, trust, and energy. He proclaimed that ***society*** (Pisces-12th) was *responsible* for making him what *he* (Aries) was! Uranus (the recognition of choice) is in Aries (the ego self identification and application), the need to wake up

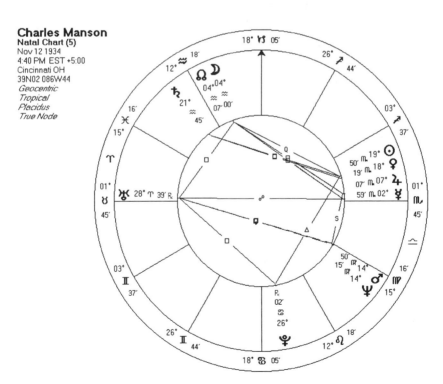

Charles Manson
Natal Chart (5)
Nov 12 1934
4:40 PM EST +5:00
Cincinnati OH
39N02 086W44
Geocentric
Tropical
Placidus
True Node

identity *definition as the form of responsibility-***natural** assertion, and spontaneity of the ***identity***.

Uranus is in the 12th (reason for incarnation) and needs reassessing (retrograde). The mode count shows a very strong energy momentum, and structure of belief (Fixed). The Sun/Moon blend reads; The establishment of identity may have experienced disruption in the early environment. An intense need to have uniqueness respected. A worthy goal needs to be defined early to apply vision in an altruistic manner. If insecurity mounts, there is a possibility of a powerfully disruptive identity expression (page 259). It is well known that his mother was absent and, the father not really known. Very disruptive early environment indeed. The ascendant is in Taurus; The self projection and definition seeks a stability and establishment in worth terms. The presentation of self is calm and focused. The identity revolves around issues of worth. Venus' position corroborates further identity definition.

His Venus (the 1st house chart ruler of identity) is in 7 in Scorpio. Now we have a powerful need for emotional significance through others as an aspect of identity definition. Venus squares Saturn (identity's greatest fears). The definition for Saturn in Aquarius; The fear that society does not allow the individuality expression. Overcompensation to get "the good opinion" of others with regard to the self's contributions. The fear of the automatic invalidation of creative extension if this acknowledgement is left to others (page 285). The reigning need, it is believed, cannot be fulfilled. This dis-empowering belief is reinforced by the low count (or disbelief) in the Fire element. The identity believes it is nonsense to have trust and faith (paranoia). The conscious mind and critical thinking (Mercury) needs to wake up (Uranus) to the recognition of a choice in the creation of it's experiences (Mercury and Uranus opposed-***across the horizon line of identity***). There is an out of sign Grand cross configuration involving Pluto in 4, Uranus in 1, Mercury in 7 and the Moon/Node conjunction in 10 in the houses of identity (1st to 7th) and its extensions status (4th and 10th)!

Pluto is retrograde in Cancer in 4. The reassessing of the need to transform and transcend the personal unconscious projections (Pluto rules the 7th and disposes of all planets in Scorpio) and take power back.

The Grand cross between Uranus in 12, Pluto in 4, Mercury in 6 conjunct the 7th, and the Moon in 10, reflects an identity crisis in perspective *about* the self's status!

The Moon rules the 4th (early environment), and is in a Grand cross pattern with Mercury ruling 2, critical degree on the 3rd, and the 6th (self worth, conscious mind thinking, and analytical discernment respectively), moon opposed Pluto (power and perspective) ruling the 7th (unconscious projections of the self), and Uranus ruler of 11 (love received). The early environmental emotional perspective, needed to be integrated with a conscious (Mercury) recognition of choice (Uranus) in the creation of his reality. A powerful belief in powerlessness and the futility of ever finding significance for individuality expression, was *his choice* in belief. The higher self chose these early environmental scenarios to challenge perspective (Grand cross) and conditions on giving of love and creative extension (Venus rules 1, is conjunct the Sun, and both square Saturn-Saturn rules 10, Sun rules 5). Neptune rules the 12th, the reason for incarnation was to dissolve ego focus (conjunct Mars) in the creative extension process.

Aries and Libra, the polarity of identity expression are intercepted (missing in reference) in 6 and 12 (the self created Imitations), and Uranus (choice) is at critical degree and being reassessed in the archetype of Aries-(*identity* definition)!

When we see planets in critical degree, as well as being retrograde, the issues experienced are a repeat performance, and need transforming urgently. There is a negative spiral that has been created by conscious mind-ego (the free will of the physical self) in the belief of reality existing outside the self. This leads to insisting on placing responsibility or experiences *on the environment* which *is* the self!

Negative expression must always be the effect of the belief

in powerlessness.

In conclusion, the higher self chose a challenging hallway by providing very little external reinforcement in the early environment to drive the identity inward in search of it's foundation. Conscious mind judgement was that the identity was somehow less equal to other co-creators (Aquarius). And in this perceived threat to establishment of identity uniqueness and significance, the identity strikes out to defeat and overthrow the perceived external threat, and in the end fulfills the belief in invalidation of creative extension. Practicing *domination of others* which reinforces the belief in the disparate ability and potentiality of all co-creators.

The Moon (personal unconscious) is conjunct the north node This could have been a life of powerful transformation, (moon rules 4) and brilliant application of the innovative expression of identity-if responsibility for actions in the past and the present life was accepted. The more the power is placed outside the self, the more of a "threat" it becomes, a catch 22.

This "blaming" turns into a negative spiral of defending the identity from itself over several lives and may eventually create a "dead end" scenario such as this, wherein the identity has nowhere else to go, but within (12 and 4). Please refer to my explanation of the overcompensatory pendulum, Chapter 1, page 25.

Perhaps confinement is the only way to stop the accelerating placement of power outside the self, and loss of recognition of the natural state of infinite creatorhood. However, a state of mind can develop *anywhere*. Full responsibility=full freedom.

Merlin the magician said after victory by King Arthur over evil throughout the land; "Be silent, be still, that's it. And look upon this moment. Savor it. Rejoice with great gladness, great gladness. Remember it always, for you are joined by it, you are **one under the stars**! Remember it well then, this night, this great victory. So that in the years ahead you can say, 'I was there that night, with Arthur the King!

For it is the doom of men that they forget."

Chapter 9

The Creation Experience
Emotion

"To be who we are, and to become
what we are capable of becoming,
is the only end in life."
Spinoza

For many years I experienced the dilemma of trying to find the purpose of living. Plato's statement that "the purpose of living is to discover the purpose of living" satisfied this need, as the overall purpose of life itself may never be known. Life is an actualiZING principle, rather than an end. The self that I am now-regardless of reincarnational or other dimensional "selves" that may be-is the only self I will be in *this* life. To be *that* self to the fullest is the primary goal and purpose in the now.

The overall master plan of an infinite Universe spanning billions of light years, and an infinite number of dimensional experiences is at our stage of awareness, incomprehensible.

In questioning the purpose of living, I became aware of the fact that by doing this I was discovering more of myself as I discovered more of life. This falls in line with the idea of the self-actualizing individual. Self-actualization is when seeking fulfillment, a person eventually recognizes that it is primarily through the *process* of becoming that they are truly fulfilled. The idea of an end in and of itself becomes secondary to the experience of living.

▸   "The general actualizing tendency, an "inherent tendency of the organism to develop all its capacities in ways which serve to maintain or enhance the organism." (Rogers, 1959, p. 196)
"The tendency toward self-actualization is a person's lifelong process of realizing his or her potentialities to become a fully functioning person." The expression of self-fulfillment is the psychological entity that becomes actualized: "to be that self which one truly is" (Rogers, 1961, p. 166)

There are characteristics which the self actualizing individual exhibits, in a recent survey using the POI (personal orientation inventory) only 1 in 3000 have the attributes of the true self actualizing individual.

Prime conditions in perspective are as follows;
1)open to experience.
2)they are time competent, stay focused regardless of judgments and are non-judgmental.
3)Awareness-the conscious apprehension of experience.
4)live in the now.
5) there is a strong level of self-congruence, meaning that the ideal self desired and the self actually expressed are congruent. Also expressed as a state of genuineness in interactions with others.
6) accurate empathy (expressed in this text as analytical discernment)i.e. being able to separate the self's beliefs from the empathic perception or discernment of another's belief system.
Maslow's (person centered psychologist) hierarchy of needs are stated thus, whatever level the individual becomes preoccupied with determines the quality of the life (expressed in this text as the positive-negative charts or philosophical structure);

In order of lesser or less actualized to greater or self actualizing;

physiological needs
safety needs
belongingness and love needs
esteem needs
self-actualization needs

Most individuals function at the levels below esteem, worrying and focusing on these primary needs associated with "survival" etc., obviously more ego focused. They correspond to the concepts of deficiency needs (lower or negative perspective) or growth needs (higher self or positive perspective). This is achieved through self-empowering perspectives.
To aid in understanding, here are some of the characteristics of the growth oriented or self actualizing person (the person actively integrating their chart).

Clear, efficient perceptions of reality and comfortable relations with it.
Acceptance of self, others, and nature.
Spontaneity, simplicity, and naturalness.
Problem centering.
Detachment and need for privacy.
Forceful will and relative independence from the environment.

(self-empowered)
>   Continued freshness of appreciation.
>   Mystic experience, peak experience.
>   Personal relations with others is characterized by deep but
>   relatively few (because they are past the needs of esteem and
>   belongingness)
>   Ethical discrimination between means and ends.
>   Philosophical, unhostile, sense of humor.
>   Creativeness.
>   Transcendence of any particular culture.

Imperfections; Usually seen as-thoughtless, socially impolite, cold, boring, irritating, stubborn, ruthless, forgetful, humorless, silly, angered, superficially prideful, naively kind, anxious, guilty, and conflicted without maladjustment.

Self actualized persons are people who fulfill themselves by making complete use of their potentialities, capacities and talents, who do the best they are capable of doing, and who develop themselves to the most complete stature possible for them. They include persons such as; Abraham Lincoln, Thomas Jefferson, Albert Einstein, Eleanor Roosevelt, Harriet Tubman, Albert Schweitzer, Jane Adams, Frederick Douglas, Caesar Chavez, Martin Luther King, Mother Teresa. (Personality Theories, Bem P. Allen, 1994, pg 253).

This view creates a different perspective, wherein the purpose of living becomes simply to be and express as fully as possible the "I" we are being at any given moment. If "All That Is" possessed the conviction to manifest the idea we are being, then we would be remiss to not trust expressing that idea as fully as possible. It is the lack of belief in identity validity and worth that deters any creation from it's full expression. If we did not deserve to exist, then we simply would not.

Therefore, as the Zodiacal template reflects, creative extension automatically manifests as an effect of identity definition (Aries to Leo trinary expression). It is our birthright, simply because we exist to effortlessly create. What special thing did we have to do in order to exist? Nothing. Therefore, what special thing must we do in order to extend that creation?

The 2nd, 5th, 8th, and 11th houses of the horoscope reflect the beliefs of the self regarding creative potential and expression of that potential based on beliefs of deservability and resource-fullness.

The belief in and trust of resource-fullness affects the

threshold of believability (please refer to definitions list, Chapter 1). We lack nothing, we have all the tools and abilities we require to be anything we are willing and bold enough to believe we can define ourselves to be.[128]

All examples and ideas can be expressed either positively (which would mean going with the flow of higher self will reflected through the chart), or negatively (which would be fighting your own ecstasy or excitement through judgement, which changes excitement into anxiety).

It is recommended at this point for those not adept with astrological principles to review astrological techniques through the recommended texts and references listed. Astrological applications are presented clearly, however *how* these methods are arrived at or calculated will not be included. There are many sources for astrological computer calculations in the back of this book. Several methods of application; secondary progressions, solar arc, solar return and transitting planetary positions may be used in analysis from here forward.

The examples simply reflect the choices of conscious mind expression of the birth path (chart). The environment one is born into does *not determine* the expression of any individual, unless of course the identity chooses to believe it does. The environment one is born into my give us insight into *why* someone may choose to take certain actions.

Creativity is the expression of the knowingness of the "All That Is" that you are. Any deviation from this idea can only be a choice in expression through conscious mind interpretation.

Our first example is the horoscope of a well known artist. Even though during his life only one painting was sold, his works now command millions. Vincent Van Gogh.

The element count reveals moderately high Fire, and absolutely zero trust of the Air element. We can use the Element count and mode count and blend them for "tone" in this manner; Low Air+low Fixed=low Aquarius or co-creator

---

[128]
Darryl Anka channeling *"Bashar"* 2/21/87, Los Angeles, California.

interaction. High Fire+high Mutable=High Pisces or dissolution of identity. This nuance gives us an overall "feel" for the identity as we begin delineation.

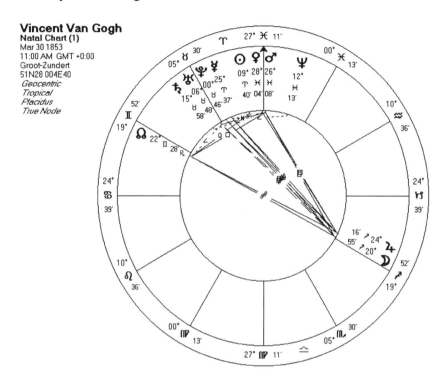

Vincent Van Gogh
Natal Chart (1)
Mar 30 1853
11:00 AM GMT +0:00
Groot-Zundert
51N28 004E40
Geocentric
Tropical
Placidus
True Node

A low count in Air reflects difficulty in seeing the self or others with analytical discernment; that the identity does not believe that self reflection will come through social or intellectual interaction. A "blinder" effect; A preoccupation with the self and it's perspectives. There is also a high count in Mutable mode; The scattering of energy and resources. Excessive fluidity, but limited idea exchange. It can be expected psychologically speaking, that where an identity perceives a lack within itself (or believes so), overcompensation will ensue. Hence, Mars (identity's need to prove the self) and Venus (personal and social reflection) conjunct the Midheaven are in developmental tension (needs fulfillment) with the reigning needs of the persona and it's expansion (moon conjunct Jupiter in 6). Mars will be very important because it is the ruler of the Sun sign, the core energy expression.

The Sun/Moon blend, Sun in Aries-Moon in Sagittarius; The Apex trine between the luminaries is always reflective of the possibility of great integrity-as long as energy and intention remain focused. This is an aspect of the expression of honesty and integrity. Following your excitement is easy. Mental influence (page 246). The reigning need might have some difficulty being fulfilled if the identity does not believe in idea interaction! We see through the Mode expression and the Sun/Moon blend, definitions of the need for far reaching philosophy and higher mind experiences, but the persona itself limiting it's own expression of it.

The Sun rules the 2nd house (self worth) and is disposed of by the Mars in Pisces on 10, which in turn rules the 10th house intercepted Aries.

Deservability enters the picture through these and other aspects, as the reason for many of the difficulties he experienced in his life.

Creative expression as the effect of worth definitions is shown through the 5th and 11th houses. One of the reasons why chose this chart as an example was because the 0 degree Pluto ruling 5 in Taurus (worth) in 11.

Extension is in a state of difficulty in belief of power-fullness (0 degree reference), and the dispositor of Pluto (Venus) is fully externalized in physical reality (10th house) and also in critical degree (28-winding up urgency), in the spiritual sign of Pisces and also rules 4, the identity establishment and security needs.

The Venus position is in a developmentally tense T-square configuration with the Moon/Jupiter conjunction and the nodal axis. Perspective about identity validity is believed separate from it's sensitive and accelerated expression (Moon ruler of the ascendant, squares Mars and squares Venus). Insecurity about the identity was probably triggered by the relationship with the mother as both archetypes of femininity are in the T-square. The path to awakening the higher self is through creative extension and value interaction (Uranus rules the 8th and is conjunct Pluto). This identity desperately needed love and expression (the rulers of the 5th and 11th house critical degrees, Mars-Venus conjunct and square Moon) and yet did not believe that it would be found through reflection, either personally or socially (Saturn and Uranus in the 11th and disposed of by Venus, air reference limited. Saturn in 11, rules 7. Mars aspects to Moon, Venus, Jupiter, and nodal axis, Pisces emphasis).

The strongest fears; Saturn is in the sign Taurus; self worth, resources. The need to be analytically correct is reflected in the Moon's placement in 6, and his opinions and intellect needed respect (Sagittarius). Emotional sensitivity was high with the Cancer ascendant and Venus in Pisces. Sensitive creative expression, *became his* form of idea interaction and extension (Venus disposes of the Pluto and is in Pisces). Unless sensitivity was as great as his of course, who would get the messages? Idealistic isolation was his tool in his work, as well as his limitation in relationship. Mars disposes of the Sun (rules worth 2nd) and Mercury (rules 4th and 10th beliefs of status). Neptune in turn disposes of Mars (empathic sensitivity) and Venus, and rules the houses reflecting the thinking profile as well (3rd and 9th cusps).

The planets around the natal chart in the first ring are the solar arc positions for his 37th birthday, the year of his suicide. (adding one degree per year of age to the natal planet positions, please refer to astrological definitions and Noel Tyl references on Solar arc theories).

The planets outside the wheel (final ring on the triwheel), are the transitting planets at the time of his suicide. Solar arcs are introduced at this point to demonstrate the profoundly obvious mechanics of astrological measurements. The incorporation of solar arcs blended with the transitting positions against the template of the birth path (natal chart) are very telling.

Let's look first at the Solar arcs first alone (2nd ring, and 2nd chart). They are only allowed one degree orb as one year equals one degree. One degree applying, exact, and one degree separating from exact, describes a three year back drop of archetypal reference.

For the year of his suicide we see immediately several exact measurements. The solar arc Midheaven (external status) is exactly upon the midpoint between Pluto (ruling 5) and Uranus

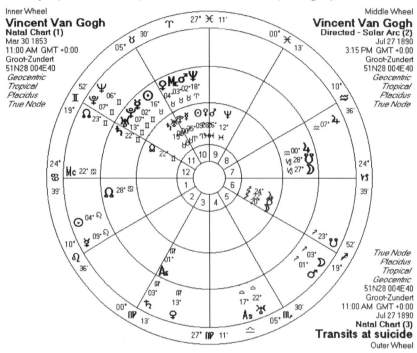

(ruling 8). Solar arc Venus, ruler of both the 4th and 11th is conjunct the 11th (co-creator interaction with others). SA Sun exactly on natal Saturn (worth, ruling 2 in co-created interaction or love received in 11). It rules the 7th of *reflection!* Social reflection is deemed not a part of the self, but outside the self (others), and incapable of receiving the sensitive expressions of the self.

Solar ARC Saturn ruler of 7 is in 12 and is exactly conjunct the nodal axis (the maternal influence reflected in the moon sign and aspects, the feminine function). The nodal axis is the midpoint between the Moon/Jupiter conjunction. This reflects the need for and incorporation of the discernment (Jupiter rules

6) and resolution (opposition) to this blinder effect (Venus and Air references) as it opposes Jupiter from the 12th, self limitation) to the 6th (the 12th of the self's mirror in 7!) or in general; perspective and view (6th/12th axis). The solar arc Moon (ascendant ruler) in the 7th has just squared Mercury in 10 in the last few years before the suicide (self expression). Solar arc Jupiter in 7 is exact in its square[129] to natal Pluto ruler of 5, which confirms the powerful need to alter perspective and understand the limitations of others views (6th is the 12th of the "others" in 7). Solar arc Sun ruler of the natal 2nd is exactly conjunct natal Saturn, ruler of the 7th, in the 11th (love received)!

Only doubt (the true opposite of love) can invalidate creation through the judgement of self worth. When we invalidate our reality, we invalidate ourselves. *THIS* is what is meant by "judge not, that you be not judged." (Matthew 7:1, New Testament, King James Version).

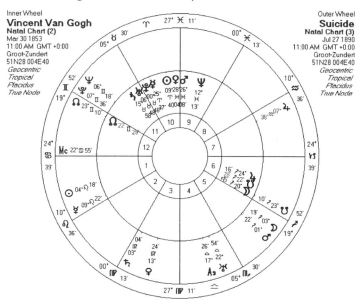

129
     Without the ability to verify his birth data to any acceptable precision, we look for corroborations to support the data we have.

The transitting aspects confirm solar arc measurements, and act through their specificity as the triggers of his developmental crisis invalidating the external as the self.

Transitting Jupiter is on the 8th house cusp (the need to transcend the ego's definitions-or physical death from the inability to believe this is possible), and rules the 6th (discernment), squares natal Uranus and Pluto in the 11th, and opposes (needs resolution) transitting Sun and Mercury, as well as solar arc Mars/Venus the rulers of houses 5/11 (see previous chart)! Transitting Mars is also opposing transit Neptune and solar arc Mercury from the 5th to the 11th. Mercury is the ruler of the 12th the (reason for incarnation), and 4th (emotional habit patterns).

In conclusion, the higher self chose a path that would allow the identity to experience itself through it's creations and the validation of self worth through reflection. The *conscious* self invalidated it's creations through a lack of belief in deservability and that the spiritual was manifestable through the physical world (Pisces 10 and planets there).

The foundational momentum of the disbelief in social appreciation or idea exchange disconnected the inner self and visions from the messages sent by the mirror *of the self;* physical reality.

The message of the Starry, Starry Night was that the painted and the actual version are one in the same. When the need to have one validate the other dissolves, so does the "distance" between them. The mirror he mistrusted now reflects his idealism brilliantly.

Horoscope #2 Private
Natal Chart (5)

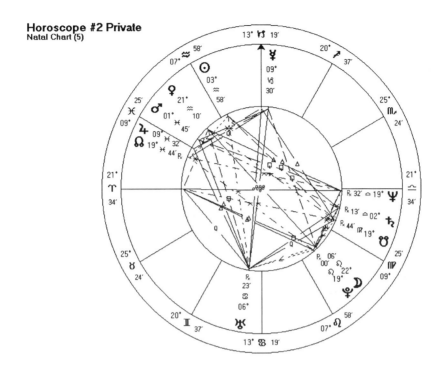

Horoscope number two is a private case, a female age 36 at the time of consultation. The element count is low in Earth, as only one planet, Mercury, and the Midheaven are in Earth signs; A lack of day-to-day stability based on the disbelief of the physical world being supportive and positive.

The Sun/Moon blend reflects a strong competition between the emotions and the intellect. Creative powers need confirmation and reinforcement. The ascendant is in Aries, assertive self projection and the need to be ego important in pioneering terms.

The ascendant ruler however, Mars, is in the sensitive and passive sign of Pisces. We sense in the momentum, contradiction and conflict. Intellect/emotions, aggressive/passive. Seeing all sides of an argument may really mean no decision. The reigning need to be dramatically ego important (Moon/Leo) is conjunct Pluto retrograde (perspective). These two planets oppose Venus ruler of 2 (self worth) and 7 (self reflection through relationship).

A powerful need for significance and dramatic ego importance (Leo/Pluto) needs to be integrated into relationship-seen through reflection (Venus+7) in order to believe in the self's worth (2).

Saturn's position, where the greatest fears as an effect of placing the power outside the self is reflected, is in Libra and retrograde. The need for social acceptance places the power in the mirror instead of the self. This is further complicated through repression reassessing (retrogradation).

Following this momentum we see that Saturn is reflecting more disintegration (belief in separateness and conflict) through it's involvement in a T-square with Mercury in 9 ruler of it's house placement (6) and Uranus in the 3rd in Cancer which is also retrograde. The recognition of choice (Uranus) and physical reality (Saturn) are believed separate and need integration into conscious mind functioning (Mercury). An information/perspective crisis (3rd, 6th, and 9th houses) through vacillating discernment (Mercury rules 6 and 3) about creative interaction or love received in relationship (Uranus rules 11 and disposes of the Venus position which in turn rules the 7th of reflection).

The Sun ruler of the 5th, and Uranus ruler of the 11th (extension, love giving) are inconjunct. This reinforces initial deductions of a powerful need to adjust perspective and thinking (3, 6, 9 information/perspective crisis pattern).

We must assume the early environment and parental structure had much to do with the triggering of these beliefs (always inspected) as the Moon rules the 4th and Saturn rules the 10th.

The impression one receives at this point, is that the parental figures were probably old fashioned especially conservative or over protective of this woman as a child (Saturn).

To find further corroboration, and to allow for a point of reference when the client arrived, the planetary positions for the Saturn opposed Saturn period are always inspected. It has proven to be invaluable in determining belief momentum in my practice, and always indicates some, if not the most important challenges in physical reality.

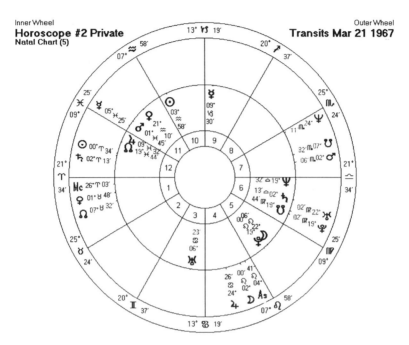

In this case transitting Saturn (at opposition) completes the natal T-square and it now becomes a Grand cross reflecting a tremendous amount of tension of issues at cross purposes or in contradiction. Since Saturn rules the 10th house (as well as the father generally) the father figure *must* have been involved in this conflict.

Transitting Mars in 7, Venus in 1, Moon in 4- complete another Grand cross with the natal Sun in the 10th! An identity/status crisis concerning creative extension or love given (Sun rules 5) social and personal reflection (Venus rules 7 relationship and 2-worth), identity definition (Mars rules 1), and emotional security (Moon rules 4).

Transitting Neptune is squaring the natal Moon/Pluto opposed Venus axis from the cusp of the 8th and rules the 12th (self limiting beliefs).

Upon her arrival I observed her to be very attractive but

overweight. Being overweight reflects over "waiting" in the application of themselves, and hence energy accumulates. We discussed the concepts of creating our own reality, and asked if there was a specific reason why she had decided to come and see me. I always trust that in consultation that whatever comes up, is what needs to come up and encourage free flow discussion. I do not use any astrological jargon unless asked to, and translate what I perceive in the horoscope in as simple and easy to understand terms as possible. She said that she was planning on getting *back* into music and art (implying that this "weighting" had been going on) and wanted to see what things looked like for her.

I pointed out we had just discussed how we create what we experience totally by what we believe, so that whatever she believed things would "look like" is what she would experience-her most likely assessment on various levels (please see the threshold of believability in the definitions section).

I asked her about the period of around age 14 (Saturn opposition) and if that had anything to do with her getting *out* of the creative endeavors that she was "trying" to get back into. I suggested what I perceived to be conflict between what she felt and what she thought could be part of her dilemma and that somehow her father may have been involved with this "doubting" conflict. Was there an early relationship at this time that might have something to do with this idea? (Saturn in Libra reference).

All deductions came out in the following disclosures; She got involved in a high school romance, experienced an early pregnancy from it, was pressured by the father to marry this young man whom she did not love, was trapped in this unhappy marriage taking care of children and had left all creative endeavors behind!

Acquiescence and repression was so great that she had never had orgasm during sex, only through fantasy during masturbation![130]

A denial of personal fulfillment of self-directed goals in order to please father with what was "socially acceptable" had detracted from fulfillment. This "waiting" had lasted more than 15 years until Saturn by transit returned to it's birthplace at age 30, when she divorced and was now re-initiating creative endeavors that she needed so badly to fulfill the reigning needs of the persona.

The reassessment (retrograde) of the powerlessness reflected by the Saturn placement had played itself out. She informed me that she had lost a considerable amount of weight since the divorce, and feelings (beliefs) of self worth were improving.

In conclusion, the momentum of acquiescence had reached a point of extreme frustration and the conscious mind (Mercury) needed to wake up to a recognition of choice in the matter (opposes Uranus) and real-ize that it was the self's judgement of external "right and wrong" that denied creative expression. As I reminded her upon leaving, no one can make you feel inferior, without your consent.[131]

In the horoscope of Walt Disney, we see exceptional integration of astrological developmental premise. Invention blends with convention. The non-physical dream is brought into the physical dream. A beautiful example of creative fulfillment, self empowerment, and proof that one's philosophy and imagination, are as solid and as "real" as a rock, and that simply by acting like they are, makes it so.

In the cartoon "Steamboat Willy", Walt incorporated the aspect of sound, which in 1925, was quite an innovation. He did not invent technologies, but he brilliantly acted upon them.

---

[130]
Abnormal sexual behavior is defined by the amount of difficulty or detraction from successful fulfillment relative to personality needs. We are not concerned with normality, we are concerned with the degree of conflict a person experiences either personally or socially with their particular needs.

[131]
Eleanor Roosevelt.

He combined an eye for detail, imagination, and breadth of vision. These characteristics were presented in the release of "Snow White And The Seven Dwarfs" in 1937, while he was only 36.

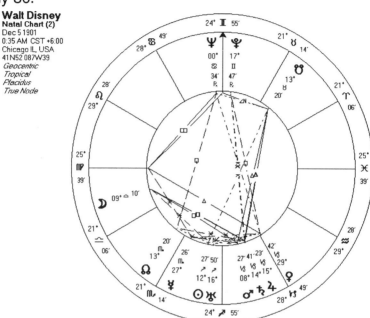

Walt Disney
Natal Chart (2)
Dec 5 1901
0:35 AM CST +6:00
Chicago IL, USA
41N52 087W39
Geocentric
Tropical
Placidus
True Node

When we act on what it excites us to do, success only fuels the fire and at age 54 "Disneyland" opened to an unprecedented 33,642,597 visitors in it's first year! Counterfeit tickets were forged in an attempt to get in on opening day as it was invitation only, and guests were out front since before sunup in anticipation. Quite an impressive response, considering it was "just his imagination" and a little cartoon mouse, that was responsible for the billion dollar conglomerate called Disney.

His chart shows a fairly balanced Element count, high Cardinal mode (action), at the expense of fixed. This reflects low energy motion (e-motion) and high motivation. It also reflects a need to develop re-source-fullness. The Sun/Moon blend in our guide reads; Expansiveness is expressed through the social mirror. A practical anchor is needed to bring ideas down to Earth. A need for external change places the power outside the self, and denies opportunity for self exploration.

Walt Disney created a wonderful and expansive atmosphere for generations to enjoy. He definitely had the practical anchor necessary with 4 planets in Capricorn-including Saturn-as well as a Virgo ascendant which reads; There is a strong sense of service toward an ideal. Self projection may be limited and focused unless the Fire element is well represented. There is also a strong need to be analytically correct-to say the "right things." Change-ability is toned down in this Mutable ascendant because of the Earth element.

His "ideal" given service to, was making the world a happier place to be in.

His horoscope has a comfortable blend. The philosophical thrust of Sagittarius is the "Fire" and expanse needed for the Virgoian projection which may preoccupy itself with details. The Moon in 1 in Libra reflects social sensitivity, and through it's square to the Capricorn planets in 4, a powerful need to establish physically a "home" for the Sagittarian philosophy. A strong need to establish the identity and it's worth through creative extension (Moon ruling 11 square Mars, Saturn, and Jupiter which rule 8, 4 and 5). The Moon squares Saturn which rules the 5th, and Venus on the cusp of 5 at critical degree rules the 2nd (worth) and disposes of the social reigning need!

To manifest the dream of Disneyland into physical reality is the ideal.

A powerful yod is formed between Neptune (fantasy) in the 10th (externalization), Mercury in 3, and the critical degree Venus in 5. A constantly emerging and adjusting of persona functions with the "other" reality could only be accomplished through the integration of the Sun/Uranus (innovation and originality needs) conjunction in 3 opposition Pluto in 9 (perspective and the thinking of others).

This configuration confirms initial deductions of the need for resourcefulness and to recognize the reason for incarnation. That reason is the incorporation of a recognition of choice in thinking (Uranus in 3) and perspective through conscious acknowledgement (Pluto). By accessing the higher self for those resources to establish the non-physical identity in physical reality (Sun/Uranus rule the 6/12 perspective axis, oppose Pluto ruler of the 3rd (conscious mind)-which is in the 9th widely trine the Moon, dispositor of Neptune in 10. The moon in turn squares the Capricorn planets in 4 (establishment). Mercury ruler of the external status 10th, sextiles (opportunity for expression) Venus in 5.

Because of his acting on the convictions of his philosophies, many of the planetary placements can accelerate to higher levels of functioning. Venus in critical degree in Capricorn in 5, becomes wisdom in material creation reflection (caution; this is not a given, it still can reflect acquisitiveness). The Libra reigning need serves the identity instead of being manipulated by reflection.

Neptune in 10; instead of disillusionment in the physicalization of the beliefs, becomes servant on equal footing with conscious mind functions of the persona. Mercury in Scorpio; instead of obsessive or defensive, now becomes incisive perception of others perspective (in mutual reception with Pluto!).

Because action was made equal to vision and acted upon, self empowerment became automatic. Perspective was the key (is always the key) to the level manifestation of consciousness. *How we look at life is profoundly important.*

When his brother came to his office very upset about meeting deadlines for investors of millions of dollars on a picture they were producing, Walt began laughing so hard that his brother was baffled. When he stopped laughing his brother asked him what he thought was so funny about this critical situation. He said "Imagine two poor old boys like us worrying about millions!" An example of the optimism (and perspective in "meaning") that *allows* expansion by removing meaning.

Many astrologers may habitually assign Neptune definitions such as; the unreal, confusion, deception and miss the positive aspects of this planet. Neptune reflects the non-physical idea template and the imagination, which is responsible for *any and every* experience in physical reality. How we envision our lives and it's unfoldment is very critical to the threshold of believability.

Walt Disney manifested tremendous self-actualization by *acting* on the imagination. The physical world became home to the philosophy of the identity (Moon in 1, sextile the Sun, disposes of Neptune and squares Mars, Saturn, and Jupiter in 4).

Walt Disney's solar return for the year of Disneyland's opening appears next.

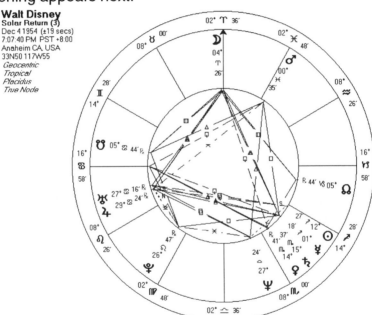

Walt Disney
Solar Return (3)
Dec 4 1954 (±19 secs)
7:07:40 PM PST +8:00
Anaheim CA, USA
33N50 117W55
Geocentric
Tropical
Placidus
True Node

The solar return is a chart cast for the exact return of the Sun to it's place at birth for each birthday.[132]

Within the return is reflected the momentum most likely to manifest during the time period of one year from the birthday until the same degree at next revolution or solar return. Our

---

[132] Please refer to Solar return under astrological definitions chapter 6. These will be used throughout this series. Also see *"The Solar Return Book of Prediction"*, Raymond Merriman, Seek It Publishing, 1977, first printing.

interpretation of the solar return begins slightly differently than that of the natal horoscope.

The ascendant sign becomes the subject that the year will "revolve" around. In this return the year revolves around the establishment of the identity, emotional security, the "home", women, children-all things nurturing.

Next we look for the ruler of the ascendant, the Moon, and blend this with the position of the Sun which is the body from which the chart is constructed. The Moon is in the 10th (physical manifestation of the establishment of identity (Aries) and the "Moon" issues as a "status" (10th) concern during the year). The Sun is in 5 (creative extension). The Jupiter/Uranus conjunction (revelation and brilliant opportunity and change) "colors" our original delineation of what the year revolves around and *disposes of the Sun in 5.* Jupiter rules 6 (work and service to the ideal), and Uranus rules 8 (the worth of projections, others money and values. The 8th is the 2nd of the 7th). It is also in the sign Cancer reflecting expansive innovation as the *mode* of identity establishment (also disposed of by the pioneering moon in 10!). This conjunction is in closing square to Neptune in the 4th, ruler of the 9th of others thinking and higher self. It then completes a Grand trine with the ruler of the year the Moon in 10 and disposes of (rules) Mercury *in* 5! The Sun, also disposed of by Jupiter, is *also* in the 5th ruling the self worth 2nd. Mars rules the 10th and opposes the ruler of the 5th, Pluto, from the 8th to 2nd (awareness) and trines Neptune in the 4th (fantasy home fulfillment). Pluto rules partnership financing.

The natal planets are placed around the solar return in the next chart (2nd ring) so that at a glance transits and important points in the solar return conjuncting natal positions can be seen. In the 3rd ring are the transits of the actual positions of planets at the opening of Disneyland.

The importance of the sign Cancer, the Moon, and Neptune in previous delineations becomes overwhelmingly obvious. Solar return Mars and Neptune complete a second Grand trine with the natal Neptune, which falls in the solar return 12th, and the transitting Moon is in Cancer exactly conjunct natal Neptune-fantasy and escape-another "world" for the family! Transitting Sun/Uranus conjunction (mirroring the same aspect in the natal) is conjunct solar return Jupiter/Uranus conjunction, and all of these oppose the very important natal Venus at 29 degrees. Transitting Jupiter, his natal Sun/Uranus conjunction *ruler* is exactly on the solar return 2nd house cusp and completes a grand trine with SR moon in 10.

The solar return horizon places his natal Jupiter/Saturn conjunction exactly on the 7 (social acceptance) and rules the solar return 6th (service) and 7th (public).

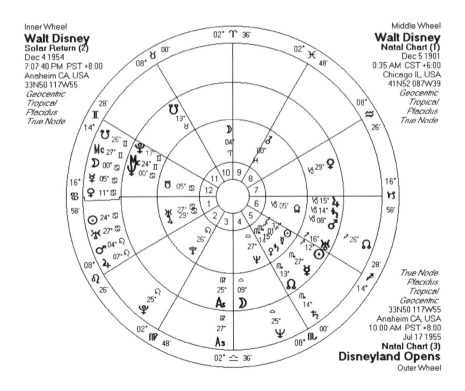

Inner Wheel
Walt Disney
Solar Return (2)
Dec 4 1954
7:07:40 PM PST +8:00
Anaheim CA, USA
33N50 117W55
Geocentric
Tropical
Placidus
True Node

Middle Wheel
Walt Disney
Natal Chart (1)
Dec 5 1901
0:35 AM CST +6:00
Chicago IL, USA
41N52 087W39
Geocentric
Tropical
Placidus
True Node

True Node
Placidus
Tropical
Geocentric
33N50 117W55
Anaheim CA, USA
10:00 AM PST +8:00
Jul 17 1955
Natal Chart (3)
Disneyland Opens
Outer Wheel

Transitting Mars in Leo in the SR 1st is exactly trine the solar return Moon, and transit Moon is exactly conjunct the natal

Neptune and trine the SR Mars!
The fulfillment of the life path is obvious.

In conclusion, the higher self chose a path wherein self empowerment could be triggered through the imagination with conviction, application and trust (as it is for everyone-in his case materially and publicly).

This life path was demonstrating that every individual is as powerful as they need to be to create whatever they desire to create in their reality without having to hurt themselves or anyone else in order to create it. Integrity and vision are the keys.

When we realize with conviction that the reality we each create and experience can be anything we are willing and bold enough to believe it can be, then each and every individual's contribution of "their" world will be as expansive, colorful, and happy, as *"The Wonderful World Of Disney."*

Chapter 10

The Mental Experience
Thought

"He who thinks he knows, doesn't.
He who knows he doesn't know-does."
Joseph Campbell
"The Power of the Myth"

The experience of mind has been described in many ways. Edgar Cayce while in the trance state said often, "mind is the builder." In this book we have referred to the mind-matter mirror. Meaning mind and matter are manifestations of the same "stuff," expressed in different formats.

The brain is to the mind, what the radio is to radio waves. The brain does not "cause" mind. The brain is the effect of mind focused in the physical dream. It receives mind (station).

Because this focus keeps mind in a particular mode during the waking state, other aspects of the mind or psychic material are ignored (other stations).

In order to allow integration on a continuous basis without interrupting focus, we sleep. During sleep, conscious mind makes connections to other aspects of the self, and incorporates them into the personal unconscious. In the dream state, physical experiences begin their way into the physical reality to educate the conscious self. We explore probabilities unfolding and begin incorporation or integration there. These connections to other portions of the self can be in the form of past self, future self, probable selves, counterpart selves, higher self and on infinitely. It is all mind on every level. As Mary Baker Eddy said; "God is mind, and God is infinite; hence all is mind."

The mental experience is *any* experience. Because in essence, no matter how "real" or "solid" an experience may seem, it is still "all in our minds." There are only different levels (stations). Therefore, what we are speaking of in this chapter, is the experience of the intermingling of unconscious psychic material with that of the conscious, and the interpretation (or misinterpretation) thereof.

Since conscious focus and physical reality manifest mind in pairs or in paradox and polarity form, misinterpretation usually occurs from conscious definitions of one aspect of the pair or polarity being the "real" or "right" one. As discussed in initial chapters of this book, there is no one truth, all truths are true. They carry in their system of "truth" the corresponding methodologies, reinforcing logic, and physical "proof"-with them and within them. It is not a matter of discovering "THE" truth, but a matter of dis-covering *which* truth you prefer to experience. If trust is placed in things you do not prefer to do the Multiverse (being unbiased), will send you plenty of opportunities to do things you do not prefer to do. This effect acts as reinforcing proof that "that's the truth about the way things are," as a reflection of the chosen set of beliefs. We return to our initial question with more answers first addressed in the preface;

> ▸ "I am able to prove," wrote the great German mathematician, Leibnitz "that not only light, color, heat, and the like, but motion, shape, and extension too are mere apparent qualities.""The Universe and Dr. Einstein"
>
> "Thus gradually philosophers and scientists arrived at the startling conclusion that since every object is simply the sum of its qualities, and since qualities exist only in the mind, the whole objective universe of matter and energy, atoms and stars, does not exist except as a construction of the consciousness, an edifice of conventional symbols shaped by the senses of man." "The Universe and Dr. Einstein"
>
> "All the choir of heaven and furniture of earth, in a word all those bodies which compose the mighty frame of the world, have not any substance without the mind....So long as they are not actually perceived by me, or do not exist in my mind, or that of any other created spirit, they must either have no existence at all, or else subsist in the mind of some eternal spirit." Berkeley

The conscious mind seeks to justify and rationalize psychic material it deems threatening to its validity and control. The

3rd, 6th, 9th, and 12th houses reflect the information/perspective of the person within the physical realm. Thinking (3/9) is the effect and counterpart of perspective (6/12). They represent the Mutable mode, the mode of re-action. The reaction meaning that our actions are just reactions to the physical experiences we create as the effect of belief. Our thinking is conscious mind's reactions to the prescriptions of our path set by higher self will. Like the hallway described previously, the conscious mind finds itself in this hallway believing (from focus) that it is separate from it, and re-acts to it. A more accurate perspective, is that the conscious mind is an *aspect* of the hallway. Mind in this way is perceived to bounce back and forth between environment and identity. Actually, it is a circle of conscious perception-reaction, unconscious creation, physical experience, back to conscious perception.

Sigmund Freud
Natal Chart (3)
May 6 1856
9:00 AM CET -1:00
Freiberg
50N54 013E20
Geocentric
Tropical
Placidus
True Node

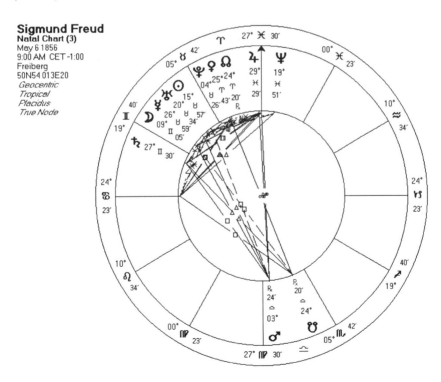

▸   Belief system="This will be one of the aspects that creates your artificial construct personality. It will be one of the cornerstones of the prism of personality. The other two will be emotion and thought. It is what is responsible for the methodology, along with the other two ideas, of how you choose to exercise your physiological mental free will in giving yourself the type of approach to your life that you do. It will be responsible for the creation of your physical reality and the reflection of that reality through your physical senses back to your mentality." Bashar in *"The New Metaphysics"*.

Our first chart sample reflects a mentality that was preoccupied with conscious mind function being the "answer" to psychic material that the ego is unwilling to accept or control. Sigmund Freud had an enormous need to objectify unconscious material and to categorize it as well. There is nothing inherently negative in this idea. However, he began analysis from the subjective perception to begin with, that competition and placing the power outside the self occurred at primal unconscious levels. This perspective however is a *conscious* mind assumption based upon his own guilt feelings (beliefs) about the "danger" of natural aggression.[133]

Much of our language (Freudian slip, anal etc) and recognition of the unconscious is obviously the result of tremendous revelation in thinking that Freud discerned simply through analysis by case histories.

The Element count reveals only one point in Fire! The delineation reads; Mistrust of the self and it's creative birthright. We observe with a quick glance the basis for his whole life's work! A disbelief in the validity of identity. The Sun/Moon blend reads; Application of the self must be in diverse terms, otherwise indecisiveness and change-ability dissipate the identity and a loss of direction will occur. The conscious and unconscious are contradictory in definition(!) But only if there is not expression of diversity within a structured format.

The focussing and structuring aspects of the Taurus Sun seek to stabilize, and the reigning need of the persona is for

---

[133]   There is much speculation on just what some of his original theories "really" were. Please see Jeffery Masson *"Assault on Truth."*

diversity. The Moon is the ruler of the ascendant (identity definition) and reinforces the need unconsciously for flexibility. The consciously aware self (the Sun, Mercury in Taurus) is being de-structurized by the unconscious self. Uranus and Mercury rule the entire unconscious matrix (4th, 8th, 12th)! Uranus is at midpoint between the Sun and Mercury in Taurus which reflects the need to awaken *his* transcendence of ego and destructurize value judgments (Uranus rules 8 and Sun rules 2).

Saturn is in Gemini in 12-his greatest fears *are* his limitation in perspective. It forms an out of sign T-square with Jupiter in 10 and Mars in 4. The limitation of total *and only* conscious mind perception of others (Saturn rules 7). Saturn squares Jupiter (disbelief in ease in the physical world) in 10 and Jupiter rules 6; the need to fulfill understanding (Pisces) and analytical discernment (6th) through self introspective (12) thought (Gemini). There is little perception of the self through the reflection of others. Little positivism is seen through others limiting perspectives (6th is the 12th of others).

Saturn rules 7 and squares critical degree Jupiter ruler of 6 (analytical discernment in preparation for the projections of self).

Mars is retrograde (repression) in Libra (projections), intercepted (missing in reference) in 4 (emotional security and the mother) and is dispositor of the only Fire reference in his chart Venus (personal and social reflection)! Boy did he need an astrologer! The parental structure needed to be understood in order to find where this profound disbelief in the validity of identity was internalized. The 3rd and 9th axis is at critical initiating degree in the perspective signs (Virgo/Pisces) and again draws Mercury into networks.

In his work he substituted free association, which is allowing the patient to speak freely whatever comes into his mind (Uranus conjunct Mercury, Moon in Gemini) instead of hypnotism (the free expression of the unconscious). His belief in sexuality as being the "root" of almost all conflicts, is *his* interpretation (being so conscious mind and externally oriented) of *his* higher self's choice of path in order to wake up (Uranus) and transform (8th) *his* extreme focus upon conscious mind and the material world (Sun, Uranus, and Mercury in Taurus). Perhaps in previous incarnations he allowed this materialism to run rampant and unconsciously felt guilt for (Mars and ego or id satisfaction).

Venus and Mars are in detriments, mutual reception and dispose of over half the planets in the chart. Venus in Aries seeks reflection that reinforces self assertion, and Mars in Libra seeks Identity reinforcement through self reflection. In the sign that places the power outside the self and in pendulum swing of overcompensation (Rx), Mars would be indicative of a sense of identity in conflict and ego frailty in his chart. We see tremendous mental preoccupation (Mercury disposes of the Moon the reigning need and Saturn the greatest fears) with the validity of identity and self assertion. Venus is conjunct the nodal axis and rules the 11th (love received) and intercepted Libra in the 4th of the *mother.* It is easy as an astrologer to see where he created these theories from. The mother would have had great influence and subconscious psychological impact on him in regard to self reflection, relationships and emotional security (regardless of *birth-time* accuracy).

Sexuality will be in high profile in any chart with strong transformational needs (Pluto/8th house). The energy of transformation on an unconscious level can be felt as the need for emotional significance. The conscious mind and ego self then seek this significance through sexual interaction to catalyze value interaction and destructurization of emotional momentum(s) (charged beliefs). This may temporarily satisfy emotional significance needs, however no true transcendence of the ego self has taken place. The answer is in insight and *trust* (Fire) through inspiration. Something Freud could not categorize or manipulate (conscious control), therefore, didn't trust. To him, not having conscious control *must* be the cause of hysteria.

The 29 degree Jupiter (urgent need to expand empathically) reflects the need to accelerate the higher self functions to merge and blend the idea of oneness of the self and others through empathy; to recognize that conscious manipulation and control is not necessarily an equivalent to ego health. He was a pessimist to a great degree and increased our beliefs about the vulnerability and powerlessness of the "human condition." I.e., that the unconscious is irrational, driven by passion and dangerous. Of course this has much to do with the current rigid beliefs regarding sexuality etc. of his time period (Jupiter/Saturn square) and still was ahead of that time (Sun conjunct Uranus).

Critical degrees on the 3rd and 9th (mental axis) in the signs of perspective reinforce this "urgent need" for perspective alteration deduction. His own 6th and 12th are extremely debilitating to perspective (Jupiter at 29 degrees Pisces rules 6, and Saturn in the conscious mind sign of Gemini) and is one of the reasons for incarnation (12). Perhaps to undo his repression and judgment through introspection with others.

Mercury is conjunct Uranus in the "Fixed" sign of Taurus-the need to maintain stability implies insecurity with abstractness and conceptual knowingness. Quite simply, his own insecurities lead us to greater acknowledgment and acceptance of the *existence of levels* of consciousness and motivational factors, and in this way was of great service.

His chart is an excellent example of how conscious focus and ego can make a "science" out of believing in victimization of the self through the environment and even by the self (please review the inverted triangle on page 21).

Saturn reflects the powerlessness derived through the separation of conscious mind from itself (the environment). The deception of the material world. By acknowledging where we place the power outside of ourselves we become consciously aware of the "limits" of physical manipulation and rationalization-hence become experts in this understanding-if we incorporate and integrate this knowledge.

It seems Freud's developmental tension was not integrated, instead conscious rationalization was accelerated. Our perspectives are changing dramatically. Now we *publicly discuss sexuality freely.*

Science does *not* equal truth. It equals physical mechanics. It only equals truth when mechanics and manipulation are necessary. Science is a methodology of investigating the world in which we live and function, not necessarily all worlds or levels.

Dis-ease is the refusal of the conscious mind to integrate higher levels or repressed levels of the self (see definitions section page 42). The dis-ease is the resistance to growth and the continuance of the belief in separation and being out of a harmonious *natural* rest state that then may have *physical effects* or consequences.

The planetary positions in the outer wheel are the Solar Arc

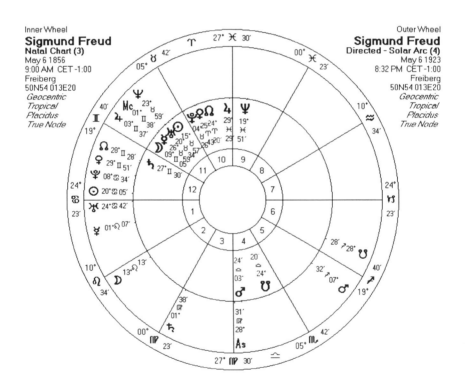

(SA) Direction positions[134] for 1923 when it was first discovered that Freud had cancer of the upper jaw (Taurus). Cancer is the dis-ease experienced when the inner self's desire to expand (Jupiter), is met by conscious mind judgement and restriction (Saturn). Thus, the over production of cells (compensation) is reflective of this cancel-ing out of the identity by itself. It could be reflected by a myriad of aspects, however, it usually is reflected through Jupiter, Saturn and Neptune (the disbelief in the ability to manifest the ideal).

Solar arc Neptune is conjunct natal Mercury/Uranus midpoint which reflects a time to dissolve physical and conscious mind focus. Solar arc Venus at critical degree in Gemini (projections) is squaring the problematic Jupiter (ruling 6) from the 12th, and solar arc Mercury (conscious focus) is squaring natal Pluto demanding transcendence of limiting ego definitions! The aspects themselves do not "predict" the cancer, it is our discernment of the law of momentum flow and demonstrated perspective that allow us to see the *probability* based on our knowledge of his *belief in* resistance and separation.

The solar arc ascendant has just squared the debilitating Saturn, opposing critical Jupiter, and is about to conjoin Mars triggering the entire T-square. The T-square bow and arrow lodges the arrow (from SA Venus in 12) in the 6th (dis-ease). Solar arc Mars is moving toward opposition to the Moon (reigning needs) and the *unconscious*! SA Uranus ruler of the 8th (reframing and psychoanalysis) is on the ascendant reflecting the need to awaken his own emotional security issues and *unconscious.*

The transit positions (on his birthday) are no less revealing (next chart).

Transitting Uranus (the awakening of unconscious knowledge) is conjunct Neptune, ruler and dispositor of the critical degree Jupiter (6th ruler) and Midheaven, and is squared by transitting Mars the co-ruler of the 10th (the

---

134
I am using this method of measurement as it would be the most accurate despite errors in birth-time.

physical manifestation of psychological dis-ease).

Transitting Neptune squares the Sun (dissolution) and T Jupiter opposes it! Transit Saturn is in a 6th house inconjunct with the Sun from 4 (using the Sun as the 1st or solar position-meaning that as a Taurus T Saturn would be in house 6).

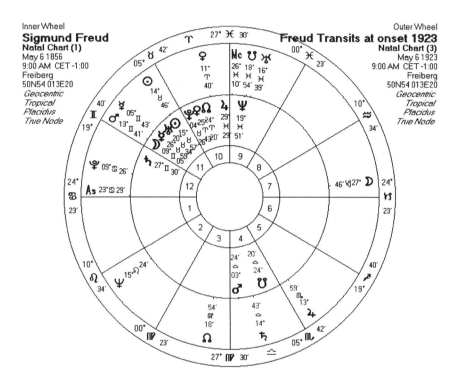

Transit Jupiter would move to oppose Uranus and Mercury in 11, Mercury and Uranus critical to the unconscious matrix as discussed.

Mars has just received the transit of Saturn; having just "physicalized" the beliefs inherent in the Mars position; is inconjuncting the developmentally tense Sun from the 4th to the 11th-the 4th=emotional security of the identity and the *unconscious*!

In conclusion, the higher self chose a path in which developmental tension would promote probing into the unconscious. However, guilt momentums from the past and the reinforcement of societal or collective belief projection, extreme focus on conscious mind functioning, and rationalization, may have contributed to an *increase in* value judgements and momentum towards a powerless spiral.

When developmental challenges are constricted through conscious mind habitual ritual, judging the higher self as an "id" full of animalistic drives, dis-ease was the unavoidable effect. When you believe that the unconscious higher self must bend to the limited prescriptions of a *component* of itself and label it irrational and dangerous, there may be no alternative than to rid ourselves of and cancel "id" out.

Everything happens for a reason, and we co-created this impact of Freud's idea expression for the sake of addressing the severity of our invalidation of *other aspects* of identity and the joyous and automatic creative extension of self, which sex is also a part.

Scientific and conscious "cogitation" must lead to understanding the overall goal and purpose (concept) of living. Straining at gnats, bowing to the letter and violating the heart, facts; addressed out of context, amounts to organizing reflections and ignoring the source.

Our next life path is a private male client. The Water element is slightly high, otherwise our point count reveals relative balance. There is not a particularly strong hemisphere emphasis, slightly clustered toward nadir (4th house) subjective inner self. The Sun is in Sagittarius, Moon in Scorpio; Opportunities become avenues for emotional significance. A belief in powerlessness can promote opportunism without regard for consequences. Obsession is always a possibility with the Moon in Scorpio.

Both the primary aspects of personalty definition are in the 2nd house of self worth (Sun and Moon). This reflects a strong preoccupation with worth on both conscious and unconscious levels. The Moon, the unconscious and feminine portion of the psyche, is under heavy developmental tension, reflecting disintegrated beliefs and conflict with that function. A powerful reigning need for emotional self worth significance, implies a powerful belief in the perceived *deprivation* of it.

Private Example (male)
Natal Chart (3)

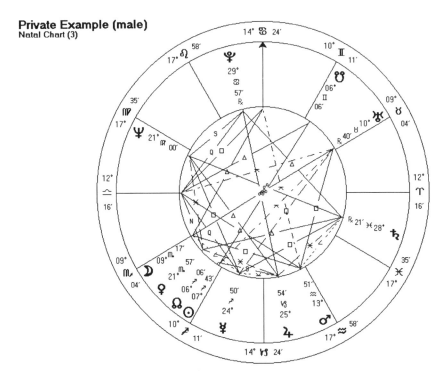

The Moon is in closing square to Mars (need to prove identity) and opposes Uranus (awakening the unconscious and integrating it). Uranus is the dispositor of the Mars in 4 and rules the 5th (creative extension). Venus is brought into this developmental network through it's rulership of the ascendant

and disposing of Uranus. It also reflects the extreme fear of being taken advantage of through it's Grand trine configuration involving Pluto retrograde in Cancer in 10 at critical degree ruling the self worth 2nd, and Saturn also at critical degree in Pisces and ruling the 4th. Pluto (again ruling the self worth 2nd) opposes Jupiter in the parental axis (4/10) exaggerating power and perspective of the worth profile.

So far we have a very defensive self protective identity

definition definitely connected to early environmental and parental perception (Pluto Rx critical degree in 10, moon disposes of it, Saturn Rx-Moon and Saturn rule 4/10).

Also revealed is the perceived threat to identity worth and expression, and much guilt and reassessment (retrograde emphasis and Water emphasis). What does this all have to do with the mental experience? All of these network's expression are totally dependent upon the mental equilibrium whether expressed integratively or disintegratively.

Which brings us to yet another planetary pattern.

Mercury (conscious mind function), Saturn (where power is placed outside the self, through fear), and Neptune (the co-fusion of non-physical reference and dissolution of identity), are in Cadent house and Mutable sign T-square developmental tension (believed separate)-a thinking/perspective crisis. The "arrow" of tension being lodged in the 9th house by Mercury, which also rules the cusp on the 9th. The "blur" of mental perceptions (Mercury in Sagittarius) operates under the belief that neither physical (Saturn) or non-physical reference ideals (Neptune) are accessible or have anything to do with aiding in the resolution of issues. The ideals (Neptune) are believed not manifestable (opposes Saturn) and defuse critical thinking (Mercury in Sagittarius in 3).

Mercury square Saturn reflects a neglect in acknowledging physical manifestations as the effect of thinking and perspective. Saturn's retrograde (not shown) and critical degree condition as the ruler of 4, indicates that preoccupation with emotional concerns and security are the reason for this ignoring perspective. Neptune rules 6 (analytical discernment) and disposes of the defensive Saturn. The non-physical reference (Neptune) is used only as an escape from harsh acceptance of reality creations.[135] An information/perspective crisis that has it's own built in defense *against* resolution!

135
All developmental aspects with Neptune reflect the disbelief in being able to find the ideal in the physical world. The tension resolution is to learn to incorporate it and find it through trust.

"Don't confuse me with the facts."

Pluto at 29 Cancer reflects this rationalizing perspective to defend emotional status, and needs to be resolved as it is accelerated powerfully (the very end of sign representation 29 degrees 57 minutes of arc, retrograde, and the apex of the emotional defense Grand trine, with Saturn as the ruler of 4 also at critical degree and in the Grand trine).

For a clearer understanding of this momentum and the powerful fears, the positions of the planets at first Saturn opposed Saturn must be inspected. They appear in the 2nd wheel outside the natal chart.

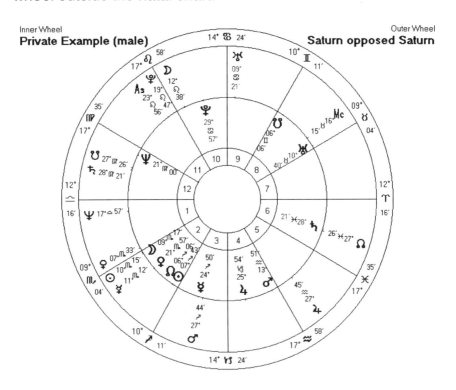

Inner Wheel
Private Example (male)

Outer Wheel
Saturn opposed Saturn

The Saturn opposition obviously occurs in the opposite point of natal Saturn, keying delineation immediately to the mother and early environment (rules 4) as well as the father (Saturn as the archetype of the father figure). The "crisis" in belief externalization (Saturn opposition Saturn) would have to do with the identity's perspective (6th and 12th) as an effect of this preoccupation with emotional security concerns (Saturn ruling 4) and disbelief in the ideal (Neptune and Pisces references).

The self worth concerns and identity definition are brought into this crisis by transitting Venus' (ruling the ascendant and 8-others values) position on the cusp of 2 triggering the natal T-square. Also by transitting Sun ruling 11 (love received and creation interaction) exactly opposing natal Uranus in 8 (the 8th would be the mother's 5th) ruler of the natal 5th (creative extension, giving love).

Transitting Mars exactly squares the problematic Saturn and triggers the mental rationalization pattern. This is definitely where belief momentum was accelerated. Transit Pluto is squaring natal Venus; emotional power struggles. There would be powerful conflicts with both parental figures at this time (Saturn and Moon aspects) triggering self worth issues, and the mental set would have been accelerated either to resolution or further disintegration.

Before his arrival I noticed that the current position of transitting Saturn at our meeting (21 Scorpio) was exactly upon the Venus position discussed, indicating the consultation would obviously revolve around relationship reflections and the early environment (Saturn rules 4).

When he arrived we discussed the premise that we create our reality by what we believe and that this premise would underlie all of our discussion. We warmed up with casual conversation, and he also stated that the reason he wanted to see me was because of a relationship experience over the last year!

I suggested the strong significance needs reflected through the chart were perhaps triggered through the relationship with the mother and father and that the period covering the Saturn opposition Saturn date would have most likely reflected an objective experience of these beliefs. He stated that because of his mother's alcoholism and subsequent beatings of him this might have been the reason he had remained homosexual, never having a relationship with a female until one year ago, which was his reason for consultation! He had become involved with his sexual surrogate therapist and he could not tolerate her interaction with other males in her work! (Scorpio emphasis).

After much discussion of the belief dynamics involved in the creation of these scenarios, his final decision was that it was much more comfortable to remain homosexual in his relationships because he could not stand the insecurity involved with female relationships (I am *not* implying this as any sort of generalizable "cause", but specifically in this case as was observed).

The rationalizing escape mechanism was overworked to replace taking responsibility for creations. A powerful e-motional momentum indeed (Water/Moon/feminine functions). The grand trine was relied upon for emotional "containment". Worth was being "protected" and the early environment taught the individual that the emotions are dangerous and to be feared.

In conclusion, higher self will was invalidated through conscious mind and physical reality fears. Discernment became *the threat* to identity emotional security and perspective contained rather than altered. This occurs often when there is no other reality or purpose except conscious mind-ego preservation. The only idea left to express in these types of encounters of extreme rigidity and fear, is the reminder that I have faith in the individual's ability to welcome life and growth no matter how miserable they insist it must be, and support the decisions made with the assumption that they must serve a purpose for now. Things are there for a reason but the client must be ready to see them in that way. Staying "stuck" still must be serving in some way, and when the individual is ready then perhaps it can be seen. There are no "shoulds."

No examination of the mental experience would be complete without observing the mental processes and beliefs of Albert Einstein. His contribution to physics through the theories of relativity were monumental. Not only because it added unifying (integrative) principles to science, but it also added force to his own statement and recognition that "Imagination is more important than knowledge." It is also supportive to the aims of this book to add the following quote;

▸ "The most beautiful and most profound emotion we can experience is the sensation of the mystical. It is the sower of all true science. He to whom this emotion is a stranger, who can no longer wonder and stand rapt in awe, is as good as dead. To know what is impenetrable to us really exists, manifesting itself as highest wisdom and the most radiant beauty which our dull faculties can comprehend only in their most primitive forms-this knowledge, this feeling is at the center of true religiousness." Albert Einstein, "The Universe and Dr. Einstein", Lincoln Barnett.

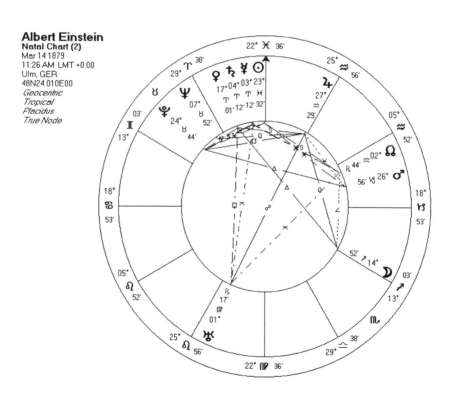

Albert Einstein
Natal Chart (2)
Mar 14 1879
11:26 AM LMT +0:00
Ulm, GER
48N24 010E00
Geocentric
Tropical
Placidus
True Node

It is this perspective that allowed him to dissolve many "apparent" barriers in the scientific world. There was not the strict adherence to conscious mind function as the "real" reality that permeates most "objective" analysis such as was Freud's discerned through the Horoscope.

The element count shows a low count in the Air element. However, this one point is carried by the largest planet in the solar system; Jupiter, and becomes a focal point in analysis. This would reflect that higher self idea interaction and the conceptual was focused upon far more than idle chit-chat.

Jupiter also rules the all important 6th house of analytical discernment and disposes of the ascendant ruler and reigning need, the Moon. In turn Jupiter is then disposed of by Uranus (innovation and "waking up" to other levels of consciousness).

The Sun is in Pisces, Moon in Sagittarius, which reads; The identity experiences the conflict of analytical understanding and the application of the intellect to intuitive recognitions. The integrative energy of these two principles represents grand intellectual awareness married to mystical awareness (page 267). Most would agree that Einstein expressed the integrative aspect of this blend. Moreover, we have a very strong momentum indicated already through the single point in Air being Jupiter ruler of the 6th, dispositor of the reigning need and ruler of the ascendant.

Next in our search for patterns, Jupiter forms a T-square (bow and arrow developmental tension) between Pluto in 11 (ruler of the 5th) and Uranus (ruler of the 9th) and dispositor of Jupiter that "shoots" developmental resolution into the 5th and 6th as well! An information/extension (Pluto in 11 ruling 5) developmental network to discharge information into creativity and extension. This is the horoscope of self-empowerment through the higher self extension par excellence.

The Jupiter/Uranus opposition is doubly applying (one forward and one Rx) and is the only focus of awareness. Jupiter closing toward critical ending degree, and Uranus retrograde closing toward initial degree in Virgo the archetype of analytical discernment! "I don't want to be right, I only want to know whether I am right."! Uranus is tied to the 8th where perspective alterations (Pluto and Scorpio and 8th) will blend with revelation (Uranus) and 9th the natural house of Jupiter and mystical or philosophic awareness (also the University system).

The only concept we have not evaluated which is essential to the application of these energies is personal focus to process them. Mercury is in Aries in the 10th (to think were no man has thought before, ego importance to be first, and in the 10th-to physically manifest pioneer thinking). It is conjunct the primary archetype of the physical dream and material focus; Saturn.

Saturn disposes of the Mars that is in strategic application Capricorn. Mars in turn disposes of Mercury, and is in *mutual reception* with Saturn from the 7th (the need to prove the self). Mars trines Pluto, the archetype of transformational energy and *perspective*! Pluto also rules atomic energy.

In 1905 he made unprecedented discoveries in three different branches of physics. He applied Planck's hypothesis (the distribution of energy in the spectrum of "black body"

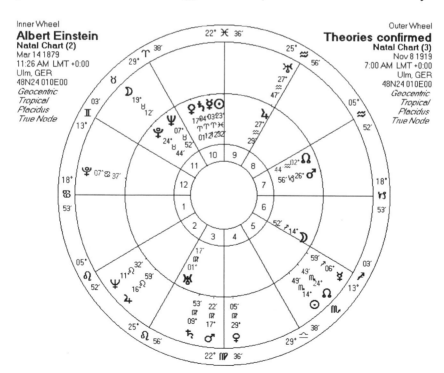

Inner Wheel
Albert Einstein
Natal Chart (2)
Mar 14 1879
11:26 AM LMT +0:00
Ulm, GER
48N24 010E00
Geocentric
Tropical
Placidus
True Node

Outer Wheel
Theories confirmed
Natal Chart (3)
Nov 8 1919
7:00 AM LMT +0:00
Ulm, GER
48N24 010E00
Geocentric
Tropical
Placidus
True Node

radiation) of the quantum to the photoelectric effect, establishing the validity of the quantum hypothesis and extending it's range; he made calculations pertaining to the Brownian movement that were instrumental in finally convincing scientists that atoms really exist and he wrote a paper on electrodynamics and motion that presented what is now called the special theory of relativity, following it with a paper deducing the formula $E=mc^2$, which, at the time, like all his ideas, seemed to have little practical application.

In the second wheel are the transits for the morning of November 8, 1919, when he awoke to worldwide recognition from the confirmation of those theories.[136] Transit Jupiter, dispositor of the reigning need (the moon ruling 1-his identity) and ruler of 6 (the worth of extension- 6th is the 2nd of the 5th) is *exactly* trine Venus in the 10th and the Moon on the 6th from 2 completing a Grand Trine. A Fire Grand Trine reflecting great inspirational self-sufficiency and identity affirmation in the material world (the 2nd, 6th and 10th is the trinity of physicality).

There is a full moon (full illumination) in the transit chart from 5th to 11th (extension interaction) on the midpoint of his natal Mars/Uranus!

Neptune, his Sun sign ruler, joins in this Grand Trine along with Mercury, which brings his natal Mercury/Saturn conjunction in as well. Transit Pluto sextiles (supports) natal Neptune (other worldly perspective) from 12 (societal institutions and reason for incarnation) ruling his 10th of status.

Transit Saturn trines natal Neptune (finds fulfilling expression of the "two" worlds of imagination and physicality) from 3 (conscious mind focus) with social recognition and acknowledgment from other co-creators (11th and reinforces the Aquarian placements).

Transit Uranus is *exactly* conjunct Jupiter in nine! Expanded recognition of his own revelations (Aquarius and Uranus) by

---

[136] They are still being proven to this day.

others thinking and opinions from the 9th (the reigning need of the moon) for his work (Jupiter rules the 6th). A tremendous triggering of the expansive networks discussed in the natal promise.

Albert Einstein lead us to the recognition of how little we use our abilities and creative potential. With Cancer on the ascendant and the ruler, the Moon in Sagittarius, it is no wonder that he is remembered for having said that "Imagination is more important than knowledge."

Albert Einstein believed wholeheartedly in simplicity. He became intrigued as a youth of 5, in the pulsations of an ordinary compass, which is what set him off on the exploration of life. He worked until his death on the unified field theory (integrative).

In conclusion, the expanse of higher self functioning and the conscious mind focus as *servant rather than director* of higher self mind, allowed integration not only to occur within the identity, but as an end to pursue in analytical service.

When the Universe is viewed from the perspective of a "child" in excitement and awe, the ego can be soothed and pacified so that it does not have to know every little detail of how things *must* fit. This relaxation can allow it to know that it's extreme fearfulness and panic is only the effect of it's *relative* and subjective perception.

"A human being is part of the whole, called by us 'universe,' limited in time and space. He experiences himself, his thoughts and feelings as something separated from the rest, a kind of optical delusion of his consciousness. This delusion is a prison, restricting us to our personal desires and to affection for a few persons close to us.

Our task must be to free ourselves from our prison by widening our circle of compassion to embrace all humanity and the whole of nature in its beauty."   Albert Einstein

"Let the mind be enlarged, according to its capacity, to the grandeur of the mysteries, and not the mysteries contracted to the narrowness of the mind. "   -SIR FRANCIS BACON

"Common sense is actually nothing more than a deposit of predjudices laid down in the mind prior to the age of 18. Every new idea one encounters in later years must combat this accretion of "self-evident" concepts."
Albert Einstein

"In mans brief tenancy on earth he egocentrically orders events in his mind according to his own feelings of past, present and future. But except on the reels of ones own consciousness, the universe, the objective world of reality, does not "happen"-it simply exists."
Lincoln Barnett

"The physicist has no need of the flow of time or the now in the world of physics. Indeed the theory of relativity rules out a universal present for all observers. If there is any meaning at all to these concepts (and many philosophers, such as McTaggart, deny that there is) then it would seem to belong to psychology rather than physics." Paul Davies on Time

"Astrology, bar sinister in the escutcheon of astronomy, maintains a unique and lonely position in human thought. It is "believed in" by a lot of people who know practically nothing about it; and it is "disbelieved in" by even more who know absolutely nothing about it. Of no other art or science can this be said." Grant Lewi, "Why I believe in Astrology"

Chapter 11

The Reincarnation Experience
Momentum

> "I believe I shall in some shape
> or other always exist, and with
> all the inconveniences human life
> is liable to, I shall not object
> to a new edition of my life,
> hoping however, that the errata
> of the last may be corrected."
> Benjamin Franklin

Re-incarnation can only occur from the perspective of a linear time frame. Since time and space are the illusion of three dimensional (3D) physical reality, all incarnations are actually "occurring" at once. The incarnation, and then reincarnation of any idea, simply reflects the linear progression of that idea (whatever the idea is-be it person or concept) from it's basic premise, to more refined specifics.

> ▸ in-car-na-tion, The act of incarnating, or the state of being incarnate, esp. assumption of human form or nature, as by a divine being; an incarnate being or form; a person or thing representing or exhibiting something, as a quality or idea, in typical form; the personification or embodiment of an idea, quality, spirit, or god. Lexicon/Webster

The incarnation of *anything* is a "spectrum" of idea manifestation in all it's probable, counterpart or parallel possible manifestations, which are infinite. The momentum of ideas can carry with them a heavy weight or little weight. Analogous to a snowball, a heavily weighted one may have much intensity or *energy-motion* (e-motion).

The basic concept of third density or dimension is the experience of separate, specific, limited and focused idea exploration. In 3D the ego self and conscious mind we defined early on in this text is believed to be all we are or have been.

I will use the analogy of a watch or clock as representing the oversoul or entire conglomerate identity or "self", physical and non-physical to explain. Remembering however, that all the marks, hands and the watch itself all exist at the same "time," only the "part's" experiences will seem separate while focus is on them, one at a time. The experience as the "mark" or the "hand" are all component aspects, counterpart polarity aspects of the overall identity called "watch." One of the minute marks on the face of the clock would stand for a single physical life. The one minute mark is unaware of it's "parent" the clock, and would only become aware of itself upon the sweeping by of the second hand over itself for that second. It's awareness would be specifically focused to that one second of experiential reality. It has a sense that the hand comes and goes, but from what and to where, is unknown. The other minute markers experience their realities in the same manner, only experiencing themselves in that moment of that second hand sweep. After sixty of these moments pass, a certain mark experiences something different, a larger hand moves overhead in conjunction with the second hand, the minute hand. During this event the mark may begin to realize that perhaps the coming and going of the second hand may have had something to do with this, and has a glimpse of some larger order that it and these hands must have something to do with. Soon the hour hand may appear at this marker along with the minute and second, and after what appeared to be quite a "separate" existence, experiences now begin to show signs of having a progression and an order. Perhaps a realization will occur that different things happen depending on these different alignments, such as a chime when the hands are all lined up on a certain marker (12=10th house?).

So it is in the experience of life in physical reality. Until we eventually become aware that all the "markers" are ourselves, and that what we once believed about being "just one little mark" was an illusion. We learn that each mark we were, was just one specific experience we chose to experience, in exploring all the different aspects of the "watch" that we are. In closing off all awareness of the "watch" that we are, and pretending to be the one mark on the face, we explore fully and without distraction the "reality" and experience of a mark. Being the mark, never detracts from being the watch, the power of the watch to drive the hands of the mark, or from measuring time. But once we've explored all the marks, gears, springs, dials, hands-we have now become a *master of limited focus* on *each*.

Because of these experiences, we can tell you any aspect of the watch with conscious clarity. How time moves, how long it takes, even what kinds of experiences a minute mark may have. We have experienced by choice every aspect of the idea we chose to express physically. We can then assist others who may wish to explore the idea of being a watch (come into physical reality). We can point out the pitfalls that are possible for example, of being a mark, wherein focus may be so sharp, that you may begin to believe that the mark is *all* you are. But this is necessary, because the expansive idea of being a clock shall be greatly refined and much more precise, through the experience of forgetting, to re-member (reintegrate) the mark.

The life we are living is the only "time" we exist. The hands are on this mark, from this mark the rest of the watch is seen and changed. The point of power is in the present. We create the future AND the past from the perspective of the present. The experience as "other marks" does not affect the experience of the present "mark," and the present mark, is not the effect of the experience of past marks. There are only three aspects of the Multiverse that are absolutes: 1) that we exist, 2) the one is all-and the all is one, and 3) that what you put into anything, is what you get back.[137]

Therefore, when we investigate past life possibilities we are free to choose whether or not to "carry" patterns or beliefs with us. Karma; simply, the experiencing of a continued momentum

---

[137] Darryl Anka channeling Bashar, "The Razor's Edge," 1993.

brought from other lives. It is not necessarily negative or positive.

> ►   "Free will, will simply be the exercising of the chosen purpose, whether from the higher consciousness level or the physiological level."
> "Karma is simply an expression of momentum in a particular direction with regard to what the higher self wishes to experience of itself. All karma is self imposed. It is not a judgment. It is the recognition of balance. It is the recognition of an idea that is being lived out, that is being experienced, and the choosing of situations that will allow for that experience to occur in physical reality." Bashar-"The New Metaphysics" 1987, page 18.

Physical reality is the mirror of mind in matter. Therefore, because beliefs are the essence of mind, they are not terminated by the cessation of the physical body. The leaving of the second hand from the "mark," does not stop the idea of the watch-only the experience of it, by that particular mark. The momentum is immediately picked up and continued by the next mark, and the next, and the next.

Changes within time, and within each life, although gradual, can also be dramatic. There could be relative silence on one mark, followed by ten chimes on the next. The primary difference between the watch and our experience of lives, is that we determine the speed, quality, and impact of these different marks. There is no mystery in discovering past life experiences, or future for that matter, whatever your present situations or circumstances are, they are a pretty good indication of what they were, and whatever you imagine them to be, is a general indication of where they are headed, unless the "mark" you are now, changes the momentum. Being aware of the momentum can in and of itself render the momentum unnecessary.

Similar ideas can be expressed in several lives, or totally different scenarios can be experienced in any number of ways. There is no one general rule. There are many variations many creations in any form, in any reality. We will not discuss whether past lives are something to believe or disbelieve in.

After thousands of horoscopes, and just plain living, it becomes quite obvious that everyone is different, at different levels of awareness, financial status, spiritual status and on and on. Levels of awareness cannot be determined by horoscopes, only the potential for it. Variations are infinite. It seems highly unlikely from this perception alone, that "All That Is" gave us all varying lives and we have one shot at it, as many religions believe. Many children starving in the world never even become aware of, or have the time to think about, their "sins," for every day is an ongoing concern for food. Another group's biggest concern may be a shopping decision. This inequity hardly seems an equal starting line for a one time race. But while countries (like the USA) help countries with physical starvation problems, the starving country helps the United States and many other countries with their *spiritual* starvation, which brings us to our first chart in the exploration of incarnation, the United States of America.[138]

The United States is the continued momentum of the collectivity incarnate during the existence of Atlantis, which ended the Age of Leo some 12,900 years ago (please see the Edgar Cayce material).

During the destruction of Atlantis caused in essence by material greed and people manipulation,[139] many Atlanteans escaped the destruction because of their awareness of the momentum. They fled Atlantis to the Yucatan, to Morocco and Egypt. The builders of the Pyramids in these locations, were Atlanteans and their descendants who blended with the local peoples. Note that on the US paper currency is the remnant pyramidal structure with the eye at it's *apex* reflecting our once

---

[138] More accurately defined as the Declaration of Independence *decision chart*. There is much controversy over which chart should be used among astrologers. To this astrologer it is irrelevant as the general idea and thrust of the new beginning will be shown clearly just in different ways in each during the period. This one accurately revealed the Northridge California quake to me, so I trust it.

[139] Please refer to Edgar Cayce on Atlantis, by Edgar Evans Cayce, or the ARE, Association for Research and Enlightenment.

conscious knowledge of the principles of integration between the physical and the spiritual. The crystal skull is an Atlantean remnant (the Mitchell-Hedges more refined one mentioned in the preface of this book).

The momentum of civilization since *recorded* history, has been a deepening enmeshment of focus in the physical world. The emergence of science and industry has been the culmination point of this focus. The collective perspective is the result, wherein we now believe that physical reality is the "real" reality and mystical and mythological awareness is the "fantasy" of imagination.

United States Declaration

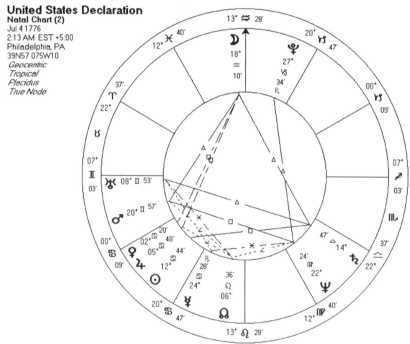

Natal Chart (2)
Jul 4 1776
2:13 AM EST +5:00
Philadelphia, PA
39N57 075W10
Geocentric
Tropical
Placidus
True Node

Continuing our watch analogy, what has actually occurred with this techno-emergence is the "mark" of the watch proclaiming it's reality as the source, and invalidating it's source-the watch. The mark then, is referring to the watch as an illusion; it's "less focused" experience at the beginning of the experience of itself as a mark.

This focus or enmeshment, reflected in what we now see as the U.S.,[140] is a more focused and specific experience of it's concept initiator, Atlantis. We will discern it's momentum as with any other chart, through sequential astrological delineation.

The Element count shows a definite disbelief in spirit, faith, and identity validity as there is 0 Fire representation! There would be an invalidation of identity and it's creative birthright! This reflects an inability to trust spirit and inspiration as "real" or as a valid way and support of the collectivity. Guilt from a past life? Obviously. Spiritual salvation until this point in history was typically with the state or heads of state. In the US declaration we have the birth of collective empowerment. Since it was the *people* as the heads of state, inspirational self sufficiency and lack of faith was replaced by strategy.

Cardinal mode is high; action, motivation, and high Air equates to the archetypal concept of Libra, the experience of self through projection, externalization, and identity reinforcement by social acceptance. The "balancing" of momentum through objective confrontation is the concept of the mirror of Libra.

The Sun/Moon blend of Cancer/Aquarius; Security is sought through innovations that liberate the self from confining structures! The self believes it is practical, others may see a little more theory than practice. Saturn, the "identity's" greatest fears and where power is placed outside the self (country) is IN Libra; Fear of not being accepted by others leads to possibly being untrue to the self-or even what the self's true position is! Natural aggression is a must with this placement to alleviate the repression. However, due to the 0 Fire representation, the "self" does not believe in natural aggression, that it must *repress* aggression (meaning natural aggression of course). The country teaching best what the country needs to learn.

---

[140] There are several versions of the "birth" of the US, the one we use is the most logical as it does not contain a void of course moon. The next in feasibility is listed.

Even the populace of the US is aware of its "double standards." There is a Grand trine in Air between Mars in Gemini in 1 (the need to prove the intelligence of the self), Saturn in Libra in 5 (guarded and defensive self-extension), and the Moon in Aquarius in 10 (the reigning need to externalize the principles of humanitarianism and free and equal validity as co-creators) as a defense against the fear of the country is not being appreciated (Air Element). This is in overcompensatory reaction to the country's disbelief in it's own identity validity (0-Fire).

The Sun ruler of 4 (emotional security) is in the sign of Cancer in the 2nd (extreme emotional self worth insecurity), and squares the Saturn in 5! The country displaces all this disbelief in self and it's worth and validity into personal worth security and money as a defense against these fears. A very insecure perspective.

Referring again to our interpretations: The ascendant is in Gemini; a conscious mind articulate projection of the identity definition. The ascendant ruler (Mercury) in the 3rd house (conscious mind function) retrograde and opposes Pluto also retrograde (the perspective and power issues in the thinking of the populace needing resolution). Pluto is in the physical externalization sign of Capricorn at critical degree, indicating a need to accelerate (urgent need to move off of the sign) and incorporate this idea so that collective perspective (Pluto) can get on with the Aquarian archetype.

Pluto rules intercepted (missing in reference) Scorpio on 6 (analytical discernment) and has just experienced opening inconjunct (perspective adjustment) from Venus (personal and social reflection) from the 2nd (worth) ruler of the Taurus interception (missing in reference) in 12. THE REASON FOR INCARNATION is the need to resolve limitations of the collective with reference to personal reflections (money/worth/materiality)!

Pluto trines Neptune in the 5th in Virgo (the analytical discernment of spiritual and other-world realities) which rules the 11th (creativity equality and validity) as the way out of this lack of perspective and discernment. This aspect supports the idea expressed by 0 fire and we see that the key to America's salvation and highest fulfillment in placing the humanitarian above the personal and material.

Mars (the ego self) also rules 12 and squares Neptune (believed separate) reinforcement of this spiritual destiny fulfillment need. Applied energy in development tension with the *non*-physical aspects of reality.

As a collective consciousness, the country believes that conscious mind "proving" will liberate individuality, when that is how it is separated (limited) to begin with! Uranus in Gemini in 1 is the way out; to wake up unconscious knowledge of the *equal validity* as co-creators and bring this unconscious knowledge to conscious mind awareness (Uranus is in Gemini and is disposed of by the retrograde Mercury, ruler of 1 *and*

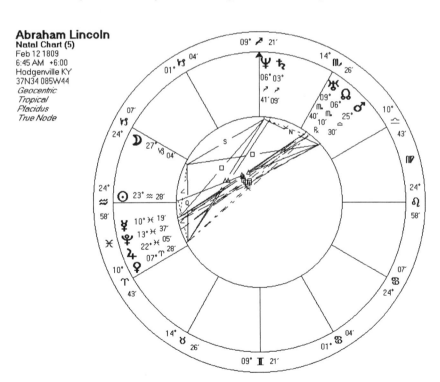

Abraham Lincoln
Natal Chart (5)
Feb 12 1809
6:45 AM +6:00
Hodgenville KY
37N34 085W44
Geocentric
Tropical
Placidus
True Node

dispositor of Mars). Uranus disposes of the Moon (reigning need) and rules 10 the physical manifestation of beliefs. Pay special attention to this *9 degree position* it is a part of important delineations to follow.

These needs will not be complete in their fulfillment-until spirit (Fire) is integrated into the collective consciousness as a *valid* and "real" element. Aries on 12 reflects this archetype as the country's introspection need that limits the birth of its aspirations (Mars squares Neptune, ruler of 11). Its Achilles heel limiting fulfillment of the reigning need.

The next chart reveals a profound connection reincarnationally with both the Atlantean concept and it's reincarnation as the United States. It is the chart of Abraham Lincoln.

The Element and Mode point count show relative balance. The Sun in Aquarius, Moon in Capricorn delineation (page 265) reads; The administration of humanitarian principles. The broad social concerns of the life energy are focused and applied by the reigning needs of the persona. Facts and an understanding of human nature can present a powerful and just persona! That both the Sun and the Moon are in the 12th house suggests idealism and compassion (along with the Pisces planets in 1).

These humanitarian principles and strategic effectiveness are applied to the self's own introspection and reflect consciously (Sun) and unconsciously (Moon) the reason for incarnation! The reigning need (Moon) square Mars in 8, the life energy (Sun) is trine Mars. Mars rules 2 reflecting self worth dependent upon and fulfilled by the Sun/Moon blend! Social acceptance (Mars) through strategic implementation (Moon in Capricorn) of the humanitarian life thrust (Sun in Aquarius). Saturn rules the 12th (understanding) and disposes of the reigning need of the Moon (strategically effective) in Sagittarius (breadth of vision) conjunct Neptune (compassion), which rules the intercepted Pisces in the ascendant.

The reason for incarnation "coloring" was to be respected for the intellect through which the incorporation of equality and oneness could be projected (12th and Neptune references).

The ascendant ruler Uranus trines Mercury ruling the 4th. The unconscious knowledge expression, reinforces identity emotional security. Both the planets connected with higher self functions, Jupiter, disposing of the Neptune/Saturn conjunction, and Pluto the 9th house ruler-are in the 1st, bringing the higher functions to the personal projection. Jupiter and Neptune are in mutual reception. Jupiter rules the 10th (physical manifestation of beliefs). Venus (social and personal reflection) trines the Neptune/Saturn conjunction and rules 3 and 8 (conscious mind-3, transcendence, death-8). Venus is also in Mutual reception with the self-worth Mars in 8. Mercury squares Saturn/Neptune conjunction and reflects the need to fulfill or integrate higher self's reason for incarnation through conscious mind function in projection (1st house placement).

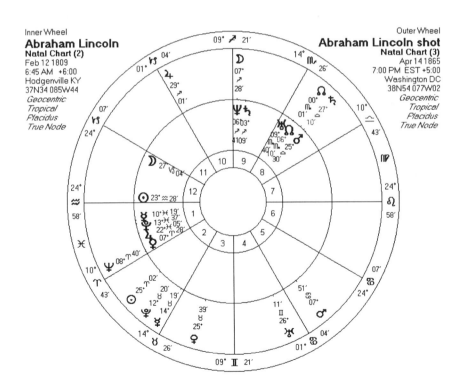

In addition, Mercury also rules the 7th of the public.

Pluto has rulership over conflicts and racial issues with the collectivity. It is conjunct Mercury in Pisces (identity sacrifice). This is a powerful projection of the higher mind through intuitive conscious mind function to bring together spirit (Neptune) and physicality (Saturn) through humanitarian strategy! The Arthurian or Arcturian energy of "I and the land are one in the same". His Mars is on the star Arcturus! The Gatekeeper at 24 Libra.

After his nomination for the U.S. Senate he declared;

▸   "A house divided against itself cannot stand. I believe this government cannot endure permanently half slave and half free"!

In the ring outside the natal chart are the transits for the time when he was shot by John Wilkes Booth at Ford's theater.

Transitting Moon ruling the 5th and 6th (the 11th and 12th house of the of the 7th-attacker) is exactly upon the Midheaven (externalized status) conjunct Neptune (camouflage, deception, dissolution of the physical) in the sign of "others opinions in the *house* of others opinions and thinking, square Mercury (conscious mind and communication-what he said) and Pluto (death, issues of power, *race* and control issues regarding others values and money).

The dispositor and ruler of the Midheaven-Jupiter, is at 29 degrees (urgent philosophical expansion differences) conjunct the 11th (the creative extensions of others), the natural house of Aquarius!

Transit Saturn (12th house ruler reason for incarnation) is retrograde conjunct natal Mars, and exactly square the natal Moon in 12! (We will see when we compare this to the US chart that this is the exact square to US Pluto!-where Lincoln's moon was tied).

Transit Sun (in Aries-head) exactly opposes natal Mars (head) and transit Saturn and rules 7. Transit Mars squares natal Venus (ruler of 8, 3) and disposes of *natal* Mars. In addition T Mars is square transit Neptune (self sacrifice) ruler of 1-in Aries, the head! Transit Mars completes a Grand trine with natal Mercury in 1, and Uranus ruler of the ascendant in

8 (the fulfillment of identity and it's extension)! Transit Venus is stationary retrograde square the Sun, inconjunct Mars, and square (needs integration) the ascendant.

Transit Pluto and Mercury oppose Uranus from the cusp of 3 (racial values (Taurus) and expression) to 9 (others thinking).

Lincoln was killed because he upset the work ethic (6th and 12th, perspective) and financial status quo (2nd, 8th and Taurus references) through his racial policies of equality.

The next chart I believe, through supporting astrological connections, is the chart of the reincarnation of Lincoln as John F. Kennedy. Lincoln represented the conceptual initiation of self-empowering example for the people of the United States, and Kennedy reflected the completion of the Uranian energy discussed in the chart of the U.S. and the racial status issues of Pluto in 9-where Lincoln's moon was in exact conjunction.

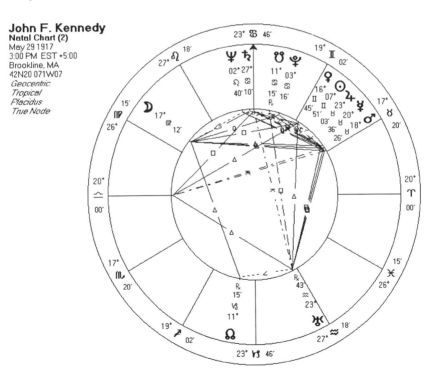

John F. Kennedy
Natal Chart (2)
May 29 1917
3:00 PM EST +5:00
Brookline, MA
42N20 071W07
Geocentric
Tropical
Placidus
True Node

The hemisphere emphasis polarizes, from subjective to objective-and so do the planets, Lincoln's chart to Kennedy's chart respectively.

A polarity is the expression other side of the same coin. Kennedy's Uranus in 4 is exactly conjunct Lincoln's Sun position (ruler polarities). Saturn is at exact polarity by sign and planet of Lincoln's Moon (and conjunct the US Pluto!). Kennedy's Moon (reigning need) is at the polarity (opposition) point of Lincoln's Pisces 1st house planets. Kennedy's Sun is at the polarity point of Lincoln's Saturn/Neptune conjunction and Midheaven. Kennedy's Mars, Mercury, and Jupiter are in the polarity signs of Lincoln's all important Uranus. The overall persona definition in Lincoln's chart in the last life, becomes the specific personal projection definition in Kennedy's chart the ascendant! Both charts have Saturn/Neptune conjunctions, Mars in 8, Venus ruling 8, the rulers of the 1st in the 8th conjunct the 9th house cusp. In addition, Mercury in the same

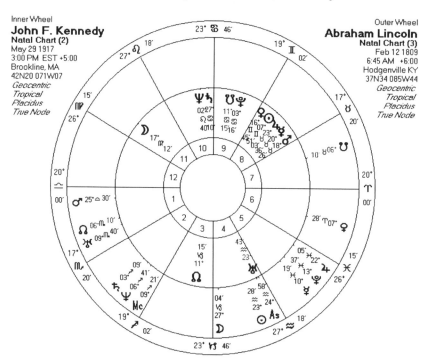

sign as Jupiter, the 27th and 23rd degrees of Capricorn and Aquarius emphasized, and 7 to 10 degrees of Gemini, Sagittarius and Pisces falling in quadrature with the U.S. Uranus!

Lincoln's 4th (unconscious) becomes Kennedy's life energy (Sun), and Lincoln's Aquarian life energy (Sun) becomes Kennedy's past unconscious knowledge in the 4th!

Here is just a very small sampling of the similarity of their momentum and expression;

▸ *Lincoln*   *Kennedy*

Lincoln	Kennedy
1836 Admitted to the Bar	1936 Entered Harvard
1860 Nominated for President	1960 Nominated for President
Lincoln-Douglas debates	Debated 4 times with Nixon on TV
1861 Elected President	1961 Elected President
1862 Ancd Emancipation Proc.-	1962 Prohibited race discrimination
1863 Emancipation Proclamation	1963 Sweeping Civil rights prohibiting discrimination of blacks

        Lincoln   **AFTER ELECTION**   *Kennedy*

▸ "In your hands my dissatisfied countrymen, and not mine, is the momentous issue of civil war"   "In your hands my fellow citizens, more than mine, will rest the final success or failure of our course"

"A nation divided against itself cannot stand....   "This country cannot afford to be to be materially rich and

(inaugural addresses)   spiritually poor.."

amnesty to appease the south   Johnson as running mate to appease south

AFTER (Lincoln's) RE-ELECTION

▸ he pleaded for poor"   "Ask not what your country can With malice toward none, do for you, but what you can do for with charity for all."   your country"

Shot in the back of the head by John Wilkes Booth?   Shot in the back of the head by Lee Harvey Oswald?

Some say no.   Some say no.

Both sought to return power to the people through principles of equality.

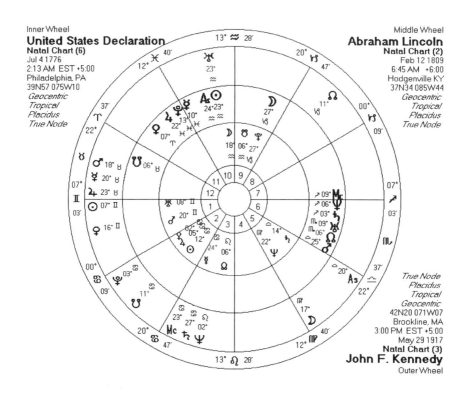

Both Jacqueline Bovier and Mary Todd were from wealthy and prominent families and interestingly upon entering the White House Jacqueline redecorated it in as a period house of the 18th and 19th centuries, making it a "museum of our countries heritage"!

John Kennedy's chart shows a low count in Fire; a disbelief in identity and it's creative birthright. The Sun is in Gemini and Moon in Virgo; There is a developmental tension to categorize information based on some sort of values. Applying the self with natural aggression will solve the indecision problems (page 249). Kennedy's indecision with the Russian buildup caused him great frustration.

The Moon in Virgo is square Venus in Gemini in 8, the reigning need to be analytically correct is in tension with the diversity of other's values! Sound familiar? Uranus in the 4th of the past and unconscious foundation is square the Mars, Mercury, and Jupiter in the sign of Taurus (money) in the 8th, another house of the past and unconscious. The same fears (beliefs) created the same effect.

Sensitivity about strategic effectiveness is reflected in Saturn in Cancer, just as the Moon in Capricorn in Lincoln's chart-Mutual reception in the exact same degree! Both are known to have had painful spine and bone problems (Saturn).

In the ring around Kennedy's natal horoscope are the transiting planets for the time of his assassination.

Transit Mercury ruler of the 12th (reason for incarnation) and 9th (other's opinions) is opposing the Sun in Gemini in 8 from the 2nd at *9 degrees Sagittarius* close to the degree of the Moon at Lincoln's assassination (7-9 Mutable). And again this degree is opposing the U.S. Uranus in Gemini in 1!

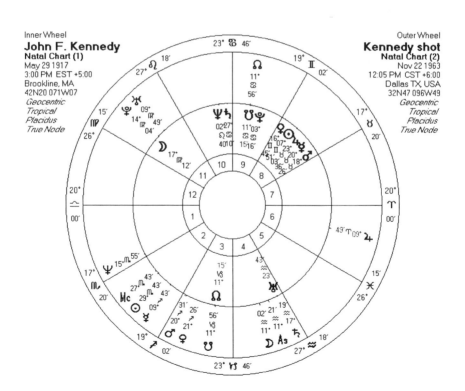

Inner Wheel
John F. Kennedy
Natal Chart (1)
May 29 1917
3:00 PM EST +5:00
Brookline, MA
42N20 071W07
Geocentric
Tropical
Placidus
True Node

Outer Wheel
Kennedy shot
Natal Chart (2)
Nov 22 1963
12:05 PM CST +6:00
Dallas TX, USA
32N47 096W49
Geocentric
Tropical
Placidus
True Node

Transit Uranus is *9 degrees Virgo* squaring the U.S. Uranus placement, and transit Mercury forming a T-square with Kennedy's Sun. Transit Jupiter is *9 degrees Aries* in the same position as Lincoln's natal Venus and transit Neptune at his assassination. Pluto in 11 ruling 2, is squaring Venus in 8 ruling 1 and 8 (resources). The Sun is at critical degree (29) in the *sign* of others resources (Scorpio). Kennedy was assassinated for similar reasons! The chart reflects *economic* (industrial) power structures and/or struggles between his and others *extension/worth powers* (Uranus and Sun as rulers of 5/11 and the Mercury/Uranus square is from the 11th-others extension. A clearer picture is revealed through his solar return for the year of his assassination which occurred in May of 63.

Scorpio; other peoples resources, death, transformation, rules the year (on the ascendant). The ruler Pluto, is at *9 degrees Virgo* in the 10th (physicalization) and squares the Sun ruler of 9 (others opinions) in the 7th!

Mercury disposes of the Sun, Uranus, Moon, MC and Pluto and is stationary direct in Taurus (values) ruler of 8 (others values) just as Venus was stationary retrograde in Taurus when Lincoln was assassinated. Mercury forms a T-square with Saturn in 3 and Mars in 9, an information perspective crisis regarding others thinking and/or knowledge (Mercury is the focus as it disposes of half the planets in the chart and rules 10). Saturn and the Moon rule the information axis of 3/9. Venus (money) opposes Neptune (camouflage) from 6 to 12 (perspective).

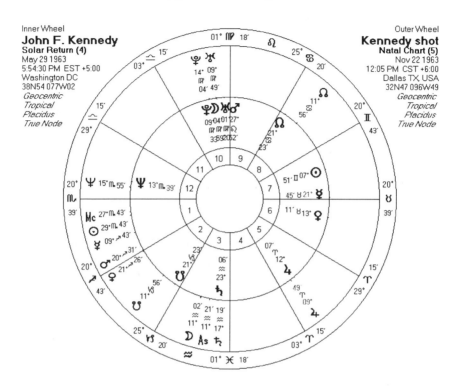

Inner Wheel
John F. Kennedy
Solar Return (4)
May 29 1963
5:54:30 PM EST +5:00
Washington DC
38N54 077W02
Geocentric
Tropical
Placidus
True Node

Outer Wheel
Kennedy shot
Natal Chart (5)
Nov 22 1963
12:05 PM CST +6:00
Dallas TX, USA
32N47 096W49
Geocentric
Tropical
Placidus
True Node

The Moon progresses approximately one degree per month in a solar return, which would put the progressed solar return Moon at *9 degrees Virgo* in 10 conjunct the ruler of the year! Here are the calculated progressions. These can be calculated by hand by taking the motions of the planets and dividing them by 365 to get a daily movement-or more conveniently, by computer;

Mon (10) Sqr Sun (7)(X)Pr-Re **Aug 21 1963** *conflict over ideology* 07°Vi51' D 07°Ge51' D

Mon (10) Qnt Asc (1)(X)Pr-Re **Sep 14 1963** *creative applications* 08°Vi39' D 20°Sc39' D
or plans

Mon (10) Pll Ura (10)(X)Pr-Re **Sep 27 1963** *individualistic thinking* 09°Vi04' D 01°Vi20' D
Parallel *(acts as a conjunction)*

Mon (10) Cnj Plu (10)(X)Pr-Re **Oct 11 1963** *threat of powerful analytical*
D9°Vi33' D   09°Vi33' D   *collective or societal impact*

Ven (6) Opp Nep (12)(X)Pr-Re **Oct 20 1963** *collusion, camouflage, deception within*
13°Ta39' D   13°Sc39' R   *relationships-the Achilles heel*
Mon (10) Pll MC (10)(X)Pr-Re **Nov 29 1963** *precision-execution of power, death*
11°Vi12' D   01°Vi18' D

The progression of these aspects show Kennedy's difficulty from the "ideas or thinking" (9th emphasis of progressed Moon square Sun from the 10th to the 7th in the SR as both rule the 9th) of an opponent (7th Sun *in Gemini*) beginning as early as August 21, 1963.

SR Venus rules the urgent critical degree Libra 12th house (and others 7th) cusp and opposes Neptune; A camouflage of blame from the economic power structures who assassinated him, to Lee Harvey Oswald who was then shot to be silenced! (camouflage, misleading). The value structure conflict is great (Taurus/Scorpio emphasis).

Mercury (the other in 7) disposes of Pluto-which disposes of the Neptune. The security of an analytical base of others (10 is the 4th of the other with the Virgo planets) was tied to some camouflaged work (Neptune in 12-the 6th of the other). Subordinates could have had much to do with this again (Venus in 6 is the ruler of 7, 11, 12). Some financial base was at risk. The moon would progress to trine SR Venus and sextile Neptune by the first months of 64 shown below reflecting success financially on the part of the camouflaged "opponent";

Mon (10)Tri Ven (6)(X) Pr-Re   **Jan 27 1964**   13°Vi11' D   13°Ta11' D

Mon (10)Sxt Nep (12)(X)Pr-Re **Feb 10 1964**   13°Vi39' D   13°Sc39' R

Evidently it was some "other's" informational and/or material base, or the President; one had to go. Virgo also rules employment.

The country's 10th house ruler (Uranus) and reigning need for equality (Aquarius Moon and is on the 10th of the US) is exactly on the solar return Midheaven, disposes of SR Saturn in the exact degree of Aquarius of Lincoln's Sun and Kennedy's Uranus in 4 (intercepted)! Mars rules the 5th (others goals as the 11th of the 7th) and 6 (subordinates) opposes Saturn in the 9/3 house axis (information, traveling) and conjoins Uranus on the 10th.

Somehow, the disruption of others' security (Mars/Uranus on 10th is the 4th of others), goals (5th is the 11th of the 7th and ruled by Mars) and limitation of ego assertion (Mars ruling 6, the 12th of the other) were being temperamentally defended-at the cost of Aquarian concepts.

The transit Mercury/Uranus square at shooting (outer wheel) falls on the Solar return Pluto in 10! The Moon/ascendant at 11 Aquarius trigger at shooting squares the SR Neptune/Venus opposition! From 3! The trigger of the opposition "shoots" the arrow of the temporary T-square (Moon, asc, Saturn Aquarius in 3) into the mind of the other (9). Transit Sun at 29 Scorpio squares Uranus in 10, Mars and the MC! Employment, economics, ego out of control (Jupiter@9 Aries inconjunct the Virgo Pluto in 10 and transit Uranus. Jupiter is the dispositor of Mercury squaring them in 1).

The equality (the Aquarian idea) is the idea everyone immortalized *both* times. These two men- counterparts of the same oversoul- gave the concept of the Aquarian ideal their all. The most frightening aspect however is the camouflaging and strategic capabilities of the power structure of the country supposedly of, by, and for the people.

Pluto at 27 degree Capricorn in the U.S. chart represents the FBI, CIA, material power structures, collective material power base and race issues. This placement has tremendous significance in a country primarily run by money.

An eclipse at 27 Cancer on July 20,1963 *exactly* opposed the U.S.'s Pluto, conjunct Kennedy's Saturn in 10 (the authority and full externalization). Transit Saturn's station on June 3,1963 was at 23 degrees Aquarius precisely conjunct Kennedy's all important Uranus in 4 (the past) and Lincoln's sun![141]

You don't have to be an astrological genius to recognize the connections these men had with the principles we discussed previously. Lincoln's Sun and Kennedy's Uranus are both conjunct the reigning need of the country (Moon). Lincoln's Moon was conjunct U.S. Pluto and Kennedy's Saturn was

---

[141] This 23-24 degree of Aquarius is one of the few factors I have been able to find in an other than accepted chart for the declaration of Independence (for the 10 pm one) found in *"The Book of The Zodiac"* by Fred Gettings, Triune Press, London England, 1972. It just may be more precise- more work needs to be done.

conjunct U.S. Mercury and opposed Pluto triggering the information aspect concerning the country's need to resolve and alter material world and conscious mind function-*at the expense of spirit*. National self-empowerment was "shot down." Kennedy's Midheaven was exactly conjunct U.S. Mercury, and his Pluto was conjunct the U.S. very important Venus (economics). His Moon was conjunct the U.S. Neptune; the much needed spiritual aspect of the nation![142]

Both men tried to get the populace to take their share of responsibility for the humanitarian effort.

Lincoln's Uranus, Mars, and Saturn/Neptune conjunction emphasized the 6th house of the nation, waking up that end of the "values" perspective. Kennedy's Taurus planets emphasized the limiting perspective that requires undoing by polarity at the other end from the 12th. The 6/12 house axis of *any* chart are the 2nd and 8th of the 5th and 11th by derivative measurement. The "value or worth" of creative extension is from perspective alteration to a greater understanding of the "All That Is", oneness, and understanding; the resource of that perspective.

Lincoln's Jupiter (expansion) was in awareness tension (opposition) with the nation's Neptune (ideal) and square Mars. The nation had the opportunity to experience expansion of compassion and triumph of spirit (Neptune) over ego (Mars). One of the issues the nation fails to resolve to this day (Mars in Gemini in 1 square Neptune in Virgo in 5).

The final chart is the U.S. with the assassination of Lincoln in the 2nd wheel and Kennedy's assassination in the outer wheel. Lincoln's assassination planets emphasize the 12th, like Kennedy's natal planets! And Kennedy's assassination planets the 6th like Lincoln's. Moreover, they emphasize the limiting perspective and reason for reincarnation of a collective society (6/12th axis of the US). This reflects the "buying into" of the preservation of ego through material domination (Pluto in 9 in Capricorn)! Kennedy's Mars/Mercury conjunction at time of

---

[142] And Militaristic informational camouflage as it is square Mars in Gemini in 1.

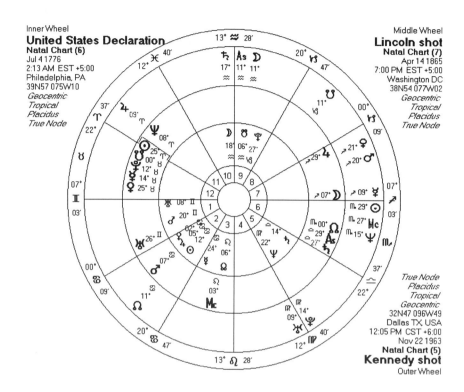

assassination oppose the nation's Mars (military/dominance/ego) ruler of 12 from the 7th; the meeting of the unconscious projections of self (collective populace)! The Moon and ascendant at the time of his shooting were conjunct the nation's 10th; the physicalization of belief momentum and "life direction" of a nation, square the Taurus planets in 12 (resources) at the time of Lincoln's shooting.

The Sun/Saturn opposition at Lincoln's assassination are *in* the nation's 6/12th ruling the 4th and Saturn disposing of, and forming a T-square with, the critical degree Pluto in Capricorn, powerfully reflecting the past life of the society in the civilization of Atlantis (material domination and "people using").

Saturn at Lincoln's assassination had just passed Saturn's return to it's natal place calling for a re-cognition of the fears of non-acceptance socially that lead to acquiescence and double standards. Transit Saturn at Kennedy assassination is conjunct the reigning need of the nation and through physical externalization, *testing* the foundation laid down by Lincoln of the society's ability to perceive *consciously* what it's beliefs about reality *have created!*

This transit Saturn of Kennedy's assassination is then disposed of by transit Uranus in 4 at *9 degrees Virgo* (analytical discernment) squaring the nation's Uranus at *8-9 degrees Gemini* (conscious mind function), opposes Lincoln's assassination Moon at *9 degrees Sagittarius* (higher self), and Kennedy's assassination Mercury at *9 degrees Sagittarius* (higher mind functioning through conscious mind) Lincoln's natal Mercury in Pisces, creating a Grand cross of contradiction, conflict and paradox with the identity/status Quadruplicity of the United States. Uranus (the recognition of choice) is it's base! The crucifixion expressed through this cross, is the freedom and equality ideal of a national perspective for the sake of material gain. With a lack of belief in the validity of identity, a whole populace agreed that "Camelot is better dreamed of, than visited".

"Ask not what your country can do for you, but what you can do for your country," was President Kennedy's plea to a complacent and prosperous country for each individual to take back their power through taking responsibility for their own creations. We did not, and Camelot remains upon the shelf.

Merlin returns for Arthur at his birth as promised by Uther for favors;

Uther to Merlin; "To kill and be King is that all?"
Merlin; "perhaps not even that."
Uther; "Merlin you strike me with words hard as steel!"
Merlin; "You betrayed the Duke, you stole his wife, you took his castle-now no one trusts you! You are not the one!"

Chapter 12

The Channeling Experience
Awakenings

"Simply, anything that will
function as a carrier wave so
to speak, a carrier idea for
another vibration, so that it
will be able to plug itself into
the particular dimensional
experience in which the carrier exists."
Darryl Anka channeling
"Bashar and The Association"

The Universe exists in holographic form. This means that any point in time or space contains within it, within this matrix, the potentiality of the entire Universe or Multiverse. The potential of the existence of any idea at any point within this structure has an equal chance of manifestation based on momentum (last chapter).

▸ In 1980 University of Connecticut psychologist Dr. Kenneth Ring proposed that near-death experiences could be explained by the holographic model. Ring, who is president of the International Association for Near-Death Studies, believes such experiences, as well as death itself, are really nothing more than the shifting of a person's consciousness from one level of the hologram of reality to another.

In 1985 Dr. Stanislav Grof, chief of psychiatric research at the Maryland Psychiatric Research Center and an assistant professor of psychiatry at the Johns Hopkins University School of Medicine, published a book in which he concluded that existing neurophysiological models of the brain are inadequate and only a holographic model can explain such things as archetypal experiences, encounters with the collective unconscious, and other unusual phenomena experienced during altered states of consciousness.

At the 1987 annual meeting of the Association for the Study of Dreams held in Washington, D.C., physicist Fred Alan Wolf delivered a talk in which he asserted that the holographic model explains lucid dreams (unusually vivid dreams in which the dreamer realizes he or she is awake). Wolf believes such dreams are actually visits to parallel realities, and the holographic model will ultimately allow us to develop a "physics of consciousness" which will enable us to begin to explore more fully these other-dimensional levels of existence.

In his 1987 book entitled Synchronicity, The Bridge Between Matter and Mind, Dr. F. David Peat, a physicist at Queen's University in Canada, asserted that synchronicities (coincidences that are so unusual and so psychologically meaningful they don't seem to be the result of chance alone) can be explained by the holographic model. Peat believes such coincidences are actually "flaws in the fabric of reality." They reveal that our thought processes are much more intimately connected to the physical world than has been hitherto suspected.

The holographic model has also received some dramatic experimental support. In the field of neurophysiology numerous studies have corroborated Pribram's various predictions about the holographic nature of memory and perception. Similarly, in 1982 a landmark experiment performed by a research team led by physicist Alain Aspect at the Institute of Theoretical and Applied Optics, in Paris, demonstrated that the web of subatomic particles that compose our physical universe-the very fabric of reality itself-possesses what appears to be an undeniable "holographic" property. "The Holographic Universe, Michael Talbot, 1992

Our languages reflect this ancient knowledge through the formations of words. Re-cognize means to re-think. We do not "really" think of anything new, it is simply a re-cognition of an idea point within this holographic matrix.

When we re-member something, we are accessing an idea that was always been a part of ourselves and is being reconnected as a "member" of the collective idea that it belongs to-us. There may be new ways to re-member ideas, events, or situations, and therefore re-create them. But they are still united with *this* member in the now.

Time and space are the illusions of three dimensional reality. Real while you are in it, but an illusion just the same. All "members" exist in the now simply at different points within the holographic matrix that correspond to "past" and "future."

In previous chapters I discussed how conscious mind focus to the exclusion of other foci, can create the appearance of dis-connection from the "All That Is," but that in actuality we will always maintain our connection with the "All That Is." In this way conscious mind and ego can create an identity or persona that seems to be separate from the infinite, and in a sense as the product of focus, it is. As the effect of this sharpness in focus, all peripheral information may be excluded. (Please refer to psychic material levels in chapters 1, page 4).

Channeling in the sense of being in a "trance state," is simply the allowance of the diffusion of focus, to access broader spectrum of levels or perspective to follow this carrier wave. There is not a bodily inhabitation of this "other" energy. First of all it is not actually another energy. It must be a part of the individual doing the channeling on some level. Second, our spirit or soul energy is not "in" our body, our body is the physical version of our spirit or soul. It is more sensible to say that our body resides in our consciousness, not the other way around. By softening focus another "entity" then is capable of flowing through this conduit. This other energy is really just impressing the channeler with the vibration of the other entity. The identity must be a part of the energy or vibration of the channel, so that an energy "pitch" can be matched to allow expression. The consciousness of the physical channel doesn't go anywhere, it is simply adjusted, usually through this diffusion of focus. The higher self can be the "identity" that is being channeled, and in the overall sense, is anyway.

In general terms, channeling is any expression of the vibration you are. If you are a dancer, you are channeling the vibration of expression of the dance you portray. If you are an artist, the medium becomes the "conduit" for the channeling of artistic effect.[143]

The following horoscopes are explored for the purpose of understanding the perspective and dynamics of astrological

---

New Metaphysics-Bashar And The Association, 1987 Light and Sound Communications Inc.

reflections of the trance channeling process; The unfoldment of this experience by the person involved and their psychological processes reflected in astrological signatures. We identify astrological significators that reflect this ability to soften focus. Of course we all soften our focus in order to connect with other aspects of ourselves, we call it sleep. But to bring this information coherently to conscious expression requires a "semi-sleep state," and it is this function we will discern through astrological reflections as probable keys to its expression.

Like any idea we experience (in concept) in physical reality, channeling in the trance state stems from general agreements made prior to the physical life to do so. We always create our own experiential reality. It always works this way as we were made in the image of an infinite creator, therefore so are we. No one's will can be forced upon another without agreement on some level, and intermingling of any energy, is always a co-creation. Are these channelings "real"? The question is rather redundant, because the experiences are. If the information allows us to expand perspective or live in an improved condition with more meaning it doesn't matter. Are there "channels" *intentionally attempting to deceive?* I am sure this is the often the case. I have chosen those I believe have demonstrated accuracy, who are being of service, and are *not* intentionally doing so as best as I can discern. Those whose message of empowerment contradicts the powerless actions reflected in "Guru like" following. Information they have channelled I have found to be useful, constructive, and applicable to the improvement of the human condition.

In the chart of Edgar Cayce known as the "sleeping prophet," we notice the element count reflects a disbelief in the idea interaction element Air representation is totally absent; Difficulty in seeing the self or others with analytical discernment. Abbreviated abilities with abstract thinking. Does not believe that self reflection can come through social or intellectual interaction; blinder effect! As child Edgar Cayce had much difficulty with his school studies, and discovered his ability to retain knowledge unconsciously after having fallen asleep on his books! In everyday life he was described as a very simple and uneducated man. A low count in Air and Fire leaves the majority of planets and points in feminine or receptive signs, Water and Earth. Perhaps this "blinder effect" was purposely induced by higher self will to remove conscious mind distraction to provide service, rather than a negative or detrimental belief system?

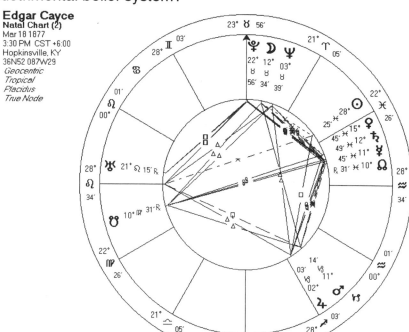

Edgar Cayce
Natal Chart (2)
Mar 18 1877
3:30 PM CST +6:00
Hopkinsville, KY
36N52 087W29
Geocentric
Tropical
Placidus
True Node

The Sun is in critical degree Pisces in an unconscious house and sign, and is the ruler of the Leo ascendant; It is at urgent degree, a masculine definition, and rules the natural Pisces house of 12. Our Sun/Moon blend reads; The mystical energy gains a practical anchor. A genuinely sincere persona. The expression of unconditional love comes easily. Conscious mind functions will need strength of will to apply unconscious understanding fully (page 266). Conscious mind function is reflected through Mercury and is strengthened by it's conjunction to Saturn (focus). However, both are also in the unconscious water sign Pisces. The Moon is in the house of others opinions and thinking and higher self (9), and exacts an opening sextile (supportive expression) to the Mercury/Saturn/Venus conjunction in 7. It rules the 11th of others extension.

The Moon also trines the ruler of the 9th (higher self), Mars exalted in Capricorn in the 5th (creative extension, love giving).

The only developmental or action aspects (squares), are between the accelerated Pisces Sun in 8 (ruling the identity projection ascendant and 12th unconscious undoing), and Jupiter in 5 the ruler of the 5th, and Pluto ruler of the personal unconscious 4th. Uranus is rising just passed the ascendant, the archetype of the awakening of unconscious knowledge! Our element count discernment does not change meaning fundamentally, but it does change probable *effect* upon our recognition of momentum or *intention* perhaps by higher self will. A life of service in higher and unconscious will expression would be possible through the supporting aspects plus the Uranus placement.

The hemisphere emphasis to the west reflects a strong need to defend, deal with, and give power to reflections and others. From the documentation available, he seems to have given much control over to the demands of others for "readings."

The trance state capabilities are easily seen through the "receptivity" of planet placements. The focal planet, however, is Uranus by placement on the ascendant, in the eastern hemisphere emphasis opposite the major planetary groupings, disposed of by the Life energy (Sun in empathic Pisces and *ruling 12*), and square the Pluto placement the ruler of 4 (inner self), on the MC (the physical manifestation of inner self) in the sign of values (Taurus).

Uranus' only "relief" from it's developmental aspect with Pluto is the Sun's disposing of it and in turn sextiling Pluto. The awakened unconscious knowledge (and identity projection as ruler of 1) *must* come through the accelerated merging and blending Pisces Sun, and through the personal unconscious

(Pluto rules 4) before physical externalization! From these placements, it is more unbelievable this man could maintain *conscious* focus than it is unconscious channeling!

Venus rules the 3rd and 10th, disposes of the Moon (11 co-creation interaction), Pluto and Neptune (rulers of the matrix of the unconscious, the 4th, 8th, and 12th), and is conjunct Saturn and Mercury-both archetypes of the conscious mind and physical reality focus in 7.

The aspects of persona are powerfully integrated into the unconscious matrix. The Venus/Mercury/Saturn conjunction in 7, is sextiled by the moon/Mars trine from the 9th to the 5th. Neptune disposes of the Pisces stellium conjunction and trines (fulfillment) Jupiter (higher self) from the 9th (higher self!) to the 5th (creative extension) and disposes of the accelerated life energy and ruler of identity definition on 1, the Sun, in the unconscious 8th!

In conclusion, the factors of the unconscious reflected by the astrological matrix of the unconscious (houses) and their placement and expression (signs and aspects) leads us very easily to an awareness of an identity's accessibility to these realms. However, the archetype of Uranus, it's position, placement, and aspects, reflects the "doorway" that acts as a catalyst to bring the unconscious into aspects of persona definition through placement on or around the ascendant, the final "stop" of the energy of the oversoul upon incarnation at physical birth. In Edgar Cayce' chart Uranus is only 7 degrees off the ascendant. Uranus, with its odd spinning-on-its-side orbit, wild magnetic fluctuations, and pole structure is the archetype of *disrupting concretized patterning and habitual ritualistic thinking.*

Our next example is the horoscope of Darryl Anka, who channels primarily extraterrestrial consciousness. The primary representative of the "Association of Worlds" is an identity named Bashar. This is not his "real" name as the civilization to which he belongs no longer uses verbiage. Communication between them is primarily telepathic. The name "Bashar" was chosen as a verbal expression that best fits the vibrational energy of this "in many ways Darryl's future self"(Bashar's own definition) entity.

The Element count reveals no particularly emphasized or de-emphasized function. The Modes however, reflect a low count in the Fixed mode; indecision. Lack of diligence (and/or fixity of e-motion or the momentum of beliefs-karma?). The Cardinal count is overemphasized primarily in the sign Libra. An exaggerated emphasis on the motivation to relate, and to acknowledge the reflections of the self. The Sun/Moon blend reads; perception of others through empathy, can allow for a good amount of psychological understanding.[144] This is the blend of a good listener, counselor, therapist. Absorption of others energy alleviates any threat, so that sharing with others comes easily (page 257).

Darryl Anka
Natal Chart (3)

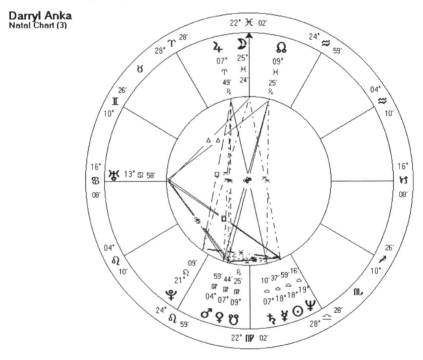

144
Obviously, the potential of personal development implies the "persona" that Darryl "becomes" in the channeling process. There is no contradiction here as these are just aspects of the higher or future selves being channeled.

This Libran sharing comes from non-physical or other worldly reality (Neptune conjunct the Sun) through the personal unconscious (4th house and disposes of the Moon) and is projected though the reflective Cancer ascendant-the natural sign of the 4th! The sensitivity of momentum flow is extreme. There are analytical placements as well with the Virgo placements in 3 (thinking). The developmental catalyst to bring this to expression is Uranus only two degrees from the ascendant square all the Libra planets in 4. The unconscious knowledge being awakened (Uranus) is profoundly caught up in the personal unconscious with regard to relationship (Libra placements).

This awakening came in the form of a close sighting of "Bashar's" craft in Los Angeles in 1972 with several friends present!

The way out of developmental tension is through the opening sextile (supportive expression) of the Mercury/Sun/Neptune conjunction in 4 (personal unconscious) to the Pluto position in 2 (other world perspective resources). Resolution is also seen through the opening sextile between Venus, the dispositor of the Libran planets, with Uranus ruler of the 8th (unconscious matrix) and 9th (higher self) on the ascendant! The Moon is disposed of by Neptune, and in turn disposes of Uranus.

These measurements reflect the personality closely tied to the other world perspective. The Sun is conjunct Neptune and disposes of Pluto. Mercury rules two houses of the unconscious matrix, is conjunct Neptune, is in Mutual reception with Venus, which is in turn conjunct the overall personality definition, Mars!

Venus is in opening inconjunct with Jupiter from the sign Virgo (analytical discernment) to the sign Aries (identity definition). Jupiter rules the 6th (analytical discernment) and is in awareness tension with Saturn (double applying opposition) the ruler of the 7th (reflections).

Uranus rules the 8th and 9th (the final unconscious house and the higher self) and is conjunct the personal projection definition of the self (ascendant).

In the outer ring of Darryl's chart are the planetary positions at the exact stationary retrograde position of Uranus in January of 1972, the year of Darryl's first sighting of "Bashar's" craft. It is not difficult to recognize the significance of Uranus as the "awakener" or the personal significance to Darryl, as the stationary retrograde degree of Uranus fell precisely upon the Sun/Mercury/Neptune conjunction in the personal unconscious 4th!

He explains before each channeling (to those unfamiliar) that what he knows now but didn't know then, was that this was Bashar's way of tapping him in the unconscious to remind him of agreements made prior to the physical life to do the work of this channeled information!

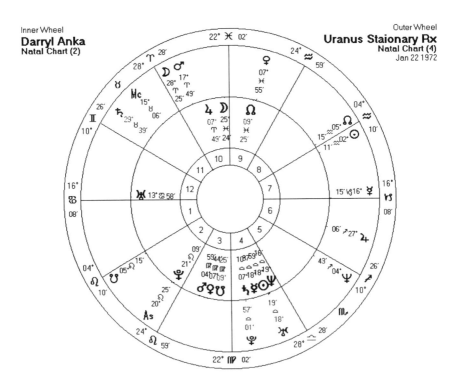

Transit Mars exactly opposes transit Uranus as well as the

stellium in 4 and rules the critical degree 11th, *the creative extension of others!*[145] The "others" in this case are definitely not the norm (Uranus).

Transit Mercury, which rules the 12th (reason for incarnation) and the 4th (personal unconscious) is exactly upon the reflective 7th cusp and completes a Grand cross with transit Uranus in 4 on the Libra stellium, Mars in 10, and the natal position of Uranus on 1, the ruler of the unconscious 8th and higher self 9th. Transit Venus is on the north node (new intake of energy in this life) and opposes natal Venus/Mars conjunction. A status/identity (1/4/7/10 houses) awakening (Grand cross-Uranus) through perspective altering (Pisces/Virgo) information (3rd/9th) from the unconscious (Venus disposes of the stellium in 4 as well as all important transit Uranus). Transit Neptune in 5 (extension) which rules the life direction and full externalization 10th, is exactly squaring the natal Mars in 3 (communication and dissemination of the self).

In this horoscope we see a maximization of expression of higher self through the merging of collective unconscious and personal unconscious. The other-world aspect is always reflected through the planets of Neptune and Pluto because these two planets represent the "end of the line" in terms of the consciousness expression of our solar system (now). Their orbits allow them to trade places wherein at certain points within their orbits Neptune becomes the furthest planet out. These planets reflect the vibrational nature of experience upon leaving and entering the system and the unseen aspects of consciousness (by the conscious mind of course).

In conclusion, the horoscope of Darryl Anka reflects a merging and blending with the self and the other world planetary vibration of the outer planets. An extreme sensitivity and permeability of personal unconscious pattern that allows the "matching" of identity perspective with that of

---

[145]
This house and the sign of Aquarius reflects all visitor and extraterrestrial alien interactions in astrology.

extraterrestrial reflection. The collectivity of mind that is much more apparent with the "visitors," can only be accessed through a broadening of not only personal self parameters, but the personal unconscious as well.

Many of the concepts in this book were accelerated through interactions personally with "Bashar" over the past few years. My introduction to Bashar co-incided with my first article in *Horoscope Magazine* entitled "Saturn Opposed Saturn-View To Reality."[146] This article was the culmination of my recognition and awakening to the "proof" I needed to see how we created our reality. Then this idea was blended with the wonderful foundational work of Noel Tyl, and Bashar. Through their work Darryl and Noel were instrumental in allowing me to piece many things together to produce this book. Although to many this seems an unlikely linking, their work completed mine.

▸   "The only means of strengthening one's intellect is to make up one's mind about nothing-to let the mind be a thoroughfare for all thoughts, not a select party."   John Keats

I must acknowledge both Darryl and "Bashar" as being conducive to my own growth in this direction. The experience of encountering one's counterpart (aspects of the same soul incarnate at the same time), is exhilarating to say the least. Thank you to Darryl and Bashar.

The horoscope of Kevin Ryerson who is best known for his appearance in "*Out On A Limb*" starring Shirley Maclaine, once again reveals the extremely powerful placement of Uranus in the 1st house.[147]

---

[146]   Dell Publishing, August 1990 issue.

[147]   This position of course in not the ONLY possible position for this unconscious knowledge to come through.

Kevin Ryerson
Natal Chart (2)

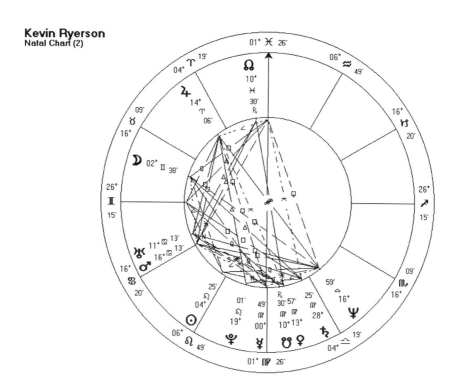

The Elements reflect a very fine balance. Mutable mode is high and reflects a strong emphasis. The possibility of scattering energy and resources-cerebration. Since the balance is slight this is not an issue-but a guide. Flexibility is also reflected through the moon in the sign of Gemini. The Sun/Moon blend delineation reads; Sextile. The light of the Sun is distributed diversely. Dramatic expression serves to reinforce the reigning needs as easily as possible. Ideas and action in harmony. This light distribution shines diversely directly into the collective unconscious house (12) and reflects the primary reason for incarnation. The Moon in 12 in *any* chart carries with it extreme sensitivity within the sign it occupies (a second layer so to speak as a Piscean element) from the blending of personal and collective unconscious archetypes.

The awakening of unconscious knowledge through the placement of Uranus in 1 is immediately seen through the

Moon's disposing of both it and Mars. This disposition ties it to the extension of others (advising-11th) and the expansion of the "others" identity and creative extension (the 11th is the 5th of others, ruling the others 1st or his 7th). Mars on the 2nd cusp reflects assertion (Mars) of unconscious (Cancer) resource (2).

Mars disposes of Jupiter (higher self) and Uranus rules the 9th (higher self-spiritual belief). Mars/Uranus exactly square Neptune. The Mars/Uranus conjunction serves as the base of the T-square bow and arrow which lodges this energy into the 7th and cusp of the 8th (projection received-others identity, ego transcendence, others values).

Neptune (spirit) is in awareness tension (opposition externalization) with Jupiter (expansion and higher self) and Neptune rules the 10th (physicalization). This is the only opposition and therefore creates the focus of the chart. Jupiter rules the 7th house Sagittarius (the reflection of higher self through others).

This diversity of the personal unconscious merged and blended with the collective unconscious, is projected through the lens of the Mars/Uranus conjunction-incorporates the awareness of the higher self and spirit (Jupiter/Neptune), and is sensitized as a projection of identity definition through the communication (Gemini on 1) through the higher self. This man channels an amazing array of other world identities, from just as equally diverse time periods (Gemini, moon in 12, Mercury).

The ways out of the developmental T-square (integrative or expressive aspects) begins with Venus the ruler of the 12th sextiling the Uranus/Mars conjunction (supportive expression, again as in Darryl's chart). It also rules 5 and disposes of Neptune from the personal unconscious 4th! Critical degree Mercury at 0 degrees Virgo implies a need for a new beginning in communication as a service through the inner self and personal unconscious from its position on the 4th house cusp ruling it and the 1st house. In this way his Venus in Virgo also reflects a finely honed capability for analytical discernment. I had the pleasure of experiencing this sensitivity through Kevin's life purpose workshop wherein he demonstrated his vast metaphysical knowledge and expertise.

Jupiter is the other expression route of this awareness of collective unconscious and other world (Neptune opposition) through it's apex trine to Pluto (transformation of perspective) and Pluto's rulership of the 6th house (service and others 12th of undoing) from the Jupiter position in 11 (others extension, humanitarianism) to the 3rd (communication/mental profile). The Sun's life energy is on the cusp of the 3rd and also rules it. It receives the integrative sextile from the Moon in 12 (diverse unconscious communication). This Moon in turn trines the accelerated Saturn at 28 degrees Virgo to the personal unconscious (4th) which rules the final unconscious house of transcendence-the 8th.

The north node in 10 (a secondary factor to delineate the unconscious) trines the symbol of unconscious awakening (Uranus) from it's placement in Pisces, the sign that reflects where our identity returns to merge and blend with "All That Is."

In conclusion, this horoscope reflects a remarkable ability to access the collective unconscious pool and act as the conscious "telephone" between these dimensions. The matrix of the unconscious-the 4th, 8th, and 12th houses, are clearly interwoven with conscious personality definitions, and all function together in tight formation through the placement of all three matrix rulers at the nadir (4th house cusp) including the self definition ruler of the ascendant and dispositor of the moon in 12, Mercury *on the nadir,* the deepest point of the personal unconscious.

The final example of this Uranian signature is again shown through the chart of Jane Roberts, author of and channeler of "Seth" and the *"Seth Material"*.

Jane Roberts
Natal Chart (3)
May 8 1929
11:31 PM EDT +4:00
Albany NY, USA
42N39 073W45
Geocentric
Tropical
Placidus
True Node

The Element count is balanced. The Sun/Moon blend reads; There can be a balanced view of one's worth. A calmness and patience in the experience of life. If in developmentally tense aspects (hers are not), there may need to be changes in the structure of the identity that may be unsettling. Insecurity so great the heels are dug in.

In this case the 4th house placements sextile the Pluto placement in 7, reflects the support of personal unconscious psychic material (4th/Cancer) values and resource (Taurus) to the perspective alteration and value structures of others and collective unconscious (Pluto in 7, Sun rules 8) in reassessing other world issues (Neptune) and creation extension (Leo). The Sun disposes of Neptune in 8.

The Saturn on 1 at urgent degree (29) of higher self and

broader perspective Sagittarius is in a reassessment state (Rx) and trine Neptune in the 8th (unconscious deep aspects of self) in the creative extension sign Leo *also* in critical degree! This lends strong support to the initial 4th house analysis of inner self and spiritual *pragmatism.*

Jupiter (higher self) is also in 4 in the sign of resource and is conjunct the north node (positive new direction in this life and maternal and unconscious reference again), disposes of critical degree Saturn on 1 (reassessment of physical reality) ruler of the self identification and definition on 1. It (Jupiter) rules the other unconscious house of blending and undoing 12, and is sextile Mars the ruler of 4 and dispositor of the Uranus and Venus in 3 in Aries (pioneering need to be first). Uranus rules the personal worth and resource 2nd house and is Novile (completion, perfection and concretization) Sun, Node, and Jupiter in 4. Mercury (communication, dissemination and thinking needs) is in Gemini in 5 (extension) and rules the 6th (work, discernment) and 9th (higher self, publicity of the self, the beliefs and opinions of others) and sextiles the Uranus in 3. Result; as Seth, she produced a tremendous amount of channeled work and detailed explanation of how we create our physical reality through beliefs! This was to lead to many channelings and others who followed and added to this Uranian pioneering of unconscious knowledge awakening.

> ▸ Each individual must examine his or her individual beliefs, or begin with feelings which will inevitably lead to them. In this area, as in all others, those of you who are proficient verbally might use the method of writing. Either write down your beliefs as they come to you, or make lists of your intellectual and emotional assumptions. You may find that they are quite different.
>
> If you have a physical symptom, do not run away from it. Feel its reality in your body. Let the emotions follow freely. These will lead you, if you allow them to flow, to the beliefs that cause the difficulty. They will take you through many aspects of your own reality that you must face and explore. These methods release your withheld natural aggressiveness. You may feel that you are swamped by emotion, but trust it-again, it is the motion of your being, and it arouses your own creativity. Followed, it will seek the answers to your problems.......each person _is creative in his or her own way, and can follow the emotions as Ruburt (Jane) did whether or not a

poem results. He will know the passage to which I refer. Use it. You must realize that your conscious mind _is competent, its ideas pertinent, and that your own beliefs affect and form your body and your experience. *"The Nature of Personal Reality",* A Seth Book, Prentice-Hall, 1974, page 251.

The last chart with transits around her natal chart once again reflects the expansion of Uranus by Jupiter's exact conjunction by transit on the day when "Seth" came through![148]

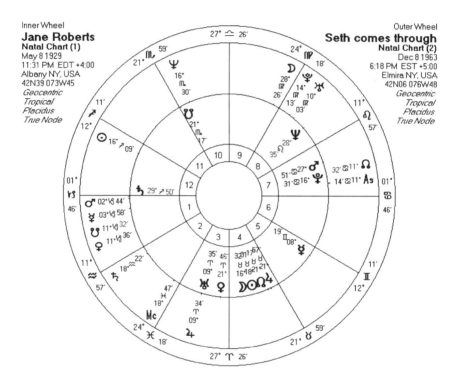

Other worldly Neptune (ruling 3 communication) is in awareness tension exact opposition with the Moon position in 4 of the personal unconscious resource. The ruler of 4, Mars has just crossed Saturn and the ascendant and is conjunct

---

148
    A reminder to the reader of this aspect in reverse with Uranus on his Jupiter by transit to Einstein's chart upon confirmation of many of his theories in the chapter on thought!

Mercury in Capricorn, the ruler of Saturn they both conjoin. Saturn is in the resource and values 2nd and is in exact apex square (full physical manifestation) to the Sun in 4! Saturn is the *archetype of physical reality* and is disposed of the Uranus awakening in 3 with Jupiter ruling 12 where we started! The counterculture beginning of the paradigm shift (the Uranus/Pluto conjunction which will be covered in the next chapter) of transit Uranus/Pluto is in 8 in Virgo and completes a Grand trine in Earth with Venus in 1, and her natal planets in 4 and squares (developmental tension to take action) her communicative and creative Mercury in 5. Transit Venus is also disposed of by Saturn and is conjunct the unconscious transit nodal axis on the horizon of awareness (ascendant/descendant axis) at the time of Seth's "arrival."

In conclusion, the identity found its natural expression and bliss through *reliance* upon the inner self to allow for the more expanded understanding of the *philosophy of physicality and its purpose* (Saturn at 29 Sagittarius and Earth references) and process of creation. As Seth she conveyed not an impractical speculation but *detailed instruction* on how to *recreate* one's reality.

In essence, this chapter has been devoted primarily to accelerate awareness of the astrological significators connected with the unconscious and collective unconscious expressed as channeling; the natural creative extension of the self. And to demonstrate astrologically the factors to look for for those who require "conscious mind validity" of the actuality of some of these "New Age" scenarios manifesting upon our planet at this time in the *transformational age*. Also, to show my appreciation for the contribution these and many other pioneers have made to concretization of the Christ/Buddha/Allah consciousness[149] as a "real" concept.

All things are discernable when we act like we were made in the image of an infinite creator. For although this "New Age"

149
   The combined collective unconscious knowledge of the entire solar system.

will certainly and can only be a new version-a new *re-creation* of ancient and unconscious understandings that have always "been there", it is still the re-*membering* of our glorious place in creation. "All That Is" is accessible in any way, shape, or form, at any point, in any way, within the holographic matrix that it is. Completely so, when we follow and channel the self we naturally are with bliss, excitement and trust.

"The theoretical idea (atomism in this case) does not arise apart from and independent of experience; nor can it be derived from experience by a purely logical procedure. It is produced by a creative act." Albert Einstein, *"On The Generalized Theory of Gravitation,"* Scientific American, Vol. 182, no. 4, April, 1950.

Chapter 13

Spectra
The Outer Limits

"I never thought I'd live to be a
hundred, I never thought I'd get
to do the things that all those
other souls do. And they do.
I never thought I'd ever have my
freedom. An age ago my maker was
refusing me the pleasure of the
view."
"The Moody Blues" To Our Children's, Children's, Children

This number 5.3937075 x 10^{58} or
5,393,707,500,000,000,000,000,000,000,000,000,000,0
00,000,000,000,000,000,000,000,000[150] is greater than the
population of a million Earths, but the SMALLEST possible
number of different astrological factor combinations, and tells
us that, what we have examined are just a few of the possible
varieties of vibrational frequencies expressed by individuals at
any given time on planet Earth. These vibrational patterns can
be similar of course, but individuality means individuality
and is based on more than either astrological measurements
or DNA alone. The number is irrelevant in my view. Life is a
conglomeration of factors all permeating one another. But
these levels and corresponding vibrations can be experienced
in an infinite variety of ways. Astrological reflections simply lay
out parameters of archetypes and perspectives both
collectively and individually. It is very difficult to measure
personal perspective and experience empirically. Astrological
indicators are reflective of probabilities of a *spectrum of*

---

[150] According to Doris Chase Doane, Astrology: 30 Years Research, page 2.

experience. What we perceive requires interpretation as we have seen, and is thus a *co-created event.* Metaphors and revelations cannot be *proven empirically.* But they are valid, reportable through experience, sometimes life changing, world changing, and powerful "factors" none-the-less.

The philosophical constructs, approach in living techniques, and self-empowerment applications I have presented cannot be proven to anyone, they can only be proven to oneself. "Reality" is a co-created event, as are all realities (science is as well). We know in psychology that diffusion of responsibility is a "real" factor (wherein helping each other in say a tug-of-war individuals exercise *less* effort than when performing alone). But whether any certain individual in any certain situation will *practice it* is an unknown.

The collective "event" of physicality is measurable because it is rather like the autonomic nervous system; a continuous creation on another level altogether so we needn't be preoccupied with it. This frees us up to focus our consciousness on the experience of *living* in this creation.

If one changes their view on life, this may or may not be measurable. If say, we quit smoking because of a change in belief and perspective, this may be measurable. If on the other hand we are economically impoverished and *just* change our perspective on whether being economically impoverished is "good" or "bad," but remain in the same economic condition, we still see, feel and experience a different reality. But there may be no way to measure that reality than by self report. By the same token, astrology may allow us recognitions that change our perspectives and life experiences dramatically by qualitative not quantitative measurements. And in that way, the statistical variables and measurements are irrelevant. It is indeed the theory that determines not only what we will observe, whether it is qualitative or quantitative, but how we measure it, obtain data about it, obtain results, and come to conclusions. The only way these experiential realities can be proven is to the self by the self with application, conviction, and trust.

Good and Bad

Many think of evil or the "Devil" and envision a being of tremendous violence and hatred. A being that "lies in wait" for any opportunity to "tempt" us to do bad, wrong, or destructive things.

This premise or belief that the Devil or Satan exists outside of us, separate from us and maintains it's own identity independent of us, is in and of itself a powerless or "Satanic" belief system. The *idea* that we must constantly defend ourselves from an external "force" that threatens our life or prosperity and *denies* the premise that we are co-creators with "All That Is" is powerless. Actually those that believe in this system of belief validate the concept that we create our own reality, because whatever "sword" you live by you must die by. When you believe in a negatively reinforcing reality, then this is precisely what you will get (create).

By addressing this I am seeking to clarify the idea that Heaven and Hell are *states of being*, and that they are experienced anywhere anytime. It is not possible to believe in victimization and self empowerment at the same time. Satan (Saturn) as an archetype simply reflects placing power outside of the self. This can happen in an infinite number of ways. The way to recognize that this is being done is to realize that the energy of re-action rather than pro-action is at work. Experiencing and perceiving whether the energy of bliss or negativity is originating outside the self as opposed to being within the self and under its control is the telling factor. In other words taking back power means taking back responsibility for our experiential reality. To keep things simple, believing is seeing. We cannot change anything we do not believe is a part of us. If we believe our governments and its administrators are a separate entity that has power *over* us, then we will see this. This idea of the power being external is exemplified in the statement "Well maybe if I had a million dollars" I would do this or that. If we believe money has the "power" then we will see this. And in waiting for the outer to change when it is changed from within, we will be waiting a long time to see the change we desire.

The negative or positive expression of any life path is determined by the fundamental issues of the beliefs in power held by the individual in question. If an individual believes they are a powerless victim of the environment, then domination of the environment is the only thing that will allow them to feel powerful. They will need to maintain this domination in order to maintain validity. If however, an individual knows that the environment is a part of them on some level and that there is a mutual reception between environment and self, then every aspect of environment must reflect aspects of self. This does not mean that if you see a negative person, you must be one. But being affected by the negative person is a different story. The idea is that you cannot *experience* anything that is not a part of you on some level. There must be agreement on your part for it to be an *issue*. Here is a clarification based on collected definitions thus far;

▸ **Self-Empowered**- Is the recognition that you lack nothing and create your reality 100% by what you believe and define yourself to be. It is created from all levels of psychic material, i.e., unconscious, conscious, collective unconscious, superconscious. You have all the tools and all the abilities that you require at any given moment to be anything you are willing and bold enough to believe you can define yourself to be. You are always in control 100% even when you use 90% to create the illusion that you only have the other 10%. No one can make you feel inferior without your consent. The recognition that the universe has no built-in meaning. The taking of responsibility (not guilt) for ones reality *because* you know it is you and your creation.

Integrity- Functioning as an integrated whole self without placing power outside of the self, since nothing is outside of the self. The recognition that you are as powerful as you need to be to create whatever you desire to create in your reality without having to hurt yourself or anyone else in order to create it. You are always a part of the problem or of the solution. If you are not part of the solution it is easy to figure out where you are on the scale (unless of course you are involved as an analytically discerning or accurate empathic observer). You are not responsible for anyone only responsible to them by being as much as you can be in integrity.

Negative beliefs do not have any more power than positive. So they are not necessarily "unfortunate", for every being creates their reality utterly as the product of what they believe or have been taught to believe is true. There is no one truth, except that THE truth is composed of all truths. Individuals can act in positive ways or in negative ways. **Positive** is simply integrative and **negative** is separative. But the positive individual, by the light by which they shine, will simply show the negative individual(s) that they are;

A) Untouchable by anything that is not of a similar vibration. And that;

B) They offer back to the negative individual(s) an offering of a choice, a choice to also be positive. If they do not choose to be positive then they can simply go their own way, for that which is negative cannot exist within the blinding[151] light of that which is positive, it is simple mechanics. That is all. Even if the negativity is intentional the positive person will still extract a positive effect.

  Action is the manifested conviction of belief-because life happens through you not to you.

No one can **interpret** a life or vibrational level at which they themselves are not capable of functioning, because all is vibration.

In this chapter we will explore a few of the infinite spectra of experience. In essence they deal with the concept of power. In general these charts reflect some issues considered to be controversial or of a specific nature or issue.

The spectrum of astrological measurement and application matches any spectrum of experience because it is a mirror.

In Analysis

Chart number one is a private client, however, not an unknown person. The Element count reflects a total disbelief in, and inability to reference emotion as there are 0 points in Water. A focus on the self and taking things extremely personally. There may be difficulty in empathizing with divergent viewpoints. Self defensive. The Sun is in Virgo and the Moon in Sagittarius; Opening square. The establishment of analytical discernment may be at odds with large concepts. Floating along with big ideas and never applying or bridging the gap between them and day-to-day reality. The incorporation of and blending of idealism and realism is necessary. The

---

151
  A blending of Bashar and The Association, Eleanor Roosevelt, Edmond H. Wollmann.

Male (private)
Natal Chart (2)

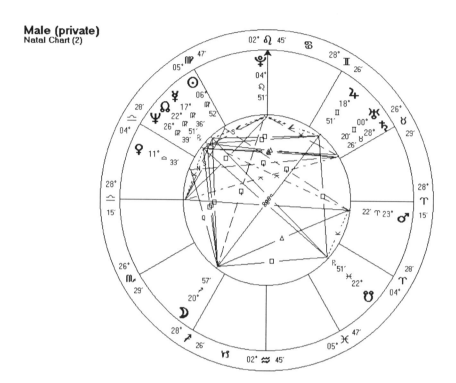

ascendant is in Libra; Amiability. The need to be socially accepted will be very apparent. Also a strong concern about the physical appearance. On the positive side, reflective tendencies take focus off the self. On the negative side, acquiescence makes the self's true stand of opinion or loyalty, elusive. Because Venus the ascendant ruler is in 12 and in Libra along with Libran the 12th house cusp, we can definitely discern that this archetype is limited in the identity's perspective (12th). The critical degree of the ascendant not only confirms this discernment, but indicates that the concept is at an urgent state of acceleration. When the ascendant and the 12th house cusp are the same sign, the reason for incarnation seems to have much to do with definitions of the self with regard to the archetype. In other words the way the person identifies themselves (1st) with regard to the sign *is* what limits that definition (12).

Our initial deduction of 0 Water reference reflects the inability for empathy. No empathy and inability for or issues with self reflection through others (Libra/12th references). A definite law of momentum establishment, Idealism and realism are believed separate (Neptune in 11 in a T-square). Six of the ten possible planet placements are in mental signs (Mutable). Yet the conscious mind function Mercury in 11 is "caught up" in the separated belief systems and forms the base of a worth/extension crisis T-square (grand cross if you include the maternal nodes) between the reigning need in 2 (Moon in Sagittarius= to have beliefs and opinions respected by others, Sagittarius reference as well as ruling intercepted Cancer in 9, the natural house of Jupiter and Sagittarius) and Jupiter in Gemini (conscious mind limiting higher self function) in 8 (ego transcendence). Intellectual self worth is exaggerated to receive accolades from others (Mercury is in 11).

The unconscious and conscious banks of psychic material are believed separate (Mercury square Moon, Sun/Moon blend, 12th house ruler (Venus=reflections) in 12 and disposes of critical degree (28) Saturn in 8. Saturn is then conjunct the final unconscious house ruler (4th) Uranus also in critical degree (0) in turn, Uranus squares the Sun in 11. External reality and inner feelings are believed to have no connection. The life energy of discernment needs waking up (Sun in Virgo square Uranus). Unconscious knowledge requires awakening regarding conscious mind function towards ego transcendence (Uranus at 0 degree Gemini in 8). There may be rigidity of habit patterning that needs awakening with reference to others values, the mysteries of life, sex, death (Saturn conjunct Uranus in 8, Uranus rules 4).

Critical degrees requiring urgent attention are on the 3rd and 9th information/thinking axis cusps. The rulers of these houses-first Mercury, rules 9 and is in the bow and arrow T-square and also rules 11 (others extension, love received). Second-Jupiter, ruler of 3 (conscious mind thinking) opposes the Moon ruler of 9 and disposes of it. Capricorn (strategy) intercepted (missing in reference) in 3 (realism) which is ruled by Saturn at critical degree in the 8th in Taurus (an accelerated urgency to real-ize the conscious mind beliefs regarding self and others worth/values and resource invalidation). Neptune (camouflage) is brought into this cerebrated developmental tension through its square to the Moon. The ideal of love received and co-creating interaction (11) is not believed attainable (square).

Inner and outer reality reference is missing in the thinking process (Capricorn/Cancer interception in 3rd/9th axis). Mars is in closing inconjunct with Neptune reflecting powerful adjustment necessary between ego self and spirit. Empathy incorporation is necessary through reflection (Mars rules critical degree 7). The Moon is in opening square to Neptune, sensitivity and empathic extension (Pisces/5th) needs integration into the personal unconscious (Moon). Self worth and the fulfillment of the need for the good opinion of others (Moon in Sagittarius, rules 9, Scorpio on 2) are in tension seeking fulfillment.

This client never made it to consultation. He was a highway patrol officer who, after two hung Juries and an FBI investigation later, was finally found guilty of violating a young woman's civil rights. The jury's conclusion; While on patrol, he fatally shot the woman in the back of the head after roadside sex.

The second ring holds the secondary progressed planetary positions for the time when he radioed headquarters that he had found an abandoned car and a woman who had possibly committed suicide. The outside the wheel are the exact transits at the time of the radio call. The secondary progressed aspects reveal the progressed ascendant in 2 exactly opposing critical degree Saturn ruler of the Capricorn interception, and progressed all important Venus ruling the Libra ascendant and 12th conjunct it, opposed both the natal and progressed Saturn/Uranus conjunction! Progressed Moon squares the natal Sun in 11 (others extension-and *their love given*), ruler of the 10th. The progressed Sun is opposed progressed Mars from 12! So far the planets do not reflect just finding a crime

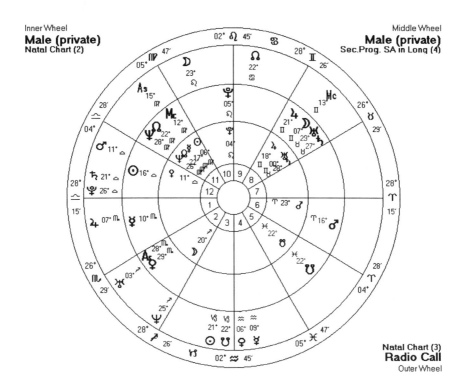

Male (private)
Natal Chart (2)

Male (private)
Sec.Prog. SA in Long (4)

Natal Chart (3)
Radio Call
Outer Wheel

but reflect personal *crisis*.

Progressed Jupiter and node form a T-square with the natal Moon (the intake of awareness tension between others values and self worth, through love received). Plus, the incontrovertible position of the Sun ruling 10, in 12 in Libra, opposing progressed retrograde Mars in 6 ruler of the critical degree 7th and 6, which would be the 12th of the other from 7! Mars, Saturn, and Uranus have all turned retrograde through progression (not shown), indicating reassessment within the life being lived.

The transits at the time of the call are even more revealing. Transit Mars ruler of the 7th is precisely on the debilitating Venus in 12! Transit Saturn and Pluto in 12, transit Sun in Capricorn in 3, and the north node in 9 form a Grand cross dilemma with Natal Mars in 6 (his work)! An information/perspective crisis through aggression (Mars) and reflection (7-others). The temptation of the external. If you believe the external separate and not you, then the messages about you, from you (external) must get louder and louder.

Transit Venus ruling the Libran 12th and 1st, and Taurean 8th is retrograde (reflection reassessing) in 4 (inner) and is applying in opposition to natal Pluto (death) in 10 (status) ruler of the self worth 2nd. Transit Mercury (which disposes of most of the planets in the chart), is square transit Jupiter (higher self) and secondary progressed Mercury in 1 (conscious self) also from the 4th. Transit Uranus opposes natal Uranus, squares the Sun and *rules* the 4th! A powerful higher self wake up call. Transit Neptune squares natal Neptune ruler of the empathic need 5th. Sex displaced compassion.

Another woman came forward and admitted to having sex with him at another time in the back of the patrol car, leaving the radio on to receive calls! We give our power to these men to protect us.

The power was placed in reflection and relationship as the determinant of worth in extreme. Being a patrolman implies a belief in the need to have power over others and that the negative aspects of human behavior need "controlling."[152] The paradox is, that only when power is placed outside the self do they need controlling.

Although these charts are quite revealing we will continue, using more astrological applications so that it can be seen that ALL forms of applications presented as valid in this text can be applied.

Next is the solar return for the year of our event. The 2nd ring holds the natal planet positions, and in the third wheel are the positions of the planets at the time he radioed.

---

[152]
I am not advocating the removal of these structures, however as individuals take responsibility for their own actions their need would diminish and dissolve accordingly.

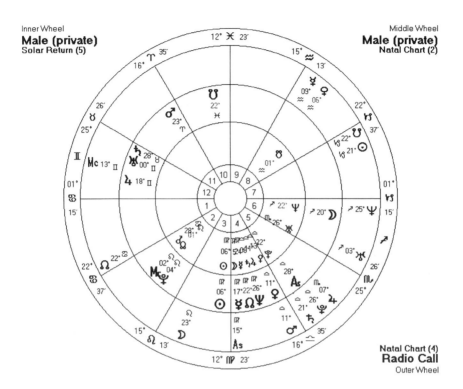

Inner Wheel
Male (private)
Solar Return (5)

Middle Wheel
Male (private)
Natal Chart (2)

Natal Chart (4)
Radio Call
Outer Wheel

We begin with solar return delineation first. The year revolves around identity emotional security, the feminine function, the personal unconscious, women, because the sign Cancer is upon the ascendant (birth) of the return. This sign also falls on the 2nd house cusp, so in some way these issues will be connected to personal worth during the year. The ruler of these houses, the Moon, falls in the 4th in Virgo conjunct the 4th house cusp!(same symbology)

The horizon line of the 1st and 7th houses are the signs "missing in reference" in the natal chart! The Moon in 4 is disposed of by Mercury in 4, both of which are square Neptune in 6, the 12th of the 7th. The Moon disposes of critical degree Mars in 2 conjunct the node (please review the Mars in Cancer interpretation). The both of them exactly square the natal Libra ascendant in 5 (and Mars rules 11 her 5th)!

The ruler of the SR 5th, Venus, is conjunct Jupiter in 4, which rules intercepted Sagittarius 6th (12th of others) and disposes of and is conjunct Saturn, the ruler of others on 7. SR Venus co-rules the solar return 12th house (Taurus), and lines up with debilitating natal Venus (relationship) and transit Mars (aggression) in 4 (emotional security)!

Solar return Moon (the feminine delineation for the year) conjunct the 4th, is also conjunct the problematic natal Mercury, and precisely the *same degree* as the rising degree at the time of the call (15 Virgo)!

Radio call transit Sun, Node, Saturn, Pluto form a Grand cross with SR Mars in 2 (ruling 11 love received) and Pluto in 5 (love given, sex) ruler of the 6th which is the 12th of the woman! Transit Moon the ruler of the year is square solar return Uranus (suddenness) on the cusp of 6 (her 12th) which rules the 9th (her 3rd of travel) and forms a T-square with his natal Saturn/Uranus conjunction in the solar return 12th! Analytical discernment (Virgo) in these charts like in the natal, needs waking up (Uranus) to perceive self through reflection (6th and 7th). He took the stand and stated he did not kill the woman. Neptune was on his Moon in the SR 6th.

Conscious mind is the only thing believed real, and all power is given to physical reality. The barrel of his service revolver he said had been stolen. No ballistics match could be made.

In the solar return, the Moon can be progressed by approximating one degree of forward movement to equal one month of time. The incident occurred five months after solar return, which places progressed solar return Moon at about twenty degrees Virgo *exactly* square natal Moon, the most prominent symbol in every chart.

Still more clarity and corroboration can be gleaned from the Lunar return covering the same period. A Lunar return is simply when the Moon returns every 27.5 days (approximation) back to the same sign and degree it occupied at birth. It **reflects and echoes the solar return**, and in the case we are discussing, the Moon has shown itself very important in delineation. We also begin to see that all our systems of measurement reinforce initial deductions; co-incident not accident-*holographically*. They must be used and approached in **order of supremacy** as I have done here. If layered in this way, it allows for the validation that all truths are true, and that at any point in the holographic matrix in the physical universe we can discern a Universe from a microbe.

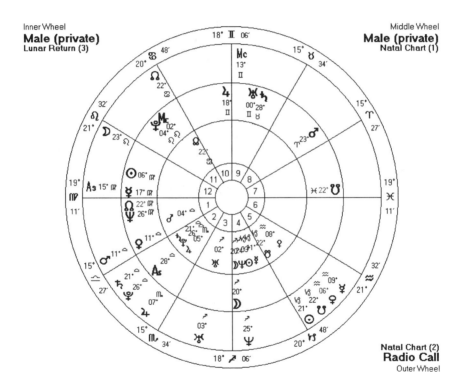

Inner Wheel
Male (private)
Lunar Return (3)

Middle Wheel
Male (private)
Natal Chart (1)

Natal Chart (2)
Radio Call
Outer Wheel

The lunar return chart reflects that the 27 day period will revolve around analytical discernment in preparation for relationship (Virgo is the 12th of the 7th in the experiential template), ideals in service, and conscious mind categorization as Virgo is on the birth time ascendant of the Moon's return. It is at 19 degrees only two degrees off the problematic Mercury position in the natal chart. The Moon as well as the ascendant ruler Mercury fall in the **4th house** of identity emotional security and personal unconscious. Mercury is at 11 degrees Capricorn in 4 *exactly* squaring the natal Venus position and transit Mars at the time of the call in 1! Mercury co-rules the 10th from the 4th at this degree, reflecting the physicalization of initial deductions from 4 and that the emotional security concerns would be referring to *status*. The Midheaven itself is precisely the degree of natal Jupiter's position in the 8th house (death), and represents a powerful point in the natal T-square that falls on the angles of this return!

Mars in the 1st house of the return reflects the juxtaposition of issues of death (rules 8) creative extension (sex) and self worth issues because Venus in 5 disposes of Mars and rules the 2nd (worth) and the 9th (others thinking and expression). Venus is then square lunar return Jupiter (in the natural 8th house sign Scorpio) in the 2nd (self worth) ruler of the 4th and dispositor of the Moon and Neptune in 4. Jupiter also rules law.

The Sun in 4 rules the 12th (the reason for the experience, and limiting perspectives during the time frame) and is *applying* in exact square to Mars in 1 (aggression), which reflects that emotional insecurity will accelerate during the period, and challenge the introspective abilities of the identity regarding assertion (Mars) in relationship (Libra). The need for acceptance in relationship severely challenges the threshold of the identity's emotional insecurities through another's values (rules 8). The transits at the time of the radio call show the Sun/Saturn square falling in the lunar return 2nd and 5th, with the Sun precisely on the cusp of the 5th and Saturn ruling it! Combined with the transit node at 22 Cancer, and natal Mars at 23 Aries, now the Sun/Saturn Grand cross falls in the worth/extension houses of the lunar return. With Saturn ruling 5, the Sun ruling 12, and Mars ruling 8. And finally, the transit retrograde Venus (in 5 Rx not shown) rules the 2nd and 9th and is applying through it's retrograde motion to a square with lunar return Jupiter ruling the emotional security issues of the month on 4, from 2.

The next chart concerning this case is the natal chart of the patrolman in center, planets at the time of the call in the 2nd ring, and outer wheel are the positions of the transits when the final federal trial jury handed down the guilty verdict. The Moon at time of the verdict is 23 degrees Virgo. During deliberation it would have passed the 17 degree point which is precisely conjunct natal Mercury, nodal axis, conjunct progressed

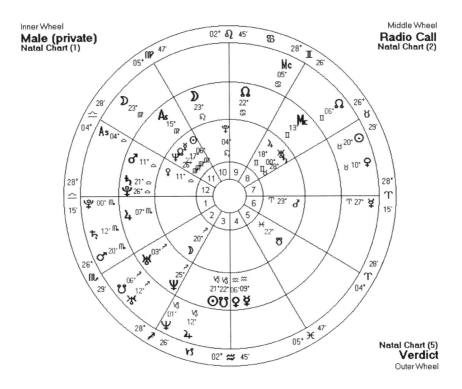

Inner Wheel
Male (private)
Natal Chart (1)

Middle Wheel
Radio Call
Natal Chart (2)

Natal Chart (5)
Verdict
Outer Wheel

Midheaven, conjunct the ascendant at the time of the radio call, conjunct the solar return Moon, and conjunct the lunar return ascendant, triggering the Mutable Grand cross!! Six of eight planets in transit at verdict capable of retrograde *are* retrograde in the self/self quadrant (houses 1-3) reflecting a powerful reassessment of subjective projection and identity definition. The verdict transit Sun and *Venus* oppose the retrograde (Mars/Saturn respectively) planets in 1 from the 7th. Transit verdict Mercury ruling 9 (the opinions of others-law) with it's critical degree, is exactly upon the 7th house cusp and is opposite the time of the radio call Pluto and the critical degree natal Libra ascendant that initiated our deductions from the beginning. Transit verdict Neptune and Pluto form a Yod with Natal Uranus at 0 degree Gemini in 8, from 0 Pluto in Scorpio on the ascendant and Neptune 1 degree Capricorn in the interception in 3, the exact degree of the solar return 7th house cusp (relationship reflection)! Pluto; death, transcendence, and perspective alteration, has just crossed the natal ascendant of "urgent" relating definition (Libra at 28).

The unconscious will now begin to wake up (Uranus rules 4) the conscious mind (it moved to square Mercury) to understand the reasons for disintegrated self projection-it will have no choice (Uranus). Power was given to the conscious mind sword through the basic belief in the need to control people's "inherently" negative nature, and therefore that is the sword conscious mind was "judged by."

We cannot escape the self through conscious mind cleverness. Therefore "judge not lest you be judged" means you judge yourself in the end.

The similarity between our next chart and the one we just completed was unobserved by myself upon selection, however my unconscious knew exactly what it was doing. The chart of Adolf Hitler reflects a similar lack of emotional reference or belief and extreme difficulty with self reflection through others, 0 water, Libra on 12 and the ascendant. Again whenever the same sign occupies the 12th and the 1st, the identity definition *itself* is the reason for incarnation and the need to incorporate and understand the archetype and how it limits the expression of the rest of the chart through the limiting definition "bought into" the life and reflected in the ascendant.

In Hitler's case, rather than self being sought or seen through reflection, power is given to the reflection as the *determinant* of identity (Venus the ruler is conjunct Mars in 7). It must dominate it to validate it's own existence, and this is always an effect of conscious mind focus *to the exclusion* of everything else (Mercury in Aries is disposed of by Mars). Although these are exaggerated examples, we all have a Saturn placement. To what extent we take back our power from the external, is in direct proportion to the limitation we experience.

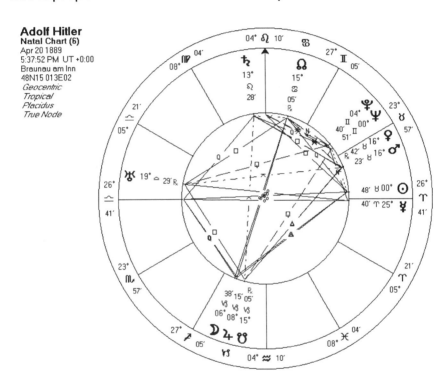

In Hitler's chart we see that Venus the ruler of the 12th, the 1st, the 8th (ego transcendence) is also the dispositor of the Sun and Mars, and is precisely conjunct Mars which disposes of *Mercury* on 7. Mars rules the 6th (the 12th of reflections) and 7th, and both Venus and Mars are retrograde *and* square Saturn ruler of intercepted Capricorn (again missing in reference) in the 3rd *conscious mind!*

Pluto and Neptune are in Gemini (conscious mind/3rd house reference again) in 8. The Sun is at critical degree in 7, disposes of Saturn in 10, which in turn disposes of the Moon/Jupiter conjunction in 3. The planet which reflects conscious mind function, Mercury, needs resolution (opposition) and waking up to reflection (Uranus in Libra) through the personal unconscious as a legacy from the mother or early environment emotional security needs (Uranus rules 4). There is no more definitive or telling aspect other than Mercury square or opposition Uranus, that the unconscious aspects of self have been have been all but negated by the conscious self. There is no access to inner self, therefore no access to higher self, and finally no *perceived* access to "All That Is." The self is all that exists. Focus on the need to prove the self (Mars) and passion for reflection is in the extreme, and all these combinations will be reflected in the chart when this is the case (Mars and Venus rule the 6/12 axis of perspective and limitations, as well as the horizon identity line).

The fall of this man *and* man is through his shutting out of "All That Is" through the belief in separateness. The separateness of ourselves from the environment and nature, and is the reason for *all* aggression expressed on this planet (Mars=singularity).

Hitler could have never gone as far as he did without the agreement of the people and their buying into this Satanic (Saturn) expression to seek validity exclusively. All of us in any situation are either a part of the solution, or a part of the problem. Taking back power by taking responsibility for our own creations is the *action* necessary to reflect acting the part of solution.

VISITORS

"Its the same kind of story that seems to come down from long ago, two friends having coffee together when something flies by their window..... Now you know it's a meaningless question to ask, if those stories are right. 'Cause what matters most is the feeling you get when you're hypnotized...and it seems like a dream-they got you hypnotized." Fleetwood Mac "Hypnotized"

The question of extraterrestrial life is actually not a question but statistically a given. As our collective "ego" socially finds more balance with other "levels" of psychic material, interaction with other civilizations will increase. *Only* because *we* have made it possible for them to interact. We cannot experience anything that is not a part of us on some level. Until we allow other more submerged levels to be a part of the self, our experiences are limited to more narrow conscious comprehension.

Science is progressing to the discovery that physics will transform into metaphysics; that space travel across great distances can only be accomplished through the blending of technology and spiritual awareness. In our Albert Einstein delineation we could intuit he was primarily a spiritually oriented person. His statement that "imagination is more important than knowledge" is key to our discussion here. Until the scientific community recognizes that mind and matter are the same thing in different forms (Quantum mechanics?), then power is placed in the external rather than the inner landscape and from this frame of reference instantaneous travel is not possible and physical propulsion, not feasible. This idea was portrayed in the movie *"Contact"* but this was a perceptual cognition already imagined by those of great sensibilities.

▸ "There is included in human nature an ingrained naturalism and materialism of mind which can only admit facts that are actually tangible sort of mind the entity called "Science" is the idol. Fondness for the word "scientist" is one of the notes by which you may know its votaries; and its short way of killing any opinion that it disbelieves in is to call it "unscientific." It must be granted that there is no slight excuse for this. Science has made such glorious leaps in the last 300 years . . . that it is no wonder if the worshippers of Science lose their heads. In this very University, accordingly, I have heard more than one teacher say that all the fundamental conceptions of truth have already been found by Science; and that the future has only the details of the picture to fill in. But the slightest reflection on the real conditions will suffice to show how barbaric such notions are. They show such a lack of scientific imagination that it is hard to see how one who is actively advancing any part of Science can make a statement so crude. Think how many absolutely new scientific conceptions have arisen in our generation, how many new problems have been formulated that were never thought of before, and then cast an eye upon the brevity of Science's career. Is this credible that such a mushroom knowledge, such a growth overnight as this, can represent more than the minutest glimpse of what the universe will really prove to be when adequately understood? No! Our Science is but a drop, our ignorance a sea. Whatever else be certain, this at least is certain: that the world of our present natural knowledge is enveloped in a larger world of some sort, of whose residual properties we at present can frame no positive idea." William James, 1895 addressing colleagues at Harvard.

Of course we cannot at this moment fathom how many civilizations may exist in the universe. The preoccupation with the physical at the expense of the spiritual would be a foreign perspective to most of them in my view. This perspective transforms at some point in evolution I believe. Our recent preoccupation with their symbolic image is the sign of our changing consciousness in this regard (alien commercialism; T-shirts etc.).

Why haven't extraterrestrials made themselves fully visible to us? Accumulated reports by observers say they have. Even though (according to current texts, please see those listed in the supplemental reading section) we have fired on UFO's with rockets and machine guns. A pretty revealing attitude on our part. Suppose we landed on another planet with our little greeting record and were immediately fired upon? I'd suppose we get back in our craft and think twice about landing again. I doubt this is the true perspective of a visitor.

Never-the-less because of their and our desire to interact (even if on our part it is more unconscious) craft sightings as well as "abductions" are reported, and have been reported on our planet apparently for many, many years.

In the same way that our ego focus keeps us from more expanded aspects of ourselves, it keeps us from experiences connected to those more expanded selves. I believe that in the least, the visitors are an unknown or higher aspect of ourselves. Therefore, as with any self-empowering development, our interaction with the "visitors" will depend solely on our individual and collective abilities to integrate these aspects of the self. We must act as one world before we can *interact* with other worlds. Thank the "All That Is" for the fact that interstellar travel is linked to integration. Think of it as an "interaction governor." Until we reach a certain level of consciousness collectively, we cannot leave the system in any significant way.

The astrological significators that reflect extraterrestrial events and interaction are primarily the outer planets. The transition point is Uranus.

Since these planets reflect the higher and more integrative aspects of ourselves, it follows that they reflect any interaction in these realms, and that these interactions are perhaps more unconscious than conscious. According to these reports, the ability of alien craft to appear, disappear, travel at velocities unheard of in our atmosphere, affect automobile electrical systems, create total blackouts of electrical power to major cities, immobilize persons, create amnesia in "abductees" so as not to remember the interaction, and on and on, are simply "natural" things to beings who are *willing* to know themselves as much as possible and perhaps have never "fallen" into the belief that the physical and spiritual are separate things. This unlimitedness seems to me to be our natural state. Conscious mind constricted perspective is not the rule, it is the *exception* to the rule. So as we re-member other aspects of our selves we have chosen to forget we will also re-member, like the beings who visit us, our creative birthright as a co-creator within the "All That Is." We must also learn that all beings possess equal power to create the reality they prefer, and that

Roswell craft crash
Natal Chart (1)
Jul 2 1947
9:57 PM MST +7:00
Roswell New
33N24 104W32
Geocentric
Tropical
Placidus
True Node

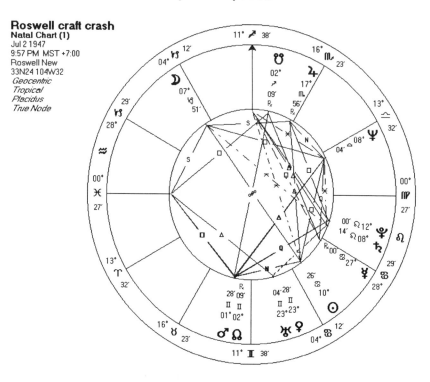

no being has anymore or less than any other.

Our first chart is the chart of the crash of an alien craft near Roswell New Mexico on July 2, 1947 at 9:57 pm MST.[153]

The birth of the event reflected through the rising sign, reveals a new beginning of spiritual awareness (0 degree Pisces ascendant). The ruler of the event Neptune, is in the 7th (reflection) in the sign Libra (reflection).[154]

This spiritual reflection of other dimensional consciousness planet is in a T-square configuration with a Full Moon (full illumination) between the Sun in Cancer (physical manifestation of inner) and the Moon in Capricorn (the

---

153
    Researched and rectified by the author.

154
    Libra has strong representation in all space exploration, i.e. Jupiter/Uranus conjunction at 0 Libra exact when we stepped upon the moon. Again reflecting we are the reality we believe we exist within.

physicalization of inner unconscious) in the 5th and 11th axis (the intermingling of co-creators). The energy of the "bow" in the configuration, the Full Moon physicalization, shoots the Neptunian energy "arrow" firmly into an identity definition into the 1st. Venus, the dispositor of the Neptune reflection and ruler of the 8th, is exactly conjunct Uranus in 4 revealing that the aliens end (4th) or death (Venus rules 8th and 3rd) was the result of lightning striking the craft (Uranus rules the 12th-the discernment of the "others") while mobile (Gemini). Mercury (Srx) dispositor of the Venus/Uranus conjunction and Mars in 3 in Gemini (travel) conjunct the node (allowed for the intake of the energy of the lightning) is retrograde (reassessment) in 5 (extension) and co-rules the reflection 7, their 1st.

Pluto (death) rules the 9th, disposes of Jupiter retrograde in the 9th (their 3rd of travel) and squares it. Pluto is conjunct Saturn in the 6th (their 12th). Saturn then disposes of the Moon's end of the bow of projection (the sun/moon opposition) into physicality (and the others extension 11th).

Critical degrees are on the 12th and 6th in the same signs as the bow! The intercepted Leo/Aquarius (extension interaction) is the missing perspective (6th and 12th) that allowed the lightning strike manifestation (Uranus ruling intercepted Aquarius). On the human perception side these critical degrees represent the profound impact on our perspective at the witnessing of such an event. The critical recognition of physical life existence elsewhere (28 degree Capricorn on 12 and the uniqueness (Aquarius) of ourselves missing in reference) the reason for the interaction.

The Venus/Uranus conjunction on our part reflects the shocking (Uranus) disruption of our emotional security (4) through the cognition of other world reflection (Venus and it's dispositorship of Neptune). Saturn exactly sextiles Neptune from 6 to 7 and reflects the materialized recognition of other world reflection and presence. The support symbolized is through the broadening of identity by recognition of other co-creators (Saturn completing closing sextile to Neptune), and the blending of the non-physical dream (Neptune) with the physical dream (Saturn).

Jupiter is precisely Novile Neptune (implying the completion or perfection between archetypes) from the higher self 9th in Scorpio (ego transcendence) and rules the purpose of manifestation 10th in Sagittarius (higher self).

Mercury is Quintile Neptune reflecting the creative application of the unconscious (rules 4) to the conscious (Mercury) to allow this necessary and imminent event. Pluto exactly trines the Midheaven representing the alteration of creative perspective (Pluto in Leo) to allow higher self function (Sagittarian Midheaven) to manifest in our reality (the 10th). Mars squares the ascendant and is conjunct the node; Piscean energy of permeation in conflict with the ego concepts, habitual thinking, and value judgements to transform (Mars rules the 2nd). Jupiter on 9 (our philosophical thinking) is in Scorpio (the occult or hidden world) on the cusp (new beginning) square Pluto (perspective) and retrograde (obviously-rethinking). Jupiter rules the physical manifestation of higher self and philosophical 10th - the "life direction" of the event (Sagittarius). Emotionally significant events challenge philosophical perspectives?

The story that is told, is that a rancher in New Mexico initially discovered the craft-or at least pieces of it-and called local authorities because he thought it was a new device of the United States. From the Sheriff's dept then to Roswell Air Force base, where investigators were sent out. The investigators leaked the story to local newspapers by releasing a statement of a captured disk in their possession on July 8, 1947. Investigators debunked the story by stating that it was only a weather balloon, retracted the base statement, and have been debunking UFO witnesses and reports, ever since.[155]

---

[155] Roswell Daily Record, July 8, 1947.

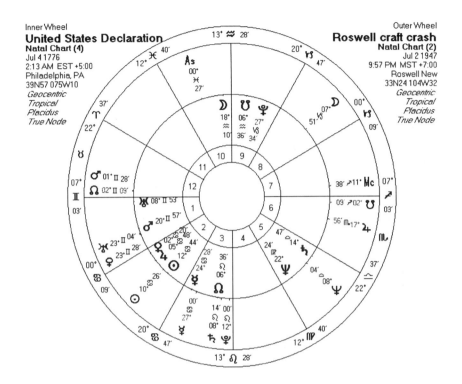

Inner Wheel
United States Declaration
Natal Chart (4)
Jul 4 1776
2:13 AM EST +5:00
Philadelphia, PA
39N57 075W10
Geocentric
Tropical
Placidus
True Node

Outer Wheel
Roswell craft crash
Natal Chart (2)
Jul 2 1947
9:57 PM MST +7:00
Roswell New
33N24 104W32
Geocentric
Tropical
Placidus
True Node

The next chart in this delineation is the United States of America introduced earlier. In the outer ring, the transit positions for the reported crash.

The U.S. chart has already been delineated and the perception of that collective momentum stands for these delineations as well.

The transits at time of crash in the ring reveal that the ascendant of crash time and the Midheaven of the crash fall in the 10th and 7th houses respectively in the U.S. chart. The Midheaven of the event trines the U.S. Venus in 2 which is the ruler of the 6th (the 12th of the public) and intercepted (missing in reference) Taurus 12th (the self introspection needs of the country). Venus also disposes of Saturn (where the country gives it's power away) in Libra (reflections) in 5 (creative extensions). The Midheaven of the crash opposes the midpoint position between the U.S. first house Uranus and Mars, from the higher mind sign of Sagittarius to conscious mind sign of Gemini.

The crash Mercury falls on the U.S. Mercury both retrograde, and opposes the U.S. critical degree Pluto in 9, which is in turn the ruler of the country's intercepted Scorpio in 6 (transformational perspective missing in reference) the 12th of the public (the unseen limitation)! The all important Venus/Uranus conjunction of the crash is conjunct the country's Mars in 1 ruler of 12 (our limiting perspective and the armed forces). This conjunction is square the country's Neptune in 5 (extension references) ruler of the 11th (the interaction of co-creators). The spiritual fears of a nation triggered?

Again as in the Lincoln/Kennedy references an event meant to trigger the spiritual awareness of the country and the true meaning of "are created equal" was it appears, shot down through fear. The fear of loss of domination (Pluto in Capricorn retrograde in 9, ruler of the public's 12th through the Scorpio interception) and control of the collective thought (9th).

Crash Pluto is exactly on the U.S. 4th house cusp which is the emotional security needs of a nation (national security) requiring resolution to experience the equality and freedom of co-creatorhood (opposes the country's Moon in 10 in Aquarius over the following years). This was what our founding fathers proclaimed as the reason for the establishment of the country (Moon and 10th house in Aquarius).

The crash Full Moon falls in the country's value interaction axis (2/8). The Sun rules the 4th (national security) and the Moon rules the 2nd (resources, worth, and values) and 3rd (communication, information). The crash Neptune T-square arrow) is conjunct the country's defensive Saturn in 5 and square the Sun in 2 ruler of the national security 4th! This apparent cover-up was predicated on the need for national security! The constriction of the country's Saturn reflected the holding back of the arrow of other dimensional recognition of co-creatorship (Neptune rules the country's 11th). The wonderful sextile of crash Saturn to the US Uranus in 1, and Neptune's trine to it remained a "military" resource only. Crash Saturn conjoins the country's north node and disposes of the transit Moon in the 8th of the country reflecting the secret possession of dead bodies (?) by "authorities." Jupiter retrograde from the crash time falls in the intercepted 6th (12th of the public) is the ruler of the 7th (the public) and squares (believed separate) the nation's reigning need; the Moon in Aquarius (equality and freedom) in the 10th (the president).

The public was not allowed to "wake up" to this momentous event (Uranus/Venus conjunct the nations Mars square the nation's Neptune and rules 10 and disposes of the Moon). We believed we needed protection from the external by the "government," and when we give this power to them they may "protect" us from things we may not necessarily desire protection from. However, it is my belief that the officials involved believed they could decipher alien technology and develop a "defense" against it so that upon announcement of the disc and alien body retrieval they could state that we have nothing to worry about if they are hostile because they would then be capable of "protecting" us from this possibility. It is probable that this technology of alien life does not include mechanics (only) as we know it (please refer to the supplemental texts and references). Spiritual knowledge is as valuable as technological awareness and our officials were doomed in the interpretation of such wizardry as they found it. Because we have created the armed services to function on the primary belief that reality exists outside of us, it is logical to maintain a "defense." Spiritual knowledge is indeed "alien" to militaristic structures as all power is given to the concept of "attack". Obviously they haven't been able to discern the workings of the alien craft to this day or we would see the technology, and hear of the event.[156]

The biggest fear the US government may now have is the publicity of the cover-up. How do you tell a nation "of the people, by the people, and for the people" that a decision was made by a *few* of the people as to whether this tremendously transformative event was ever even to be known?!

Unknowingly they have sealed the inevitable though this and other events, that the reigning need of the founding fathers must be fulfilled and the public will, through the natural progression of spiritual growth and awareness, cease giving their power to another "entity" and will take it back. History demonstrates that awareness expands not decreases.

The transits outside the second US wheel represent the

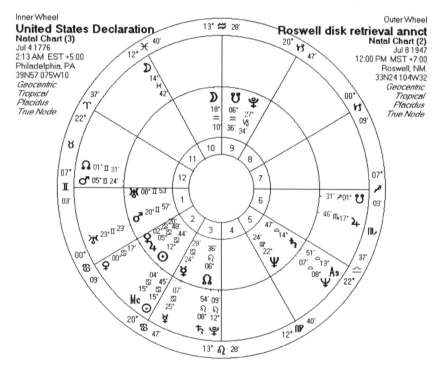

Inner Wheel
United States Declaration
Natal Chart (3)
Jul 4 1776
2:13 AM EST +5:00
Philadelphia, PA
39N57 075W10
Geocentric
Tropical
Placidus
True Node

Outer Wheel
Roswell disk retrieval annct
Natal Chart (2)
Jul 8 1947
12:00 PM MST +7:00
Roswell, NM.
33N24 104W32
Geocentric
Tropical
Placidus
True Node

---

[156]
    Recent allegations from former enlisted military officials and government employees imply some of our current technology has been derived from this alien technology. This has yet to be confirmed.

planetary positions of the leaked statement that "the Air Force has a flying disc in it's possession." Since only 5 days had passed since the crash, many positions, especially the slower planets remain the same. The Moon however, moves very quickly and it's exact inconjunct to Saturn (out of control aspect-or adjustment) implies that this wasn't a "leak" at all, but that this was an intentional decoy to thwart or divert attention from the location of the actual site of the crash (and opinion as Saturn rules 9). Further confirmation of this is shown through the ascendant at the time of announcement which is applying to a conjunction with the country's defensive Saturn! The announcement Moon also forms a Grand trine in Water with the Sun in Cancer in 2 and Jupiter in Scorpio in 6 (the public's 12th), a closed circuit of emotional self sufficiency to defend against the fear of advantage![157]

The thrust of the announcement was to deny the crashed disc was still there! Venus of the announcement is exactly on the nation's 2nd house cusp at 0 degree (a need to initiate a new start) and rules the announcement ascendant (the birth idea) conjunct announcement Neptune (camouflage) and Venus rules 6 the limiting 12th of the public. Once security was established at the site officials came out with the story that it was only a weather balloon that the rancher found pieces of, and as far as they were concerned case closed (it is my opinion that once the entire craft was located that this decision was made).

The President at that time, Harry Truman, had a chart however-and does not reflect case closed. Let's start at the beginning in this with his personal delineation.

The Element count reflects low Fire! Mistrust of the self and it's creative birthright. Difficulty in entering experiences energetically and with trust! The Sun is in Taurus, Moon in Scorpio; A powerful momentum of rigidity. Full illumination of

---

[157] The midpoint structure does however confirm the possession of a valuable resource. Venus=MC/Asc, Sun/MC=Mercury/Jupiter, Pluto=Venus/Neptune. Midpoints will be expanded upon in Volume 2.

subjective value judgements that need transforming. Insecurity may not allow interaction with others, or sharing not possible! And this blend falls in the United States of America's 6th and 12th house axis!

The Sun is in 8 (ego transcendence) and squares the *only Fire reference* Mars in Leo (powerful ego need to prove the self) the Sun rules the 11th (co-creation interaction) and Mars rules the 7th-the public! This Mars position falls in the national

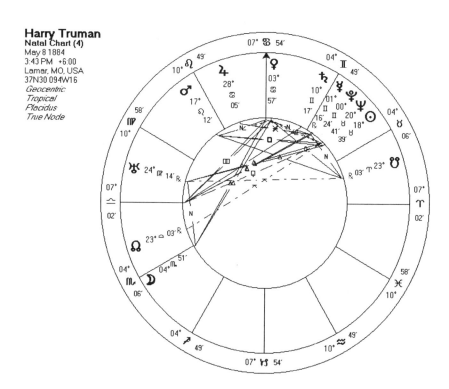

Harry Truman
Natal Chart (4)
May 8 1884
3:43 PM +6:00
Lamar, MO, USA
37N30 094W16
Geocentric
Tropical
Placidus
True Node

security U.S. 4th. The Sun (exactly square the US moon!) is conjunct Neptune (other world and camouflage) and is the ruler of the 6th, his work, and the 12th of others. Because of the square developmental tension requiring fulfillment, there is the need to prove the self (Mars) though camouflage and the spiritual resources of others (Neptune)! Saturn is in Gemini (gives power to conscious mind function) in the 9th reflecting his greatest fears (beliefs) are the opinions of others (9th house), their view of his intelligence, legality, and higher self or "publicity" issues. Saturn rules the 4th of the self's emotional security needs. Mercury (conscious mind function) is retrograde (reassessment, repression) in the 8th (ego transcendence and death issues!) and is conjunct Pluto. Both at critical degrees at the beginning of Gemini (conscious mind), reflecting a tremendous need to transform conscious mind dependency and alter perspective towards other world recognition! This also reflects propaganda-like information control (Gemini, Pluto, 8th. Refer to the Hitler chart just reviewed). Issues of death are very prominent in his chart-other worldly death (Neptune).

The Libra ascendant confirms the perception that the fear of personal popularity and the issues with opinions of others is

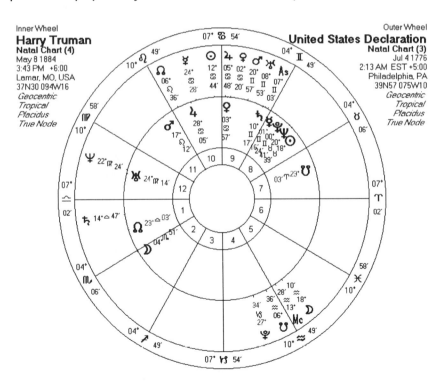

Inner Wheel
Harry Truman
Natal Chart (4)
May 8 1884
3:43 PM +6:00
Lamar, MO, USA
37N30 094W16
Geocentric
Tropical
Placidus
True Node

Outer Wheel
United States Declaration
Natal Chart (3)
Jul 4 1776
2:13 AM EST +5:00
Philadelphia, PA
39N57 075W10
Geocentric
Tropical
Placidus
True Node

tremendous. Venus is in 9 (publicity), trines the moon, which in turn is disposed of by the propagandic Pluto in 8 and rules 8. The Sun/Moon blend is moving toward full illumination in the resource houses with the Sun ruling 11. There are no oppositions (awareness) and only the Moon is below the horizon; all power is given to the external. The power of discrimination, discernment and critical thinking are his limitations and reason for incarnation (Virgo on 12 with Uranus there retrograde). In the life to be lived "correctness" and the "proper" perspective would be disrupted and challenged. The discrimination (Virgo) of how to express oneself (Uranus rules 5) without rocking the boat (Libra ascendant and western hemisphere emphasis). The spiritual aspects of the U.S. is what he could not discern as this Uranus falls on the U.S. Neptune in 5 (creative extension) and his Uranus rules his 5th! Spiritual awakening denied? The limitation of discernment in the ability for a recognition of choice in self-empowerment (5th). Four planets of the US declaration fall in his 9th including the ascendant. Philosophical, religious, information (Gemini) issues with this country would be his lot. This event challenged the very basis of his belief systems (9th emphasis). The US Moon forms a T-square with his Sun in 8 (death, secrets others values) opposes his Mars in 11 (social issues, co-creator interaction, and the extension of others) rules his 10th and disposes of US Jupiter in 9 (the information issue).

Natal Jupiter is at urgent acceleration degree in 10 (28 Cancer) reflecting a need to wind up this emotionally insecure exaggerated (Cancer) thinking (rules 3) to allow higher self manifestation (Jupiter in the 10th). It opposes the US Pluto! The collective consciousness! What philosophical (Sagittarius on 3) information or issue would be in awareness tension with the collective (Pluto) perspective...be in his mind as a status issue (from his 4th to 10th)? His Saturn (limitation-fear) is on the US Uranus (the avant garde) and rules his 4th (security). Mars (ego self) opposes the US Moon (the founding equality principle) and rules 7 (opponents, others).

The transits of the crash reflect beyond a shadow of a doubt

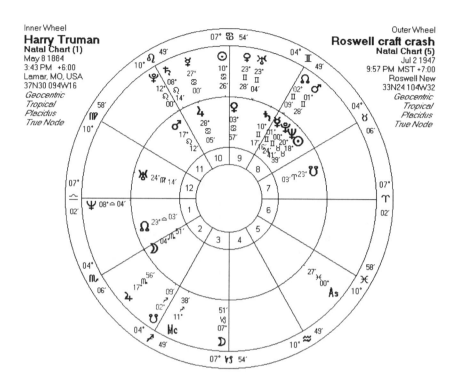

that this man had much more to do with the time of the crash than just the downing of a weather balloon.

The crash ascendant squares Truman's natal Pluto/Mercury (information/perspective and thoughts on the death of others, and their resources) conjunction in 8 exactly, and the crash Mars/node conjunction is right on it! The birth of the event challenged perspective powerfully. The crash Jupiter in Scorpio (philosophical issues about death-mysteries) makes a T-square with his Mars/Sun and a Grand cross if you place the US moon in! A cross to bear with regard to resources (2/8) and extension (5/11) in the *signs* of worth/extension. Crash Sun is conjunct his Midheaven and square his ascendant! An Identity/status crisis! (note transit Neptune on the ascendant!). Crash Mercury rules his natal 12th (discernment limitation) and 9th (others opinions) and is stationary retrograde conjunct critical Jupiter in 10 (focus)! Is this philosophical security issues accelerated? Crash Saturn/Pluto conjunction is on the 11th (creator interaction) and conjunct his Mars ruler of the 7th (reflection, the public). Crash Jupiter ruling his 3rd, completes a T-square of worth and information crisis with his natal Sun/Mars square and Mars "shoots" the arrow into the 5th of creative extension. The 5th house is ruled by Aquarius with its ruler Uranus in the 12th-*one of the main reason's for incarnation!* The crash Uranus/Venus conjunction is square this Uranus in 12 from 9.

Crash Neptune(other worldly consciousness **and** camouflage) is **on** the ascendant and rules the 6th of discernment (*Virgo*) and discretion.

The crash Midheaven opposes his natal Saturn where he gives his power to public opinion from identity insecurity (Capricorn on 4) with regard to intelligence (Gemini). Crash

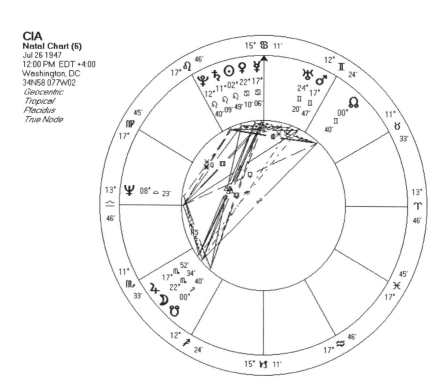

CIA
Natal Chart (6)
Jul 26 1947
12:00 PM EDT +4:00
Washington, DC
34N58 077W02
Geocentric
Tropical
Placidus
True Node

Moon is precisely conjunct the 4th showing mental preoccupation and stress (natal Jupiter is disposed of by the moon) about status (4/10) with this powerful responsibility (the Moon rules the natal 10th!). The Venus/Uranus conjunction in 9 (the *sign of extraterrestrial interaction*) squares his Uranus in 12 and was conjunct the US Mars (the military!). I have only seen clients with major event self reports have this type of powerful corroboration between planetary momentum in the natal chart and extended measurements through transit or progressions.

As Uranus came to precisely square his natal Uranus, the CIA was formed 24 days later; to study the issue of this profound resource? Mercury is in Cancer trine Jupiter in Scorpio from 10 to 2, Saturn rules 4, and is conjunct Pluto ruling that resource house 2. The Moon having just left conjunction with this "stroke of luck" Jupiter death, and trine to Venus-*ruling 8, the ascendant, and dispositor of Neptune.* Mars is in Gemini (information) conjunct Uranus (the avant garde) and rules the opponent 7th and inconjuncts (out of control adjustments) the Jupiter in Scorpio in 2 resource. Mars conjunct Uranus in Gemini in 9; applied energy to the thinking of others with reference to the avant garde?!

The next chart we have is Truman's natal chart (center) with the planets of the United States in 2nd ring and the transits at the initiation of the top secret *Majestic 12* project in the outermost wheel which supposedly consisted of scientists, physicists, and biologists to examine and report on the disc and it's occupants.

For review; Truman's Saturn is conjunct the U.S. Uranus and ascendant. His fears of others thinking (Gemini/9th) limited the reasons for the birth of the country, which is the awakening of unconscious knowledge and the freedom and recognition of choice (Uranus) *thought.*

His Jupiter in critical degree rules the U.S. 7th of the public and exactly opposes US Pluto (giving away of power to materiality Capricorn). His need to prove himself (Moon), his ego focus (Mars), and his life energy (Sun), are believed

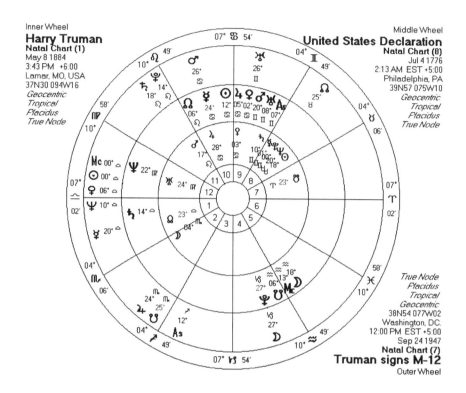

Inner Wheel
Harry Truman
Natal Chart (1)
May 8 1884
3:43 PM +6:00
Lamar, MO, USA
37N30 094W16
Geocentric
Tropical
Placidus
True Node

Middle Wheel
United States Declaration
Natal Chart (8)
Jul 4 1776
2:13 AM EST +5:00
Philadelphia, PA
39N57 075W10
Geocentric
Tropical
Placidus
True Node

True Node
Placidus
Tropical
Geocentric
38N54 077W02
Washington, DC.
12:00 PM EST +5:00
Sep 24 1947
Natal Chart (7)
Truman signs M-12
Outer Wheel

separate (square) and need resolution (opposition) with the reigning need of the country with its Moon in Aquarius. The U.S. reigning needs (Uranian) were his limitations in expression remember?

The U.S. Midheaven, the purpose and direction for the country (Aquarius) is conjunct his 5th of self empowerment. He would not only have fulfilled his *personal* reason for incarnation but the nation's also, had he transformed perspective along with the country and event.

The transits of the initiation of Majestic reveal a Grand cross of worth/extension between Majestic Jupiter, Saturn, his natal Mars and Sun/Neptune and the reigning needs of the entire country (US Moon in 5 in Aquarius) being crucified on the cross of matter! Obviously this issue was unresolvable and not an easy technology, task, or perspective to understand. Saturn opposing the US Moon and in 4th house aspect to his Sun (Leo is the 4th of Taurus) reflects insecurities all around.

Saturn is exactly opposing the U.S. Moon and is the dispositor of the country's critical degree Pluto at 27 degrees Capricorn, where control seems to be the order of the day. All major propaganda and ideological conflicts will be seen when this planet (Pluto) in the US chart is triggered.

The only way power can be taken back from governmental structures *anywhere* is by each and every person taking complete responsibility for their reality and the creations

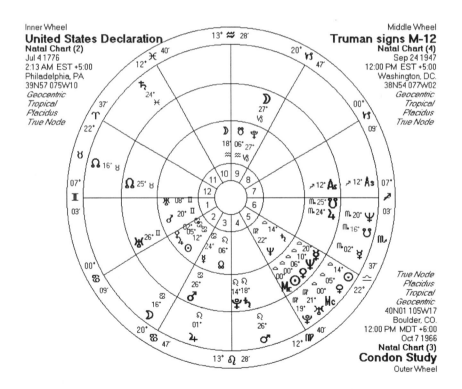

Inner Wheel
United States Declaration
Natal Chart (2)
Jul 4 1776
2:13 AM EST +5:00
Philadelphia, PA
39N57 075W10
Geocentric
Tropical
Placidus
True Node

Middle Wheel
Truman signs M-12
Natal Chart (4)
Sep 24 1947
12:00 PM EST +5:00
Washington, DC.
38N54 077W02
Geocentric
Tropical
Placidus
True Node

True Node
Placidus
Tropical
Geocentric
40N01 105W17
Boulder, CO.
12:00 PM MDT +6:00
Oct 7 1966
Natal Chart (3)
Condon Study
Outer Wheel

therein. This can only happen by each individual recognizing that they are as powerful as they need to be to create whatever they desire to create in their reality without having to hurt, deny, or malign anyone else in order to create it. (please refer to integrity definitions).

A grand cross *can* represent the merging and blending of polarities to create a birth of awareness when all of the components of the cross are given *equal power*. When they are recognized as the polarization of all *one* thing. "All That Is" is all-one-thing (at-one-ment).

The Majestic Midheaven and Sun are exactly trining the Pluto/Mercury conjunction in Truman's 8th at 0 Libra.[158] Neptune is precisely trining his Saturn! Majestic Mars is on his Jupiter and the US Mercury and opposition the U.S. Pluto. Majestic Moon precisely on it. What were the findings? Where is the information?

Our next chart is the U.S. in the center, the Majestic project in the 2nd wheel, and the outside wheel the seemingly unconnected announcement by the Air Force of the University of Colorado at Boulder, *The Condon Study* in 1966, 19 years later!

Observe the "self extension" 5th house of a government of, for, and by the people. Was this another attempt at indoctrinating the youth (5)? Transit (Condon study) Saturn exactly opposes Truman's Uranus position, squares the Uranus of the CIA and opposes Condon Uranus that has just conjoined Condon Pluto in 5.[159]

The Condon study announcement ascendant is the same degree as Majestic ascendant. The Condon report tried to bury the subject once and for all by scientist's statements that there was absolutely nothing to thousands of UFO sightings or

---

158
    This degree will become important for space exploration in future delineation for the US and reflective of our initiation into the association of worlds.

159
    This Uranus/Pluto planetary configuration will be explored at the end of the book. It is a reflection of a consciousness shift and is the symbol of the counterculture that began to take root at this time.

reports! This, as a final attempt of the government to protect itself (and strategy of discounting) is easily seen through the conjunction of the Condon report Sun and the U.S. self defensive Saturn ruler of 8 (others values) and 9 (the thinking and opinions of the public)!

This report was in response to the 1965 wave of sightings around the world. Almost unbelievably, credible witnesses such as airline pilots and Air traffic controllers were invalidated by the government's position that all reports were simply explainable as Venus, weather balloons, satellites, cloud formations, or other natural phenomenon.

The Air Force announcement and the initiation of Majestic Midheavens are both 0 degree Libra. The attempt to make a new beginning in public opinion. The Condon study Neptune (camouflage) is conjunct not only the Jupiter of Majestic (rules the public 7) but also the Jupiter position of the Roswell crash. Condon study Mars is inconjunct the country's critical Pluto from the national security 4th (adjustment of the public thought, the 9th is the 3rd of the public 7th). Condon study Uranus is conjunct the US Neptune, Neptune just squared US Moon in 10, Jupiter has just opposed US Pluto in 9, and Saturn is Rx to oppose the US Neptune for a second time.

Condon study Saturn is retrograde forming a T-square with the country's Mars (need to prove conscious mind) ruler of 12 (a limiting perspective and Mars *is the Military*) and opposes the other dimensional symbol Neptune in 5. Condon study Moon ruling the worth and communication of the country 2nd and 3rd, is conjunct the Sun the ruler of the national security 4th.

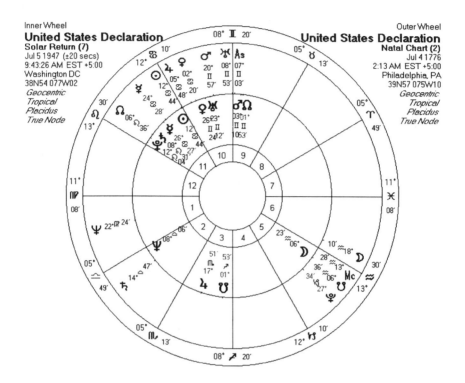

Inner Wheel
United States Declaration
Solar Return (7)
Jul 5 1947 (±20 secs)
9:43:26 AM EST +5:00
Washington DC
38N54 077W02
Geocentric
Tropical
Placidus
True Node

Outer Wheel
United States Declaration
Natal Chart (2)
Jul 4 1776
2:13 AM EST +5:00
Philadelphia, PA
39N57 075W10
Geocentric
Tropical
Placidus
True Node

The Pluto/Uranus conjunction of the announcement for the Condon study is also opposed by the announcement Saturn and falls on the country's Neptune, the reason for increased awareness of UFO's by the public! Perhaps awareness is what needs deterring to control the public?

Our next chart is the solar return of the United States for the year 1947 (2 days after the crash at Roswell) and the U.S. natal planets in the second wheel.

The year revolves around issues of analysis and categorization of material information, work service of possibly missing the forest for the trees as Virgo at 11 degrees occupies the ascendant of the year. It's ruler, Mercury is retrograde (reassessment, repression), in the sign Cancer (emotional security) in the 11th of social interaction! Mercury also rules the 10th and disposes of Venus ruler of 2 (resources) and 9 (thinking and philosophical profile of the public).

Uranus (the planetary archetype of creator interaction) is the ruler of 6 (the issues the year revolves around, as well as the limits of public perspective) and is in 10 (status) and conjunct Venus. Mars/Node is in 9 (public opinion) and is ruling the Aries 8th (ego transcendence, death, the values of the public- the 2nd of the 7th). The year ruler Mercury is disposed of by the Moon in Aquarius (extension interaction) in 5 which trines Neptune in 2 (the "others" ruler of 7) reflecting the possible possession of the craft.

The 12th house degree of the solar return is the exact degree of the national security 4th of the US declaration chart and is ruled by the Sun in 11 (creation interaction again). The Sun in turn disposes of the Saturn/Pluto conjunction on the 12th, Saturn ruling 5.

Pluto on the 12th also disposes of the 4th house ruler Jupiter (national security) also repressed (retrograde) in the 3rd (conscious mind opportunity for transformative investigation; Scorpio). The Aquarian focal point of the chart is the opposition from the co-creation Moon in 5 (country's creative extension) to the Saturn/Pluto conjunction on the 12th cusp.

If we progress the solar return Moon one degree for one month it makes it's exact opposition to Saturn in two months. Precisely the month of the initiation of the Majestic operation by Truman!! Saturn and the Moon rule the 5th and 11th house axis of creative extension and interaction, and the Moon's opposition to Saturn (limited, focused physicality) shows that there would have been serious concerns with others extension capabilities, strategy, defense?

This opposition reflects tremendous frustration on the part of the U.S. government, and perhaps tremendous paranoia. How can we defend ourselves against something we don't have the slightest inkling or understanding of?

Pluto rules the 3rd and connects security issues to it by

disposing of Jupiter ruling 4. If we progress this important Moon position in the solar return to it's opposition with Pluto it would have become exact 6 months later, which co-incides with one of the most, if not *the* most, traumatic UFO encounters in history by Captain Mantell of the United States Air Force.[160] Six months later, the date is January 7, 1945;

> ▸   "The time was one-fifteen in the afternoon. The place: Godman Air Force Base, just outside of Louisville, Kentucky. Control tower personnel received a call from State-highway Patrol; did Godman tower know anything about strange aircraft hovering in the vicinity? The Godman tower replied in the negative. Nothing airborne in the vicinity. As a check, they called Flight Service at the Wright-Patterson Air Force Base. Still no response or record of anything in the area. State Highway Patrol reluctantly concluded there was nothing more they could do about calls they'd had from Maysville, a small town 500 miles east of Louisville. But twenty minutes later" they were back on the phone to Godman Tower with reports from two towns west of Louisville. The reports from each town seemed to jibe. A flat, circular object, about 300 feet in diameter, was moving westward at an appreciable rate of speed. Although they'd been looking since the first report, Godman tower still saw nothing. They checked Wright-Patterson again and got another negative response. Then, at 1:45 p.m. it happened. The assistant tower operator saw the object for several minutes before reporting it to the chief. Both men tried to convince themselves the object was a balloon but could not. Key personnel were alerted to the tower where they all viewed the object through 6x50 binoculars. None could identify the object, but all saw it. Then the base commander arrived and he, too, saw the object.
>
> At two-thirty, a flight of four F-51's hove into view, and the base commander made up his mind. He called Captain Mantell, the flight leader, and asked him to identify the object. After one of the F-51s dropped out of the flight because his fuel level was low, the three remaining aircraft took a heading from Godman tower and headed south. By the time the F-51s reached 10,000 feet, Mantell was well ahead of his wing men and barely visible to them. He called into the tower. "I saw something ahead of me and I'm still climbing." Everyone in the tower heard this. They also heard one of the wing men say, "What the hell are we looking for?"

160
        After this was written, this story was also told on the television show "Sightings" by his son.

Godman tower called Mantell now for a description. To this day, there is controversy over most of what he told them. Yet they do agree on one thing. "It's above me and I'm gaining on it. I'm going to 20,000 feet." None of the pilots had oxygen, and Mantell's announcement that he was climbing to 20,000 feet meant immediate trouble. Twelve thousand feet is an altitude where oxygen is definitely indicated, at 15,000 feet and over, it is essential. His two wing men tried desperately to call Mantell, but he did not answer. They levelled off at 15,000 feet, made other efforts to call their leader, then started down, their own fuel level dangerously low. The two remaining aircraft returned to their base, and at 3:50 Godman tower lost sight of the UFO. Minutes later, the reports came in that Mantell's plane had crashed; he was dead. Later that evening, airfields throughout the Midwest sent in UFO reports, and newspapers carrying the story of the Mantell tragedy linked the subsequent sightings with the Kentucky sightings, claiming it was one object and that it had led Mantell to his death.[161]

This event occurred precisely 6 months after the U.S. solar return and in the next chart outside the US return and US Declaration placements are the transits for Mantell's pursuit of the UFO in the third wheel. First, we must look at the U.S. natal placements to observe where the solar return planets fall in that chart (this process should be done with any solar return interpretation).

The Midheaven of the solar return falls exactly on the US's Uranus, the symbol of the need to wake up unconscious knowledge, thinking and communication. This planet would be powerfully emphasized during the year we are discussing 7/47 to 7/48. Uranus disposes of the country's reigning need, the Moon, as well as the solar return Moon, now progressed to the time of Mantell's crash opposing Pluto the ruler of the 3rd house of conscious mind. We now have evidence from reports that UFO's exhibit inter-dimensional characteristics, and cannot be chased with a jet aircraft. As the scientist Jacques Vallee has pointed out in his book *"Revelations"* we have no scientific proof that they are even alien.

The opposition to Pluto by the Moon in the solar return was

---

[161] Howard V. Chambers, UFOs For The Millions, Sherbourne Press 1967

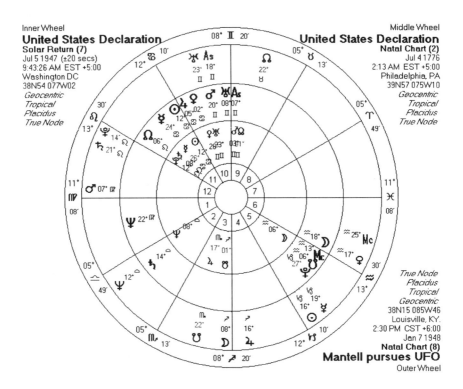

calling for the transformation of perspective to liberate ego focus. Pluto also has rulership of the atomic bomb which President Truman had just finished using on Hiroshima August 6, 1945. Would an alien presence have been likely after such an event? Perhaps atomic energy would attract attention upon detonation? Humans who demonstrate careless ego, armed with such a devastating capability is perhaps good reason and cause for alarm.[162]

The transits at the pursuit by Mantell, reflect aggression on the part of the U.S.. Transit Mars (military) at pursuit is 7 degrees Virgo on the SR ascendant and pursuit Moon is at 8 degrees Sagittarius forming a T-square with the powerfully

162
     Please see "The Great Jupiter/Saturn Earth Conjunctions" Dell Horoscope Magazine, May 1996 Issue, also by the author, for the significance of these events historically.

positioned U.S. Uranus on 10, ascendant, and solar return Midheaven. Mars becomes an aggression arrow aimed at the visitors (7th-8th). The ascendant of the pursuit is conjunct the U.S. Mars and SR Uranus. Pursuit Venus opposes Saturn, squares the solar return Jupiter and is conjunct the Moon of the country, which is the dispositor of the Cancer SR Sun and Mercury. We need to see co-creators through reflection not conscious mind security needs (Jupiter rules the 4th of the solar return). Pursuit Sun opposes solar return Sun (awareness) ruler of the 12th (the limits of perspective). Whatever we put into scenarios in terms of energy (negative/positive) is what determines the effect extracted from it. Why the government is still debunking UFO sightings is not clear. Except of course, the strain this would place on our cherished beliefs. Why extraterrestrials keep *their distance* is quite clear to this writer. It is because of the distance we maintain from *ourselves.*

Our next chart for study on this subject is the chart for the time of the historic Betty and Barney Hill abduction case. First let me clarify from the empowered view, there can be no such thing as an "abduction." All creations of reality are the effect of higher self agreement between the parties previous to incarnation and/or made at an unconscious level. No being is more powerful than another in this overall sense.[163]

The Hill case was widely publicized in the October 4th and 18th issues of *LOOK* Magazine in 1961. Under hypnosis, separately by Dr. Benjamin Simon a distinguished Boston Psychiatrist and neurologist at the time, Betty and Barney both recalled an alien encounter after recurring dreams and an unaccounted-for time period the night of September 19th and early morning hours of September 20th, 1961.

They recalled being taken aboard the alien's craft and given numerous examinations. Betty recalled conversing in a telepathic manner with the occupants, seeing a map of stars,

---

[163] Please refer to "Bashar and The Association," by Darryl Anka, and "Abduction," by John E. Mack.

and an explanation of the aliens origin. This was perhaps the first well documented close encounter. They have been reported ever since with amazing similarity.(see Budd Hopkins *"Missing Time"*).

The event horoscope for the time of their experience appears below. As in the crash of the craft in 1947, we again see the archetype of reflection, Venus, conjunct the symbol for unconscious knowledge, Uranus. Any valid contact will have these two archetypes in powerful configuration as this reflects the awakening of *forgotten* relationship (not necessarily the only aspect). All planets past Saturn-Uranus, Neptune, Pluto, will be strongly emphasized in other world encounters because these planets reflect the aspects of the higher and non-physical aspects of the self. These same planets are then incorporated through the quadratures and conjunctions to the inner planets of persona and physicality.

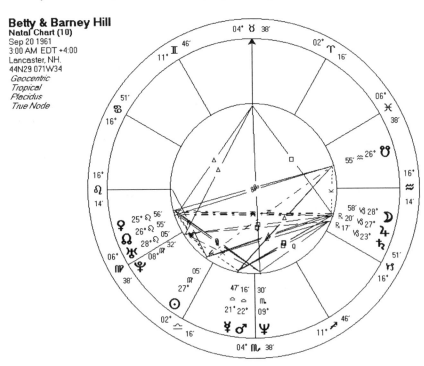

Betty & Barney Hill
Natal Chart (10)
Sep 20 1961
3:00 AM EDT +4:00
Lancaster, NH.
44N29 071W34
Geocentric
Tropical
Placidus
True Node

In the Hill chart we see Jupiter (higher self) is conjunct the Moon the ruler of the 12th (reason for incarnation) reflecting a higher self chosen event. The expansion of discernment of other world presence physically (in the 6th in Capricorn-conjunct the US Pluto!). All the planets in the 6th are trine the Sun in 2, which is the dispositor of the Uranus/Venus conjunction, indicating absence of negative intent. The conscious mind planets are square these 6th house placements (Mars/Mercury). Evidence that any discomfort experienced by the Hills, was an effect of the resistance to the developmental growth in relationship awareness (Libra) from definitions of the way things "really" are or "should" be.

Whenever any being willing to know itself all that it can (the Visitors) comes in contact with a being that represses fears and aspects of the self (us) the higher vibration of the more integrative being has the effect of somewhat overwhelming or accelerating the vibration of the lower vibrating being which allows these fears and repressed energies to come to the surface. (see the section on fear, Bashar page 11). This can be a frightening experience if you are not willing or capable of believing in your own power when it occurs. All pain is the effect of resisting growth, developmental tension and the belief in separation.

The "clinical" attitude of aliens reported by abductees is the effect of a higher vibrational being not necessarily adhering to the "shoulds" of cultural expectations which are not natural, but are learned.

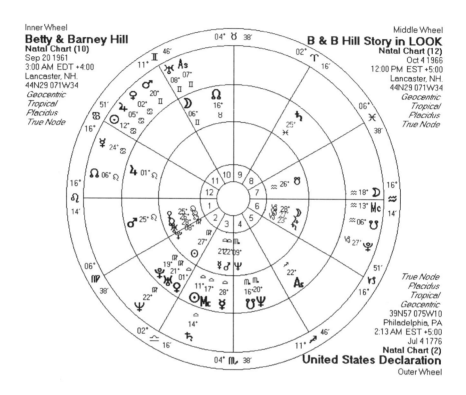

Inner Wheel
Betty & Barney Hill
Natal Chart (10)
Sep 20 1961
3:00 AM EDT +4:00
Lancaster, NH.
44N29 071W34
Geocentric
Tropical
Placidus
True Node

Middle Wheel
B & B Hill Story in LOOK
Natal Chart (12)
Oct 4 1966
12:00 PM EST +5:00
Lancaster, NH.
44N29 071W34
Geocentric
Tropical
Placidus
True Node

True Node
Placidus
Tropical
Geocentric
39N57 075W10
Philadelphia, PA
2:13 AM EST +5:00
Jul 4 1776
Natal Chart (2)
United States Declaration
Outer Wheel

In the second ring are the planetary positions at the time of the publication of their experiences in *LOOK* magazine, and in the outside are the U.S. natal positions.

This article was published as transit Uranus exactly conjoined the U.S. Neptune! The Moon/Jupiter conjunction of the event is precisely on the U.S. Pluto, insuring the broad attention and publicity of the event and triggering the much needed perspective alteration of the country. This event was destined by higher self agreement to do just that (the Moon rules the 12th of incarnational purpose). Publication Mercury is in quadrature to U.S. Pluto (square) and the event Moon, as well as the 27 degree Cancer Mercury of the crash at Roswell in 1947. We have seen the significance of the 27th and 24th degree of the signs because of the U.S. placements of Mercury at 24 Cancer and Pluto 27 Capricorn.

This country must lead in perspective alteration. Changes will be powerful in 2015 (discussed in Projections page 457).

The Capricorn planets square the Mars/Mercury conjunction in the 3rd (communication) in the Hill chart and form a T-square with the addition of the U.S. Mercury. The Pluto of the Hill chart is exactly square the U.S. Uranus. The publication Saturn (physicalization) opposes the U.S. Neptune. Publication Mars (assertion) is conjunct the Venus/Uranus conjunction of the event and Mars rules the 9th of publication!

Remember the planetary positions for the University of Colorado at Boulder the "Condon Study" report on the significance of UFO reports? According to the report, none was found, but it is easy to see the primary significance of this announcement is that it came *three days* after the Hill story came out in *LOOK* magazine!

We discussed the study's Sun being precisely on the U.S. defensive Saturn! It seems there was never any objectivity intended in this report but was initiated primarily to defend against the threat of contradiction to the government's stance on the issue. To "spin" the idea that it was stupid to believe anything but the report.

The announcement of the study Moon (please refer back to that chart page 437) is exactly on the 12th house cusp of the Hill experience, a definite reflection of the attempt to "limit" the life of the experience!

Finally, as the effect of petitions signed and delivered to United States Congressman Steven Schiff of Albuquerque, New Mexico on January 12, 1994 (The Roswell Declaration, *Omni Magazine*) the time for the press conference to release Air-Force report "Case Closed" on the Roswell incident appears as the next chart. In the outer wheel is the chart for the US.

Mail to; Omni Magazine, 324 West Wendover Ave, suite 205, Greensboro, North Carolina 27408. They will forward it to the organizers. Must be signed and returned by November 30, 1994.

Please Copy and Circulate

THE ROSWELL DECLARATION

Forty-seven years ago, an incident occurred in the southwestern desert of the United States that could have significant implications for all mankind. It involved the recovery by the U.S. military of material alleged to be of extraterrestrial origin. The event was announced by the U.S. military on July 8, 1947, through a press release that was carried by newspapers throughout the country. It was subsequently denied by what is now believed to be a cover story claiming the material was nothing more than a weather balloon. It has remained veiled in government secrecy ever since.

The press release announcing the unusual event was issued by the commander of the 509th Bomb Group at Roswell Army Air Field, Colonel William Blanchard, who later went on to become a four-star general and vice chief of staff of the United States Air Force. That the weather balloon story was a cover-up has been confirmed by individuals directly involved, including the late General Thomas DuBose who took the telephone call from Washington, DC. ordering that the original press re-

lease was correct and the Roswell wreckage was of extraterrestrial origin. One such individual was Major Jesse Marcel, the intelligence officer of the 509th Bomb Group and one of the first military officers at the scene.

On January 12, 1994, United States Congressman Steven Schiff of Albuquerque, New Mexico, announced to the press that he had been stonewalled by the Defense Department when requesting information regarding the 1947 Roswell event on behalf of constituents and witnesses. Indicating that he was seeking further investigation into the matter, Congressman Schiff called the Defense Department's lack of response "astounding" and concluded it was apparently "another government cover-up."

History has shown that unsubstantiated official assurances or denials by government are often meaningless. There is a logical and straightforward way to ensure that the truth about Roswell will emerge: an Executive Order declassifying any information regarding the existence of UFOs or extraterrestrial intelligence. Because this is a unique issue of universal concern, such an action would be appropriate and warranted. To provide positive assur-

ance for all potential witnesses, it would need to be clearly stated and written into law. Such a measure is essentially what presidential candidate Jimmy Carter promised and then failed to deliver to the American people 18 years ago in 1976.

If, as is officially claimed, no information on Roswell, UFOs, or extraterrestrial intelligence is being withheld, an Executive Order declassifying it would be a mere formality, as there would be nothing to disclose. The order would, however, have the positive effect of setting the record straight once and for all. Years of controversy and suspicion would be ended, both in the eyes of the United States' own citizens and in the eyes of the world.

If, on the other hand, the Roswell witnesses are telling the truth and information on extraterrestrial intelligence does exist, it is not something to which a privileged few in the United States government should have exclusive rights. It is knowledge of profound importance to which all people throughout the world should have an inalienable right. Its release would unquestionably be universally acknowledged as an historic act of honesty and goodwill.

I support the request, as outlined above, for an executive order declassifying any U.S. government information regarding the existence of UFOs or extraterrestrial intelligence. Whether such information exists or whether it does not, I feel that the people of the world have a right to know the truth about this issue and that it is time to put an end to the controversy surrounding it.

Signature / Date / Name (Please Print)

Occupation/Title / Street

City / State / Zip

Degrees/Credentials (if applicable) / U.S. Representative (if known)

In the branch of astrology known as *Horary astrology* (please refer to the glossary end of chapter 6) the Moon is said to be *Void-of-course* if it does not make any major aspects (trine, sextile, conjunction, square or opposition) before it leaves the sign it is in. When this occurs it is delineated that *nothing will come of the event!*

It is not "Case Closed" because this condition exists in the "Case Closed" chart. This reflects the impotency of the report and it was immediately laughed at because the Air Force asserted that the aliens that were said to be found in 1947 were *really* dummies used in testing that the Air Force did not use until *the 50's!* The Moon in Aquarius (the avant garde) ruling 11 (co-creator interaction) will make no aspects before it leaves that sign. The conjunction of the moon immediately before the press conference tells us what generated it, and the next conjunction tells us the future. The last conjunction it

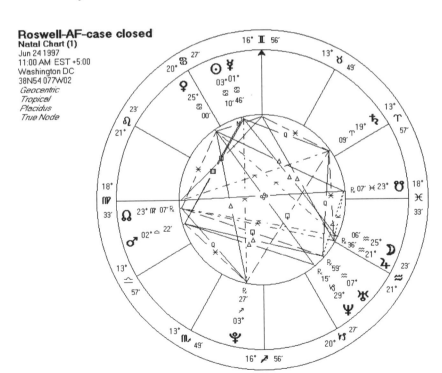

Roswell–AF–case closed
Natal Chart (1)
Jun 24 1997
11:00 AM EST +5:00
Washington DC
38N54 077W02
Geocentric
Tropical
Placidus
True Node

made (the past) was a conjunction to Jupiter ruling 4 (national security with regard to extraterrestrial interaction-Aquarius!) in the 6th the 12th of the public (expansion and opportunity).

The next conjunction the moon will make is to Saturn in 8. The testing of ego strategies and control of secrets (Saturn in Aries in 8). This degree of Cardinal signs will be seen to be significant in our next section on projections. This spin doctoring will prove to be fatal to public trust.

Mars (ego defense) ruling 8 and disposing of Saturn is in 1 square Mercury in 10 (information-the press conference itself) and the Sun ruling 12 (the reason for the report) in Cancer (security). The Sun is applying to inconjunct Pluto in 3 in Sagittarius (out of control limitations 12, and forced communication, Pluto and 3). Venus opposition Neptune (camouflage, i.e., Kennedy's solar return page 375) from 11 to

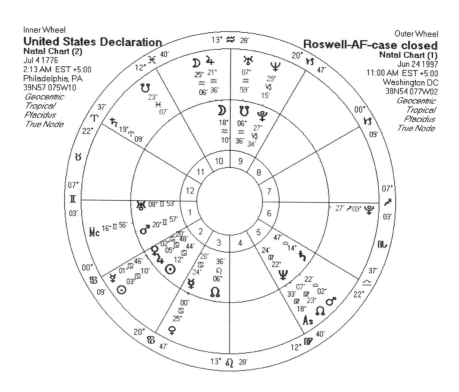

Inner Wheel
United States Declaration
Natal Chart (2)
Jul 4 1776
2:13 AM EST +5:00
Philadelphia, PA
39N57 075W10
Geocentric
Tropical
Placidus
True Node

Outer Wheel
Roswell-AF-case closed
Natal Chart (1)
Jun 24 1997
11:00 AM EST +5:00
Washington DC
38N54 077W02
Geocentric
Tropical
Placidus
True Node

5 (creator interaction) sums it up! Neptune rules the public 7th and Venus rules the resource 2nd and thinking of the public 9th. Venus disposes of the Mars (military) defensiveness and need to prove intelligence (square Mercury) in Libra (social acceptance). Lets look at this press conference when placed around the US declaration.

The Case Closed chart (from here referred to as CC) Sun and Mercury are conjunct the US Venus/Jupiter conjunction in the 2nd house of resource and squares the Mars in 5 of extension. The Sun rules the national security 4th and Mars rules 12 (limitations)! The Moon in Aquarius in 10 rules the 2nd (resource) and 3rd (communication) and is leaving conjunction with Rx Jupiter ruler of 7 (the reassessment of co-creator interaction from the public!). And of course the camouflage

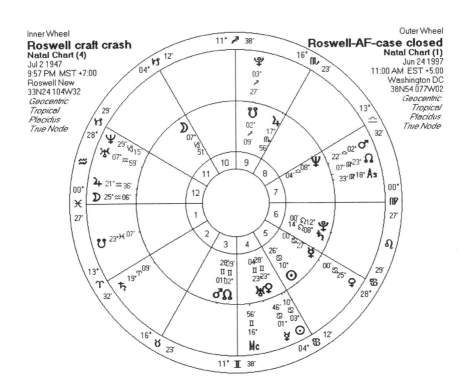

Inner Wheel
Roswell craft crash
Natal Chart (4)
Jul 2 1947
9:57 PM MST +7:00
Roswell New
33N24 104W32
Geocentric
Tropical
Placidus
True Node

Outer Wheel
Roswell-AF-case closed
Natal Chart (1)
Jun 24 1997
11:00 AM EST +5:00
Washington DC
38N54 077W02
Geocentric
Tropical
Placidus
True Node

Venus/Neptune opposition falls on the power and controlling Pluto in 9, that limits the public (rules the intercepted Scorpio in 6-the 12th of the public).
Here the CC surrounds the Roswell crash itself.

Neptune has moved forward over the 12th cusp and is retrograding back (the dissolution of the reason for the event and a camouflaged limitation) to oppose Mercury in 5 a second time (communication and awareness consciously of the event) *and back over the US Pluto in 9.* Uranus moved to 8Aquarius40 opposing the crash Saturn bringing the fears of creator interaction into awareness as we moved into the early months of 1998 as Pluto crossed the US 7th cusp and opposed US Uranus in 1. Events will accelerate with this issue by December 25, 1998 and again October 24, 1999. January of 2000 begins an era of paranormal acceleration in many areas.

▸   Friends and Neighbors, Bashar and The Association. 1/28/87
         Who is the Alien?
         "Let us begin by speaking about the concepts you have held on your planet regarding what you colloquially call extraterrestrials. Even before that, however, from another point of view allow us to delineate a time when we first discovered a civilization, one that had a life form upon it that was, to use our term, Essassani-ish. But instead of our average height of 5 feet, they ranged on an average from 5 to 6-1/2 feet. Whereas we exhibit generally overall white/whitish-gray skin color, this civilization exhibited a wide range of colors. . . . Well, are you all catching on so far?   (Yes!)
         All right. This is to give you the perspective that, considered from other points of view, you yourselves are the aliens. Your world to many other civilizations is unknown, different, unusual, unique in many ways. There really is no need when considering us, or any other civilization, to think any more highly of us than you are willing to think of yourselves-for you are unique and different in your own way. You are just as valid an expression of a form of life as any other form of life that has chosen to express itself-in physical reality or in any other level of consciousness.
         You are an alien civilization to us; we are an alien civilization to you. But on other levels we are the same. The way we choose to express that sameness is what creates the different societies, and it is that sameness that allows us the opportunity to create different expressions. It is because we all draw from the same source of

Infinite Creation; it is because we are all the same type of soul, if you will, that we allow ourselves the opportunity to express ourselves in such a broad, diversified range of experience and life.

Many of your years ago, any time your culture even thought of the idea of an extraterrestrial, you usually designed your awareness regarding what these extraterrestrials looked like to be something quite different from your own human physical form. And from what we have observed, since you imbued in these non-human physical forms typically a certain degree of malevolence toward your society, you thus created these extraterrestrial forms to be terrorizing things. Now that you are beginning to change your attitudes and ideas about how other life forms can be experienced and possibly be encountered by you, you are beginning to think more in terms of your own human form. You have discovered that many of the interactions and contacts that have taken place more often than not seem to involve extraterrestrials who are human-ish, or humanoid in form.

There may be many individuals who say, "Well, why should this be so? Just because we might now think that extraterrestrials may be friendly, as opposed to possessing a desire to consume us, does not necessarily mean that they must appear in humanoid form." And this is so. The reason basically why you are coming closer and closer to the reality wherein you can interact with extraterrestrial consciousness; the reason why you are now seeing many of these contacts take place between your form and forms that are not truly very dissimilar to your own, is because of the nature of reality, the nature of the universe.

As we have discussed, everything is the product of different rates of frequency, and it is those different frequencies that determine the material constructs designed and created out of the primal energy. Therefore recognize that when any other civilizations-at least among the majority we have encountered- first begin to venture into space, first begin to realize that they may in fact encounter other forms of life, they usually at first encounter and attract those forms operating closest to their own frequency. And thus by definition those attracted usually reflect a similar physical structure."

"If a man doesn't keep pace with his companions, perhaps it's because he hears a different drummer. Let him step to the music he hears, however measured or far away." Henry David Thoreau, 1854

"There is no bar to knowledge greater than contempt prior to examination." Herbert Spencer

"True goodness springs from a man's own heart. All men are born good." Confucius

"The man who acts never has any conscience; no one has any conscience but the man who thinks." Goethe, Spruch in Prosa.

"Your saying to me, "I do not understand you," is praise beyond my worth, and an insult you do not deserve." Kahlil Gibran

"Genius, that power which dazzles mortal eyes, Is oft but perseverance in disguise." Henry Austin "Perseverance Conquers All"

"To see what is right and not to do it is want of courage." Confucius

"A wise and good man can suffer no disgrace." Fabius Maximus

"The best known evil is the most tolerable." Livy

"Fear is the parent of cruelty." James Anthony Froude

"Whom they fear they hate." Quintus Ennius "Thyestes"

"Rules and models destroy genius and art." William Hazlitt

"The only means of strengthening one's intellect is to make up one's mind about nothing-to let the mind be a thoroughfare for all thoughts, not a select party."   John Keats

Part 2

Projections

Projections

The future holds many surprises. It is often much more surprising than we can imagine. Understanding how those surprises come about has always held a fascination for us. Astrology can be used as guide to trends and probabilities. We still must change the source of the reflection-ourselves. Working between the two, understanding the self and understanding how that self(s) unfoldment is most likely to manifest, is really what astrology is about. Because reality is not completely an independent entity outside of us but is intimately connected to our views, beliefs, and aspirations, our attitude toward life is critical. Understanding how we limit those aspirations through habitual ritualistic thinking patterns and bias (or as we spoke of in the beginning, encoding) allows us to change levels in our interpretation of planetary aspects that act as a template of probabilities-not fixed fate.

Our first subject under consideration is extraterrestrial interaction. In order to project the future probability and unfoldment of momentum of these interactions we must first clarify the overall astrological design of this inevitable intermingling. We seek to answer the question; What planetary "pictures" illustrate this?

According to our template, before we can "get" to Pluto (4th dimensional perspective), we must integrate the forgotten unconscious knowledge (Uranus), of our co-creatorhood with "All-That-Is" (Neptune). It is the developmental pattern between Uranus/Neptune that will allow us to experience Pluto. All three work to expand our collective reality. Their quadrature aspects (conjunction, square, opposition) will be our first subject of analysis as well as their combinations in events.

These two planets along with Pluto have enormously long revolutions. The last cycle actually began in the early 1800s, but the last opposition and closing square will be sufficient to demonstrate the validity of connection of extraterrestrial sighting waves as well as quantum leaps of consciousness and expansion in recent history.

Much of our future interaction with other worlds depends on (1) our governments willingness to acknowledge and share information (which I believe is little) and (2) on our ability to be all that we can be. Primarily number 2.

Transformation of perspective is the primary ingredient and the goal. Transformation is not the product of mediocrity (Bashar). It can be an ecstatic or traumatic transformation. Judging by our easing into the recognition that we are not alone with the discovery of planets around other stars recently, it can be natural. But there will be major transformations especially in 1999, 2000, 2006 and 2012, with the major shift in consciousness at 2015.

When we give power to the government to protect us from things we are not willing to take responsibility for, they may also "protect" us from things we do not necessarily wish to be protected from. This is why the need for restructuring governments more in line with that idea is becoming a need collectively.[164]

URANUS With NEPTUNE/PLUTO CONJUNCTIONS

On the following page, our foundational vibrational pattern chart for our study appears around the chart for the U.S.. The first wake-up call of Uranus (not shown) in the US chart, was at the beginning of the century in 1897, at 8 degrees Sagittarius opposing the US Uranus. Uranus opposition Uranus breaks up rigid patterns. In the case of the US this is reflected in travel, knowledge and thought in general. It coincided with the first wave of sightings, although it should be

---

164
    The US government, it seems to me, was more accurately defined by the founding fathers to be a republic, not a democracy.

noted, that sightings since dates B.C.E. have been recorded.

The quadrature aspects of Uranus/Neptune reflect collective consciousness leaps in awareness.

We begin with the first of three Uranus/Neptune oppositions that occurred from February 28, 1906, to February 1, 1907 (this also coincides with the publication of Einstein's Special Theory of Relativity). Only the first and the last (third) oppositions are used to save space and reduce complication. In the fourth wheel the planets at the time of the Roswell crash in 1947. Our analysis can be extended to world application but we are primarily delineating interaction with the U. S.. If we were to do this for other countries, the chart for the specific country in question would be used. Mundane astrology is a complex field all on its own.

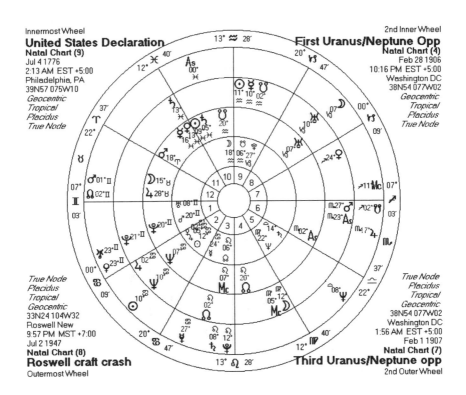

Major planetary transit patterns leave "imprints." These holographic imprints are then triggered by future planetary patterns and transits. The opposition points in the 2/8 axis of the US chart of Uranus/Neptune during 1906/7 should be studied carefully because this reflects a striking precision of astrological premise as the degrees of the opposition are exactly the degree manifestation of the full illumination Sun/Moon/Neptune T-square of the Roswell crash in 1947!!! The 1st was 7 and the third 10 Capricorn/Cancer. Pluto at the time of the opposition is exactly on the U.S. Mars (Military) and awakened by the Venus/Uranus conjunction of the crash. Jupiter at first Uranus/Neptune opposition trines the U.S. Pluto-the opportunity for tremendous perspective alteration though expanded consciousness (also the possession of nuclear power).

Even the obscure explosion of June 30, 1908, when something huge exploded with the force of a 20 megaton

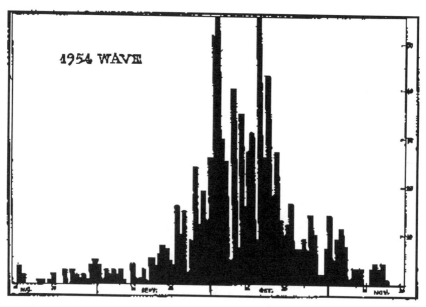

Fɪɢ. 21.—Daily number of unidentified aerial phenomena reported during the 1954 wave.

nuclear bomb over Siberia in the region known as Tunguska, transit Sun was 8 degrees Cancer square transit Saturn at 8 degrees Aries, signaling that rumors that this explosion possibly being a UFO, may be more than just rumors.

The peak of UFO sightings and reports of the wave of 1954, was October 2, when the Sun was at 8 degrees Libra! (See graph, from *Challenge to Science, The UFO Enigma, Jacques and Janine Vallee, 1966*).

The opposition points conjoin the U.S. Sun the ruler of 4, reflecting great emotional and national security concerns being triggered for this period and culminating at the next quadrature, the square that became exact and applying as indicated in the next wheels-from July 15 1954, though June 11, 1955.

The degrees emphasized at the square are from 23 Cancer/Libra, to 27 Cancer/Libra falling on the U.S. 3rd and 9th (information/perspective crisis) precisely the degree of the country's important Mercury opposed Pluto at critical degree Cancer/Capricorn axis in the 3rd and 9th.

The U.S. 6th is the 12th of the public by derivative house measurement and Pluto rules intercepted Scorpio in the 6th (hidden information). The degrees listed above must also be noted as they are profoundly connected to the US' future and always will be.

Pluto at the time of the first Uranus/Neptune closing square was 23 degrees Leo opposing the U.S. Moon in 10 (our freedom symbol as well as co-creator interaction) from the 4th of national security. Jupiter at the first Uranus/Neptune square is on the opposition points of Uranus/Neptune in 1906, the crash full moon of 1947, the U.S. natal Sun, and is the ruler of the 7th of the public. The peak of the 1954 wave extended to mid-October covering the degrees of Cancer/Capricorn/Libra from 8 to 27, including the Sun, Moon, Mars, Jupiter, Uranus and Neptune, while Saturn occupied 8 degrees of Scorpio, the first quadrature to it's position at the time of the crash in 1947. This Saturn quadrature will be in a similar phase in early May 1999, triggering the eclipse in January of the same year.

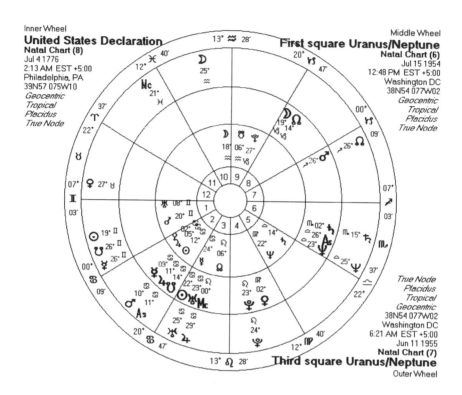

Inner Wheel
United States Declaration
Natal Chart (8)
Jul 4 1776
2:13 AM EST +5:00
Philadelphia, PA
39N57 075W10
Geocentric
Tropical
Placidus
True Node

Middle Wheel
First square Uranus/Neptune
Natal Chart (6)
Jul 15 1954
12:48 PM EST +5:00
Washington DC
38N54 077W02
Geocentric
Tropical
Placidus
True Node

True Node
Placidus
Tropical
Geocentric
38N54 077W02
Washington DC
6:21 AM EST +5:00
Jun 11 1955
Natal Chart (7)
Third square Uranus/Neptune
Outer Wheel

With this pattern establishment, we now turn our attention to the Uranus/Neptune conjunction that became exact on February 2, 1993, which occurred at 19 degrees Capricorn,[165] exactly on the 9th house cusp of the U.S. and is precisely conjunct the midpoint degree (halfway point) that falls between the powerful 1906 opposition, and the 1954 closing square! This reflects the integration of the two quadrature points and the initiation of a powerful change in U.S. philosophy, and the thinking and mental awareness profile of the public mind. Shortly after this conjunction the public consciousness became inundated with movies such as *"Alien"*, *"Contact"* *"Men in Black"*, *"Independence Day"*, *"Fire in The Sky"*............ Uranus

---

[165]
      If the reader will recall the announcement of "Roswell Case Closed" had Saturn exactly square this degree. It is the dispositor of the conjunction and rules the 9th.

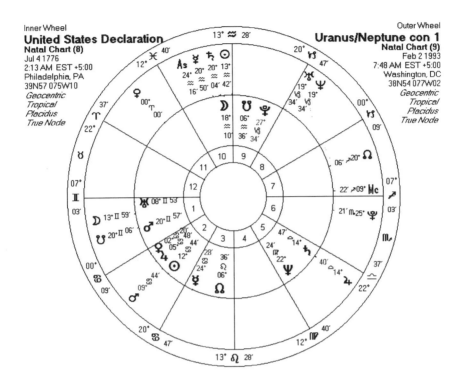

Inner Wheel
United States Declaration
Natal Chart (8)
Jul 4 1776
2:13 AM EST +5:00
Philadelphia, PA
39N57 075W10
Geocentric
Tropical
Placidus
True Node

Outer Wheel
Uranus/Neptune con 1
Natal Chart (9)
Feb 2 1993
7:48 AM EST +5:00
Washington, DC
38N54 077W02
Geocentric
Tropical
Placidus
True Node

rules the 10th of the U.S. chart, the country's "life direction." Neptune rules the 11th, co-creator interaction (the 11th also rules congress, the party in power).

The degrees of the Uranus/Neptune imprint will be the sensitive points of future quantum leaps in consciousness until next quadrature in approximately 2040.

Transit Jupiter at 93 conjunction is retrograde and conjunct U.S. Saturn in 5 the ruler of the national 8th and 9th cusps and rules the 7th (other countries and the public reception). An opportunity for the U.S. to reassess its defense policies and creative extensions by the force of public opinion.

Saturn at 93 conjunction was conjunct the reigning need of the country, the Moon; testing human rights and equality. This was the testing of the country's true commitment to these principles.

The Jupiter/Saturn Conjunction May 2000

Values (Taurus) give birth to judgement (Virgo). Judgement gives birth to status (Capricorn), status to inequality. We made no special effort in order to exist. These judgments and limitations are the effect of the illusions of the physical world (Saturn=to sow/Satan=to oppose or the adversary of spirit, the adversary of Neptune). But good and bad are subjective value judgments. There is no THE truth, except that the truth is composed of all truths (Bashar). There is only positive (unifying) and negative (separating) energy. White light is composed of all colors and in that form reflects the unifying effect of positive energy.

The experience of Earth is not something to be shunned and escaped from, it is a spiritual experience. The Earth element formed by the three signs Taurus, Virgo, and Capricorn reflect the spiritual experience of materiality and spirit in a version that is simply different-material. Our belief that it must be difficult is simply choice. This choice of definition has arisen from the perspective "deus ex machina" (deity separate from the machine) when we lost the recognition that God, man and nature were one and the same. The end of the native American tribes was the beginning of the industrial/territorial perspectives in the Americas and the reflection of this "delusion of grandeur" wherein manipulation of the world into a "better" format technologically is considered to be the sign of intelligence and "better".

Functional adequacy when taken to extremes becomes dogmatic science. We must reawaken our connection to nature. Nature intends the grail, and is the thrust of this book. We tend to focus on facts and data as the solution to everything. They are not. The reasons for this is because of the materialistic structure we have built around us and our survival needs being confused with *survival of the ego and identity*. These structures are reflective of the need to have shells of definitions that remove us further and further from our source internally and is paralleled by our distance from nature. We create defenses as shells that hide our true intention and true need for harmony with our environment. We then build upon the structures and create more shells to hide the fact that we do so. This is reflected in the negative expression of the archetype of Taurus/Libra (Venus) with the need to maintain the familiarity of habit and reliance upon personal reflection. It is a *momentum* ritual that then becomes the accepted norm as values become structured. These value structures imprison us and restrict us from the release from hell, from discovery. Maintaining sameness is necessary for physical survival but detracts from personal developmental dynamics.

The word hell is derived from the root word in old English Helan, meaning to *cover over or to hide*. It is our own unconscious knowledge of instinctual harmony (and other aspects of our psyche) that we collectively and individually hide. Therefore, *dis-covery* leads us to heaven and away from the judgement of the world in which we live (Uranus means *heavens*).

All orbits of bodies from the Sun to the Oort cloud increase reflectiveness of the depth of our consciousness as we move away from the center, the Sun. This is why the planet Uranus is outside of Saturn's orbit and before Neptune's. The farther into space we go, the more expanded aspects of ourselves we discover. It is this discovery that when thwarted becomes the catalyst of *dis-aster* (separated from the stars) and the resultant forced awakening and termination of fruitless momentums Uranus).

The Jupiter/Saturn conjunction which occurs on May 28, 2000, reflects dramatic value judgement de-structurization of this momentum and hence the transformation of many material views, relied upon value judgments, and economic conditions.

Natural dis-asters have a way of becoming the ultimate "dissolvers" of status barriers (Capricorn). This is necessary for the next mutation (Element change of a conjunction pattern) of conjunctions (Jupiter/Saturn) in the air signs (the trinity of idea interaction).

The United States cannot fulfill its founding premise with a material perspective as its driving force. We are becoming aware now that we can have a prosperous world without conflict. The stock markets soar with no "real" corroborating reasons. With Capricorn on the 9th cusp, this country's philosophical profile is one of materialism. As Uranus/Neptune conjoined the 9th cusp and transit Pluto moves through Sagittarius, the public perspective has made a radical shift (Pluto rules the 6th, which is the 12th of the public 7th) to philosophic, ideological and religious issues.

This comes about through the gradual recognition of the true seat of power in our government (the people not the material power structure), or through citizens of unusual power or uniqueness (Uranus rules the country's 10th) which began in February 1995. Other countries perspective will begin to be given more inclusion in the US policy profile beginning in 98 as we move with Neptune into the sign of co-creation interaction Aquarius. They may have to as each country rises in technological prowess.

As Uranus moves to the MC the US will accelerate the innovative and forward thinking premise, slowed from its lack of Fire (spirit). The Presidential position will become a seat of humanitarian equity. Relinquishing control and trusting the people is the only answer. International policy will begin to undergo a long term dramatic change toward world integration.

On 3/6/94 the UN reported that 1 out of 3 people on the planet were unemployed. Taking responsibility for our own creations is the only way to take back power from governmental and material or industrial structures. Following one's bliss is the key to self directed development and response-ability. The shift from the corporate to individual creative application and service is the only way for each person to be fulfilled and accelerate the whole. This idea is happening largely from the advent of the personal computer (Uranus) which allows many types of work to be done from *anywhere.*

The Jupiter (Mind) and Saturn (Matter) Conjunction Mutation

Since the beginning of the twentieth century this aspect has occurred in;
14 Capricorn (November 28, 1901)
26 Virgo (September 9, 1921)
14, 12, 9, degrees Taurus (August 7, 1940, October 20, 1940, February 15, 1941)
25 Capricorn (February 18, 1961)
9, 8, and 5 Libra, a grand mutation (December 31, 1980, March 4, 1981, July 24, 1981).

All of them co-incide with economic and social growth restructuring. The focus is always upon the archetype (sign) in which the conjunction occurs and either conflict or ease with these archetypes (aspects). This planetary pair has much to do with the organizational and procedural notions of societal

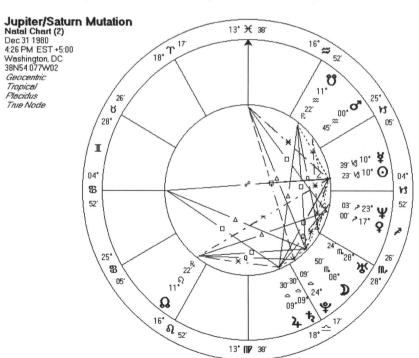

Jupiter/Saturn Mutation
Natal Chart (2)
Dec 31 1980
4:26 PM EST +5:00
Washington, DC
38N54 077W02
Geocentric
Tropical
Placidus
True Node

advance. In this way, society reorganizes itself and these conjunctions reflect the fundamental issues around which will take place.

In this century the Jupiter/Saturn conjunction focus has been upon the Earth family or the archetype of physicality. Everyday issues and trends revolved around material concerns and the industrial system gained power.

The mutation conjunction of 1980 in Libra accelerated to the trinity of idea interaction (Air sign emphasis). Relationships will now be more important than material. The children born during this mutation represent a quantum leap in understanding, a preparation towards interaction with other worlds, and a tremendous preoccupation and orientation to relationship. The Sun/Mercury conjunction square the Jupiter/Saturn conjunction has manifested as the reflection of an era of economic

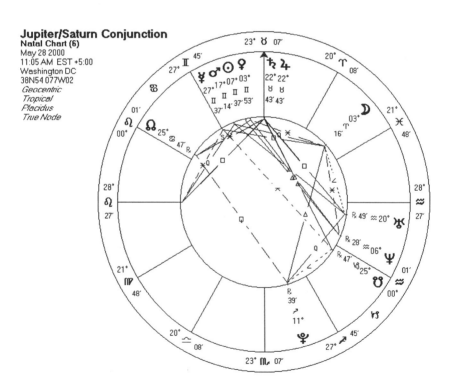

Jupiter/Saturn Conjunction
Natal Chart (6)
May 28 2000
11:05 AM EST +5:00
Washington DC
38N54 077W02
Geocentric
Tropical
Placidus
True Node

difficulties and social issues in dynamic tension. Homelessness, aids, ballooning deficits. The most profound changes have been in our relationships to each other and to outer space (The Movie *"Star Wars" initiated this movement*). Libra always reflects the marriage of the apparently separate entity with itself in the outer reflection. This is because we are the reality we believe we exist within. The singularity is really just a point of focus within the all, not truly separate from it.

Technology has served its purpose-to free us from preoccupation with material and the shells that separate us from ourselves. Because it is us, this allows us to relinquish the shield in the battle against ourselves (the environment). The Jupiter/Uranus Conjunction[166] of 1997 in Aquarius brought us the relationship and identity issues of *cloning.* With this is the question of just what determines individuality.

The Jupiter/Saturn conjunction of May 28, 2000, is the last Earth conjunction. It is square Uranus, and depending upon the ability for collective integrity, could be quite disruptive.

Jupiter and Saturn are the only planets in Earth and are squared by Uranus in Aquarius. Unexpected social changes shatter every resource base and powerful changes are imminent. Venus, the dispositor of the conjunction, the Sun, and Mars, all oppose Pluto from the information/conceptual signs of Gemini/Sagittarius. Propagandic power struggles are very prominent and likely. Jupiter disposes of the Sagittarius Pluto revealing an information and communication transformation and powerful focus on the collective opinion with regard to law, religions, and philosophical profile in general (refer to the Uranus/Neptune conjunction previous). Quantum leaps in thought will be necessary and a blending of all nations begins in earnest. Uranus has just transitted the US moon. The position of the presidency undergoes revolutionary changes.

There will be great economic destructurization which will

---

[166] Please see the February 1997 Issue of "Horoscope Magazine" for the article entitled *"The Jupiter/Uranus Conjunction, A Global leap in Consciousness"* also by the author.

necessitate power decentralization and hopefully lead us out of material dependence when the "beast" (referred to in Revelations) is seen to have usurped much unnecessarily.

The greatest difficulties will come from governmental and economic disarray and the final recognition that we have given far to much power to those in authority. Revelation and new aspects of the higher self mind will have to be put to use by each individual by taking back power and relinquishing complacency. How will the populace deal with resource bases will be the primary issue.

Philosophical and religious beliefs will be shattered (Uranus square Jupiter) and business will not be "as usual" (Uranus square Saturn). The unsoundness of our values (Taurus) and economic structures leads to destruction (Saturn square Uranus) through power struggles and war (Sun/Mars opposition Pluto, Pluto opposing Sun/Mars midpoint. (Noel Tyl has pointed to the middle east as an area of major concern, please refer to *"Prediction in Astrology"* by that author.)

The computer age accelerates and creates a new arena for crime, independence, and enlightenment. The trine of the Sun to Neptune in the Air element promises some exciting artistic and spiritual enlightenment and is the way out of some difficult dilemmas. Computers will bring the unreal aspects of virtual reality into greater application. Discovery of alien life accelerates and is the base for the dramatic perspective alterations. The US presidency will undergo revision and that president will have their hands full economically.

The Jupiter/Saturn Earth conjunctions have been our test of believing that the material world and the identity we believe ourselves to be, *is all we are.* Heaven and hell are choices in perspective. We will recognize that the matter and mind are one thing, even when the material appears to be empirically real and externally oppositional (Saturn, Helan). Dis-covery returns us to our heaven (Uranus), and hell is diminished to a negative state of mind.

Paradigm Shift Uranus Square Pluto 2012-15

As we move into the transformational age after 2000, our mobility both physically and mentally will accelerate. This will depend upon the psychological strength we nurture through understanding the self and its co-created part in the collective consciousness.

In 1923 Carl G. Jung published his works on *Psychological Types* and introduced us to the idea of groups of thought or collections of thoughts that we experience on an unconscious level en mass, through archetypes. The collective unconscious contains the inherited or ancestral memories and archetypes that the individual taps into as a reference to the world around him. These primal images are the *"real" template*. We carry these ancestral memories and continually build upon them in our ever expanding awareness and perspective. Significance within this reference is the goal of the identity, the understanding and conscious cognition of the implicate order and the self's place within it.

Pluto is a very small planet at the edge of the solar system with an orbital tilt that allows for a different view or *perspective* of the rest of the solar system, far removed from the light of our consciousness center (Sun). Much of our *perspective* is determined by this collective reference as a starting point for transformation of that collective identity. The powerless position of such a small body is reflected in the need for *significant impact* as the overcompensation to "make itself felt". This arises from the fear of insignificance in such an isolated position. This is the psychological key to Pluto and Scorpio. The transformation that is pursued is the attempt to validate the ego within this larger group of like thinkers and is usually felt by that generation as the *thing that society lacks and needs.* That generation then adds to society its contribution in perspective. In astrology the planet Pluto reflects the generational collective unconscious and acts as the guide to the collective development of this system's (the solar system) ever expanding awareness.

The group we are born into by Pluto's sign reference carries with it tremendous change in the sign it is so placed. But curiously, this impact is felt as the generation matures. We must first seek to expand the influence of our self (Jupiter) through strategy necessary for physical realization (Saturn), realize these barriers are self created and imposed (Uranus) and dissolve them (Neptune), leading us to this collective transformative recognition, with altered perspectives and attitudes of our place within the system (Pluto).

In the early sixties the generation that was born with Pluto in Leo (1939-57) became the "do your own thing" generation and creative applications were the order of the day. Why? Because the generation that preceded them had their focus on security concerns (Cancer-1914-39) and they needed to move off that perspective (Cancer limits Leo), because the previous generation concentrated on dispersing and creating a global community (Gemini limits Cancer) through the power of communication that the Cancer generation had to secure... Of course this repeats over and over each time at a higher and more expanded level but with different configurations of the planets inside it's orbit and perhaps those outside of its orbit marking a larger frame of reference (Nibiru?, the undiscovered planet-see *"Contact Cards"* listed in the bibliography and recommended reading list).

A paradigm is a conceptual framework or set of assumptions under which we make rules, and determine inquiry.[167] In this sense, Pluto reflects the current paradigm collectively that we are "agreeing" to be our parameter of focus and development. The issues of the period by sign and aspects are reflected through it. But the individuals born under a certain paradigm manifest that paradigm as the *current* paradigm when they reach adult age 20 years or so later. That imprint seems to exist then and is brought forward in time.

Conjunctions of the outer planets to Pluto reflects the periods when these paradigms shift in focus or content. Since

---

[167] Please refer to Thomas Kuhn and *"The Structure of Scientific Revolutions."*

Neptune's orbit and Pluto's orbit[168] cover some of the same space sometimes (because of the off center shape of their orbits) they work together in this dissolution and reformation of global and collective perspective development. The solar system itself is in a state of developmental awareness and consciousness expansion that is reflected in the collective perspective. It *is* the collective consciousness in material form.

Uranus is the planet that reflects the primary energies of dislodging the old paradigm sets, so this change can take place. The quadratures between Uranus and Pluto are very significant indicators of these collective shifts. The Pluto in Leo

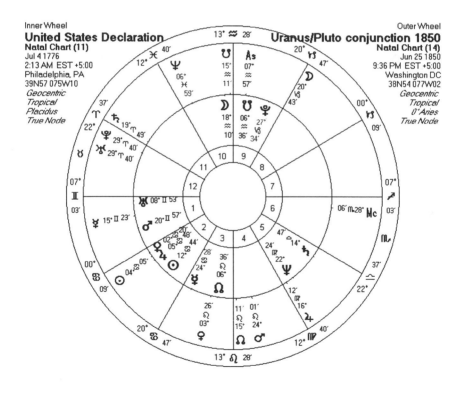

Inner Wheel
United States Declaration
Natal Chart (11)
Jul 4 1776
2:13 AM EST +5:00
Philadelphia, PA
39N57 075W10
Geocentric
Tropical
Placidus
True Node

Outer Wheel
Uranus/Pluto conjunction 1850
Natal Chart (14)
Jun 25 1850
9:36 PM EST +5:00
Washington DC
38N54 077W02
Geocentric
Tropical
0°Aries
True Node

Neptune's orbit is about twice and Pluto's about three times that of Uranus, but the tilts are different and none are circular, they are variations of ellipses.

generation therefore was able to take advantage of a paradigm shift with which to express their specific change[169] as the major paradigm of creative awakening during the Uranus/Pluto conjunction of 1965.

The last conjunction of Uranus/Pluto was at 29 Aries which preceded the Civil War. The threat to the disruption of the union easily seen by the square to the materialistic position of Pluto in Capricorn in the chart of the US at 27 Capricorn. Here we had a revolution in ego dominance (Aries) of the collective and racial perspective. Uranus rules 10 (the president) and Pluto rules 6 (service and servants, work and the 12th of the public). It was also the time that California became a state. California has always been known for its "conglomeration"

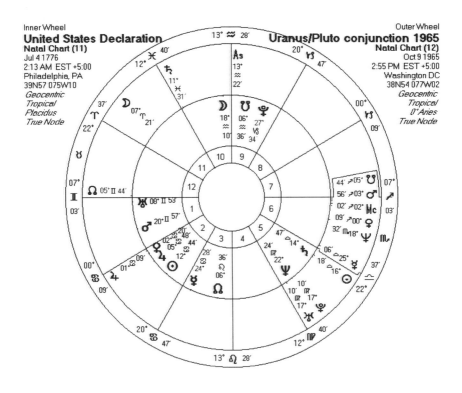

169
Pluto is exalted in Leo according to some astrological schools of thought.

populace and avant garde lifestyles. The seal of California depicts a Grizzly bear as the symbol of the early American struggle for *independence.*

In 1965 the conjunction occurred in Virgo (critical thinking) in the 5th of the US chart (the youth of the nation) and the rebellion against the "establishment" began. Square the US Mars (the military) the protest against military maneuvers and the Vietnam efforts begins to get serious. Its conjunction to Neptune easily identifies drugs and counterculture activities as being a part of this rebellion. The 17th degree of the Mutable signs remains a sensitive point until the next squares in 2012.

The generation born with Pluto in Virgo (1957-72) pushed for the transformation of perspective with the emphasis on technological service oriented devices, health and fitness issues. This generation found practical uses for the creations of the previous generation. But this generation awakened technological service that will dramatically change future paradigms or systems of belief (Uranus and computers) because of the conjunction of Uranus to this Pluto cycle. This is the predominating paradigm that will carry until the first square in 2012. The illusory effects of what we do for a living will be where this breakup will occur-does my service really reflect me? Hence, an identity crisis must follow. When this occurs we wake up to the recognition of unlimited choice in our creative prowess. The period immediately preceding this first square will begin to seem oppressive in this "Virgoian"system. The overthrowing of the current paradigm is the effect of the Uranus/Pluto quadratures and this generation made drastic changes through computers, medicine, psychology and the entire service industry. Downsizing and right-sizing of corporations and workplaces and all types of efficiency concerns have been the effect of this Virgoian generational perspective. Making things easier through technology leaves more time for relationship concerns. This is what the next generation will "feel" was missing and begin to promote as its most predominant paradigm. The critical and refining, or discriminating and efficiency oriented Virgo perspective, will be overthrown and overshadowed by the sudden surge in relationship and identity concerns.

Pluto in Libra (1971-84) will be the generation who's perspective and collective orientation will probably be the most influencing and influenced by the next quadrature of Uranus/Pluto which occurs in 2012. This generation's need for social change will dramatically alter the present assumptions about all sorts of commonly accepted beliefs about relationship and interaction. It may have to as we discover new life in space.

With the last square around 1932, Pluto itself was discovered and the mobster mentality and world domination by one country became a possibility from many directions. As we can see, all of these quadratures corresponded to some sort of

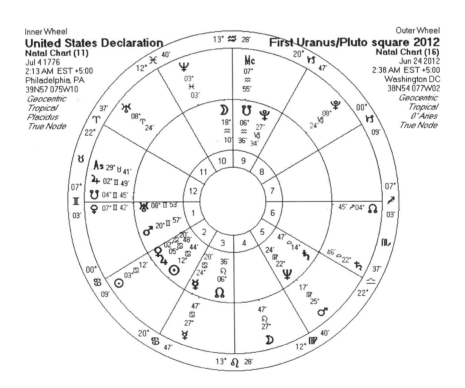

Inner Wheel
United States Declaration
Natal Chart (11)
Jul 4 1776
2:13 AM EST +5:00
Philadelphia, PA
39N57 075W10
Geocentric
Tropical
Placidus
True Node

Outer Wheel
First Uranus/Pluto square 2012
Natal Chart (16)
Jun 24 2012
2:38 AM EST +5:00
Washington DC
38N54 077W02
Geocentric
Tropical
0° Aries
True Node

power struggles within the mass consciousness, usually but not always having to do with race or nationality (as is the case with Neptune as well, refer to Hitler's chart on page 417). The generation that will be right in the middle of the next square will be the Pluto in Libra generation. And as shown by the placement of this square around the US chart, the issues will be again revolving around the status and ego (Aries and Capricorn) a competitive struggle for dominance.

The past has shown us that this quadrature brings some sort of redistribution of power within the masses or at least the need to remove power from some group who has usurped it. This power realignment as we will call it, will take place in economic functions and sharing, the death rate or issues of life and death, and the advising segments for the president(8th house). The death of a president while in office would be the entirely possible under such an aspect. The 11th house of the US chart deals with congressional issues and no doubt there will be major power struggles here. The difference in this quadrature as opposed to other historically recent ones is the fact that this one falls within orb of a grand cross with the US radix Venus, Jupiter, Sun, and Saturn, this will be an extremely difficult time in US history. Economic and political issues will no doubt be powerful. The squares get closer to the US Saturn by 2015 and reflect tremendous difficulties and power struggles as the direction of the country's extension (5th house Saturn) and relationship to other powers is challenged by the Pluto in Libra generation. This also coincides with a Saturn return for the US as well and it appears that the military structures are where power will be taken back from.

In the natural horoscope the signs of Scorpio (Pluto) and Aquarius (Uranus) are square each other and reflect the externalized "versions" of Taurus (Venus) and Leo (Sun). Since these two signs reflect our worth and creative extension respectively, their externalized versions are just reflections of our own creations interacting with the apparent other. It is a question of abundance typically-or rather the belief or disbelief in that idea, that is the cause of these power struggles. The only resolution to such difficulties is usually what transpires; A redistribution of power (Pluto) to allow for a greater experience of liberty (Uranus) and justice for all. It is never entirely justice and rarely for all. But this distribution itself is essentially an illusion, because our realities are created by us day in and day out. It is the giving away of power that begins the cycle. Perhaps sometime in the present or the future we can allow for the recognition that we don't need to give it away to begin with. We can create whatever we desire without detracting from someone else. We cannot be responsible for others only to them. This is why Pluto's exaltation in Leo (see Table of Dignities page 238) tells us that our greatest power to change the world is through the individual's power to extend themselves. In this way, if we take responsibility for our creations day to day, one group or another will not have to be fighting to get it back sometime in the future, and even if they are, it won't be a group we belong to.

The paradigm shift of 2012 will be from material or scientific standards of validity, to quality of life and relationship standards. Of course this takes power from certain groups that are no longer necessary or fair. The battle of the egos may be great, but as history has shown through these quadratures in the past, transforming has never been the result of mediocre people or events. If there was only one truth, or one basis to form our assumptions about the nature of existence from, obviously paradigms would never shift and discovery would not exist. It is from tiny Pluto's perspective the only way to find significance and meaning in the vast sea of time and space.

> ▸ The threshold we are referring to is the transformation taking place on your planet from third to fourth density. That is the overall threshold. Every single symbol within your reality that has any relationship to transformation is all generally a part of that. The specifics are up to you to determine for yourselves, although as we have said, the idea of your moon does to some degree represent the idea of your subconscious and unconscious awareness coming to the surface. The idea of Pluto is the actual journey involved across the threshold itself. In this same archetypical manner you have described the myth you call the crossing of the River Styx. This puts you in touch with what you previously assumed to be the

darker regions of your consciousness. It is another way of saying that you enter the blending of your positive and negative polarities, and therefore allow yourselves, in the crossing of that threshold, to glean only a positive effect out of the blending of the positive and the negative. This is why you have intuitively labeled Pluto's moon with the same name as the ferryboat driver that drives you across the mythological river Styx . . . Charon.
Bashar "Blueprint for Change"

"And there appeared a great wonder in heaven, a woman clothed with the sun, and the moon under her feet, and upon her head a crown of twelve stars; and she being with child cried, travailing in birth, and pained to be delivered."

Sites on the Internet

Astrological Consulting
http://www.astroconsulting.com/
Bookwire
http://www.bookwire.com
Online Atlas
http://www.astro.ch/atlas
Timezone Information
http://aa.usno.navy.mil/AA/faq/docs/world_tzones.html
Celebrity Birthdata
Matrix Database - contains 30,000 names
http://205.186.189.2/ms/ms_astro_search.html
Matrix Encyclopedia
http://205.186.189.2/cgi-win/elib.exe?sql=1&orig=/astrology/
avirgo.htm
The Magical Blend
http://www.themagicalblend.com/catalog/books/astro.html
http://www.astrostar.com/books.htm
Association for Astrological Networking
http://www.afan.org
Dell Horoscope Magazine
http://www.bdd.com/horo1/bddhoro1.cgi/horo1
ISAR
http://thenewage.com/na/ISAR.html
NCGR: National Council for Geocosmic Research (USA)
http://www.geocosmic.org
Astrology.Net: Guest Astrologers
http://www.astrology.net/astrozine/guests.html
YAHOO
http://www.yahoo.com
   (search keyword: astrology)

Bibliography and Supplementary Reading List

Allen, Bem P. Personality Theories.
Massachusetts: Allyn & Bacon.
      1994
Allgeier, Elizabeth and Albert. Sexual Interactions, fourth edition.
Massachusetts: D.C. Heath and Company.
      1995
Amend, Karen, and Ruiz, Mary. Handwriting Analysis.
California: Newcastle Publishing.
      1980
Anka, Darryl. The New Metaphysics.
California: Light & Sound Communications Inc.,
      1987
Anka, Darryl. Bashar: Blueprint for Change.
Seattle: New Solutions Publishing.
      1990
Arguelles, Jose'. The Mayan Factor.
New Mexico: Bear & Company.
      1987
Arroyo, Stephen. Astrology, Karma and Transformation.
Washington: CRCS Publications.
      1978
Bach, Richard. Illusions; The Adventures of a Reluctant Messiah.
New York: Dell Publishing
      1977
Barnett, Lincoln. The Universe And Dr. Einstein.
New York: William Morrow & Co., Inc..
      1966 second edition.
Barr, David L.. An Introduction-New Testament Story. Second edition.
California: Wadsworth Publishing.
      1995
Brill, E.J.. The Gospel According To Thomas.
New York: Harper and Row.
      1959
Bruder, Kenneth and Moore, Noel Brooke. Philosophy, The Power of Ideas.
California: Mayfield Publishing Co.
      1993
Campbell, Joseph. Myths To Live By.
New York: Bantam Books.
      1972
Campbell, Joseph. The Power Of The Myth, W/Bill Moyers.
New York: Doubleday.
      1988

Campbell, Bernard G.. Humankind Emerging.
New York: HarperCollins Publishers Inc.
        1992
Carlsberg, Kim, & Anka, Darryl. Contact Cards
New Mexico: Bear & Company
        1996
Cayce, Edgar Evans. Edgar Cayce On Atlantis.
New York: Paperback Library.
        1968
Cerminara, Gina. Many Mansions, The Edgar Cayce Story on
Reincarnation.
New York: William Morrow and Company.
        1978
Chambers, Howard V.. UFO's For The Millions.
California: Sherbourne Press
        1967
Chance, Paul. Learning and Behavior. Third edition
California: Brooks/Cole Publishing Co.
        1994
Chopra, Deepak, M.D.. Ageless Body, Timeless Mind.
San Diego: Harmony Books
        1993
Cole, Sheila R., and Michael. The Development of Children. Second edition.
New York: Scientific American Books.
        1993
Davidson, Gerald C., and Neale John M.. Abnormal Psychology. Sixth
edition.
New York: John Wiley and Sons, Inc.
        1996
De Laszlo, Violet Staub. The Basic Writings of Carl Jung.
New York: The Modern Library.
        1959
DSM-IV. Diagnostic and Statistical Manual of Mental Disorders. Fourth
edition.
Washington DC: The American Psychiatric Association.
        1994
Einstein, Albert. On The Generalized Theory of Gravitation.
Scientific American: Volume 182, No. 4,
        April 1950
Evans, Richard I.. Conversations With Carl Jung.
New Jersey: Van Nostrand Company Inc.
        1964
Fischer, Mary Pat. Living Religions.
New Jersey: Prentice Hall.
        1994

Fix, William R. Pyramid Odyssey
Virginia: Mercury Media.
     1984
Freedman, Russell. Lincoln; A Photobiography.
New York: Houghton Mifflin Company.
     1987
Freud, Sigmund. A General Introduction to Psychoanalysis.
New York: Garden City Publishing.
     1943
Fuller, John G. The Interrupted Journey.
New York: Dial Press.
     1966
Garvin, Richard. The Crystal Skull.
New York: Pocket Books.
     1974
Goswami, Amit. The Self Aware Universe.
New York: G. P. Putnam's Sons
     1995
Haich, Elisabeth. Initiation.
California: Seed Center.
     1974
Hand, Robert. Planets in Transit.
Massachusetts: Para Research Inc.
     1976
Holy Bible. Bible. With Apocrypha.
New York: Oxford University Press.
     1989
Hopkins, Budd. Missing Time.
New York: Ballantine.
     1981
Hull, R.F.C.. Flying Saucers, A Modern Myth of Things Seen in The Sky.
New York: MJF Books, Princeton University Press.
     1978
Hurley, Patrick J.. A concise Introduction to Logic. Fourth edition.
California: Wadsworth Publishing.
     1991
Hynek, J. Allen. The UFO Experience. A Scientific Enquiry.
New York: Ballantine Books
     1974
Jaffe, Aniela. Jung's Last Years.
Texas: Spring Publications.
     1984
Jung, Carl G.. Psychological Types. Volume 6, Collected Works.
New Jersey: Princeton University Press.
     1971

Kalat, James W.. Biological Psychology. Fourth edition.
California: Wadsworth Publishing.
     1992
Kaplan, J.D.. Dialogues of Plato.
New York: Pocket Books.
     1951
Keirsey David, and Bates, Marilyn. Please Understand Me.
San Diego: Promtheus/Nemesis Book Co.
     1978
Kennedy, John F.. Profiles In Courage.
New York: Original-Harper & Brothers.
     1956
Kolak, Daniel and Martin, Raymond. The Experience of Philosophy. Second
edition.
California: Wadsworth Publishing.
     1993
Kuhn, Thomas S., The Structure of Scientific Revolutions. Second edition,
enlarged.
London: The University of Chicago Press.
     1970
Kuhn, Thomas S. The Copernican Revolution.
England: Harvard University Press.
     1985
Lenderman, Leon and Schramm, David. From Quarks To The Cosmos.
New York: Scientific American Library.
     1989
Lewi, Grant. Heaven Knows What.
Minnesota: Llewellyn Publications.
     1977
Lewi, Grant. Astrology For The Millions.
Minnesota: Llewellyn Publications. Bantam Edition
     1980
Lewis, James R. The Astrology Encyclopedia.
Michigan: Invisible Ink Press.
     1994
Mack, John E. M.D.. Abduction.
New York: Charles Scribner's Sons
     1994
Mader, Sylvia S.. Inquiry Into Life. Seventh edition.
Iowa: Wm. C. Brown Publishers.
     1994
Manchester, William. The Death of a President.
New York: Harper & Row Publishers.
     1967

Matthiessen, Peter. Indian Country.
New York: Penguin Books.
　　　1992
Merriman, Raymond A. The Solar Return Book of Prediction.
Michigan: Seek-It Publishing
　　　1977
Millman, Dan. The Way of The Peaceful Warrior.
California: H J Kramer Inc.
　　　1980
Mischel, Walter. Introduction to Personality. Fifth edition.
Texas: Harcourt Brace Jovanovich Publishers
　　　1993
Nemett, Barry. Images, Objects and Ideas. Viewing the Visual Arts.
San Diego: Harcourt Brace Jovanovich College Publishers.
　　　1992
Pelletier, Robert. Planets in Aspect.
Massachusetts: Para Research Inc.
　　　1974
Randle, Kevin D., and Schmitt, Donald R.. UFO Crash At Roswell
New York: Avon Books.
　　　1991
Roberts, Jane. The Nature Of Personal Reality, A Seth Book.
New Jersey: Prentice Hall.
　　　1974
The Coming of Seth.
New York: Pocket Books.
　　　1966
The Seth Material.
New York: Bantam Books.
　　　1970
Ruperti, Alexander. Cycles Of Becoming.
Washington: CRCS Publications.
　　　1978
Sakoian, Frances & Acker, Louis. The Astrologers Handbook
New York: Harper & Row Inc.
　　　1989
Sagan, Carl. Cosmos.
New York: Random House
　　　1980
Skinner, B. F., About Behaviorism.
New York: Vintage Books, A Division of Random House.
　　　1976
Sorensen, Theodore, Special Counsel To The Late President Kennedy.
New York: Harper & Row.
　　　1965

Stearn, Jess. Edgar Cayce; The Sleeping Prophet.
New York: Bantam Books.
    1967
Stevenson, Leslie. Seven Theories of Human Nature. Second edition.
New York: Oxford University Press.
    1974
Strieber, Whitley. Majestic.
New York: Berkley.
    1990
    Majestic.
    1990
Communion
New York: Morrow
    1987
Transformation
New York: Avon
    1988
Talbot, Michael. The Holographic Universe
New York: HarperCollins
    1991
Thorne, Kip S.. Black Holes & Time Warps.
New York: W W Norton & Company.
    1994
Tyl, Noel. Astrology 1-2-3.
Minnesota: Llewellyn Publications.
    1980
    Holistic Astrology.
    1984
    Astrology 1-2-3.
    1991
    Prediction In Astrology.
    The Horoscope as Identity
    1974
Vallee, Jacques. Revelations.
New York: Ballentine Books.
    1991
    UFO Chronicles of the Soviet Union.
    1992
    Challenge to Science; The UFO Enigma
    1974
Yott, Donald H.. Astrology and Reincarnation
York Beach Maine: Samuel Weiser Inc.
    1989

Secondary Reading Suggestions

Astrology
  Beginners:
The Rulership Book - Bills
Interpret Your Chart - Ludlam
Astrological Insights into Personality - Lunsted
The Only Way to Learn Astrology (3 Vols) - March & McEvers
Basic Astrology: A Guide - Negus
Basic Astrology: A Workbook - Negus
Cosmic Combinations - Negus
Astrodeck (a unique way to learn keywords) - ACS
Handbook for the Humanistic Astrologer - Meyer
Alan Oken's Complete Astrology - Oken
Astrology: The Divine Science - Moore & Douglas
A Spiritual Approach to Astrology - Lofthus
Spiritual Astrology- Jan Spiller
Psychology, Astrology and the Four Elements - Arroyo
Horoscope Symbols - Hand
Astrological Keywords - Hall
Useful Outline of Signs of the Zodiac - King
Child Signs - Gloria Starr
Guide to Horoscope Interpretation - Jones
How to Learn Astrology - Jones
Astrology, How and Why it Works - Jones
New Mansions for New Men - Rudhyar
The Astrology of Personality - Rudhyar
The Practice of Astrology- a technique in understanding - Rudhyar
The Astrological Houses -Rudhyar
Transit of Saturn - Robertson
Sex, Mind, Habit, and Other Relationships - Robertson
Cosmopsychology - Robertson
The Theory of Celestial Influence - Collins
Astrologer's Handbook - Sakoian & Acker
The Inconjunct-Quincunx - Sakoian & Acker
Astrology 1-2-3 - Tyl
Pluto - Marks
Neptune - Marks
Cardinal Squares - Marks
Squares - Marks
Transits: the times of your life - Marks
The Twelfth House - Marks
Turning Oppositions into Conjunctions - Marks
Chart Synthesis - Marks
Astrology: a New Age guide - Perrone

The Inner Sky - Forrest
Astrology - Davison
A Time for Astrology - Stearn
Twelve Doors to the Soul - Evans
Principles of Astrology - Carter
Heaven Knows What- Grant Lewi
Astrology For The Millions- Grant Lewi

Intermediate and Expert:
An Astrological Mandala - Rudhyar
Person-Centered Astrology - Rudhyar
Planets in Transit - Hand
Planets in Youth - Hand
Essays in Astrology - Hand
Relationships - Guttman
AstroDice (Astrology's parallel to the I-Ching) - ACS
Psychology of the Planets - Gauquelin
The Cosmic Clocks - Gauquelin
Healing with the Horoscope - Pottenger
The American Book of Nutrition and Medical Astrology - Nauman
Interpreting the Eclipses - Jansky
The Fortunes of Astrology - Granite
Winning! Zodiacal Timing - Wehrman
Planetary Planting - Riotte
The Lively Circle - Koval
Recent Advances in Natal Astrology - Dean
The Larousse Encyclopedia of Astrology
Combinations of Stellar Influences - Ebertin
Directions - Ebertin
Cosmic Marriage - Ebertin
Profiles of Women - Rodden
Relating - Greene
Saturn: a new look at an old devil - Greene
Jupiter/Saturn Conference Lectures - Greene & Arroyo
The Cycles of the Outer Planets - Greene
Expanding Astrology's Universe - Dobyns
Transpluto or Should We Call Him Bacchus - Hawkins
Career Astrology - Puotinen
Phases of the Moon - Busteen, et al.
Taking the Kid Gloves Off Astrology - Alan
Cosmic Influences on Human Behavior - Gauquelin
Vocational Guidance by Astrology - Luntz
Solar and Lunar Returns - Bradley
Solar Return Book of Prediction-Merriman
Holistic Astrology - Tyl

The Principles and Practice of Astrology- 12 volumes- Tyl
Esoteric Astrology - Bailey
Astrology, Karma, and Transformation - Arroyo
Relationships - Arroyo
Cycles of Becoming-Ruperti
Toward a New Astrology-Ry Redd
Handbook for the Humanistic Astrologer- Michael R. Meyer
The Astrology of Human Relationships- Sakoian and Acker

Reference books for all astrologers:
The American Ephemeris - ACS
The Astroid Ephemeris - ACS
The American Sidereal Ephemeris - ACS
The American Book of Tables - ACS
The American Atlas (best on the market, and the most accurate)- ACS
The International Atlas - ACS
The American Book of Charts - Rodden
The Gauquelin Book of American Charts - Gauquelin
The Koch Table of Houses - AFA
The Placidus Table of Houses - AFA

Organizations:
The American Federation of Astrologers
PO Box 22040
Tempe, AZ. 85285-2040
(602)838-1751....... e-mail AFA@msn.com.........FAX (602)838-8293

The AFAN Association for Astrological Networking
8306 Wilshire Blvd, suite 537
Beverly Hills, CA. 90211

ISAR International Society for Astrological research
PO Box 38613
Los Angeles, CA. 90038-0613
(805)525-0461   Fax (805)933-0301

Kepler College of Astrological Arts and Sciences
4518 University Way NE #215
Seattle WA. 98105
(206)547-0136   Fax (206)643-7416

NCGR National Concil for Geocosmic Research, Membership
Margaret Meister
PO Box 501078
Malabar, Florida   32950-1078
(407) 722-9500 fax (407) 728-2244

Astrology Computer Software
Matrix Software
315 Marion Ave
Big Rapids, Michigan 49307
(616) 796-2483   FAX (616) 796-3060

Astrolabe Inc.
350 Underpass Rd
PO Box 1750
Brewster, MA. 02631
(508) 896-5081   FAX (508) 896-5289

Index

ii

Chapter 4

Chapter 9

About the Author

Edmond Wollmann was born in Cleveland, Ohio. At the age of 9 he moved to New Mexico where he lived with his family on a ranch in Los Chavez, New Mexico until the age of 21 when he moved to southern California.

At the age of 15 he became interested in astrology, and received his professional certification in August of 1981 from the *American Federation of Astrologers*. A graduate of San Diego Miramar College in psychology, he currently attends San Diego State University where he is completing degrees in psychology and art.

His articles on astrology/psychology have been published in Dell Horoscope Magazine, and Aspects Magazine since 1990.

He is an accomplished life drawing artist and Falconer, and has been researching the UFO phenomenon since early sightings as a youth in the New Mexico deserts.

Correspondence should be mailed to:
Edmond Wollmann
PO Box 221000
San Diego, CA. 92192-1000
E-mail.... *letters@astroconsulting.com*

Book And Horoscope Order Form

☎ To order by phone call toll free............................**1(888)85FLYER**

Please have your credit card ready.......................................1(888)853-5937

🖥 To order by e-mail send to ***services@astroconsulting.com*** or visit our site at; ***http://www.astroconsulting.com***

✉ To order by mail send to: Astrological Consulting/Altair Publications, PO Box 221000, San Diego, CA. 92192-1000

Please send____copies of The Integrated Astrological Guide @ $20.95. Please add 7.75% for books shipped to California addresses. Shipping: Book Rate: $2.00 for the first book and 75 cents for each additional book (Surface shipping may take three to four weeks) Air Mail: $3.50 per book.

Horoscope Chart Orders; charts $3.00 per page + postage and handling.
First and last name_____

BirthDate_____/_____/_____/_____

^{1}*Time_____:____ am/pm   Male/Female

Place (City, State, Country)_____,_____
Extra Chart(s)
For all credit card orders please include:
Card number:_____
Name on card:_____
Expiration date_____
Amount enclosed_____ (+$1.00 postage and handling per order)
Return address:_____
Send to;
Astrological Consulting
PO Box 221000
San Diego, CA. 92192-1000   Make checks or money orders payable to;
Astrological Consulting/Altair Publications
               Call Toll Free For All Orders Today!
Add my name to astrological mailing lists___
Send me the Astrological Consulting Computer services list___

1

*Time indicated on birth certificate, if unknown we will use Sun sign ascendant·